T0256117

COMPUTATIONALLY INTELLIGENT HYBRID SYSTEMS

COMPUTATIONALLY INTELLIGENT HYBRID SYSTEMS

The Fusion of Soft Computing and Hard Computing

Edited by

Seppo J. Ovaska
Helsinki University of Technology

IEEE Series on Computational Intelligence
David B. Fogel, Series Editor

IEEE PRESS

A JOHN WILEY & SONS, INC., PUBLICATION

For general information on our other products and services please contact our Customer Care Department within the U.S. at 877-762-2974, outside the U.S. at 317-572-3993 or fax 317-572-4002.

Wiley also publishes its books in a variety of electronic formats. Some content that appears in print, however, may not be available in electronic format.

Library of Congress Cataloging-in-Publication Data is available.

ISBN 0-471-47668-4

10 9 8 7 6 5 4 3 2 1

To Helena, my dear wife; this one is for you

CONTENTS

Editor's Introduction to Chapter 4   89

4   SENSORLESS CONTROL OF SWITCHED RELUCTANCE MOTORS   93

Adrian David Cheok

Editor's Introduction to Chapter 7   199

7 PREDICTIVE FILTERING METHODS FOR POWER
SYSTEMS APPLICATIONS   203

Seppo J. Ovaska

Editor's Introduction to Chapter 10   313

10 INTRODUCTION TO SCIENTIFIC DATA MINING: DIRECT KERNEL METHODS AND APPLICATIONS   317

Mark J. Embrechts, Boleslaw Szymanski, and Karsten Sternickel

CONTRIBUTORS

AJITH ABRAHAM, Oklahoma State University, Tulsa, Oklahoma

GREGORY D. BUCKNER, North Carolina State University, Raleigh, North Carolina

ADRIAN DAVID CHEOK, National University of Singapore, Singapore

SUNG-BAE CHO, Yonsei University, Seoul, Korea

MARK J. EMBRECHTS, Rensselaer Polytechnic Institute, Troy, New York

SANG-JUN HAN, Yonsei University, Seoul, Korea

TAKUMI ICHIMURA, Hiroshima City University, Hiroshima, Japan

AKIMOTO KAMIYA, Kushiro National College of Technology, Kushiro, Japan

KAZUYA MERA, Hiroshima City University, Hiroshima, Japan

SEPPO J. OVASKA, Helsinki University of Technology, Espoo, Finland

RICHARD E. SAEKS, Accurate Automation Corporation, Chattanooga, Tennessee

BERNHARD SICK, Micro-Hybrid Electronics GmbH, Hermsdorf, Germany

KARSTEN STERNICKEL, Cardiomag Imaging Inc., Schenectady, New York

BOLESLAW SZYMANSKI, Rensselaer Polytechnic Institute, Troy, New York

FOREWORD

Intelligent machines are no longer a dream of the future, because we already can create computers that teach themselves how to solve our problems. Yet, this was not always so. For decades, computer scientists attempted to inject so-called "artificial intelligence" into machines, programming them to follow rules divined from human experts. And this is still done, albeit not with the same irrational exuberance as was once evidenced. Years of experience with knowledge engineering, case-based reasoning, common-sense reasoning, and other related endeavors has shown these techniques to be useful in some limited domains, but they do not address the fundamental problem of how to solve problems, which is at the core of the future of intelligent machines.

The methods that have achieved success in addressing new problems without relying on existing human expertise are altogether different from traditional artificial intelligence techniques. They conform to a broad set of principles gleaned from learning systems observed in nature. Among these are neural networks, fuzzy systems, evolutionary computation, and other techniques that collectively form the field of *computational intelligence.* Within this field, there is an improper subset of methods that model primarily human information processing, and these are described by the term *soft computing*, first coined by Lotfi A. Zadeh in the early 1990s.

Although the boundaries of these terms are themselves fuzzy, their success is not. This is particularly true of the last 15 years, in which the number of applications of soft computing and computational intelligence has increased dramatically. More recently, within the last three years, research programs have developed computationally intelligent self-learning systems that can teach themselves to play games of skill at high levels—on par with human experts—without knowing much more than the rules of the game. Other research has shown that these techniques can discover real-world designs—in one case, involving electronic circuits—that have either been patented previously or might be patentable currently, this evidencing a level of competence that might exceed what would be obvious to an engineer trained in the art.

Specific inventions are valuable contributions to our collective intellectual property, but real-world problem solving demands more than useful inventions. That soft computing and computational intelligence provide the necessary tool set that allows a computer to invent something new is fundamentally important. Using that set of tools to generate efficient solutions to real-world problems is an altogether different challenge of engineering.

Good engineering requires understanding the purpose to be achieved, the available resources, and the manner in which they may be allocated collectively to achieve the objective. Now that our understanding of neural networks, fuzzy systems, evolutionary computation, and other related methods is maturing, the next synthesis must come in understanding how to combine these techniques, as well as traditional methods, which are also described as *hard computing* in contrast with soft computing, to generate synergistic improvements. In essence, the immediate challenge is to understand how to collectively allocate soft- and hard-computing techniques to create hybrid methods that are more effective than either alone.

This book, *Computationally Intelligent Hybrid Systems: The Fusion of Soft Computing and Hard Computing*, edited by Seppo J. Ovaska, is an important contribution in the effort to meet this challenge. The book is a uniquely crafted work, combining the experience of many soft-computing experts with illustrations across diverse problems. Each chapter provides insight into a combination of soft and hard computing that will leave the perceptive reader with much to consider. Professor Ovaska has taken the important additional step of writing an introduction to each chapter, placing each in overall context and weaving a common thread throughout the edited collection. Thus, this book is more than a collection of individual chapters: It is an integrated whole that serves as an example of the synergy it seeks to promote.

It is my pleasure to see this book in the IEEE Computational Intelligence Society's series on computational intelligence. I expect it will be of long-lasting value to researchers and practitioners in diverse aspects of engineering and computer science.

DAVID B. FOGEL

Vice President, Publications
IEEE Computational Intelligence Society
Computational Intelligence Series Editor

PREFACE

Computationally intelligent hybrid systems comprise a diverse field that could be presented in numerous different ways. The subtitle, *The Fusion of Soft Computing and Hard Computing*, reflects the viewpoint of the present treatment. Over the past six years, I have been developing and promoting the new concept "Fusion of Soft Computing and Hard Computing" with my colleagues. This term was invented in 1998, the first review article on the topic was presented in 1999 [1], and in 2002 a special issue on "Fusion of Soft Computing and Hard Computing in Industrial Applications" was published in the *IEEE Transactions on Systems, Man, and Cybernetics—Part C: Applications and Reviews* [2]. Moreover, several invited sessions, panel discussions, and tutorials were organized for international conferences in Finland, Japan, and the United States.

World Wide Web (WWW) search engines give a reasonable idea on the global spreading of some term or concept; I used the Google search engine to find the number of WWW pages where the term *fusion of soft computing and hard computing* is mentioned. In November 2001, the number was only 27; in November 2002, it was already 50; and in November 2003, there were altogether 70 WWW pages containing the specific term. Nevertheless, each major concept needs a comprehensive book that is fully devoted to the emerging topic, because books do usually receive more attention than conference or even journal contributions. In that way, the concept becomes better known and appreciated throughout the international research and development (R&D) community.

It is with pride and a sense of accomplishment that I am presenting this edited volume to the soft-computing and hard-computing communities. Unlike previous books on soft computing or computational intelligence, this timely book can be considered unique. The soft-computing and hard-computing research communities are quite separated; but from the practicing engineers' point of view, all the available methodologies are needed for developing innovative and competitive solutions to demanding real-world problems. Thus, both soft-computing and hard-computing people have to look at the complementary fusion concept. This fusion approach can be seen as a classical two-culture problem, where bridging the two cultures would eventually benefit them both.

Throughout this book, the methodological fusion or integration scheme is discussed with a collection of examples from the following fields of application:

- Aerospace
- Computer security
- Data mining
- Electric power systems
- Large-scale plants
- Motor drives
- Robust control
- Tool wear monitoring
- User interfaces
- World Wide Web

A diverse set of multidisciplinary applications was carefully chosen to illustrate the wide-ranging applicability of the fusion concept. To prepare an edited volume instead of a monograph was a natural choice, because it is practically impossible for one or two individuals to write a thorough book covering such a broad range of applications. On the other hand, the fusion of soft computing and hard computing is essentially linked to applications. Therefore, I have identified distinguished specialists in those important fields and invited them to contribute a chapter in their respective areas of expertise. The contributors come from Finland, Germany, Japan, Korea, Singapore, and the United States. In fact, four of the 11 chapters are modified and expanded versions of articles published in the above-mentioned special issue [2]. The chapter authors follow a common structure in their contributions. In addition, I have coupled the individual chapters together by introductions to every chapter. Although the range of application fields is wide, it is a redeeming feature of life that we are able to use many things without understanding every detail of them. That is also true with these illustrative examples of the fusion of soft computing and hard computing.

This book is targeted for graduate students, practicing engineers, researchers, and R&D managers who wish to enhance or deepen their knowledge on the fusion of soft computing and hard computing. It is expected that the reader is a graduate of computer engineering, computer science, electrical engineering, or systems engineering study program with a modest mathematical background. The potential group of people who could be interested in this book is considerable, because the book is the very first volume on the emerging area of fusion of soft computing and hard computing. My intent has been to make this book a "guiding star" of the complementary fusion schemes between soft computing and hard computing. It will aid readers in developing their own computationally intelligent hybrid systems, as well as understanding those designed by others. And I want to recommend the volume for the following purposes as a graduate textbook, a continuing education reference book, or supplemental reading:

- Textbook in M.S./Ph.D. level courses and seminars on soft computing or computational intelligence applications (graduate students)
- State-of-the-art source of computational hybrid structures for real-world engineering applications (practicing engineers)
- Basis for new research directions in this area, where the symbiosis of soft computing and hard computing offers great potential for developing efficient algorithms and methods (researchers)
- Pool of fresh ideas for creating competitive systems and commercial products with high machine IQ (R&D managers)

Sample course titles where the book could be used were searched from the Internet, and they include:

- Advanced course in neural computing
- Advanced topics in soft computing
- Artificial neural systems
- Computational intelligence in control engineering
- Engineering applications of artificial intelligence
- Evolutionary computation
- Neuro-fuzzy intelligent decision systems
- Signal processing and soft computing in industrial electronics
- Soft computing
- Special topics in artificial intelligence

Next, some words about the structure of this book. The book is organized into 11 self-contained chapters; thus, the material could be rearranged depending on the preferences of the instructor or reader. It is advised, however, that Chapter 1 would be explored first, because it contains a pragmatic introduction to the fusion concept. Below is a list of the chapter titles and contributing authors. Motivating introductions to individual chapters are available before each chapter. Chapter 1, "Introduction to Fusion of Soft Computing and Hard Computing," is contributed by me. Chapter 2, "General Model for Large-Scale Plant Application," is by Akimoto Kamiya. Chapter 3, "Adaptive Flight Control: Soft Computing with Hard Constraints," is by Richard E. Saeks. Chapter 4, "Sensorless Control of Switched Reluctance Motors," is by Adrian David Cheok. Chapter 5, "Estimation of Uncertainty Bounds for Linear and Nonlinear Robust Control," is by Gregory D. Buckner. Chapter 6, "Indirect On-Line Tool Wear Monitoring," is by Bernhard Sick. Chapter 7, "Predictive Filtering Methods for Power Systems Applications," is contributed by me. Chapter 8, "Intrusion Detection for Computer Security," is by Sung-Bae Cho and Sang-Jun Han. Chapter 9, "Emotion Generating Method on Human–Computer Interfaces," is by Kazuya Mera and Takumi Ichimura. Chapter 10, "Introduction to Scientific Data Mining: Direct Kernel

The editor and the following chapter authors had a meeting at the SMC '03 conference on October 6, 2003 at the Hyatt Regency Crystal City, Arlington, Virginia. *From left*: Seppo J. Ovaska (Chapters 1 and 7), Akimoto Kamiya (Chapter 2), Sang-Jun Han (Chapter 8), Mark J. Embrechts (Chapter 10), and Bernhard Sick (Chapter 6). Also Gregory D. Buckner (Chapter 5) and Richard E. Saeks (Chapter 3) attended the conference, but were not available when the photo was taken.

Methods and Applications," is by Mark J. Embrechts, Boleslaw Szymanski, and Karsten Sternickel. Chapter 11, "World Wide Web Usage Mining," is by Ajith Abraham.

During the past six years, I have had excellent opportunities to collaborate with many recognized scholars in the fields of soft computing and computational intelligence. Of those colleagues and friends, I want to thank Drs. Hugh F. VanLandingham (Virginia Polytechnic Institute and State University), Yasuhiko Dote (Muroran Institute of Technology), and Akimoto Kamiya (Kushiro National College of Technology). Their insightful advices and stimulating enthusiasm have guided me in the dynamic field of computationally intelligent hybrid systems.

As a final thought, I attended the 2003 IEEE International Conference on Systems, Man, and Cybernetics (SMC '03). The last conference day began with an inspiring panel discussion on "New Research Directions in Systems, Man, and Cybernetics." The distinguished panel members expressed and discussed their views on emerging research topics. Dr. Richard E. Saeks, senior past president of the IEEE SMC Society, emphasized in his opening talk the fundamental role of the fusion of soft computing and hard computing in developing computationally intelligent systems for aerospace and other safety-critical applications. Saeks' strong message was delivered to the audience of some 400 conference partici-pants. It was certainly an important step in making the *fusion* concept recognized by the worldwide research community. During the conference, I had a chance to meet six of the chapter contributors (see the group photograph). Such an informal face-to-face meeting was really valuable, and it enforced the "we" spirit of the attending book team.

SEPPO J. OVASKA

Helsinki University of Technology
August 2004

REFERENCES TO PREFACE

1. S. J. Ovaska, Y. Dote, T. Furuhashi, A. Kamiya, and H. F. VanLandingham, "Fusion of Soft Computing and Hard Computing Techniques: A Review of Applications," *Proceedings of the IEEE International Conference on Systems, Man, and Cybernetics*, Tokyo, Japan, Oct. 1999, **1**, pp. 370–375.

2. S. J. Ovaska and H. F. VanLandingham, "Guest Editorial: Special Issue on Fusion of Soft Computing and Hard Computing in Industrial Applications," *IEEE Transactions on Systems, Man, and Cybernetics—Part C: Applications and Reviews* **32**, 69–71 (2002).

EDITOR'S INTRODUCTION TO CHAPTER 1

Fusion of soft-computing (SC) and hard-computing (HC) methodologies is a well-known approach for practicing engineers. Since the utilization of evolutionary computation, fuzzy logic, and neural networks began to emerge in various applications, also complementary unions of SC and HC have been in common use. Nevertheless, the actual term "Fusion of Soft Computing and Hard Computing" was invented as recently as 1998. But why do we need such a term *now* if the basic ideas have been in applications use already for more than a decade? We will return to this relevant question at the end of the following discussion.

Soft computing is sometimes called—particularly in Japan—"human-like information processing." This is a somewhat misleading description, because the human brain has two specialized hemispheres, the left one (logic, mathematics, analysis, serial processing, etc.) and the right one (creativity, recognition, synthesis, parallel processing, etc.), and they are connected closely to one another through the *corpus callosum*, which consists of over 200 million nerves [1]. Each hemisphere is continually supporting and complementing the activity of the other. Roger W. Sperry shared the 1981 Nobel Prize in Medicine for his discoveries concerning "the functional specialization of the cerebral hemispheres" [2]. Based on his brilliant work that enhanced our comprehension of the higher functions of human brain, obvious analogies have been established between the left brain and HC, as well as between the right brain and SC. Furthermore, the massive bundle of connecting nerves corresponds to the fusion interface between the two computing paradigms; this crucial communications extension to the above brain analogy is hardly ever mentioned in the literature.

Computationally Intelligent Hybrid Systems. Edited by Seppo J. Ovaska
ISBN 0-471-47668-4 © 2005 the Institute of Electrical and Electronics Engineers, Inc.

The aims of human-like *hybrid* information processing are directed toward developing either computationally intelligent (CI) or artificially intelligent (AI) systems—that is, computer-based implementations with high machine IQ. The key distinction between these two common terms was defined by Bezdek in 1994 [3]. In his practical definition, CI is a subset of AI; and the term "artificially intelligent" is reserved for systems where computational intelligence is augmented by "incorporating knowledge (tidbits) in a non-numerical way."

Hayashi and Umano published a seminal article on fusing fuzzy logic and neural networks in 1993 [4]. Their pragmatic discussion on different fusion categories was an activator for the fuzzy-neuro boom of the late 1990s. By explicitly emphasizing the complementary fusion approach, they stimulated the (Japanese) engineering community to develop *hybrid intelligent systems*. Besides, they wisely pointed out that to combine individual methodologies effectively, considerable attention should be paid to the interface section; it is generally not effective to force two algorithms together.

Chapter 1 of the present book, "Introduction to Fusion of Soft Computing and Hard Computing," is authored by Seppo J. Ovaska. It forms a solid basis for the complementary fusion of soft computing and hard computing methodologies by introducing a representative set of fusion architectures and defining their functional mappings. In addition, it gives a concise definition of "Fusion of Soft Computing and Hard Computing" and offers a rationale for the term. Most of the reviewed real-world examples contain *loose* connections of SC and HC algorithms, while the more *intimate* connections offer future research and development (R&D) potential. As an interpretation of Chapter 1, the principal R&D challenges of this fusion field can be summarized as follows:

- Interface sophistication beyond the current means
- True symbiosis of soft computing and hard computing techniques
- Fusion implementations at different levels of hierarchy (algorithm, subsystem, system, and entity)

Let us now return to the question, *Why* do we need the term "Fusion of Soft Computing and Hard Computing"? This concept needs to be recognized explicitly, because in that way we can highlight that there is a lot of unused R&D potential in the *interface section* between SC and HC methodologies. In the highly successful human brain, the left and right hemispheres are linked closely together. By following such an analogy, it could be anticipated that a high degree of interaction between soft and hard computing would lead to better implementation economy of CI and AI systems, improved tolerance against incomplete or uncertain sensor data, enhanced learning and adaptation capabilities, and increased machine IQ. All those characteristics are needed for developing autonomously intelligent systems. Furthermore, the fuzzy-neuro era of the 1990s started after Hayashi and Umano summarized the principal fusion structures with an insightful discussion on the entire fusion approach [4].

A similar boost in the R&D of computationally or artificially intelligent hybrid systems could follow the present book.

REFERENCES

1. P. Russell, *The Brain Book*, Routledge & Kegan Paul, London, UK, 1979, pp. 48–63.
2. The Nobel Assembly at the Karolinska Institute, "Press Release: The 1981 Nobel Prize in Physiology or Medicine," Oct. 1981, Stockholm, Sweden. WWW page. Available from <http://www.nobel.se/medicine/laureates/1981/press.html>.
3. J. C. Bezdek, "What is Computational Intelligence?" in J. M. Zurada, R. J. Marks II, and C. J. Robinson, eds., *Computational Intelligence: Imitating Life*, IEEE Press, Piscataway, NJ, 1994, pp. 1–11.
4. I. Hayashi and M. Umano, "Perspectives and Trends of Fuzzy-Neural Networks," *Journal of the Japan Society of Fuzzy Theory and Systems* **5**, 178–190 (1993), in Japanese.

CHAPTER 1

INTRODUCTION TO FUSION OF SOFT COMPUTING AND HARD COMPUTING

SEPPO J. OVASKA
Helsinki University of Technology, Espoo, Finland

1.1 INTRODUCTION

The roots of this book on the fusion of soft computing and hard computing method-ologies can be traced back to the IEEE International Conference on Systems, Man, and Cybernetics that was held in San Diego, California, in 1998. One of the highlights of that conference was the panel discussion on "New Frontiers in Information/Intelligent Systems." Lotfi A. Zadeh, the father of fuzzy logic and soft computing, was the moderator of the panel, and the panelists were all world-class scholars in the field of soft computing. While the discussion was surely stimu-lating and provided inspiring visions, something was missing—the dominating and continuing role of conventional hard computing in developing successful products and profitable services was not recognized at all—and that caused us to focus our research interests on the complementary *fusion* of these two principal methodologies.

1.1.1 Soft Computing

From the practicing engineer's point of view, a large amount of real-world problems can be solved competitively by hard computing. The term "hard comput-ing" is not nearly as widely accepted or known as "soft computing," but Zadeh used it already in his original definition of soft computing (quoted from a memo [1] written in 1991 and updated in 1994; references 2–4 added by the author of the present chapter):

Computationally Intelligent Hybrid Systems. Edited by Seppo J. Ovaska
ISBN 0-471-47668-4 © 2005 the Institute of Electrical and Electronics Engineers, Inc.

Soft computing differs from conventional (hard) computing in that, unlike hard computing, it is tolerant of imprecision, uncertainty, partial truth, and approximation. In effect, the role model for soft computing is the human mind. The guiding principle of soft computing is: Exploit the tolerance for imprecision, uncertainty, partial truth, and approximation to achieve tractability, robustness and low solution cost. The basic ideas underlying soft computing in its current incarnation have links to many earlier influences, among them Zadeh's 1965 paper on fuzzy sets [2]; the 1973 paper on the analysis of complex systems and decision processes [3]; and the 1981 paper on possibility theory and soft data analysis [4]. The inclusion of neural computing and genetic computing in soft computing came at a later point.

At this juncture, the principal constituents of soft computing (SC) are fuzzy logic (FL), neural computing (NC), genetic computing (GC) and probabilistic reasoning (PR), with the latter subsuming belief networks, chaos theory and parts of learning theory. What is important to note is that soft computing is not a mélange. Rather, it is a partnership in which each of the partners contributes a distinct methodology for addressing problems in its domain. In this perspective, the principal constituent methodologies in SC are complementary rather than competitive. Furthermore, soft computing may be viewed as a foundation component for the emerging field of conceptual intelligence.

In the present chapter, however, we use consistently the term "neural networks" (NN) instead of "neural computing," and we use the more general "evolutionary computation" (EC) as a replacement for "genetic computing." Otherwise, we follow strictly Zadeh's original definition of soft computing (SC). Furthermore, it should be pointed out that many people actually use the word "computing" when they mean hard computing (HC) and that they use "computational intelligence" as a substitute of soft computing. Soft computing is a low-level cognition in the style of the human mind as well as evolution of species in the nature, and it is in contrast to symbolic artificial intelligence (AI) that consists of expert systems, machine learning, and case-based reasoning. The mainstream AI is firmly committed to hard computing instead of soft computing.

SC is already a significant field of research and development; nearly 64,000 soft computing-related journal and conference papers were published between 1989 and 2002 by the IEEE and IEE together. Figure 1.1 illustrates the growth of published journal and conference articles on soft computing during those 14 years (based on the IEEE *Xplore*™ database; data collected on December 10, 2003). From 1989 to 1994, the number of conference papers was growing rather linearly, while the five-year period 1994–1998 was surprisingly flat. The year 2002 set a new record of conference publishing—nearly 6000 publications in one year. On the other hand, the number of journal articles has remained practically constant (around 1100) during the past few years. Therefore, it can be stated that soft computing has an established position in the research community, as well as a stabilizing publishing volume. It should be remembered, however, that in parallel with the recognized IEEE and IEE journals, there is a growing number of new journals on soft computing and its constituents.

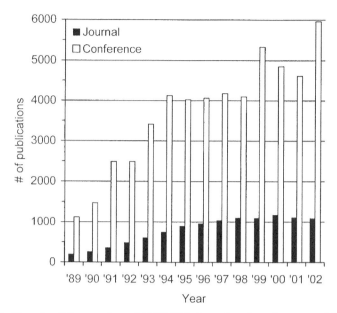

Figure 1.1. Growth of the number of IEEE/IEE journal and conference articles on soft computing and its applications.

Soft computing methods are penetrating gradually to industrial applications: They are no longer just in Japan and South Korea, but also in the United States and Europe. In the majority of such applications, SC is hidden inside systems or subsystems, and the end user does not necessarily know that soft computing methods are used in control, fault diagnosis, pattern recognition, signal processing, and so on. This is the case when SC is mainly utilized for improving the performance of conventional HC algorithms or even replacing them. Another class of applications uses soft computing for implementing computationally intelligent and user-friendly features that could not be realized competitively by HC. One important reason behind the growing industrial acceptance of SC is the existence of advantageous combinations of individual SC methods, such as fuzzy-neuro, genetic algorithm (GA) like fuzzy, and neuro-GA [5,6]. From the applications point of view, those combined constituents of SC are often more efficient than pure evolutionary computation, fuzzy logic, or neural networks.

1.1.2 Fusion of Soft-Computing and Hard-Computing Methodologies

Soft-computing methods are also commonly fused to more conventional hard-computing techniques in industrial products, instead of using SC unaccompanied. While academic researchers typically prefer *either* SC *or* HC methodologies, the complementary fusion of SC and HC is, increasingly, a natural way of thinking for practicing engineers, who are facing demanding real-world problems to be solved competitively. Recently, Goldberg presented three principal requirements that are essential in making SC widespread among different applications [7]:

- Scalable results
- Practicality
- Little models or theory

Besides, he emphasized the importance of more complex integration of individual SC methods in developing autonomously intelligent systems. We would definitely include the complementary fusion of SC and HC in that requirements list.

There exist several vague ideas and informal definitions of the new concept "Fusion of Soft Computing and Hard Computing" in the researchers' and engineers' minds, but none of the used ones has yet obtained a dominating position. Our specific definition of this emerging concept can be stated as follows:

> An algorithm- or system-level union of particular soft computing and hard computing methodologies, in which either methodology is signal-, parameter-, or structure-wise dependent upon and receives functional reinforcement from the other.

The noteworthy role of the fusion of SC and HC was highlighted in a recent special issue, edited by Ovaska and VanLandingham, on "Fusion of Soft Computing and Hard Computing in Industrial Applications" that was published in the *IEEE Transactions on Systems, Man, and Cybernetics—Part C: Applications and Reviews* [8]. A summarizing overview article [9] and eight original contributions [10–17], discussing advanced applications, were presented in that pioneering special issue. The feedback from the research and development community that the guest editors received during and after the editing process was mostly positive but also somewhat negative. This negative feedback was consistently related to the *vagueness* of the entire fusion concept, because, at that time, there was not available any systematic treatment on different fusion categories or their characteristic features in the context of integrated SC and HC. The qualitative work of Agarwal on combining neural and conventional paradigms for modeling, prediction, and control is a partial attempt toward that direction [18]. On the other hand, in the context of pure SC, a landmark discussion on various fusion categories was presented by Hayashi and Umano in 1993 [19] (in Japanese), and a discussion on the characteristic features for knowledge acquisition was presented by Furuhashi in 2001 [20]. An extended discussion of Hayashi's and Umano's fusion categories, including also genetic algorithms, is available in reference 5 (in English).

To establish a theoretical framework for the fusion of SC and HC, we will analyze below both the structural categories and characteristic features of the core fusion topologies, and thus provide a similar basis for the fusion of SC and HC that already exists for the fusion or hybridization of individual SC methods [5,20]. It is crucial for the successful development of computationally intelligent hybrid systems to pay particular attention to the integration and interaction of SC and HC constituents. Our aim is to remove the criticized vagueness aspect that was mentioned above. In this way, the fusion of SC and HC may obtain a similar solid position in the research and development community as the fusion of individual SC methods attained already in the middle of the 1990s. The ultimate motivation behind our fusion discussion is naturally to advance the global use of SC in real-world applications.

This chapter is organized as follows. In Section 1.2, we introduce the structural categories of the fusion of SC and HC, as well as provide a brief discussion on the procedure how these categories were identified. Next, in Section 1.3, we discuss the characteristic features of SC and HC constituents in a few representative fusion applications. Section 1.4 gives a demonstrative categorization of several published fusions of SC and HC in industrial applications. Finally, Section 1.5 closes this chapter with a conclusion and a brief discussion on the acceptance of SC methods to industrial use.

1.2 STRUCTURAL CATEGORIES

By following the original and pragmatic thinking of Hayashi and Umano [19] and after analyzing a substantial number of application articles, we will next introduce 12 core categories for the complementary fusion of SC and HC. They belong to the class of "little models or theory" that was emphasized by Goldberg in the keynote address of reference 7. In his practical view, only little but sufficient models or theory are advancing the spread of SC, because research and development engineers prefer plain and straightforward solutions. Our core fusion categories are first summarized in Table 1.1. The adopted qualitative measure, *fusion grade* [5], describes the strength of a particular connection between SC and HC constituents. Table 1.2 gives brief definitions of the employed fusion grades: low, moderate, high, and very

TABLE 1.1. Structural Fusion Categories

#	Acronym	Description	Fusion Grade
1	SC&HC	SC and HC are isolated from each other	Low
2	SC/HC	SC and HC are connected in parallel	Moderate
3	SC\HC	SC with HC feedback	Moderate
4	HC\SC	HC with SC feedback	Moderate
5	SC-HC	SC is cascaded with HC	Moderate
6	HC-SC	HC is cascaded with SC	Moderate
7	HC=SC	HC-designed SC	High/very high
8	SC=HC	SC-designed HC	High/very high
9	HC+SC	HC-augmented SC	Very high
10	SC+HC	SC-augmented HC	Very high
11	HC//SC	HC-assisted SC	Very high
12	SC//HC	SC-assisted HC	Very high

TABLE 1.2. Definitions of Fusion Grades

Fusion Grade	Qualitative Definition
Low	SC and HC in simultaneous or alternative use without explicit connections
Moderate	Connections on input/output signal level only
High	SC or HC used for determining values of internal parameters
Very high	HC or SC used for determining internal structure or generating/ manipulating internal data

high. Below is a description of each core fusion category, as well as an introductory discussion on six supplementary categories.

1.2.1   Soft Computing and Hard Computing Are Isolated from Each Other

In SC&HC-type systems (Fig. 1.2), both the SC and HC constituents have their independent roles, and there is no explicit connection between them. A descriptive example of such a loose union is an advanced elevator group dispatcher, where the primary call allocation algorithm is usually based on SC methods (NN, FL, or EC), while the backup algorithm, which becomes effective should the hall call interface have a serious failure, is typically a simple HC procedure (finite-state machine). In such cases, the fusion grade is naturally low, because there is no direct information exchange between the individual SC and HC blocks. The mathematical mappings realized by SC&HC are formulated below:

$$\mathbf{y}_1(n) = f_{SC}(\boldsymbol{\theta}_{SC}; \mathbf{x}_1(n))$$
$$\mathbf{y}_2(n) = f_{HC}(\boldsymbol{\theta}_{HC}; \mathbf{x}_2(n))$$

(1.1)

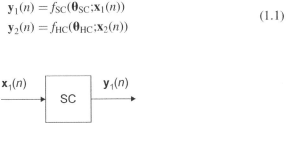

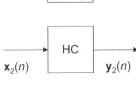

Figure 1.2. Partnership of soft computing and hard computing without explicit connection. All the arrow lines may contain several individual signals or data/parameter elements.

where $f_{SC}(\cdot;\cdot)$ and $f_{HC}(\cdot;\cdot)$ are arbitrary SC and HC algorithms (mapping functions), respectively; $\mathbf{x}(n)$ is the input and $\mathbf{y}(n)$ the output of such an algorithm; and $\boldsymbol{\theta}_{SC}$ and $\boldsymbol{\theta}_{HC}$ are the corresponding system parameters (coefficients, weights, etc.). All the boldface symbols represent vectors in this discussion; multiple inputs and outputs are identified by a subscript; and n is a discrete-time index. Although we are assuming that the SC and HC blocks are discrete-time systems, the presented fusion structures could straightforwardly be modified for continuous-time systems as well.

1.2.2 Soft Computing and Hard Computing Are Connected in Parallel

The second category, SC/HC, is presently of moderate practical interest. It offers possibilities for creating versatile combinations of SC and HC. In this parallel-connected topology, SC is complementing the behavior and capabilities of a primary HC system, or vice versa (Fig. 1.3). A typical example of such a configuration is an augmented linear controller (HC-type), where the nonlinearities and possible uncertainties of a plant are compensated by a parallel-connected SC-type controller. Such a closed-loop system could often be stabilized even without the supplementary SC controller, and the role of SC is merely to fine-tune the control performance and provide additional robustness. Besides, such parallel SC and HC systems are often considerably easier to design and more efficient to implement than pure HC systems with comparable performance. In this important category, the fusion grade is moderate. The characteristic function of SC/HC is defined as

$$\mathbf{y}(n) = f_{SC}(\boldsymbol{\theta}_{SC};\mathbf{x}_1(n)) \oplus f_{HC}(\boldsymbol{\theta}_{HC};\mathbf{x}_2(n)) \tag{1.2}$$

where the merging operator, $\oplus$, denotes either addition or combining of data/signal vectors, that is, $\mathbf{a} \oplus \mathbf{b}$ is either $\mathbf{a} + \mathbf{b}$ or $[\mathbf{a}\,\mathbf{b}]$, where $\mathbf{a}$ and $\mathbf{b}$ are arbitrary row/column vectors.

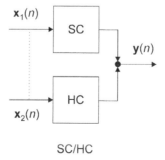

SC/HC

Figure 1.3. Soft computing and hard computing in parallel. Dotted line shows a typical connection.

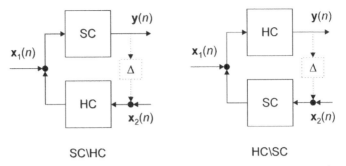

SC\HC   HC\SC

Figure 1.4. Soft computing with hard computing feedback and hard computing with soft computing feedback. Dotted line shows a typical connection.

1.2.3   Soft Computing with Hard-Computing Feedback and Hard Computing with Soft-Computing Feedback

Also the feedback parallel connections, SC\HC and HC\SC, are currently of some applications use. In these cases, the output of HC feedback or SC feedback is added to the input of the primary SC and HC blocks, respectively (Fig. 1.4). Notice that all fusion structures containing feedback must have a delay element Δ on the feedback loop to make the system realizable. The reversed parallel connections are used in a variety of control applications—for example, for improving the transient performance of a closed control loop. As with the forward parallel connection, SC/HC, the feedback parallel connections have also moderate fusion grades. The input–output mappings of SC\HC and HC\SC can be expressed in the following compact form:

$$y(n) = f_{SC}(\theta_{SC};[x_1(n) \oplus f_{HC}(\theta_{HC};x_2(n))]) \tag{1.3}$$

$$y(n) = f_{HC}(\theta_{HC};[x_1(n) \oplus f_{SC}(\theta_{SC};x_2(n))]) \tag{1.4}$$

1.2.4   Soft Computing Is Cascaded with Hard Computing or Hard Computing Is Cascaded with Soft Computing

There are two obvious alternatives to form hybrid cascades of SC and HC algorithms, SC-HC or HC-SC, depending on the sequential order of those functional blocks (Fig. 1.5). In these widespread configurations, the first block is usually a kind of pre-processor and the second one acts as a post-processor. A typical example of the SC-HC configuration is a dual-stage optimization procedure, where the initial optimization phase is carried out by evolutionary computation (global search), and the intermediate result is then refined by some gradient-based algorithm (local search) to yield the final optimum. This kind of complementary fusion leads to computationally efficient "global" optimization. It should be pointed out, however, that such a hybrid method cannot be applied if the local gradient of the criterion function is incalculable or difficult to obtain. Besides, when the

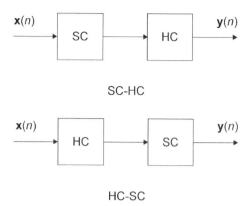

Figure 1.5. Cascades of soft computing and hard computing.

surface of the criterion function is very complicated, local gradient plays a smaller role even in the local search. Therefore, the dual-stage optimization procedure may offer clear advantages in specific applications, but is not as general-purpose a technique as EC alone. Moreover, instead of using a gradient-based algorithm in the second optimization stage, also other local-information-based algorithms (e.g., the simplex algorithm [21]) are applicable. On the other hand, a typical HC-SC configuration is an SC-based pattern recognition system, where the feature vectors are first constructed by HC-based linear/nonlinear filters or interdomain transforms. Soft computing techniques are then used for automatic pattern recognition or classification tasks. Also these cascade configurations have moderate fusion grades. Equations (1.5) and (1.6) describe the cascade structures SC-HC and HC-SC, respectively:

$$\mathbf{y}(n) = f_{HC}(\boldsymbol{\theta}_{HC}; f_{SC}(\boldsymbol{\theta}_{SC}; \mathbf{x}(n))) \tag{1.5}$$

$$\mathbf{y}(n) = f_{SC}(\boldsymbol{\theta}_{SC}; f_{HC}(\boldsymbol{\theta}_{HC}; \mathbf{x}(n))) \tag{1.6}$$

1.2.5 Soft-Computing-Designed Hard Computing and Hard-Computing-Designed Soft Computing

The next two combinations, SC=HC and HC=SC, have high or very high fusion grades. This is because SC is explicitly assisting the design or configuring of a HC system, or vice versa (Fig. 1.6). A usual example of SC=HC is a simple linear controller with SC-based gain scheduling for improved handling of varying dynamical characteristics. Such a hybrid controller could be tuned coarsely by experienced human operators; and the gain scheduling extension is further adjusting the control parameters within the predefined stability and performance range. In contrast, the conventional back-propagation training of layered neural networks is actually an HC=SC-type fusion. Another example of the HC=SC-type fusion is a dynamic neural network model with the computational structure and possibly

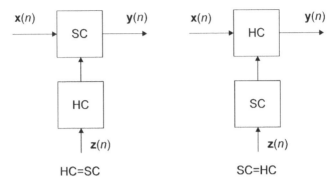

Figure 1.6. Hard-computing-designed soft computing and soft-computing-designed hard computing.

some physical parameters taken from a traditional differential or difference equations-based model. The SC=HC and HC=SC mappings can be expressed conveniently by the following formulae:

$$y(n) = f_{SC}\left(\overbrace{\tilde{\boldsymbol{\theta}}_{SC}, f_{HC}(\boldsymbol{\theta}_{HC}; \mathbf{z}(n))}^{\text{Parameters}}; \mathbf{x}(n) \right) \tag{1.7}$$

$$y(n) = f_{HC}\left(\overbrace{\tilde{\boldsymbol{\theta}}_{HC}, f_{SC}(\boldsymbol{\theta}_{SC}; \mathbf{z}(n))}^{\text{Parameters}}; \mathbf{x}(n) \right) \tag{1.8}$$

Here, the principal SC (or HC) algorithm has two classes of parameters: internal parameters, $\tilde{\boldsymbol{\theta}}_{\cdot C}$, and externally supplied parameters, $f_{\cdot C}(\boldsymbol{\theta}_{\cdot C}, \mathbf{z}(n))$. They both are needed for providing the final output. In some applications, however, the principal SC (or HC) algorithm may not have any internal parameters, but all the necessary parameters are provided by an external HC (or SC) algorithm.

1.2.6   Hard-Computing-Augmented Soft Computing and Soft-Computing-Augmented Hard Computing

The next intimate structures, HC+SC and SC+HC, have very high fusion grades (Fig. 1.7). In the former case, the HC block is first extracting some internal data, $\mathbf{z}(n)$, from the SC algorithm and, after some further processing, the resulting HC output is added or combined to the principal SC output. Moreover, in the latter case, the SC block is processing certain internal data from the HC algorithm, and the final output is the sum or combination of the individual HC and SC outputs. These two categories are not widely used in real-world applications, but they offer great potential for developing advanced fusions of SC and HC methodologies.

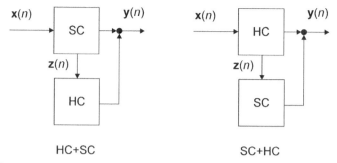

Figure 1.7. Hard-computing-augmented soft computing and soft-computing-augmented hard computing.

In Section 1.3, we will identify one promising HC+SC-type fusion with emerging application interest. HC+SC and SC+HC structures are formulated as

$$\mathbf{y}(n) = f_{SC}(\boldsymbol{\theta}_{SC};\mathbf{x}(n)) \oplus f_{HC}(\boldsymbol{\theta}_{HC};\mathbf{z}(n)) \tag{1.9}$$

$$\mathbf{y}(n) = f_{HC}(\boldsymbol{\theta}_{HC};\mathbf{x}(n)) \oplus f_{SC}(\boldsymbol{\theta}_{SC};\mathbf{z}(n)) \tag{1.10}$$

1.2.7 Hard-Computing-Assisted Soft Computing and Soft-Computing-Assisted Hard Computing

HC-assisted SC and SC-assisted HC are master–slave-type structures that are used moderately/sparsely in real-world applications. In HC/SC, some internal data are first extracted from the SC algorithm (master), processed by the specific HC algorithm (slave), and fed back into the SC algorithm, which completes the primary task. Thus, the HC constituent is an integral part of the computational procedure. An example of this kind of fusion is a hybrid genetic algorithm with Lamarckian or Baldwinian local search strategies [22], where a local search is following the selection–crossover–mutation chain in the repeated evolution loop; and the role of local search is to refine the chromosome population yielding to a new population for fitness evaluation and further genetic manipulations. SC//HC, on the other hand, is an analogous symbiosis between a principal HC algorithm and an assisting SC algorithm. Both of these structures (Fig. 1.8) have very high fusion grades, and they carry out the following input–output mappings:

$$\mathbf{y}(n) = f_{SC}\left(\tilde{\boldsymbol{\theta}}_{SC}; \overbrace{\mathbf{x}(n), f_{HC}(\boldsymbol{\theta}_{HC};\mathbf{z}(n))}^{\text{Inputs}} \right) \tag{1.11}$$

$$\mathbf{y}(n) = f_{HC}\left(\tilde{\boldsymbol{\theta}}_{HC}; \overbrace{\mathbf{x}(n), f_{SC}(\boldsymbol{\theta}_{SC};\mathbf{z}(n))}^{\text{Inputs}} \right) \tag{1.12}$$

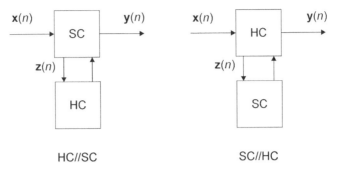

Figure 1.8. Hard-computing-assisted soft computing and soft-computing-assisted hard computing.

1.2.8   Supplementary Categories

In classifying the different kind of fusions of neural networks and fuzzy logic, Hayashi et al. proposed 11 structural categories [5]. This is about the same as our 12 core categories for the fusion of SC and HC. On the other hand, Agarwal identified only the three most obvious fusion structures of neural networks and conventional paradigms (i.e., NN/HC, NN-HC, and HC-NN) in his article that was published in 1995 [18]. Another relevant discussion on integration architectures, related to symbolic artificial intelligence (SA), FL, GA, and NN, was presented by Fu in his 1996 conference tutorial [23]. He identified five integration architectures with three coupling strengths. Those hybrid architectures share obvious similarities with our core categories.

Because the field of HC is much wider and more heterogeneous than the field of SC, we decided to classify only the universal categories. If the very details of specific HC algorithms were taken into consideration, the number of fusion categories could be increased considerably. Since the fusion structures of Figs. 1.2–1.8 have the minimum number of SC and HC blocks—only one of each type—they are said to be canonic. It should be pointed out that more complex, large-scale systems are naturally modeled as interconnections of these canonic building blocks.

Most of the fusion categories discussed above were created following the synergy between the fusion of SC and HC and the fusion of individual SC methods [5,19]. In addition, numerous journal and conference articles were thoroughly analyzed to verify the coverage of intermediate category sets. After identifying a relevant structural category, like HC\SC, its reverse category, SC\HC, was also carefully considered for the final category set. This particular reverse category, although not in wide use among practicing engineers, offers apparent potential for developing advantageous fusions of SC and HC. Moreover, Fig. 1.9 illustrates the reverse categories of HC+SC and SC+HC. Due to the small number of existing applications, these two categories were not included in the core category set of Table 1.1. Equations (1.13) and (1.14) give the mappings of the reversed SC+HC and

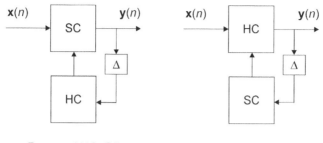

Figure 1.9. Reversed HC+SC and SC+HC structures.

HC+SC structures, respectively:

$$\mathbf{y}(n) = f_{SC}\left(\boldsymbol{\theta}_{SC}; \overbrace{\mathbf{x}(n), f_{HC}(\boldsymbol{\theta}_{HC};\mathbf{y}(n - \Delta))}^{\text{Inputs}}\right) \tag{1.13}$$

$$\mathbf{y}(n) = f_{HC}\left(\boldsymbol{\theta}_{HC}; \overbrace{\mathbf{x}(n), f_{SC}(\boldsymbol{\theta}_{SC};\mathbf{y}(n - \Delta))}^{\text{Inputs}}\right) \tag{1.14}$$

It should be noted that here the fusion structures contain a feedback loop and, therefore, the value of $\mathbf{y}(n)$ must be delayed at least by one sampling period—that is, $\Delta \geq 1$—to make the systems realizable. These reversed structures have two kinds of inputs: the primary input, $\mathbf{x}(n)$, and the auxiliary input, $f_{\bullet C}(\boldsymbol{\theta}_{\bullet C};\mathbf{y}(n - \Delta))$.

Structural transposition or flow-graph reversal of the defined core categories leads to two additional structures (Fig. 1.7 → Fig. 1.10) that may offer innovation potential. Their mathematical mappings are formulated in Eqs. (1.15) and (1.16). However, to our best knowledge, they are not commonly in applications use and,

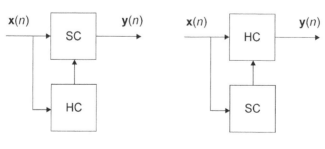

Figure 1.10. Transposed HC+SC and SC+HC structures.

therefore, we decided to omit them from Table 1.1. On the other hand, the fusion categories of Fig. 1.10 could be used at least for initializing the internal states or memory of SC or HC models.

$$\mathbf{y}(n) = f_{SC}\left(\boldsymbol{\theta}_{SC}; \overbrace{\mathbf{x}(n), f_{HC}(\boldsymbol{\theta}_{HC}; \mathbf{x}(n))}^{\text{Inputs}}\right) \tag{1.15}$$

$$\mathbf{y}(n) = f_{HC}\left(\boldsymbol{\theta}_{HC}; \overbrace{\mathbf{x}(n), f_{SC}(\boldsymbol{\theta}_{SC}; \mathbf{x}(n))}^{\text{Inputs}}\right) \tag{1.16}$$

For completeness of this category presentation, reversed versions of the transposed HC+SC and SC+HC are depicted in Fig. 1.11. Both of these structures have also a feedback loop that must contain a delay element Δ. Moreover, they can be expressed mathematically as

$$\mathbf{y}(n) = f_{SC}(\boldsymbol{\theta}_{SC}; [\mathbf{x}(n) \oplus f_{HC}^{\Delta}(\boldsymbol{\theta}_{HC}; \mathbf{z}(n))]) \tag{1.17}$$

$$\mathbf{y}(n) = f_{HC}(\boldsymbol{\theta}_{HC}; [\mathbf{x}(n) \oplus f_{SC}^{\Delta}(\boldsymbol{\theta}_{SC}; \mathbf{z}(n))]) \tag{1.18}$$

In Eqs. (1.17) and (1.18), the necessary loop delay, Δ, is shown as a superscript of the HC and SC algorithms, respectively.

It should be pointed out that similar to the core HC+SC and SC+HC structures of Fig. 1.7, the six supplementary fusion structures of Figs. 1.9–1.11 are also intimate fusions of SC and HC and, therefore, have very high fusion grades. In Section 1.4, we will classify a representative collection of application papers on the fusion of SC and HC according to the structural categories of Table 1.1.

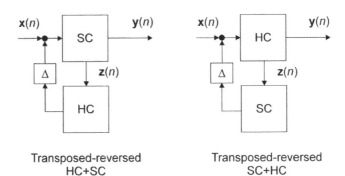

Figure 1.11. Transposed-reversed HC+SC and SC+HC structures.

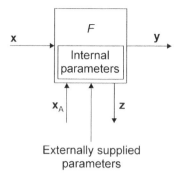

Figure 1.12. Generic SC or HC system with signal/data inputs and outputs, as well as externally supplied system parameters.

1.2.9 General Soft-Computing and Hard-Computing Mapping Functions

We will next define mathematically the general mapping functions (algorithms), $f_{SC}(\cdot;\cdot)$ and $f_{HC}(\cdot;\cdot)$, used in Eqs. (1.1)–(1.18). Our compact definition follows the operational structure and notations of Fig. 1.12. It should be noticed, however, that only SC=HC- and HC=SC-type fusions use the externally supplied parameters that are shown in Fig. 1.12. The nonlinear or linear mapping function, $F \in \{f_{SC}, f_{HC}\}$, from the primary input vector, $\mathbf{x} \in \Re^{N}$, and the auxiliary input vector (optional), $\mathbf{x}_A \in \Re^{K}$, to the internal output vector (optional), $\mathbf{z} \in \Re^{L}$, and the primary output vector, $\mathbf{y} \in \Re^{M}$, can be expressed as

$$F:\langle \mathbf{x} \in \Re^{N}, \mathbf{x}_A \in \Re^{K} \rangle \longrightarrow \langle \mathbf{z} \in \Re^{L}, \mathbf{y} \in \Re^{M} \rangle \tag{1.19}$$

where $\mathbf{x} = [x_1, x_2, \ldots, x_N]^{\mathrm{T}}$, $\mathbf{x}_A = [x_{A,1}, x_{A,2}, \ldots, x_{A,K}]^{\mathrm{T}}$, $\mathbf{z} = [z_1, z_2, \ldots, z_L]^{\mathrm{T}}$, and $\mathbf{y} = [y_1, y_2, \ldots, y_M]^{\mathrm{T}}$. Here, the auxiliary input vector, $\mathbf{x}_A$, and the internal output vector, $\mathbf{z}$, can be considered as partial- or full-state data of the dynamical mapping function, F. All the input and output spaces may naturally have different dimensions; therefore, this general definition covers both single-input single-output (SISO)-type and multiple-input multiple-output (MIMO)-type systems.

1.3 CHARACTERISTIC FEATURES

The central motivation behind fusing elemental SC and HC methods is the aim to overcome the limitations of individual methods. This applies to all fusion categories; the resulting hybrid systems are expected to have such valuable characteristics that would not be either possible or practical to obtain by using a single methodological class only. Table 1.3 contains the most important characteristic features of evolutionary computation [24], fuzzy logic [25], and neural networks [26]. All these constituents of SC have useful functional characteristics that are potentially needed in

TABLE 1.3. Characteristic Features of EC, FL, and NN Methods

SC Method	Characteristic Features
EC	• Search methods inspired by the Neo-Darwinian paradigm • No gradient of the error surface needed • Avoidance of local optima through random perturbations • Computationally intensive
FL	• Rule-based approach • Tolerance for imprecision, partial truth, and uncertainty • Capability to approximate any continuous function or system • Possibility to utilize human intuition
NN	• Black box approach • Massively parallel distributed structure • Supervised or unsupervised learning from data • Generalization ability • Capability to approximate any continuous function or system

real-world applications, because the conceptual structure of HC is overly precise in relation to the imprecision of the world around us, and there is a growing demand for computationally intelligent hybrid systems.

The HC field, on the other hand, is more diverse than the SC field, and thus it is not feasible to create a comprehensive table that would contain the characteristic features of all specific classes of hard computing methods. Therefore, we built Table 1.4, which lists only five representative HC methods with their primary characteristic features. The fusion needs and potential of these HC methods are discussed below.

1.3.1 Proportional Integral Derivative Controllers

Proportional integral derivative (PID) controllers are certainly the most widely used control algorithms in industrial applications. Thus, practicing engineers favor them also in developing future products and systems. However, the requirements of control performance are continuously increasing, and they cannot always be met by using a fixed linear approximation unaccompanied. This problem has been solved successfully, for example, by complementary EC=HC-, FL=HC-, and NN=HC-type fusions of SC and HC [27–29]. In such hybrid systems, the SC constituent is tuning the PI(D) control parameters either incrementally or continuously. To ensure the stability of auto-tuning PI(D) systems, the range and tuning interval of control parameters must be constrained appropriately.

1.3.2 Physical Models

A variety of process models for estimation, prediction, control, and simulation is developed by modeling the entire physical system using its characteristic differential

TABLE 1.4. Characteristic Features of Specific HC Methods

HC Method	Characteristic Features
PID controller	• Simplified linear approximation • Manual tuning possible • Computationally efficient
s-domain models with physical origin	• Solid physical basis (differential equations) • Sensitivity to parameter variation • Tedious derivation of high-order models
Fletcher–Powell optimization algorithm	• Makes use of derivatives of the error surface • Variable metric method • Efficient unconstrained optimization
General parameter adaptation method	• Reduced-rank adaptation • Computationally efficient • Applicable with many computational structures
Stochastic system simulation	• Suitable for various kind of complex systems • Demanding phase of model building • Time-consuming brute force technique

or difference equations. This requires a thorough understanding of the entire system to be modeled. On the other hand, such core knowledge is usually available in matured research and development organizations. Nevertheless, differential equation models and their s-domain counterparts become cumbersome to deal with if the system to be modeled is considerably nonlinear or time-variant, or a high-order model, including also critical secondary effects, is needed to obtain the required accuracy. In these demanding cases, the physics-originated low- or moderate-order linear models have been complemented by neural networks or fuzzy logic-based nonlinear models [30]. The linear approximation remains the "backbone," and its behavior is enhanced by NN/HC- or FL/HC-type fusions, where the SC constituent compensates for system nonlinearities, parameter uncertainty, or other inadequacies of the primary HC model.

1.3.3 Optimization Utilizing Local Information

The Fletcher–Powell optimization algorithm [31] is a widely used unconstrained optimization method that makes use of derivatives of the error surface. This kind of variable-metric algorithm works usually well when the error surface is moderately difficult. However, with highly peaky error landscapes that are typical for complex nonlinear optimization problems, all the derivatives-based methods have a notable possibility of getting stuck on some (poor) local optimum. This undesired possibility has been reduced substantially in advanced HC//EC- and EC-HC-type hybrid optimization procedures [17,32].

1.3.4 General Parameter Adaptation Algorithm

Various neural network models are used frequently for time-series prediction in embedded real-time systems—for example, in automatic fault detection and systems' state estimation. In many applications, however, the predicted time series has specific time-varying characteristics that would actually need an adaptive model for maximizing the prediction accuracy. Unfortunately, fully adaptive neural network implementations have high computational burden. Thus, they are rarely used in real-time applications. With radial basis function networks (RBFNs), such a disturbing time-variance problem was relieved considerably by introducing an intimate HC+NN-type fusion structure [33]. In that hybrid structure, the HC constituent is a simple reduced-rank adaptation scheme, the general parameter (GP) method, which tunes the behavior of the RBFN model around a nominal operation point. The desired input–output mapping at the nominal operation point is represented accurately by the fixed RBFN part, and the simple general parameter extension is able to compensate for reasonable time-varying characteristics in the time series. Similar intimate fusion schemes could also be applied with other layered neural networks that are used in predictive configurations. For example, the fixed output layer of multilayer perceptron (MLP) networks could be complemented by a least-mean-square (LMS)-type adaptive linear combiner [34].

1.3.5 Stochastic System Simulators

Stochastic system simulation is a widely applied technique for analyzing and optimizing complex systems that do not have tractable analytical models. There are several commercial simulation packages available with efficient model building functions and versatile visualization capabilities of simulation results. Monte Carlo-method-based stochastic simulation is considered as a "brute force" technique for optimizing parameters of complex systems. From the computation time point of view, it would be desired to keep the number of simulation cycles at a minimum. On the other hand, that would affect directly the statistical reliability of the simulation results. Such a problem could be reduced by combining evolutionary computation with stochastic system simulation. In an HC//EC-type fusion, the stochastic system simulator is used to compute the values of the fitness function needed in evolutionary optimization [17], and the EC constituent provides an intelligent search of the enormous solution base.

1.3.6 Discussion and Extended Fusion Schemes

Table 1.5 summarizes the principal characteristic features of the fusions of SC and HC that were discussed above. The constructive fusion approaches have provided improved results over nonhybrid techniques. These improvements are chiefly in such areas as computational efficiency, design cost, robustness, and tractability. In addition, the SC-enhanced HC algorithms form a natural intermediate step on the methodological evolution path from pure HC toward dominating SC. Such an

TABLE 1.5. Characteristic Features of Representative Fusions

HC Constituent	Characteristic Features of the Fusion
PID controller	*General* • Automatic tuning of control parameters • Manual tuning still possible • Stability predictable *EC=HC* • Global search of control parameters *FL=HC* • Possibility to utilize human intuition *NN=HC* • Learning from data
s-domain models with physical origin	*General* • Solid physical basis • Ability to handle nonlinearities *FL/HC* • Possibility to utilize human intuition *NN/HC* • Learning from data
Fletcher–Powell optimization algorithm	*EC-HC* • Global search • Efficient unconstrained optimization
General parameter adaptation method	*HC+NN* • Partially adaptive neural network model • Computationally efficient
Stochastic system simulation	*HC//EC* • Optimization method for complex systems • Global search • Demanding phase of model building

evolutionary multistep path is highly preferred in industrial R&D organizations and among practicing engineers.

As mentioned earlier in this chapter, our structural categorization is based on a little model approach. In this approach, each SC or HC constituent is represented by a compact model, and the categorization is based on the types of *interconnections* of these models. However, the fusion of SC and HC could further be extended into "Soft Computing in a Hard Computing Framework" or "Hard Computing in a Soft Computing Framework." In such extended fusion schemes, the resulting system contains only SC constituents that are being implemented in an HC framework, or only HC constituents that are being embedded in an SC framework. Representative examples of such fusions are: genetic algorithms formulated in an object-oriented framework [35]; fuzzy rules coded in a Petri net [36]; neural networks embedded in inverse-model-based control techniques [37]; and various mathematical programming methods combined in a genetic algorithm architecture [38].

1.4 CHARACTERIZATION OF HYBRID APPLICATIONS

In Table 1.6, we list a demonstrative collection of reference articles that contain some fusion structure(s) belonging to one of the core categories of Table 1.1 [10,17,27,32,33,39–54]. To make the reference table more instructive, the SC constituent was divided into three subconstituents: evolutionary computation, fuzzy logic, and neural networks. Because the first category, SC&HC, was not included in this consideration, Table 1.6 contains all together 33 possible fusions of SC and HC methodologies. The carefully selected reference articles, as well as the

TABLE 1.6. Fusion Examples from the Literature

Category	SC	HC	Reference
SC/HC	EC	Mixed-integer linear programming	39
	FL	P-type controller	40
	NN	Two PI controllers with cascaded notch filters	41
SC\HC	EC	Linear combination of visual perception	42
	FL	First-order linear filter	43
	NN	Noise filter	44
HC\SC	EC	Spacecraft navigation and control	45
	FL	Feedback linearization controller	46
	NN	Linearizing control	47
SC-HC	EC	Powell's unconstrained optimization method	32
	FL	Linear quadratic Gaussian-type controller	48
	NN	Narrow-band lowpass filters (integrators)	49
HC-SC	EC	Linear programming for initial population	50
	FL	Extended Kalman filter	48
	NN	Feature extraction algorithm	10
HC=SC	EC	Constraint satisfaction techniques	51
	FL	Gradient-descent method	40
	NN	Newton–Gauss optimization algorithm	52
SC=HC	EC	Two PI controllers with cross-coupling	27
	FL	Dynamic programming algorithm	53
	NN	Optimizing long-range predictive controller	54
HC+SC	EC	—	—
	FL	—	—
	NN	General parameter adaptation algorithm	33
SC+HC	EC	—	—
	FL	—	—
	NN	—	—
HC//SC	EC	Stochastic system simulator	17
	FL	—	—
	NN	—	—
SC//HC	EC	—	—
	FL	—	—
	NN	—	—

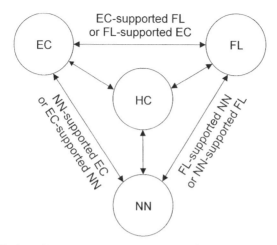

Figure 1.13. Fusion of hard-computing and individual/fused soft-computing methods.

recent overview article [9], guide the reader to the realm of specific fusion implementations. Besides, advanced implementation aspects are discussed systematically in the subsequent chapters of the present book.

As shown in Table 1.6, the number of reported applications with respect to HC+SC, SC+HC, HC//SC, and SC//HC is still very limited. However, as research and development on various applications with respect to the fusion of SC and HC further evolve, these intimate structures will likely become a promising area to be explored.

One noticeable trend in the fusion of SC and HC is the simultaneous partnership of HC and *multiple* SC methodologies as illustrated in Fig. 1.13 [6]. Here, the fused SC methodologies are targeted to provide intelligent behavior or high machine IQ (MIQ) for a variety of advanced systems and products. This attractive goal of intelligent behavior was defined by Fogel et al. in 1965 [55]:

> ... intelligent behavior can result from an ability to predict the environment coupled with the selection of an algorithm which permits the translation of each prediction into a suitable response.

Already in that early definition, intelligent behavior was seen as a coupling of some reliable predictor and a robust translator; and these individual units could be realized efficiently and competitively using the constructive fusion of SC and HC.

1.5 CONCLUSIONS AND DISCUSSION

We introduced 12 structural core categories for the fusion of SC and HC. Figure 1.14 shows a qualitative diagram, where each of these categories is positioned according

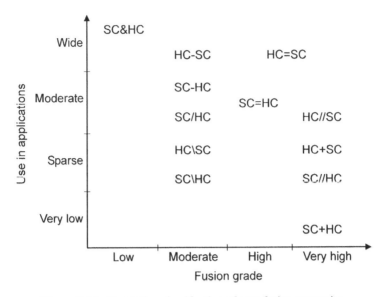

Figure 1.14. Qualitative classification of core fusion categories.

to its fusion grade and current use in engineering applications. By comparing our core categories to those related to the fusion of individual SC methods and after reviewing a large amount of application articles, it can be concluded that the fusion of SC and HC is already a well-defined concept for developing computationally intelligent hybrid systems that largely overcome the shortages and limitations of individual SC and HC methods. In addition to those 12 core categories, we also identified six supplementary categories that offer considerable innovation potential for future applications.

Although the HC and SC research communities are quite separated, it is good to observe that many SC-oriented researchers and engineers are openly favoring the various fusion opportunities. However, the HC community generally seems to be more reluctant in applying the complementing SC techniques. This situation may change progressively following positive experiences, along with the associated evolving emphasis in various engineering curricula. Currently, there is usually an unfortunate division between HC- and SC-oriented courses related to major application topics like electric power systems, industrial electronics, systems engineering, and telecommunications. This separation is clearly hindering the industrial acceptance of SC, because those separated courses do not typically consider the methodological fusion approach at all, but mostly neglect totally the other class of available methodologies.

As a final thought, this fusion discussion is closely related to Zadeh's original aims of fuzzy logic providing an advanced interface between imprecise human reasoning and the highly precise calculations of digital computers.

ACKNOWLEDGMENTS

This work was supported by the Academy of Finland under Grants 80100 and 203436. The author wishes to thank Drs. Randy L. Haupt and Tamal Bose (Electrical and Computer Engineering, Utah State University) for providing the visiting scientist position that made it possible to complete this manuscript in the summer of 2003. Many discussions with Drs. Akimoto Kamiya (Information Engineering, Kushiro National College of Technology) and Hugh F. VanLandingham (Electrical and Computer Engineering, Virginia Polytechnic Institute and State University) were extremely useful.

REFERENCES

1. L. A. Zadeh, "A Definition of Soft Computing in Greater Detail," WWW page, 1991/ 1994. Available from <http://www.cs.berkeley.edu/~mazlack/BISC/BISC-DBM-soft.html>.

2. L. A. Zadeh, "Fuzzy Sets," *Information and Control* **8**, 338–353 (1965).

3. L. A. Zadeh, "Outline of a New Approach to the Analysis of Complex Systems and Decision Processes," *IEEE Transactions on Systems, Man, and Cybernetics* **3**, 28–44 (1973).

4. L. A. Zadeh, "Possibility Theory and Soft Data Analysis," in L. Cobb and R. M. Thrall, eds., *Mathematical Frontiers of the Social and Policy Sciences*, Westview Press, Boulder, CO, 1981, pp. 69–129.

5. I. Hayashi, M. Umano, T. Maeda, A. Bastian, and L. C. Jain, "Acquisition of Fuzzy Knowledge by NN and GA—a Survey of the Fusion and Union Methods Proposed in Japan," *Proceedings of the 2nd International Conference on Knowledge-Based Intelligent Electronic Systems*, Adelaide, Australia, Apr. 1998, pp. 69–78.

6. H. Takagi, "R&D in Intelligent Technologies: Fusion of NN, FS, GA, Chaos, and Human," *Half-Day Tutorial/Workshop, IEEE International Conference on Systems, Man, and Cybernetics*, Orlando, FL, Oct. 11, 1997.

7. D. E. Goldberg, "A Meditation on the Application of Soft Computing and Its Future," in R. Roy, M. Köppen, S. Ovaska, T. Furuhashi, and F. Hoffmann, eds., *Soft Computing and Industry: Recent Applications*, Springer-Verlag, London, UK, 2002, pp. XV–XVIII.

8. S. J. Ovaska and H. F. VanLandingham, "Guest Editorial: Special Issue on Fusion of Soft Computing and Hard Computing in Industrial Applications," *IEEE Transactions on Systems, Man, and Cybernetics—Part C: Applications and Reviews* **32**, 69–71 (2002).

9. S. J. Ovaska, H. F. VanLandingham, and A. Kamiya, "Fusion of Soft Computing and Hard Computing in Industrial Applications: An Overview," *IEEE Transactions on Systems, Man, and Cybernetics—Part C: Applications and Reviews* **32**, 72–79 (2002).

10. B. Sick, "Fusion of Hard and Soft Computing Techniques in Indirect, Online Tool Wear Monitoring," *IEEE Transactions on Systems, Man, and Cybernetics—Part C: Applications and Reviews* **32**, 80—91 (2002).

11. C. Shi and A. D. Cheok, "Performance Comparison of Fused Soft Control/Hard Observer Type Controller with Hard Control/Hard Observer Type Controller for Switched

Reluctance Motors," *IEEE Transactions on Systems, Man, and Cybernetics—Part C: Applications and Reviews* **32**, 99–112 (2002).

12. G. D. Buckner, "Intelligent Bounds on Modeling Uncertainties: Applications to Sliding Mode Control," *IEEE Transactions on Systems, Man, and Cybernetics—Part C: Applications and Reviews* **32**, 113–124 (2002).

13. R. Sterritt and D. W. Bustard, "Fusing Hard and Soft Computing for Fault Management in Telecommunications Systems," *IEEE Transactions on Systems, Man, and Cybernetics—Part C: Applications and Reviews* **32**, 92–98 (2002).

14. M. Oosterom, R. Babuska, and H. B. Verbruggen, "Soft Computing Applications in Aircraft Sensor Management and Flight Control Law Reconfiguration," *IEEE Transactions on Systems, Man, and Cybernetics—Part C: Applications and Reviews* **32**, 125–139 (2002).

15. J. J. Murray, C. J. Cox, G. G. Lendaris, and R. Saeks, "Adaptive Dynamic Programming," *IEEE Transactions on Systems, Man, and Cybernetics—Part C: Applications and Reviews* **32**, 140–153 (2002).

16. S.-B. Cho, "Incorporating Soft Computing Techniques into a Probabilistic Intrusion Detection System," *IEEE Transactions on Systems, Man, and Cybernetics—Part C: Applications and Reviews* **32**, 154–160 (2002).

17. R. H. Kewley and M. J. Embrechts, "Computational Military Tactical Planning System," *IEEE Transactions on Systems, Man, and Cybernetics—Part C: Applications and Reviews* **32**, 161–171 (2002).

18. M. Agarwal, "Combining Neural and Conventional Paradigms for Modeling, Prediction, and Control," *Proceedings of the 4th IEEE Conference on Control Applications*, Albany, NY, Sept. 1995, pp. 566–571.

19. I. Hayashi and M. Umano, "Perspectives and Trends of Fuzzy-Neural Networks," *Journal of the Japan Society of Fuzzy Theory and Systems* **5**, 178–190 (1993), in Japanese.

20. T. Furuhashi, "Fusion of Fuzzy/Neuro/Evolutionary Computing for Knowledge Acquisition," *Proceedings of the IEEE* **89**, 1266–1274 (2001).

21. L. Yang, J. Yen, A. Rajesh, and K. D. Kihm, "A supervisory Architecture and Hybrid GA for the Identifications of Complex Systems," *Proceedings of the 1999 Congress on Evolutionary Computation*, Washington, DC, July 1999, pp. 862–869.

22. D. Newth, M. Kirley, and D. G. Green, "An Investigation of the Use of Local Search in NP-Hard Problems," *Proceedings of the 26th Annual Conference of the IEEE Industrial Electronics Society*, Nagoya, Japan, Oct. 2000, **4**, pp. 2710–2715.

23. L. M. Fu, "Tutorial 5: Knowledge & Neural Heuristics," *Half-Day Tutorial/ Workshop, IEEE International Conference on Neural Networks*, Washington, DC, June 2, 1996.

24. D. B. Fogel, *Evolutionary Computation: Toward a New Philosophy of Machine Intelligence*, IEEE Press, Piscataway, NJ, 2000.

25. B. Kosko, *Fuzzy Engineering*, Prentice Hall, Upper Saddle River, NJ, 1996.

26. S. Haykin, *Neural Networks: A Comprehensive Foundation*, Prentice Hall, Upper Saddle River, NJ, 1999.

27. Y. Zhao, R. M. Edwards, and K. Y. Lee, "Hybrid Feedforward and Feedback Controller Design for Nuclear Steam Generators over Wide Range Operation Using Genetic Algorithm," *IEEE Transactions on Energy Conversion* **12**, 100–105 (1997).

28. K. C. Jeong, S. H. Kwon, D. H. Lee, M. W. Lee, and J. Y. Choi, "A Fuzzy Logic-Based Gain Tuner for PID Controllers," *Proceedings of the FUZZ-IEEE*, Anchorage, AK, May 1998, pp. 551–554.

29. S. Omatu, T. Iwasa, and M. Yoshioka, "Skill-Based PID Control by Using Neural Networks," *Proceedings of the IEEE International Conference on Systems, Man, and Cybernetics*, San Diego, CA, Oct. 1998, pp. 1972–1977.

30. Y. Tipsuwan and M.-Y. Chow, "Analysis of Training Neural Compensation Model for System Dynamics Modeling," *Proceedings of the International Joint Conference on Neural Networks*, Washington, DC, July 2001, pp. 1250–1255.

31. R. Fletcher and M. J. D. Powell, "A Rapidly Convergent Descent Method for Minimization," *Computer Journal* **6**, 163–168 (1963).

32. T. S. Kim and G. S. May, "Optimization of Via Formation in Photosensitive Dielectric Layers Using Neural Networks and Genetic Algorithms," *IEEE Transactions on Electronics Packaging and Manufacturing* **22**, 128–136 (1999).

33. D. F. Akhmetov, Y. Dote, and S. J. Ovaska, "Fuzzy Neural Network with General Parameter Adaptation for Modeling of Nonlinear Time-Series," *IEEE Transactions on Neural Networks* **12**, 148–152 (2001), errata published in *IEEE Transactions on Neural Networks* **12**, 443 (2001).

34. B. Widrow and S. D. Stearns, *Adaptive Signal Processing*, Prentice-Hall, Englewood Cliffs, NJ, 1985.

35. C. S. Krishnamoorthy, P. P. Venkatesh, and R. Sudarshan, "Object-Oriented Framework for Genetic Algorithms with Application to Space Truss Optimization," *Journal of Computing in Civil Engineering* **16**, 66–75 (2002).

36. W. Chiang, K. F. R. Liu, and J. Lee, "Bridge Damage Assessment Through Fuzzy Petri Net Based Expert System," *Journal of Computing in Civil Engineering* **14**, 141–149 (2000).

37. M. A. Hussain, "Review of the Applications of Neural Networks in Chemical Process Control—Simulation and Online Implementation," *Artificial Intelligence in Engineering* **13**, 55–68 (1999).

38. J. Rachlin, R. Goodwin, S. Murthy, R. Akkiraju, F. Wu, S. Kumaran, and R. Das, "A-Teams: An Agent Architecture for Optimization and Decision Support," in J. Mueller, M. Singh, and A. Rao, eds., *Lecture Notes in Artificial Intelligence: Intelligent Agents V*, Springer-Verlag, Heidelberg, Germany, 1999, **1555**, pp. 261–276.

39. T. Nishi, T. Inoue, and Y. Hattori, "Development of a Decentralized Supply Chain Optimization System," *Proceedings of the International Symposium on Design, Operation and Control of Next Generation Chemical Plants*, Kyoto, Japan, Dec. 2000, pp. 141–151.

40. J. Abonyi, L. Nagy, and F. Szeifert, "Adaptive Sugeno Fuzzy Control: A Case Study," in R. Roy, T. Furuhashi, and P. K. Chawdhry, eds., *Advances in Soft Computing: Engineering Design and Manufacturing*, Springer-Verlag, London, UK, 1999, pp. 135–146.

41. D. M. McDowell, G. W. Irwin, G. Lightbody, and G. McConnell, "Hybrid Neural Adaptive Control for Bank-to-Turn Missiles," *IEEE Transactions on Control Systems Technology* **5**, 297–308 (1997).

42. S. Schaal and D. Sternad, "Learning of Passive Motor Control Strategies with Genetic Algorithms," in L. Nadel and D. Stein, eds., *Lectures in Complex Systems*, Addison-Wesley, Boston, MA, 1992, pp. 631–643.

43. J. Abonyi, R. Babuska, M. Ayala Botto, F. Szeifert, and L. Nagy, "Identification and Control of Nonlinear Systems Using Fuzzy Hammerstein Models," *Industrial & Engineering Chemistry Research* **39**, 4302–4314 (2000).

44. Q. Zhang and S. J. Stanley, "Real-Time Water Treatment Process Control with Artificial Neural Networks," *Journal of Environmental Engineering* **125**, 153–160 (1999).

45. S. McClintock, T. Lunney, and A. Hashim, "A Genetic Algorithm Environment for Star Pattern Recognition," *Journal of Intelligent & Fuzzy Systems* **6**, 3–16 (1998).

46. L.-C. Lin and T.-B. Gau, "Feedback Linearization and Fuzzy Control for Conical Magnetic Bearings," *IEEE Transactions on Control Systems Technology* **5**, 417–426 (1997).

47. K. Fregene and D. Kennedy, "Control of a High-Order Power System by Neural Adaptive Feedback Linearization," *Proceedings of the IEEE International Symposium on Intelligent Control/Intelligent Systems and Semiotics*, Cambridge, MA, Sept. 1999, pp. 34–39.

48. A. Ben-Abdennour and K. Y. Lee, "An Autonomous Control System for Boiler Turbine Units," *IEEE Transactions on Energy Conversion* **11**, 401–406 (1996).

49. M. G. Simões and B. K. Bose, "Neural Network Based Estimation of Feedback Signals for a Vector Controlled Induction Motor Drive," *IEEE Transactions on Industry Applications* **31**, 620–629 (1995).

50. G. R. Raidl, "An Improved Genetic Algorithm for the Multiconstrained 0–1 Knapsack Problem," *Proceedings of the IEEE International Conference on Evolutionary Computation*, Anchorage, AK, May 1998, pp. 207–211.

51. N. Barnier and P. Brisset, "Optimization by Hybridization of a Genetic Algorithm with Constraint Satisfaction Techniques," *Proceedings of the IEEE International Conference on Evolutionary Computation*, Anchorage, AK, May 1998, pp. 645–649.

52. D. Gorinevsky, A. Kapitanovsky, and A. Goldenberg, "Neural Network Architecture for Trajectory Generation and Control of Automated Car Parking," *IEEE Transactions on Control Systems Technology* **4**, 50–56 (1996).

53. F.-C. Lu and Y.-Y. Hsu, "Fuzzy Dynamic Programming Approach to Reactive Power/Voltage Control in a Distribution Substation," *IEEE Transactions on Power Systems* **12**, 681–688 (1997).

54. G. Prasad, E. Swidenbank, and B. W. Hogg, "A Neural Net Model-Based Multivariable Long-Range Predictive Control Strategy Applied in Thermal Power Plant Control," *IEEE Transactions on Energy Conversion* **13**, 176–182 (1998).

55. L. J. Fogel, A. J. Owens, and M. J. Walsh, "Artificial Intelligence through a Simulation of Evolution," in D. B. Fogel, ed., *Evolutionary Computation: The Fossil Record*, IEEE Press, Piscataway, NJ, 1998, pp. 230–254.

EDITOR'S INTRODUCTION TO CHAPTER 2

Large-scale systems are highly potential users of soft computing, because their planning, operation, control, supervision, and fault diagnostics tasks have traditionally employed a significant amount of human expertise. To minimize the need of human specialists and increase the operational efficiency, it is beneficial to introduce computational and artificial intelligence on different levels of system hierarchy.

But what is a large-scale system? *The Random House Dictionary of the English Language* (2nd ed., 1987) defines "large-scale" as *very extensive or encompassing.* On the other hand, Vernon lists five properties that belong to any "system" [1]:

1. A system is an assembly of components connected together in an organized way.
2. A system is fundamentally altered if a component joins or leaves it.
3. It has a purpose.
4. It has a degree of permanence.
5. It has been defined as being of particular interest.

Our environment, society, economy, transportation, power grid, telephone network, and Internet are all representative large-scale systems. Such complex systems can be further divided into multiple subsystems [2].

Chapter 2 of the present book, "General Model for Large-Scale Plant Application," is authored by Akimoto Kamiya. It considers a vital subclass of large-scale systems—that is, large-scale plants. The word "plant" is defined in *The Random House Dictionary of the English Language* as *the complete equipment or apparatus for a particular mechanical process or operation.* For instance, a gener-

Computationally Intelligent Hybrid Systems. Edited by Seppo J. Ovaska
ISBN 0-471-47668-4 © 2005 the Institute of Electrical and Electronics Engineers, Inc.

ating station is a large-scale plant consisting of a steam generator, turbine, alternator, feedwater heaters, piping, and so on. The operation of such plants is complicated and involves numerous trade-off problems—for example, accuracy, costs, efficiency, environmental impact, human safety, and reliability.

Chapter 2 is devoted to control systems related to large-scale plants. It presents a survey of hierarchical control system architectures; forecasting of the market demand; scheduling of processes; supervisory control; and local control. Based on the survey, Kamiya introduces a general model with regard to the fusion of soft computing (SC) and hard computing (HC) methodologies for the control of large-scale plants.

Usually when some researcher is proposing a forecasting method that provides 1% more accurate predictions than a competing scheme, the improvement may be considered negligible by the prediction-oriented peers. However, in the context of power systems load forecasting, even this small improvement may have a notable economical impact as pointed out by Kamiya. Therefore, it is of great importance to develop forecasting models with high accuracy and online adaptivity. To achieve these desired characteristics, multiple individual forecasting models are typically fused together by an adaptive linear combiner. The individual models are implemented using either SC or HC.

The unit commitment problem involves finding an optimal commitment schedule with respect to a set of generating units so that specific constraints are satisfied while the total fuel consumption is minimized. Such an optimal schedule could also reduce CO_2 emission, which is the principal contributor to global warming. Iterative multi-level optimization methods are applied to solve unit commitment problems. Those methods are usually cooperative fusions of HC and SC—for example, the Lagrangian relaxation method and evolutionary computation. To achieve practical computation time, heuristics are used to guide evolutionary algorithms to search over the feasible space.

In hierarchical control systems, the supervisory control monitors processes and performs a coordinated control by providing commands and setpoints to local controllers. The aim is to ensure that all the processes are operating according to the optimized schedule. Computationally or artificially intelligent supervisory control is used—for example, to modify setpoints of local controllers in abnormal conditions. To achieve an *operatorless* plant is the ultimate goal for the development of industrial control systems. In most large-scale plants, however, this is merely an asymptotic goal, because the safety regulations may require a human operator to supervise even the most advanced autonomic systems.

Local control is typically implemented using HC algorithms. This makes it possible to develop control loops with guaranteed stability. Although the field of control engineering provides us with a variety of sophisticated control techniques, more than 95% of local control loops in industrial processes are still implemented with proportional integral derivative (PID) control methods. Nevertheless, SC-based gain scheduling is used to enhance the behavior of PID controllers.

At the end of the chapter, a general model for the fusion of SC and HC in large-scale plants is created and discussed. From that insightful model, the following concise remarks can be made:

- *Forecasting.* SC-based methods outperform traditional HC methods
- *Scheduling.* Most successful optimization schemes are fusions of HC techniques and evolutionary computation
- *Supervisory Control.* To achieve autonomous control, a combination of symbolic artificial intelligence and SC is suggested
- *Local Control.* SC methods are effectively complementing the performance of primary HC controllers

Thus, it can be concluded that large-scale plants are active all-around users of computationally intelligent hybrid systems.

REFERENCES

1. P. Vernon, "Systems in Engineering," *IEE Review* **35**, 383–385 (1989).
2. M. Kayton, "A Practitioner's View of System Engineering," *IEEE Transactions on Aerospace and Electronic Systems* **33**, 579–586 (1997).

CHAPTER 2

GENERAL MODEL FOR LARGE-SCALE PLANT APPLICATION

AKIMOTO KAMIYA
Kushiro National College of Technology, Kushiro, Japan

2.1 INTRODUCTION

Large-scale plants such as chemical, electrical power, and water treatment plants are complex systems, consisting of many interconnected subsystems, subprocesses, or components presenting a wide range of different properties. They can be, for example, linear or nonlinear, well-defined or ill-defined, measurable or unmeasurable, predictable or unpredictable, continuous or discrete, time-variant or time-invariant, static or dynamic, short-term or long-term, centralized or distributed. Moreover, the operation of such plants always involves numerous trade-off problems such as costs, quality, efficiency, complexity, environmental impact, human safety, reliability, and accuracy, problems that are often conflicting or noncommensurate. For decades, large-scale, complex, and hybrid systems have been a class of special interest systems among researchers and engineers from various disciplines, and the subject of large-scale systems is still growing [1]. The methodology for large-scale systems based on the system engineering approach was introduced by Sage in 1977 [2]. The control theory and optimization methods for large-scale systems have been addressed by Siljak [3] and Wismer et al. [4]. In order to achieve intelligent control of large-scale systems, in addition to those hard computing approaches, fusion with fuzzy theory has been explored by Jamshidi [1]. The term *intelligent control* in reference 1 refers to the integration of artificial intelligence (expert systems, neural networks, fuzzy logic, genetic algorithms, probabilistic reasoning, etc.), operations research, and control theory. In line with this fusion thinking, Ovaska et al. proposed the concept of "fusion of soft computing and hard computing" and conducted a condense survey on such applications. There was, however, only limited discussion on its applicability to large-scale plants [5]. This

Computationally Intelligent Hybrid Systems. Edited by Seppo J. Ovaska
ISBN 0-471-47668-4 © 2005 the Institute of Electrical and Electronics Engineers, Inc.

is what this chapter intends to remedy, as an extended study and qualitative analysis of the fusion approach. Although our society, the economy, the environment, transportation, aerospace, the Internet, and so on, are all large-scale, complex systems, this chapter is limited, for the sake of focus, to the discussion of control systems related to large-scale plants. Along with the survey results, this chapter introduces a general model and discusses the fusion categories for the control of large-scale plants.

2.2 CONTROL SYSTEM ARCHITECTURE

For the sake of economy, computability, reliability, flexibility, and manageability, the design of a control system for large-scale plants is often based on a hierarchical approach and implemented on a computationally distributed platform [1,6]. It should be noted that the distributed architecture is not limited within a single plant, but extended into a wide area as seen in power systems, or around the world as in the case of global manufacturing systems [7]. A conceptual diagram of a control system based on a hierarchical structure is given in Fig. 2.1. As shown in the figure, the forecasting task is carried out at the top level to predict the market demand with respect to the plant's output. The scheduling task is employed to optimize operations of large-scale processes based both on the forecast demand given by the higher level and on various operation constraints, aiming at achieving lower costs, less environmental and mechanical impacts, higher quality, and so on. The supervisory control task is to (a) monitor the local controllers and the processes based on a given schedule from the higher level and (b) carry out the tasks of coordination by generating set points or commands for the local control task. The role of the local control is to respond to the dynamic change of the process, based on the setpoints or commands given by the supervisory control.

Although it is not shown in Fig. 2.1, human operators always play an important role in the control of large-scale plants. In general, the higher the level is, the more

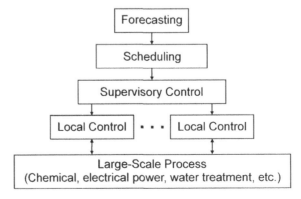

Figure 2.1. Control system based on a hierarchical structure for a large-scale plant.

human interventions are required to deal with those complex and ill-defined tasks in order to achieve a high level of reliability and safety. At the forecasting and scheduling levels, even with the state-of-the-art computing techniques, the machine-based forecasting and scheduling results have to be evaluated and modified (if necessary) by human operators before the results are introduced to the lower level. At the supervisory control level, even in with a fully automated large-scale plant, human operators are still required to deal with abnormal situations in which machines fail to respond appropriately. Hence, interactions between humans and machines or humans in the loop through easy-to-understand and easy-to-use human machine interfaces are also an important issue with respect to the control of large-scale plants. In this chapter, however, discussions will focus on the fusion of soft computing and hard computing for the control of large-scale plants with a few discussions on the roles of human operators.

2.3 FORECASTING OF MARKET DEMAND

In order to optimize the operations of large-scale plants, demand forecasting is an important task. In power systems, a conservative estimate is that a 1% reduction in forecasting error for a 10-GW utility can save up to $1.6 million annually [8]. To formulate a forecasting model with high prediction accuracy is challenging work. The art of building a forecasting model lies in employing an appropriate function to map demands with the determining factors such as seasonal parameters based on given historical data. Traditionally, linear or nonlinear autoregression methods have been applied to build such forecasting models [9,10]. The difficulty with these hard-computing-based methods is that the relationship between the demand forecasts and the determining factors is highly nonlinear and uncertain. Thus, to form a particular function with the autoregression approach is usually a tedious work, and the results may lack accuracy and robustness.

Neural networks are data-driven self-adaptive methods without depending much on prior knowledge about the structural relationship between demand forecasts and the determining factors. It has been proved that given a sufficient number of hidden units each with a monotone increasing and bounded activation function, neural networks can approximate any continuous function arbitrarily well to any given accuracy [11]. Other than the financial field (which is not discussed in this chapter), a major application of neural-networks-based forecasting is in an electricity load consumption study [12]. As an approximator, similar to neural networks, given a sufficient number of fuzzy sets and rules, fuzzy systems can also approximate any continuous function to any degree of accuracy [13]. Based on a simulation study, it has been shown that both neural networks and fuzzy systems offer similar performance [14,15], while both outperform the autoregression model with a higher forecasting accuracy of up to 6% [14]. Although the performance is similar, neural networks, which are known for their simplicity and model-free approach, have been well accepted in practice and used by many utilities for load forecasting [16].

The generally accepted forecasting method in many utilities is based on multiple neural networks combined with a recursive least-squares algorithm (RLS). This multiple networks approach is aimed at extracting various load patterns implicitly embedded in the training data. Figure 2.2 shows the case for two combined neural networks [16]. As depicted in the figure, with the same input, the base load forecaster emphasizes regular load patterns (long term), whereas the change load forecaster puts a stronger emphasis on yesterday's load (short term). The two forecasters are adaptively combined using a recursive least-squares algorithm, which produces coefficients that minimize the weighted sum of squared errors of past forecasts. This multiple forecaster approach has already been supported by many hard-computing-based forecasting applications and theories [17], an indication that through the combination of multiple individual forecasts, the forecast accuracy can be substantially improved.

Forecasting accuracy can be improved further by using the knowledge of experienced human forecasters. Note that by incorporating such knowledge, the hard-computing-based Box–Jenkins Autoregressive Integrated Moving Average (ARIMA) method can outperform the stand-alone neural networks approach [18]. In order to further improve the forecasting performance, a fusion of neural networks and fuzzy inference models with a linear combiner has been proposed [19]. A simplified diagram of this fusion approach is shown in Fig. 2.3. This approach has been verified with actual load data, achieving better forecasting accuracy than stand-alone neural networks or a stand-alone expert system by 0.36%, or 1.60% on an overall average. A knowledge-based approach is somehow site-dependent, and the knowledge acquisition process can be tedious. In order to make this approach truly useful and easily implemented at different sites, a user interface including a highly easy-to-use explanation module for neural-networks-and-fuzzy-systems-based load forecasting has been developed [20].

Instead of being integrated in a loose scheme where each component works as an individual forecaster as shown above, neural networks and fuzzy systems can be

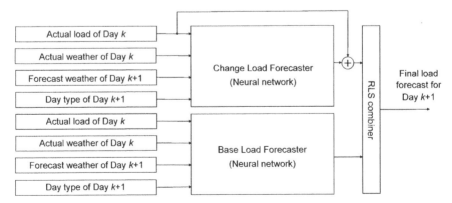

Figure 2.2. Electric load forecasting with neural networks and a recursive least-squares algorithm [16].

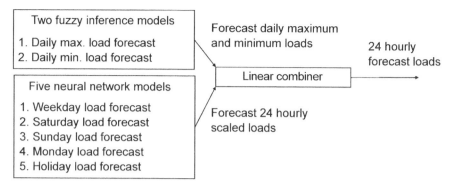

Figure 2.3. Fuzzy inference models and neural networks integrated with a linear combiner for load forecasting.

combined closely together to yield one single forecasting result. In reference 15, neural networks are integrated with fuzzy systems using expert knowledge as a front-end preprocessor for the neural networks' input layer and output layer. This intimate integration approach can be further extended, where fuzzy membership functions are incorporated within the neural nodes of the networks to form a neural-networks-based fuzzy system [21]. Based on historical data, the neural networks learning algorithms are used to determine the parameters of the expert-knowledge-based fuzzy systems for electric load forecasting [22] and product demand forecasting [23]. These intimate integration schemes have also been verified to produce better forecasting accuracy than stand-alone neural networks [15,22,23], stand-alone fuzzy systems [15], and the traditional ARIMA method [22].

2.4 SCHEDULING OF PROCESSES

2.4.1 Problem Decomposition

A successful design of large-scale, complex systems invariably involves decomposing the system into a number of smaller subsystems, each with its own goals and constraints. The resulting interconnection of subsystems may take on many forms, but one of the most common, as shown in Fig. 2.4, is the hierarchical form in which a higher-level unit controls or coordinates the units on the level below it and, in turn, is controlled by the units on the level above it [4].

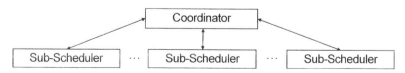

Figure 2.4. Scheduling based on a hierarchical–multilevel approach.

For the physical structure of power systems with a set of distributed electrical power generating units controlled by a load dispatch center, power utilities traditionally employ this hierarchical–multilevel approach based on a Lagrangian relaxation method to solve the unit commitment problem [24]. The unit commitment problem involves finding an optimal or near-optimal commitment schedule with respect to a set of generating units so that certain constraints are satisfied and the total fuel cost is minimized. Recently, genetic algorithms with the Lagrangian relaxation method have been applied to this problem in order to improve the commitment schedule [25]. The coupling constraints of the primal problem are relaxed and decomposed into a set of generating-unit-wise subscheduling problems through a set of Lagrangian multipliers and local constraints. Each subproblem is solved individually by a subscheduler at the low level using dynamic programming and nonlinear programming to minimize the fuel cost over a specified scheduling horizon. A Lagrangian coordinator and a genetic-algorithms coordinator are employed at the high lever, adjusting the Lagrangian multipliers and the local constraints to reduce the schedule infeasibility with respect to the coupling constraints. The process repeats until all coupling constraints are satisfied. This approach has been verified to efficiently find an optimal or near-optimal commitment schedule over a seven-day planning horizon in 38 minutes and 17 seconds of computing time, a time frame that is acceptable to power system operators [25].

Decomposition of the scheduling problem is not necessarily limited to the machine level. Managers of efficient large-scale plants also take a hierarchical decomposition approach, where planning and scheduling are performed at various levels, from the very bottom decisions at the machine level, to top-level strategic decisions. In the traditional hierarchical management structure, the decisions are taken in sequence and in a top-down approach. The decisions taken at some level of hierarchy are constrained by those already taken at upper levels, and since there is often only a little interaction between different levels, the resulting plans or schedules may not be feasible for the entire system. In order to achieve efficient operations of large-scale plants, an integrated and interactive approach in production planning and scheduling across various levels is desired, so that a decision taken at some level in the hierarchy translates into a feasible objective for the next level of decision-making [26]. Such an integrated and interactive approach has been implemented successfully in a supply chain optimization system [27]. As shown in Fig. 2.5, the supply chain optimization system consists of three subsystems. The purpose of the material resource planning subsystem is to decide the material order plan to minimize the material shipping costs and the inventory costs of the feed materials. On the other hand, the scheduling subsystem determines the production sequence and the starting time of jobs to minimize changeover costs and the due date penalties. The order and supply planning subsystem is to decide the delivery plan of each product so as to maximize the profit including the inventory cost based on a given production demand over a planning horizon. Each subsystem generates a production schedule with its own goals and constraints, and therefore the resulting solutions may not be feasible for the entire system.

To make this scheme feasible, the optimization at each subsystem and the data exchange among the subsystems are repeated to gradually reduce the range of

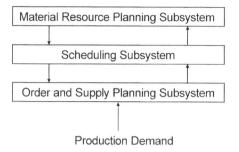

Figure 2.5. Decentralized supply chain optimization system [27].

infeasibility. In this approach, the two planning subsystems were based on the traditional Mixed Integer Linear Programming method (MILP), while the scheduling subsystem adopted a simulated annealing search method in order not to be trapped in a poor local optimum. As supported by the "no free lunch" theorems [28], since there is no single algorithm that can fit all types of optimization problems, it reinforces the concept of fusion of soft computing and hard computing by uniting different classes of search methods to solve a complex and distributed scheduling problem.

As argued by Morton and Pentico [29], it is possible to consider a broadened concept of genetic algorithms as a very general class of techniques that can include simulated annealing and tabu search as special cases. For example, if the offspring selected varies to some extent from the fittest, we have simulated annealing. If we keep a memory about not repeating offspring under certain conditions, we have tabu search. In this chapter, similar to genetic algorithms, simulated annealing and tabu search are also regarded as a class of soft-computing methods to exploit tolerance for imprecision, uncertainty, and partial truth to achieve tractability, robustness, and low solution cost. Unlike mathematical programming that is based on mathematical theories and can find a local optimum precisely, genetic algorithms are a low-cost solution using easy-to-implement genetic operators to solve difficult optimization problems by finding a global optimum though imprecisely or uncertainly.

Easy modifiability of the scheduling system is essential in order to deal with rapidly varying environments such as changing production line, organization, management, or customer's requirements under the pressure of local or global competition. Therefore, a scheduling system with a high degree of modularity and flexibility is required, so that modification of a particular subsystem will not require the modification of the other subsystems or reconfiguration of the whole system. For this purpose, a multi-agent-based approach has been applied in order to achieve an autonomous and cooperative scheduling system with a high degree of modularity and flexibility in an enterprise-wide or global manufacturing environment [7]. This multi-agent-based approach has been successfully employed in a number of commercial products such as trim optimization tool for paper industries, load planning and distribution optimization tool for distribution planners, and global scheduling tool for enterprises [30]. In reference 31, an extended neighborhood search [29] such as evolutionary algorithms, simulated annealing, and tabu search, embedded in a constraint programming framework, is applied to direct the autonomous agent's reasoning (by manipulating a set of global constraints) to perform cooperative planning and scheduling in order to achieve global search in a dynamic environment.

2.4.2   Hybrid Genetic Algorithms

It is very unlikely that pure genetic algorithms would outperform a specialized scheme tailored to a particular problem. However, a combination of the two as shown in Fig. 2.6 usually performs better than either one alone. This occurs because on a hybrid scheme there is the possibility of incorporating domain knowledge, which gives it an advantage over a pure blind searcher such as genetic algorithms. This is why most successful applications of genetic algorithms have been hybrids [32]. There are two basic strategies for using hybrid genetic algorithms. One is Lamarckian learning, where the genetic representation is updated to match the solution found by the improvement procedure. The other is Baldwinian learning, where improvement procedures are used to change the fitness landscape, but the solution found is not encoded back into the chromosome string [33]. Both use the metaphor that an individual learns during its lifetime [32]. These two types of learning can be combined with genetic algorithms in various forms—for example, 95% of Baldwinian steps and 5% of Lamarckian steps [34], 20% to 40% partial Lamarckianism search strategies [33], pure Lamarckian learning [35], or pure Baldwinian learning [36], depending on the specific class of problems. All these approaches have been verified to yield a better performance than pure genetic algorithms [32–36].

The improvement procedures cited in the articles above are based on some local search algorithm aimed at leading an individual toward a local optimum in one generation. For this reason, hybrid genetic algorithms based on Lamarckian learning tend to converge to a local optimum. By testing with numerical optimization

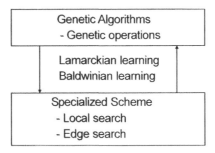

Figure 2.6. Hybrid genetic algorithms.

problems such as Rastrigin and Schwelfel, it has been verified that Baldwinian strategy converges to a global optimum, but Baldwinian search is much slower than Lamarckian search [36]. Based on the observation that the global optimum often lies on the boundary of the feasible space, genetic algorithms hybridized with edge search strategies have been proposed to search the boundary area precisely [37] or approximately [38] between the feasible and infeasible space. Such edge search strategy has been applied to a power plant start-up scheduling problem successfully. In the power plant start-up scheduling problem, it has been proved theoretically that the global optimum stays somewhere on the boundary of the feasible space. By searching along the boundary instead of the whole space, this edge-search hybrid approach has been verified to improve the search efficiency significantly without being trapped in a local optimum [38].

2.4.3 Multiobjective Optimization

Scheduling in large-scale plants is often required to deal with multiobjective optimization problems, making decisions based on several criteria such as time, costs, efficiency, reliability, and environmental impact. In general, the methodologies related to multiobjective optimization can be divided into two categories: (1) generation of a set of noninferior solutions and (2) determination of the best-compromise solution [39]. The noninferior solution (also known as Pareto optimal, efficient, or nondominated solution) is one where any improvement of one objective function can be achieved only at the expense of another. The best-compromise solution is generally a noninferior solution, which is preferred by human decision-makers. A conceptual landscape of a multiobjective optimization problem on a two-objective space is shown in Fig. 2.7. In this figure, a solution with a smaller objective function value is regarded as superior.

Genetic algorithms seem particularly desirable to solve multiobjective optimization problems because they deal simultaneously with a set of possible solutions, which allow finding an entire set of Pareto optimal solutions in a single run of the algorithm, instead of performing a series of separate runs as in the case of traditional mathematical programming techniques [40]. Given a set of Pareto solutions, it can help the final decision-maker narrow down the choice for the best-compromise solution. The first hybrid genetic algorithms with local search for multiobjective problem were proposed by Ishibuchi [41]. The hybrid algorithm uses a weighted sum of multiple objectives as a fitness function, which is utilized when a pair of parent solutions is selected for generating a new solution by genetic operations. A local search procedure is applied to the new solution to maximize its fitness value. In order to search an entire set of Pareto solutions, the hybrid algorithm is to randomly specify weight values whenever a pair of parent solutions are selected. That is, each selection is performed by a different weight vector. High performance of the hybrid approach has been demonstrated by applying it to multiobjective flow-shop scheduling problems. Instead of local search, hybrid genetic algorithms with heuristics have been proposed to solve the multiobjective unit commitment problem with a set of complex constraints. Heuristics are used to guide genetic

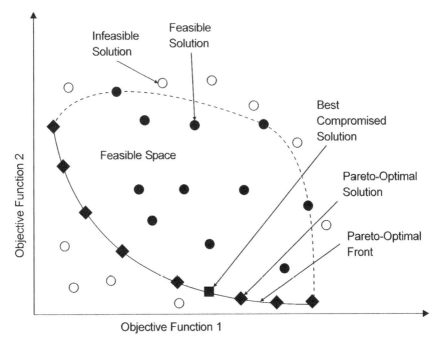

Figure 2.7. Conceptual landscape of a multiobjective optimization problem.

algorithms to search over the feasible space to reduce computation time. As a result, the computation time increases almost linearly with number of generating units, thus making the hybrid approach suitable for large-scale problems [42].

In general, there are two types of approach, noninteractive or interactive, to determine the best-compromise solution from the set of Pareto solutions. The noninteractive approach assumes that the decision-maker can specify the "preference function" with respect to the combination of the individual objective functions in advance, either as "weights" (utilities) or as "distance functions" (concerning the distance from the goal) [43]. With this approach, the multiobjective optimization problem is eventually converted into a single-objective optimization problem in advance by the human decision-maker, and it can be solved by single-objective optimization methods. The interactive approach assumes that the decision-maker can only give some preference information on a local level to a particular noninferior solution. In this approach, one noninferior solution is generated for each iteration. The decision-maker then acts on this solution by assigning some kind of preference that will determine the desired direction to move away from the current point. The process stops if the decision-maker is satisfied with the solution [39]. Since human preference is fuzzy in nature and its precise descriptions are not easy, fuzzy sets are recognized as a better choice to describe human preference [44]. An interactive fuzzy multiobjective decision-making system has been applied to solve a fuel ethanol production planning problem [45]. In this approach, fuzzy goal programming [43] integrated with hybrid genetic algorithms methods are applied. For each iteration, a decision-maker is asked if a particular noninferior solution is satisfactory. If not, the decision-maker is asked to update the aspiration levels. With a new set of aspiration levels that specify the degree of individual goal satisfaction, hybrid genetic algorithms are used to find the corresponding noninferior solution. This process repeats, until a best compromise solution with respect to the optimal feed concentrations of glucose and xylose is found. For a multiobjective unit commitment problem, an interactive approach based on fuzzy goals and a traditional gradient-based optimization method for finding noninferior solutions is applied in order to obtain a compromise solution, reducing generation costs while satisfying irrigation needs [46]. In this approach, in order to assist the decision-maker in updating the aspiration levels of each fuzzy goal, the trade-off rates among each goal's membership function are also supplied with each noninferior solution.

2.5 SUPERVISORY CONTROL

In a hierarchical control system, the supervisory control is to monitor entire processes and to provide setpoints and commands for the local controllers, ensuring that the entire processes are operated with a high level of efficiency and safety based on a given schedule provided by the upper layer. To achieve an operatorless plant is the ultimate goal for the development of industrial control systems. Such systems are already available in many fully automated small-scale plants. However, even with state-of-the-art technologies, human operators still play an important role in the operation of large-scale and complex plants for many years to come. Nevertheless, with the development of control systems, the role of operators in a large-scale plant has shifted from the laborious local control level to the sophisticated supervisory control level, to monitor all the processes and handle abnormal situations (like machine failures) that today's machine-based supervisory control system is not capable of handling with a high level of reliability. To identify the cause of the abnormal situations is the key to take effective countermeasures to bring the system back to the normal conditions. Therefore, in order to assist human operators in reacting properly and timely in the presence of abnormal situations, fault diagnosis is an important task at the supervisory control level.

The operation of large-scale plants at a supervisory control level requires a great deal of expertise. The traditional supervisory control system applied in automated large-scale plants is mostly implemented with crisp-type expertise encoded in a set of Plant Tables (in a condition-action-trigger format) [47] or with the Sequential Function Chart language [48]. In order to achieve a control system with a high degree of autonomy that can deal effectively with significant uncertainties or unanticipated changes in plants while depending on limited or no human assistance, a combination of conventional and intelligent decision-making methods is required at the supervisory control level [49]. Based on the observation that experienced operators can skillfully control highly nonlinear processes by adjusting the PID setpoints, a fuzzy supervisory control has been applied successfully to a demonstration power plant with multiple inputs and outputs [50] and a commercial petroleum plant with a long-delay-and-dead-time process [51]. In both systems, a fuzzy logic supervisory control is used to adjust setpoints of local PID controllers, and they have been proved to work very effectively or show better performance than human supervisory control. In the petroleum plant [51], supervisory control is implemented with a hybrid approach: a fuzzy logic combined with a statistical model. The statistical model is used to estimate the plant's condition and give a rough control target, while the fuzzy logic is applied to compensate the control target based on control know-how acquired from experienced operators. In order to achieve an autonomous control system, a fuzzy supervisor combined with conventional local controller has been proposed for a boiler–turbine system [52] and for a water treatment plant [53]. In the boiler–turbine system, the fuzzy-logic-based operator monitors the overall plant operation and carries out the tasks of coordination, fault diagnostics, fault isolation, and fault accommodation, while the local controller maintains the plant variables close to the setpoints given by the fuzzy-logic-based supervisor. Based on simulation results with a feedwater valve failure, this method has been verified to provide significant improvements in the plant performance. In this approach, the fault detection is implemented with (a) a mathematical process model serving as a nominal plant and (b) a Kalman filter for actual plant variables. A fault is detected by observing the discrepancy between the mathematical process model output and the Kalman filter output. The fault diagnosis and accommodation are encoded explicitly in fuzzy rules.

Control expert systems are often based on a shallow reasoning model, in the sense that conclusions are drawn directly from the presented situations using a set of explicit casual rules. Based on this shallow reasoning approach, in order to achieve an autonomous control system, all situations have to be accounted and encoded explicitly into the system, ensuring that the control system can deal with any presented situations. However, such a system requires a huge number of control rules and is difficult to be achieved. As a complement to a shallow-reasoning-based control, a control expert system using a model-based deep reasoning method has been proposed in order to cope with unanticipated situations [54]. The unanticipated situations in this context mean situations for which no explicit control rules were prepared in advance. As shown in Fig. 2.8, in this approach, the supervisory control consists of a deep-knowledge-based supervisor and a traditional crisp-rule-based supervisor. Using deep reasoning based on (a) plant functional-and-structure models and (b) general operating goals and principles, the proposed system has been verified successfully to generate a set of executable control rules to cope with a simulated boiler feedwater pump failure. The attempt to apply deep knowledge for dealing with unanticipated situations is based on the observation that during unfamiliar situations, faced with an environment for which no know-how or rules for control are available from previous encounters, the control of performance of skilled operators must move from rule-based behavior to knowledge-based behavior [55]. In order to achieve an autonomous control system for large-scale and complex plants, the

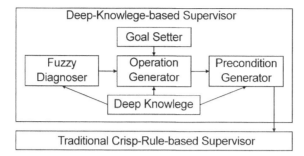

Figure 2.8. Sketch diagram of deep-knowledge-based supervisory control [54].

incorporation of deep knowledge at the supervisory control level should be considered and deserves further research.

Inspired by the well-known MYCIN project in medical work [56], knowledge-based diagnosis systems have been applied to various industrial areas. In the case of industrial application, as shown in the boiler-turbine system [52] cited above or in a DC motor diagnosis system [57], an integration approach by combining human expertise for fault diagnosis and a mathematical process model for fault detection is often employed. However, it should be noted that although a well-designed mathematical model can provide accurate information, statistical analysis and neural networks also play an ever-increasing role in this integration approach, particularly in systems where information about the process may be scarce and estimates need to be made [58].

2.6 LOCAL CONTROL

The local controller at the lowest level in the hierarchy is used to control the process based on a setpoint given by a supervisory controller from the higher level. At the local control level, the hard-computing-based control methods such as the conventional PID control and the advanced model-based control were developed in the past decades to control dynamic systems, the behavior of which is primarily described by linear differential or difference equations. Note that this mathematical framework may not be general enough in certain cases. In fact, it is well known that there are control problems that cannot be adequately described in a linear differential/difference equations framework [59]. Examples include thermodynamic phase changes and the starting/stopping of a pump. For such problems, soft computing techniques, which are formulated in neither linear nor differential/difference equations framework, are likely a better choice than the traditional hard computing approach. Because there is a wide range of control problems in a large-scale and complex plant, as shown below, a local controller based on the integration of the two types of methods can be a better choice for a class of control problems that is difficult to be handled satisfactorily by either one of them.

PID control, being simple and easy to understand, is still widely used in various industrial processes since it was introduced decades ago. As a matter of fact, more than 95% of control loops are implemented with PID control methods in industrial processes [60]. However, it basically either works for the process that is linear or works only at one operational point for a nonlinear process. To overcome this shortage, PID with a gain scheduling scheme is often used. As shown in Fig. 2.9, in this scheme the control gains—proportional, integral, and/or derivative—are adapted by a gain scheduler based on a set of process measurements. Soft-computing-based gain scheduling PID controllers have been recognized in recent years as a powerful and easy-to-implement solution to deal with the control of complex systems for which no easy mathematical descriptions can be provided. In reference 61, a fuzzy-logic-based scheduler, a neural-networks-based scheduler, and a neuro-fuzzy-based scheduler have been implemented in a systematic way such that each of the schedulers is based on the type of data available to the designer (knowledge base, experimental data, or a combination of both). For a highly non-linear fan control problem, it has been verified that all three soft-computing-based controllers outperform the conventional gain scheduling PID based on a simple lookup table approach. The cumulative tracking error of the fuzzy-logic-based scheduler, the neural-networks-based scheduler, and the neuro-fuzzy-based scheduler are 20%, 39%, and 44% smaller than the simple-lookup-table-based scheduler, respectively. As shown in references 62 and 63, the neural-networks and neuro-fuzzy-based schedulers work well for tuning PID with an unstable nonlinear plant, provided that the values of plant inputs/outputs are known at any given time. When linguistic information for tuning PID is available, as shown in reference 64, the fuzzy logic can be applied efficiently with quick response to the change of the plant parameters.

Recently, model-based control techniques such as MPC (Model Predictive Control) have been applied successfully for the control of a process with a long delay or dead time. Among various modern control-theory-based methods such as LQG (Linear Quadratic Gaussian) regulator, Kalman-filter, and H_∞ control, MPC is most widely used in Japanese industry [65]. MPC is defined as a control scheme in which the controller based on a plant model determines a manipulated variable profile that optimizes some performance objectives on a time interval, from the current time up to a prediction horizon. The optimization is repeated at each sampling time based on updated information (measurements) from the plant. Figure 2.10 shows the basic structure of MPC [66].

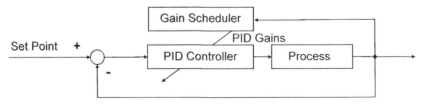

Figure 2.9. Gain scheduling PID controller.

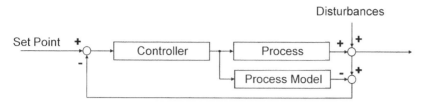

Figure 2.10. Basic model predictive control structure.

In a nonlinear MPC, neural networks are popularly used as convenient identified models to replace the normal first-principle plant models (mathematical models) in the optimization formulation. Numerous industrial applications of such neural-networks-based MPC can be found in a review article [67]. Although neural networks are commonly used, fuzzy logic can also be applied effectively to form an MPC. In reference 68, Fuzzy Hammerstein models are implemented in MPC for the nonlinear temperature control of a simulated electrical water heater. The Fuzzy Hammerstein model consists of a series connection of a fuzzy static nonlinear submodel and a differential-equation-based dynamic linear submodel. Therefore, the hybrid model is transparent and linguistically interpretable, and it can be identified with the help of linguistic rules and data gathered from the process. Simulation results show that not only good dynamic modeling performance is achieved but also the steady-state behavior of the system is well captured by the proposed Fuzzy Hammerstein model.

2.7 GENERAL FUSION MODEL AND FUSION CATEGORIES

A general model with respect to the fusion of soft computing and hard computing for hierarchical control system of a large-scale plant is shown in Fig. 2.11 and Table 2.1. As illustrated in the figure and the table, the fusion of soft computing and hard computing can be implemented at the system level and at the algorithm level. In the system level, soft computing should be applied to the upper and middle levels, performing human-like tasks such as forecasting and diagnosis, and also to the lower level for control loops that are based on the control know-how of experienced operators and difficult to be implemented by the conventional hard computing approach. On the other hand, hard computing is employed at the middle and lower levels, performing supervisory control and local control with those well-defined control procedures and process models. With respect to the algorithm level, fusion of soft computing and hard computing is applied to the middle level for scheduling and is applied to the lower level for highly nonlinear process control. In terms of fusion categories of Chapter 1, the typical fusion categories at each control level of large-scale and complex plants can be summarized as shown in Table 2.1. Along with Fig. 2.11, this table indicates that the higher the level, the more important the role played by soft computing techniques; while the lower

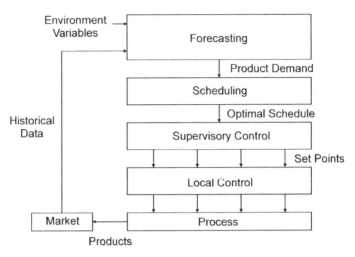

Figure 2.11. Fusion of soft computing and hard computing for large-scale plant control system.

the level, the more suitable the hard computing techniques. However, soft computing and hard computing techniques are both important and should be fused in low or high fusion grade or in system or algorithm level so as to achieve a control system with a high level of quality, efficiency, less environmental impact, human safety, reliability, and accuracy for the operations of large-scale and complex plants.

TABLE 2.1. Fusion Categories of Soft Computing and Hard Computing for Large-Scale Plants

Tasks	Categories	Descriptions
Forecasting	SC	Combing forecasts based on multiple data-driven neural networks, multiple knowledge-driven fuzzy inference models, or their combination [16,19].
Scheduling	SC-HC//SC	Human preference is described by fuzzy goals, which are solved by using hybrid GA [32,44].
Supervisory control	HC/SC	A combination of conventional and intelligent decision-making methods is required for autonomous control [49].
Local control	HC	More than 95% of control loops are implemented with PID methods [60].
	SC//HC	Soft-computing-based gain scheduling PID controller is a powerful solution to deal with the control of complex systems [61–64].
	HC-SC	Neural-networks- or fuzzy-logic-based MPC for nonlinear optimization control [67,68].

2.8 CONCLUSIONS

In order to gain advantages in today's highly competitive global market, research and development of a next-generation intelligent manufacturing system is in great demand worldwide [69]. Since the control of a large-scale complex plant involves a wide range of tasks, fusion of soft computing and hard computing appears to be an efficient approach to develop an intelligent control system for a large-scale plant. Based on a survey of published theoretical and application literature, this chapter presented a general model with respect to the fusion of soft computing and hard computing for large-scale plants. Although we focused on Fuzzy Systems, Neural Networks, and Genetic Algorithms, other important soft computing techniques such as Rough Sets, Probabilistic Reasoning, and Reinforcement Learning should be explored in the future.

REFERENCES

1. M. Jamshidi, *Large-Scale Systems: Modeling, Control, and Fuzzy Logic*, Prentice-Hall, Upper Saddle River, NJ, 1997.

2. A. P. Sage, *Methodology for Large-Scale Systems*, McGraw-Hill, New York, 1977.

3. D. D. Siljak, *Decentralized Control of Complex Systems*, Academic Press, Boston, 1991.

4. D. A. Wismer, ed., *Optimization Methods for Large-Scale Systems*, McGraw-Hill, New York, 1971.

5. S. J. Ovaska, H. F. VanLandingham, and A. Kamiya, "Fusion of Soft Computing and Hard Computing in Industrial Applications: An Overview," *IEEE Transactions on Systems, Man, and Cybernetics—Part C: Applications and Reviews* **32**, 72–79 (2002).

6. K. T. Erickson and J. L. Hedrick, *Plantwide Process Control*, Wiley, New York, 1999.

7. B. P.-C. Yen, "Agent-Based Distributed Planning and Scheduling in Global Manufacturing," *Proceedings of the 3rd Annual International Conference on Industrial Engineering Theories, Application and Practice*, Hong Kong, 1998, pp. PN259.1–PN259.9.

8. B. F. Hobbs, S. Jitprapaikulsarn, and D. J. Maratukulam, "Analysis of the Value for Unit Commitment of Improved Load Forecasts," *IEEE Transactions on Power Systems* **14**, 1342–1348 (1999).

9. J. G. De Gooijer and K. Kumar, "Some Recent Developments in Non-Linear Time Series Modelling, Testing, and Forecasting," *International Journal of Forecasting* **8**, 135–156 (1992).

10. A. D. Papalexopoulos and T. C. Hesterberg, "A Regression-based Approach to Short-Term System Load Forecasting," *IEEE Transactions on Power Systems* **5**, 1535–1547 (1990).

11. A. Pinkus, "Approximation Theory of the MLP Model in Neural Networks," *Acta Numerica* **8**, 143–196 (1999).

12. G. Zhang, B. E. Patuwo, and M. Y. Hu, "Forecasting with Artificial Neural Networks: The State of the Art," *International Journal of Forecasting* **14**, 35–62 (1998).

13. H. Ying, Y. Ding, S. Li, and S. Shao, "Comparison of Necessary Conditions for Typical Takagi–Sugeno and Mamdani Fuzzy Systems as Universal Approximators," *IEEE*

Transactions on Systems, Man, and Cybernetics—Part A: Systems and Humans **29**, 508–514 (1999).

14. K. Liu, S. Subbarayan, R. R. Shoults, M. T. Manry, C. Kwan, F. I. Lewis, and J. Naccarino, "Comparison of Very Short-Term Load Forecasting Techniques," *IEEE Transactions on Power Systems* **11**, 877–882 (1996).

15. M. R. Khan and A. Abraham, "Short Term Load Forecasting Models in Czech Republic Using Soft Computing Paradigms," *International Journal of Knowledge-Based Intelligent Engineering Systems* **7** (2003).

16. A. Khotanzad, R. Afkhami-Rohani, and D. Maratukulam, "ANNSTLF—Artificial Neural Network Short-Term Load Forecaster—Generation Three," *IEEE Transactions on Power Systems* **13**, 1413–1422 (1998).

17. R. T. Clemen, "Combining Forecasts: A Review and Annotated Bibliography," *International Journal of Forecasting* **5**, 559–583 (1989).

18. N. Amjady, "Short-Term Hourly Load Forecasting Using Time-Series Modeling with Peak Load Estimation Capability," *IEEE Transactions on Power Systems* **16**, 798–805 (2001).

19. K.-H. Kim, H.-S. Youn, and Y.-C. Kang, "Short-Term Load Forecasting for Special Days in Anomalous Load Conditions Using Neural Networks and Fuzzy Inference Method," *IEEE Transactions on Power Systems* **15**, 559–565 (2000).

20. H. W. Lewis III, "Intelligent Hybrid Load Forecasting System for an Electric Power Company," *Proceedings of the IEEE Mountain Workshop on Soft Computing in Industrial Applications*, Blacksburg, VA, 2001, pp. 23–27.

21. J.-S. R. Jang, "ANFIS: Adaptive-Network-Based Fuzzy Inference System," *IEEE Transactions on Systems, Man, and Cybernetics* **23**, 665–685 (1993).

22. A. Abraham and B. Nath, "A Neuro-Fuzzy Approach for Modelling Electricity Demand in Victoria," *Applied Soft Computing* **1**, 127–138 (2001).

23. I. Escoda, A. Ortega, A. Sanz, and A. Herms, "Demand Forecast by Neuro-Fuzzy Techniques," *Proceedings of the 6th IEEE International Conference on Fuzzy Systems*, Barcelona, Spain, 1997, **3**, pp. 1381–1386.

24. G. B. Sheble and G. N. Fahd, "Unit Commitment Literature Synopsis," *IEEE Transactions on Power Systems* **9**, 128–135 (1994).

25. A. Kamiya, M. Kato, K. Shimada, and S. Kobayashi, "Soft Computing-Based Optimal Operation in Power Energy System," in S. J. Ovaska and L. M. Sztandera, eds., *Soft Computing in Industrial Electronics*, Physica-Verlag, Heidelberg, Germany, 2002, pp. 196–230.

26. S. Dauzere-Peres and J.-B. Lasserre, *An Integrated Approach in Production Planning and Scheduling*, Springer-Verlag, Berlin, Germany, 1994.

27. T. Nishi, T. Inoue, and Y. Hattori, "Development of a Decentralized Supply Chain Optimization System," *Proceedings of the International Symposium on Design, Operation and Control of Next Generation Chemical Plants*, Kyoto, Japan, 2000, pp. 141–151.

28. D. H. Wolpert and W. G. Macready, "No Free Lunch Theorems for Optimization," *IEEE Transactions on Evolutionary Computation* **1**, 67–82 (1997).

29. T. E. Morton and D. W. Pentico, *Heuristic Scheduling Systems: With Applications to Production Systems and Project Management*, Wiley, New York, 1993.

30. J. Rachlin, R. Goodwin, S. Murthy, R. Akkiraju, F. Wu, S. Kumaran, and R. Das, "A-Teams: An Agent Architecture for Optimization and Decision-Support," in J. Mueller, M. Singh, and A. Rao, eds., *Lecture Notes in Artificial Intelligence: Intelligent Agents V*, Springer-Verlag, Berlin, Germany, 1999, **1555**.

31. A. Nareyek, *Constraint-Based Agents: An Architecture for Constraint-Based Modeling and Local-Search-Based Reasoning for Planning and Scheduling in Open and Dynamic Worlds*, Springer-Verlag, Berlin, Germany, 2001.

32. F. Lobo and D. E. Goldberg, "Decision Making in a Hybrid Genetic Algorithm," *Proceedings of the IEEE International Conference on Evolutionary Computation*, Indianapolis, IN, 1997, pp. 121–125.

33. C. R. Houck, J. A. Joines, M. G. Kay, and J. R. Wilson, "Empirical Investigation of the Benefits of Partial Lamarckianism," *Evolutionary Computation* **5**, 31–60 (1997).

34. D. Orvosh and L. Davis, "Using a Genetic Algorithm to Optimize Problems with Feasibility Constraints," *Proceedings of the 1st IEEE Conference on Evolutionary Computation*, Orlando, FL, 1994, pp. 548–553.

35. B. A. Julstrom, "Comparing Darwinian, Baldwinian, and Lamarckian Search in a Genetic Algorithm for the 4-Cycle Problem," *Late Breaking Papers at the Genetic and Evolutionary Computation Conference*, Orlando, FL, 1999, pp. 134–138.

36. D. Whitley, S. Gordon, and K. Mathias, "Lamarckian Evolution, the Baldwin Effect and Function Optimization," *Parallel Problem Solving from Nature—PPSN III*, pp. 6–15 (1994).

37. M. Schoenauer and Z. Michalewicz, "Boundary Operators for Constrained Parameter Optimization Problems," *Proceedings of the 7th International Conference on Genetic Algorithms*, East Lansing, MI, 1997, pp. 322–329.

38. A. Kamiya, K. Kawai, I. Ono, and S. Kobayashi, "Theoretical Proof of Edge Search Strategy Applied to Power Plant Start-up Scheduling," *IEEE Transactions on Systems, Man, and Cybernetics—Part B: Cybernetics* **32**, 316–331 (2002).

39. V. Chankong and Y. Y. Haimes, "Optimization-Based Methods for Multiobjective Decision-Making: An Overview," *Large Scale Systems* **5**, 1–33 (1983).

40. C. A. Coello Coello, "A Comprehensive Survey of Evolutionary-Based Multi-objective Optimization Techniques," *Knowledge and Information Systems* **1**, 269–308 (1999).

41. H. Ishibuchi and T. Murata, "A Multi-objective Genetic Local Search Algorithm and Its Application to Flowshop Scheduling," *IEEE Transactions on Systems, Man, and Cybernetics—Part C: Applications and Reviews* **28**, 392–403 (1998).

42. D. Srinivasan and A. Tettamanzi, "An Evolutionary Algorithm for Evaluation of Emission Compliance Options in View of the Clean Air Act Amendments," *IEEE Transactions on Power Systems* **12**, 336–341 (1997).

43. H.-J. Zimmermann, "Fuzzy Programming and Linear Programming with Several Objective Functions," *Fuzzy Sets and Systems* **1**, 45–55 (1978).

44. R. E. Bellman and L. A. Zadeh, "Decision-Making in a Fuzzy Environment," *Management Science* **17**, 141–166 (1970).

45. F. S. Wang, C. H. Jing, and G. T. Tsao, "Fuzzy Decision Making Problems of Fuel Ethanol Production Using a Genetically Engineered Yeast," *Industrial & Engineering Chemistry Research* **37**, 3434–3443 (1998).

46. L. F. B. Baptistella and A. Ollero, "Fuzzy Methodologies for Interactive Multicriteria Optimization," *IEEE Transactions on Systems, Man, and Cybernetics* **10**, 335–365 (1980).

47. K. Kawai, "Knowledge Engineering in Power-Plant Control and Operation," *Control Engineering Practice* **4**, 1199–1208 (1996).

48. E. van der Wal, "Standardization in Industrial Control Programming: What's in It for Me?," *Proceedings of the International Conference and Exposition for Advancing Instrumentation, System, and Automation*, New Orleans, LA, 2000.

49. P. J. Antsaklis, M. Lemmon, and J. A. Stiver, "Learning to Be Autonomous Intelligent Supervisory Control," in M. M. Gupta and N. K. Sinha, eds., *Intelligent Control Systems*, IEEE Press, Piscataway, NJ, 1996, pp. 28–62.

50. D. Pruessmann, B. Krause, and C. von Altrock, "Fuzzy Logic Supervisory Control for Coal Power Plant," *Proceedings of the 6th IEEE International Conference on Fuzzy Systems*, Barcelona, Spain, 1997, pp. 921–925.

51. T. Kobayashi, T. Tani, N. Abe, and S. Miyamoto, "Comparison between Human Supervisory Control and Hierarchical Control System Based on Human's Knowledge in Petroleum Plant," *Proceedings of the IEEE International Conference on Fuzzy Systems*, Anchorage, AK, 1998, pp. 200–204.

52. A. Ben-Abdennour and K. Y. Lee, "An Autonomous Control System for Boiler–Turbine Units," *IEEE Transaction on Energy Conversion* **11**, 401–406 (1996).

53. H. Voos, "Intelligent Agents for Supervision and Control: A Perspective," *Proceedings of the IEEE International Symposium on Intelligent Control*, Rio, Greece, 2000, pp. 339–344.

54. T. Kohno, J. Suzuki, M. Iwamasa, N. Sueda, and A. Kamiya, "A Plant Control Expert System to Cope with Unforeseen Situations," *Transactions of the Society of Instrument and Control Engineers* **29**, 833–842 (1993), in Japanese.

55. J. Rasmussen, "Skills, Rules, and Knowledge; Signals, Signs, and Symbols, and Other Distinctions in Human Performance Models," *IEEE Transactions on Systems, Man, and Cybernetics* **13**, 257–266 (1983).

56. B. G. Buchanan and E. H. Shortliffe, *Rule-Based Expert Systems: The MYCIN Experiments of the Stanford Heuristic Programming Project*, Addison-Wesley, Reading, MA, 1984.

57. M. Ulieru and R. Isermann, "Design of a Fuzzy-Logic Based Diagnostic Model for Technical Processes," *Fuzzy Sets and Systems* **58**, 249–271 (1993).

58. S. Edwards, A. W. Lees, and M. I. Friswell, "Fault Diagnosis of Rotating Machinery," *Shock and Vibration Digest* **30**, 4–13 (1998).

59. P. Antsaklis, "Defining Intelligent Control," *IEEE Control Systems* **14**, 4–5 and 58–66 (Jan. 1994).

60. K. J. Åström and T. H. Hägglund, "New Tuning Methods for PID Controllers," *Proceedings of the 3rd European Control Conference*, Rome, Italy, 1995, pp. 2456–2462.

61. F. Karray, W. Gueaieb, and S. Al-Sharhan, "The Hierarchical Expert Tuning of PID Controllers Using Tools of Soft Computing," *IEEE Transactions on Systems, Man, and Cybernetics—Part B: Cybernetics* **32**, 77–90 (2002).

62. E. M. Hemerly and C. L. Nascimento, Jr., "An NN-Based Approach for Tuning Servocontrollers," *Neural Networks* **12**, 113–118 (1999).

63. C.-H. Lee and C.-C. Teng, "Tuning of PID Controller for Stable and Unstable Processes with Specifications on Gain and Phase Margins," *International Journal of Fuzzy Systems* **3**, 346–355 (2001).

64. Y.-Y. Tzou and S.-Y. Lin, "Fuzzy-Tuning Current-Vector Control of a Three-Phase PWM Inverter for High-Performance AC Drives," *IEEE Transactions on Industrial Electronics* **45**, 782–791 (1998).

65. H. Takatsu and T. Itoh, "Future Needs for Control Theory in Industry—Report of the Control Technology Survey in Japanese Industry," *IEEE Transactions on Control Systems Technology* **7**, 298–305 (1999).

66. C. E. Garcia, D. M. Prett, and M. Morari, "Model Predictive Control: Theory and Practice—a Survey," *Automatica* **25**, 335–348 (1989).

67. M. A. Hussain, "Review of the Applications of Neural Networks in Chemical Process Control—Simulation and Online Implementation," *Artificial Intelligence in Engineering* **13**, 55–68 (1999).

68. J. Abonyi, R. Babuska, M. Ayala Botto, F. Szeifert, and L. Nagy, "Identification and Control of Nonlinear Systems Using Fuzzy Hammerstein Models," *Industrial & Engineering Chemistry Research* **39**, 4302–4314 (2000).

69. "Intelligent Manufacturing Systems, an International Research and Development Program," WWW page, 2001. Available from <http://www.ims.org/>.

EDITOR'S INTRODUCTION TO CHAPTER 3

The first adaptive control systems, autopilots, were experimentally installed on high-performance aircraft about 50 years ago. Typical aircraft operate over a broad range of altitudes and speeds, and their dynamics are both nonlinear and time-varying [1]. On the other hand, soft-computing methods—that is, neural networks and fuzzy logic—offer effective means for handling nonlinearities and uncertainties. Thus, they could be potential techniques also for the control of aircraft.

"Since the safety of the aircraft is dependent on its flight control system, no airline or government will certify a pure soft-computing-based flight control system, where one does not have an absolute guarantee of stability and (at least) asymptotic tracking." I first learned this understandable fact from Richard E. Saeks, the author of Chapter 3, "Adaptive Flight Control: Soft Computing with Hard Constraints," in a soft-computing workshop [2]. Similar thinking applies actually to any adaptive or learning controller in a critical application, where the overall stability must be guaranteed strictly. Therefore, it is natural to see an adaptive and possibly nonlinear control system as a symbiosis of two functional modules: the *controller* itself and a *supervision unit* that verifies the stability and transient/tracking behavior. Such closely cooperative modules could be implemented as a fusion of soft-computing (SC) and hard-computing (HC) methodologies.

Saeks points out in his chapter that modern control system design is best performed with a fusion of SC and HC. This is a contradictory opinion compared to the usual thinking of numerous control engineers favoring HC unaccompanied, or those academic researchers and practicing engineers who, on the other hand,

Computationally Intelligent Hybrid Systems. Edited by Seppo J. Ovaska
ISBN 0-471-47668-4   © 2005 the Institute of Electrical and Electronics Engineers, Inc.

57

prefer pure SC methods. Nonetheless, the illustrative case examples of the present chapter give qualitative evidence to support that pragmatic view.

Chapter 3 introduces two computationally intelligent hybrid algorithms, Adaptive Dynamic Programming (ADP) and Neural Adaptive Controller (NAC^{TM}), and their application in aircraft flight control systems. In ADP, neural network techniques are used to learn the optimal control law in real time for a stabilizable nonlinear system with unknown or time-varying dynamics, and HC techniques to verify the convergence and stability of the control algorithm. The adaptation algorithm is globally convergent to the optimal cost functional, and the optimal control law is stepwise stable. Thus, it fulfills the most important requirements of adaptive aircraft control. Challenging applications to flight control of advanced unmanned aerial vehicles (UAVs) illustrate the successful operation and high performance of the ADP algorithm:

- Autolander for a Mach 10 lifting body (NASA X-43)
- Optimal inner loop controller for a Mach 5 waverider (LoFLYTE$^{®}$)

NAC^{TM}, a nonlinear multivariate controller, has its roots in the work of Seraji on adaptive control of robotic manipulators [3]. It uses an HC-type Lyapunov synthesis technique to asymptotically track a predefined state trajectory, and it uses neural network techniques to control the short-/medium-term response of the overall system. The control gains are adapted within specific bounds in real time to automatically compensate for modeling uncertainties and possible changes in plant dynamics caused by component damage, environmental variations, or system failures. This nonlinear adaptive control scheme is applied to a stability augmentation system for the above Mach 5 waverider. The simulated NAC^{TM} flight controller was able to reconfigure itself successfully to compensate for moderate in-flight damage and destabilize the aircraft.

Both the proposed Adaptive Dynamic Programming and Neural Adaptive Control share the following significant advantages:

- Minimal prior knowledge of the plant dynamics is needed.
- It has applicability to a wide variety of nonlinear multivariate systems.

The innovativeness of ADP and NAC^{TM} emerges largely from the fusion of SC and HC methodologies. Saeks uses effectively the SC-HC and transposed SC+HC structures of Chapter 1. Nevertheless, it is important to realize that such a novel fusion was possible only because of thorough understanding of the *application domain*, as well as *control theory* and *SC* techniques.

The hybrid control methods of this chapter form a general model to follow for engineers and researchers who are solving demanding control problems in various critical environments. Here the word "critical" is referring to substantial monetary losses, environmental disasters, or safety threats. Although Chapter 3 is built on extensive simulations only, all the presented techniques have either been successfully flight tested or are in the process of flight testing at Edwards Air Force Base in California.

REFERENCES

1. P. A. Ioannou and E. B. Kosmatopoulos, "Adaptive Control," in J. G. Webster, ed., *Wiley Encyclopedia of Electrical and Electronics Engineering*, Wiley-Interscience, New York, 1999, **1**, pp. 240–253.
2. R. E. Saeks, "Three Applications of (Hard/Soft) Computing to Flight Control and the Degree of 'Softness' Which Can Be Tolerated," *Opening Talk in Panel Discussion, IEEE Midnight-Sun Workshop on Soft Computing Methods in Industrial Applications*, Kuusamo, Finland, June 16, 1999.
3. H. Seraji, "Decentralized Adaptive Control of Manipulators: Theory, Simulation, and Experimentation," *IEEE Transactions on Robotics and Automation* **5**, 183–201 (1989).

CHAPTER 3

ADAPTIVE FLIGHT CONTROL: SOFT COMPUTING WITH HARD CONSTRAINTS

RICHARD E. SAEKS

Accurate Automation Corporation, Chattanooga, Tennessee

3.1 INTRODUCTION

Over the past half century the focus of control engineering has evolved from simply meeting a performance goal to *design for uncertainty*. Indeed, the primary role of a stable feedback loop is to compensate for unknown disturbances, driving the system back to its setpoint. More recently, robust control systems which meet their performance goals for all plants which are sufficiently close to a nominal plant, and adaptive control systems which adapt their gains in real time to compensate for unknown or changing plant dynamics have been developed.

Soft-computing techniques, with their ability to deal with incompletely defined and/or qualitative concepts, are well-suited to design for uncertainty, and they have been widely used in modern control system design. Hard-computing techniques may, however, be required to meet the performance goals. In particular, the hard constraint that *every control system must be stable* cannot be delegated to soft-computing techniques, which are designed to achieve a "good approximation most of the time" while an "exact solution all of the time" is required by the stability constraint. As such, modern control system design is often best performed with a *fusion of soft- and hard-computing techniques.*

The purpose of this chapter is to describe two adaptive control algorithms and their application in advanced aircraft flight control systems:

- Adaptive Dynamic Programming (ADP)
- Neural Adaptive Controller (NAC[TM])

Computationally Intelligent Hybrid Systems. Edited by Seppo J. Ovaska
ISBN 0-471-47668-4 © 2005 the Institute of Electrical and Electronics Engineers, Inc.

Both algorithms use a fusion of soft- and hard-computing techniques to meet their performance goals, while simultaneously dealing with the uncertainty intrinsic in a modern control system. They are applicable to a broad class of nonlinear multivariate systems with minimal a priori knowledge of the plant dynamics; and by virtue of their adaptivity, they can be used to control systems with unknown and/or changing dynamics (due to changes in the operating environment, changing loads, aging, system failures, etc.). Moreover, these algorithms require minimal a priori information about the plant dynamics; and they are readily ported from one plant to another with minimal modification, thereby reducing the cost of control law development.

Adaptive Dynamic Programming (ADP) uses a soft-computing algorithm to learn the optimal control law in real time [1], while circumventing the computationally intensive solution of the Hamilton–Jacobi–Bellman (HJB) Equation, which traditionally limits the applicability of dynamic programming techniques [2,3]. On the other hand, the Neural Adaptive Controller (NAC^{TM}) uses a Lyapunov synthesis technique to asymptotically track a prescribed state trajectory, with soft-computing techniques used to control the short and intermediate time response of the system [4].

A more detailed description of the Adaptive Dynamic Programming and Neural Adaptive Control algorithms is provided in Section 3.2, while the flight control problem is introduced in Section 3.3. The application of the two adaptive control algorithms to the control of two advanced unmanned aircraft vehicles (UAVs) is described in Sections 3.4–3.6:

- An ADP autolander for a Mach 10 lifting body
- An ADP optimal inner loop controller for a Mach 5 waverider
- An NAC^{TM} stability augmentation system for a Mach 5 waverider

The implications of the fused soft/hard-computing techniques used in these algorithms are discussed in Sections 3.7 and 3.8, while our conclusions are summarized in Section 3.9.

3.2 THE ADAPTIVE CONTROL ALGORITHMS

In the following sections we provide an overview of the Adaptive Dynamic Programming and Neural Adaptive Control algorithms. Although the performance goals and the techniques used to achieve these goals are radically different for the two algorithms, both algorithms share the following characteristics:

- Are applicable to a broad class of input affine nonlinear multivariate systems
- Require minimal a priori knowledge of the plant dynamics
- Use a fusion of soft- and hard-computing techniques

Moreover, the common thread of Lyapunov's second theorem runs through both algorithms, via (a) the Lyapunov synthesis technique used in the NAC^{TM} to achieve its asymptotic performance goals and (b) the optimal cost function for the ADP, which is in fact a Lyapunov function for the resultant controller [1].

3.2.1 Adaptive Dynamic Programming

The centerpiece of Dynamic Programming is the Hamilton–Jacobi–Bellman Equation [2,3,5], which one solves for the *optimal cost functional*, $V^o(x_0)$, which characterizes the cost to drive the initial state of the plant, x_0 (at $t_0 = 0$), to a prescribed final state using the optimal control. Given the optimal cost functional, one may then solve a second partial differential equation [6] (derived from the HJB Equation) for the corresponding optimal control law, $k^o(x)$, yielding an optimal cost functional/optimal control law pair, (V^o, k^o).

Although the direct solution of the HJB Equation is computationally intense due to the so-called "curse of dimensionality," the HJB Equation and the relationship between V^o and the corresponding control law, k_0, derived therefrom [6], serve as the basis of the Adaptive Dynamic Programming Algorithm. In this algorithm, we start with an initial cost functional/control law pair, (V_0, k_0), where k_0 is a stabilizing control law for the plant, and construct a sequence of cost functional/control law pairs, (V_i, k_i), in real time, which converge to the optimal cost functional/control law pair, (V^o, k^o), as follows.

- Given (V_i, k_i); $i = 0, 1, 2, \ldots$; we run the system using control law k_i from an array of initial conditions, x_0, covering the entire state space (or that portion of the state space where one expects to operate the system).
- Record the state, $x_i(x_0, \cdot)$, and control trajectories, $u_i(x_0, \cdot)$, for each initial condition.
- Given this data, we define V_{i+1} to be the cost to take the initial state x_0 to the final state, using control law, k_i.
- Take k_{i+1} to be the corresponding control law derived from V_{i+1} via the HJB Equation.
- Iterate the process until it converges.

Although this algorithmic process is similar to many of the soft computing algorithms that have been proposed for optimal control [7–10], it is supported by a hard convergence and stability proof [1,11]. Indeed, with the appropriate technical assumptions, this process is as follows:

- *Globally convergent* to the *optimal cost functional*, V^o, and the optimal control law, k^o.
- *Stepwise stable*; that is, k_i, is a stabilizing controller at every iteration with Lyapunov function, V_i.

A detailed list of the technical assumptions required to implement the Adaptive Dynamic Programming algorithm appears in references 1 and 11 with an outline of the proof of the convergence theorem in reference 1 and a detailed proof in reference 11.

Since stability is an asymptotic property, technically it is sufficient that k_i be stabilizing in the limit. In practice, however, if one is going to run the system for any length of time with control law k_i to generate data for the next iteration, it is necessary that k_i be a stabilizing controller at each step of the iterative process. As such, for this class of adaptive control problems we require stepwise stability—that is, stability at each iteration of the adaptive process—rather than simply requiring stability in the limit [1].

An analysis of the above algorithm will reveal that a priori knowledge of the state dynamics matrix is not required to implement the algorithm [1]. Moreover, the requirement that the input matrix be known (to compute k_{i+1} from V_{i+1}) can be circumvented by the pre-compensator technique of references 1 and 6. As such, the above-described Adaptive Dynamic Programming Algorithm achieves the primary goal of soft-computing control: applicability to plants with unknown and/or changing dynamics [8,12].

While one must eventually explore the entire state space (probably repeatedly) in any truly nonlinear control problem with unknown dynamics, in the above algorithm one is required to explore the entire state space at each iteration of the algorithm (by running the system from an array of initial states which cover the entire state space). Unfortunately, this is not feasible and is tantamount to fully identifying the plant dynamics at each iteration of the algorithm. As such, an approximate implementation of the algorithm, which does not require global exploration of the state space at each iteration, is required. Some of the implementation techniques that have been developed for the ADP algorithm include:

- The *linear case* [1,13], employed in the linear autolander example of Section 3.4, where one can evaluate k_{i+1} and V_{i+1} from n local observations of the system state at each iteration.
- An approximation of the nonlinear control law at each point of the state space, derived using a *quadratic approximation of the cost functional* at that point, requiring $n(n-1)/2$ local observations of the system state at each iteration [1].
- A nonlinear control law employed in the optimal inner-loop control example of Section 3.5, derived at each iteration of the algorithm from a *radial basis function approximation* (RBF) of the cost functional, which is updated locally at each iteration using data obtained along a single state trajectory [1,14].
- An *analytic continuation* technique that is applicable to systems with real analytic plants [1,15].

3.2.2   Neural Adaptive Control

A Lyapunov function, $V(x)$, is a positive definite functional defined on the state space of a (nonlinear) system such that

$$\frac{d}{dt}V(x(t)) < 0 \qquad (3.1)$$

where x is any state trajectory of the system starting at an arbitrary initial state, x_0. If such a function exists and satisfies the appropriate technicalities [3], it follows from Lyapunov's second theorem that the system is stable [3]. Although Lyapunov's second theorem was originally intended for stability analysis, as a practical matter one can only construct a Lyapunov function in the linear case and a few (usually low order) nonlinear cases.

The real power of Lyapunov's second theorem, however, resides in its application to system design. In these Lyapunov synthesis techniques, one hypothesizes the form of the control law and a Lyapunov function and chooses the control gains to satisfy Eq. (3.1) [16–18]. Indeed, these techniques are well-suited to the design of a control system, which is stable and asymptotically tracks a prescribed state trajectory, while a hybrid of a Lyapunov-synthesis-based design technique with soft-computing methods, to deal with uncertainty and the short and intermediate time response of the system, is well-suited for adaptive control [4,19–22].

For the Neural Adaptive Controller [4] (NAC^{TM}) we assume a nonlinear multi-variate plant of the form

$$x^{(n)} + a(x, \ldots, x^{(n-1)}) = b(x, \ldots, x^{(n-1)})u \tag{3.2}$$

where superscript (i) denotes ith derivative of a function. Here, x and u are the system state and input vectors, while $a = a(x, \ldots, x^{(n-1)})$ and $b = b(x, \ldots, x^{(n-1)})$ are the state dynamics and input matrices, which are assumed to be slow-varying functions of the system state. See reference 4 for a precise definition of the "slow-varying" concept, which is readily satisfied by the mechanical and aerospace systems to which the NAC^{TM} is normally applied.

Now let x_r be the reference trajectory one desires to track (a flight path through a set of way points, a minimal energy trajectory, etc.), and assume a control law of the form

$$u(t) = f(t) + \sum_{i=0}^{n-1} k_i(t)e^{(i)}(t) + \sum_{i=0}^{n} q_i(t)x_r^{(i)}(t) \tag{3.3}$$

where $e^{(i)} = x_r^{(i)} - x^{(i)}$ is the ith derivative of the error between the reference and actual state trajectories. Then with the aid of the rather complex Lyapunov function defined in references 4 and 17, one can compute the required gain matrices: $f, k_i, i = 0, 1, \ldots, n-1$, and $q_i, i = 0, 1, \ldots, n$; to guarantee that:

- The control system is *stable*.
- It asymptotically tracks the prescribed reference trajectory.

The reference trajectory can be expressed as

$$f(t) = f(0) + \int_0^t \delta\theta^T r(\psi) \, d\psi = \rho u^T r(t) \tag{3.4}$$

$$k_i(t) = k_i(0) + \int_0^t \alpha_i \theta^T r(\psi) [e^{(i)}(\psi)]^T \, d\psi + \beta_i \theta^T r(t) [e^{(i)}(t)]^T ;$$

$$i = 0, \ldots, n-1 \tag{3.5}$$

$$q_i(t) = q_i(0) + \int_0^t \gamma_i \theta^T r(\psi) [\theta_r^{(i)}(\psi)]^T \, d\psi + \lambda_i \theta^T r(t) [\theta_r^{(i)}(t)]^T ;$$

$$i = 0, \ldots, n \tag{3.6}$$

Here, $\theta = \theta(x, \ldots, x^{(n-1)})$ is the orthogonal part of the input matrix; $b = \theta p$; $\theta^T \theta = 1$, $p \geq 0$; r is a linear combination of the state error vector, $e^{(i)}$, and its derivatives with coefficients derived from a stable reference model [4,17]; while δ, α_i, and γ_i are arbitrary positive constants, ρ, β_i, and λ_i are arbitrary non-negative constants, and $f(0)$, $k_i(0)$, and $q_i(0)$, are arbitrary constants.

Although we have glossed over the details (see reference 4 for a detailed derivation of this algorithm), the expressions of Eqs. (3.3)–(3.6) define a straightforward real-time control algorithm for a nonlinear multivariate system.

Moreover, an analysis of Eqs. (3.3)–(3.6) will reveal that the only a priori knowledge of the state dynamics required by the algorithm is the orthogonal part of the input matrix, θ, which is normally known. Indeed, in the single-variate case θ is either $+1$ or -1, while even this requirement can be circumvented by the techniques of reference 23. As such, the Neural Adaptive Controller is a true adaptive controller, which is applicable to plants with unknown and/or changing dynamics.

Although the performance goals for a control system are often stated in terms of its asymptotic properties, in practice the short and intermediate time response of the system (ringing, overshoot, undershoot, etc.) must be well-behaved in some practical sense. To this end, we combine the above-described Lyapunov-synthesis-based asymptotic design technique with soft-computing techniques to control the short and intermediate time response of the system.

This is best illustrated by the NAC^{TM} flight control example of Fig. 3.1 (based on the 6-degree-of-freedom (6-DoF) LoFLYTE® dynamics model used in Section 3.6). In this example, simultaneous pitch, roll, and yaw commands are executed three times in sequence, with the short and intermediate time response of the system improving each time the command is executed. A careful review of this example will, however, reveal that the only differences between the state of the system at the first, second, and third time the command is executed are the initial values of the gain matrices: $f(0)$, $k_i(0)$, and $q_i(0)$. As such, one can learn to improve the short- and intermediate-time performance of the controller, by monitoring its performance and remembering the initial values of the control gains that yield the best performance for future use.

In the NAC^{TM} this process is implemented by a neural network that operates in a self-learning mode, learning from the prior performance of the NAC^{TM} to initialize the gain matrices in the future. As such, the NAC^{TM} uses a fusion of hard- and soft-computing techniques, with the hard-computing Lyapunov synthesis technique

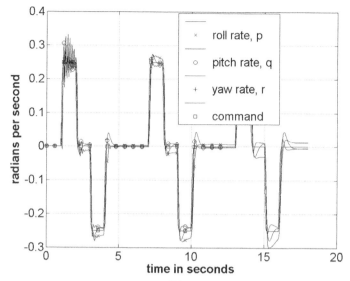

Figure 3.1. NAC^{TM} learning process.

controlling the asymptotic response of the system and soft-computing techniques controlling its short and intermediate time response.

3.3 FLIGHT CONTROL

The Adaptive Dynamic Programming and Neural Adaptive Control algorithms have been applied to a variety of mechanical and aerospace systems: servoactuators [4], robotic joint control [4,5], a hybrid electric vehicle [24], and several flight control systems [1,13,25,26]. In the present chapter, however, we will restrict consideration to their application to flight control for two advanced UAVs. For this purpose a generic flight control system is illustrated in Fig. 3.2. Here the aircraft model is organized as a cascade of three separate subsystems. The first subsystem characterizes the control surface actuator dynamics that map the torque applied to the control surface actuators to the resultant control surface deflection angles. The second subsystem models the inner-loop aircraft dynamics that map the control surface deflection angles to the aircraft state (angle-of-attack, pitch rate, side-slip, etc.), while the third system defines the aircraft kinematics that map the aircraft state to its position and altitude.

Similarly, the flight control system is organized as a cascade of three separate controllers. The outer-loop controller (or autopilot) observes the error between the actual and desired aircraft position and altitude, and it computes the desired values for the aircraft state to correct the position and altitude error. The error between the actual and desired aircraft states serves as the input to the inner-loop controller (or stability augmentation system), which computes the desired control surface deflection angles to correct the state error. Finally, the error between the

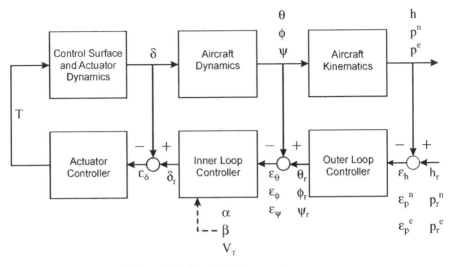

Figure 3.2. Generic flight control system.

actual and desired control surface deflection angles is the input to the actuator controller, which computes the desired actuator torque required to control the aircraft.

The actuator dynamics are made up of one or more servoactuators for each controlled surface, normally using second-order (or lower, depending on the required fidelity) sevoactuator models, while the aircraft kinematics are typically modeled by a set of algebraic equations dependent on the geometry of the aircraft and the coordinate system employed. For flight control the aircraft dynamics are, however, of paramount importance. In a full 6-DoF model the aircraft's pitch, roll, and yaw dynamics are typically modeled by a ninth- to twelfth-order system, while a fourth-order longitudinal model (pitch, pitch rate, horizontal and vertical velocity) may be used to simplify the analysis. (See Sections 3.4 and 3.6 for a typical 6-DoF model, and see Section 3.5 for a typical longitudinal model.) In practice, the aircraft dynamics are always nonlinear, although a linearized model may be used if one restricts consideration to a limited flight regime, or gain schedules a linear model as a function of altitude and air speed.

3.4   X-43A-LS AUTOLANDER

To illustrate the implementation of the Adaptive Dynamic Programming algorithm in the linear case, we developed an autolander for the NASA X-43A-LS [27]. The X-43A [28] (or HyperX), shown in Fig. 3.3a, is an unmanned experimental aircraft for an advanced scramjet engine, operating in the Mach 7–10 range [28]. In its present configuration, the X-43A is an expendable test vehicle, which will be launched from a Pegasus missile, perform a flight test program using its scramjet engine, and then crash into the ocean. The purpose of the simulation described

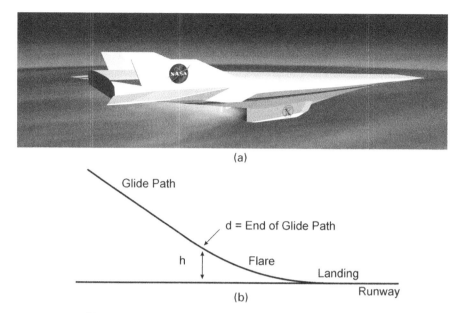

Figure 3.3. (**a**) NASA X-43 (HyperX) and (**b**) its glide path.

below was to evaluate the feasibility of landing the planned X-43B. To this end, we designed, fabricated, and are in the process of flight testing the X-43A-LS, a full-size subsonic version of the X43-A with increased wingspan, designed to evaluate the low-speed performance, landing, and take-off characteristics of the X-43 design. The 12-ft-long X-43A-LS is powered by a 130-lb thrust AT-1500 Phoenix turbojet engine and is designed to fly at 250 kts [27].

The initial flight test of the X-43A-LS was performed in the fall of 2001, while we are presently preparing for a flight test program that will include testing the X-43A-LS with both the Adaptive Dynamic Programming and Neural Adaptive Control algorithms. As a first step in this process we developed an autolander [13] for the X-43A-LS—that is, a special-purpose flight control system designed to track a glide path from low altitude to the flare just above the end of the runway, as indicated in Fig. 3.3b.

Since the operation of the autolander is restricted to a low-speed/low-altitude flight regime, it suffices to design the autolander around a linearized version of the X-43A-LS flight dynamics, characterized by a classical linear time-invariant state space model with 11 states (listed in Table 3.1) and four inputs (listed in Table 3.2). A trim routine was used to calculate the steady-state settings of the aircraft control surfaces required to achieve the desired flight conditions, with the state variables and controlled inputs for the flight control system taken to be the deviations from the trim point. In the present example, the trim was calculated to put the aircraft on the specified glide slope.

The performance of the Adaptive Dynamic Programming (ADP) algorithm was simulated using this 6-DoF linearized X-43A-LS model, together with a linear

TABLE 3.1. States of Linearized 6-DoF X-43A-LS Model

State	Symbol	Units	Trim Value	Initial Error
Roll rate	P	rad/s	0.0	0.0850
Yaw rate	R	rad/s	0.0	0.0850
Pitch rate	Q	rad/s	0.0	0.0850
Roll	ϕ	rad	0.0	0.0850
Yaw	ψ	rad	−0.0778	0.0850
Pitch	θ	rad	0.0	0.0850
Vertical component of airspeed	W	ft/s (positive in down direction)	96.1442	−20.0000
Horizontal/forward component of airspeed	U	ft/s	0.0	−20.0000
Side component of airspeed	V	ft/s	30.6225	−20.0000
Side tracking error (side deviation from desired glide-path)	—	ft	—	0.0850
Altitude tracking error (vertical deviation from desired glide-path)	—	ft	—	0.0850

implementation of the ADP algorithm [1]. To stress the adaptive controller, the simulation uses an extremely steep glide path angle—indeed, so steep that the drag of the aircraft was initially insufficient to cause the aircraft to fall fast enough, requiring negative thrust. Of course, in practice one would never use such a steep glide slope, alleviating the requirement for thrust reversers. To illustrate the adaptivity of the controller, neither an initial guess nor any a priori knowledge of the state dynamics or input matrices for the X-43A-LS model was provided to the controller.

The performance of the X-43A-LS autolander is summarized in Fig. 3.4, where the altitude and lateral errors from the glide path and the vertical component of the aircraft velocity (sink rate) along the glide path are plotted. After correcting for the initial deviation from trim, the autolander brings the aircraft to, and maintains it on, the glide path. The control values employed by the autolander to achieve this level of performance are shown in Fig. 3.5a, all of which are well within the dynamic range of the X-43A-LS's controls, while the remaining states of the aircraft during landing are shown in Figs. 3.5b, 3.5c, and 3.5d.

TABLE 3.2. Inputs (Symbol, Units) of Linearized 6-DoF X-43A-LS Model

Control	Symbol	Units	Trim Value	Control	Symbol	Units	Trim Value
Elevator deflection	de	deg	−15.86	Aileron deflection	da	deg	0.0
Rudder deflection	dr	deg	0.0	Thrust	T	lb	−10.728

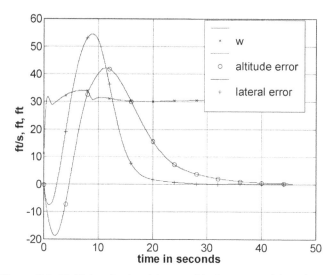

Figure 3.4. X-43 Autolander sink rate, altitude error, and lateral error.

To evaluate the adaptation rate of the autolander, the cost-to-go from the initial state is plotted as a function of time as the controller adapts in Fig. 3.6. As expected, the cost-to-go jumps from the low initial guess for the optimal cost function to a relatively high value, and then it decays monotonically to the optimal value as the controller adapts. Although the theory predicts [1] that the cost-to-go jump

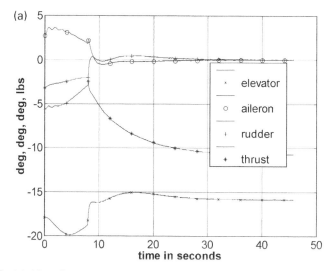

Figure 3.5. (a) Aircraft controls (de, da, dr, and T); (b) orientation rates (p, q, and r); (c) orientation angles (phi, theta, and psi); and (d) airspeed components (u, v, and w).

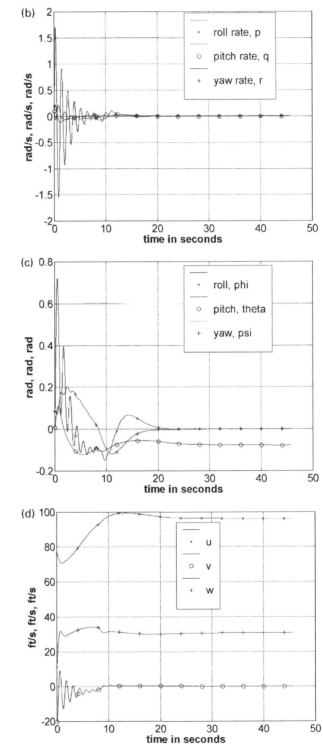

Figure 3.5. *Continued*

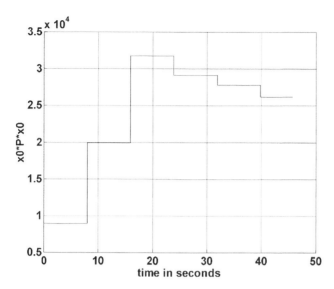

Figure 3.6. Cost-to-go from initial state as a function of time.

should occur in a single iteration, a lowpass filter was used to smooth the adaptive process in our implementation, which spreads the initial cost-to-go jump over several iterations.

3.5 LoFLYTE® OPTIMAL CONTROL

The purpose of section is to describe an implementation of the Adaptive Dynamic Programming algorithm in the nonlinear case using the fourth-order longitudinal dynamics of the LoFLYTE® UAV [29–31], illustrated in Fig. 3.7, with a nonlinear pitching moment coefficient. LoFLYTE® is an unmanned subsonic testbed for a Mach 5 waverider that was built to evaluate the low-speed, landing, and take-off performance of the waverider design. It is 8 ft long, powered by a 40-lb thrust

Figure 3.7. LoFLYTE® UAV at Edwards Air Force Base.

AMT Olympus turbojet, and designed to fly at 150 kts. LoFLYTE® was extensively flight tested in the late nineties. An upgraded version of LoFLYTE®, which is presently being prepared for flight testing, will be used as an adaptive flight control testbed for both the Adaptive Dynamic Programming and Neural Adaptive Control algorithms.

In this implementation of the ADP algorithm, LoFLYTE®'s longitudinal flight dynamics are modeled by a fourth-order input affine nonlinear state model with an input quadratic performance measure [32]. The states for this model are indicated in Table 3.3, with the zero point in the state space shifted to correspond to a selected trim point for the aircraft, while the input for this model was the elevator deflection, with $\delta_e = 0$ in the model corresponding to a downward elevator deflection of $-2.784°$.

Unlike the linear case where the optimal cost functional is a quadratic form on the state space, no simple parameterization of the optimal cost functional exists in the nonlinear case. As such, to implement the ADP algorithm for LoFLYTE®'s nonlinear longitudinal dynamics, we approximated the cost functional by a linear combination of radial basis functions. Indeed, one can achieve any desired degree of numerical accuracy with such an approximation. Moreover, since a linear combination of radial basis functions is a local approximator, one can update the approximation locally at each iteration of the ADP algorithm, circumventing the requirement that one explores the entire state space at each iteration of the algorithm.

The performance of the Adaptive Dynamic Programming algorithm was simulated using the radial basis function implementation of the ADP algorithm [1,14] with LoFLYTE®'s fourth-order nonlinear longitudinal dynamics. For this simulation, each axis of the state space was covered by 21 radial basis functions, from a predetermined minimum to a predetermined maximum value indicated in Table 3.3. As such, that part of state space where the UAV operates is covered by 21 × 21 × 21 × 21 = 194,481 radial basis functions, corresponding to a 4-cube in state space centered at x with $\Delta u = \pm 4.76$ ft/s, $\Delta w = \pm 4.76$ ft/s, $\Delta q = \pm 0.083$ rad/s,

TABLE 3.3. States of Nonlinear Longitudinal LoFLYTE® Model

State	Symbol	Units	Min	Trim Point	Max
Pitch rate	Q	rad/s	−0.3491	0.0000	0.3491
Pitch	θ	rad	−0.6850	−0.3359	0.0132
Vertical component of airspeed	W	ft/s (positive in down direction)	−4.116	16.12	36.12
Horizontal/forward component of airspeed	U	ft/s	95.97	115.97	135.97

and $\Delta\theta = \pm 0.083$ rad. Given the local nature of the radial basis functions, however, at any point, x, in the state space the cost functional is computed by summing the values of a smaller $5 \times 5 \times 5 \times 5 = 625$ block of radial basis functions in a neighborhood of x.

To illustrate the adaptivity of the controller, no a priori knowledge of LoFLYTE®'s flight dynamics was provided to the controller. The following figures illustrate the performance of the radial basis function implementation of the Adaptive Dynamic Programming algorithm, learning an "optimal" control strategy from a given initial point in the state space. The algorithm was initiated on the zeroth iteration with a "zero" controller. After the state converged to the trim point, the iteration count was incriminated, updated radial basis function approximations of the cost functional and the corresponding control law were computed, and the system was restarted at the same initial state. In these simulations, the aircraft state was updated 100 times per second while the elevator deflection angle was updated 10 times per second. The performance of the radial basis function implementation of the Adaptive Dynamic Programming algorithm is illustrated in Figs. 3.8 through 3.11, where we have plotted each of the key system variables on the zeroth to fifth iterations of the algorithm and plotted the limiting value of these plots at the 60th iteration.

The state variables of the aircraft are plotted in Fig. 3.8. For each state variable the initial (zeroth) response (indicated by "x"s) is at one extreme (high for the vertical velocity, pitch, and pitch rate; and low for the horizontal velocity), with the response jumping to the opposite extreme on the first iteration (indicated by "o"s) and then converging back toward the limiting value, with the adaptation process effectively convergent after 10 iterations. The elevator deflection required to achieve these responses is shown in Fig. 3.9. Since $k_0(x) = 0$ the initial (zeroth) elevator deflection remains constant at the trim point of $-2.784°$ (indicated by "x"s). The elevator deflection then jumps to a high value on the first iteration (indicated by "o"s) and then converges back toward the limiting value. All variables are well within a reasonable dynamic range for the LoFLYTE® UAV, except for the initial drop of the aircraft (indicated by the initial positive spike in the vertical velocity curve of Fig. 3.8a), due to the use of a "zero" controller on the first iteration (which would not be the case for the actual aircraft where $k_0(x)$ would be selected on the basis of prior simulation).

The performance of the Adaptive Dynamic Programming algorithm is illustrated in Fig. 3.10, where the computed (Fig. 3.10a) and radial basis function approximation (Fig. 3.10b) of the optimal cost functional are plotted as a function of time along the state trajectory, on the zeroth, first, second, third, fourth, fifth, and 60th (limiting) iteration of the algorithm. In both cases, the initial estimate (indicated by "x"s) is low and converges upward to the limiting value, with the RBF approximation error decreasing in parallel with the adaptation process. Finally, the cost-to-go based on the computed ("x"s) and radial basis function approximation ("o"s) of the optimal cost functional is plotted as a function of the iteration number in Fig. 3.11. As predicted by the theory, the cost-to-go has an initial spike and then declines monotonically to the limiting value.

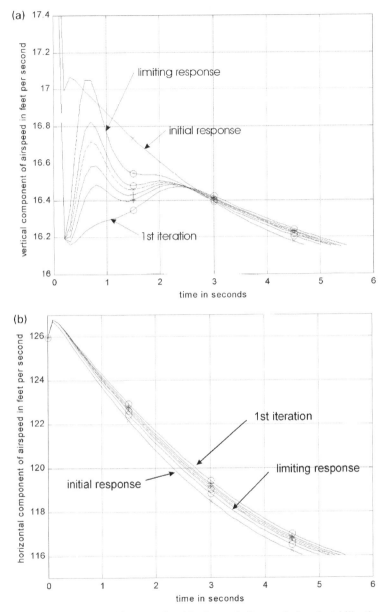

Figure 3.8. Elevator, aileron, and rudder inputs before and after destabilization.

3.6   LoFLYTE® STABILITY AUGMENTATION

Our third flight control example is a 6-DoF simulation of the performance of an NAC™ inner-loop controller for the LoFLYTE® UAV [29,30] using a nonlinear

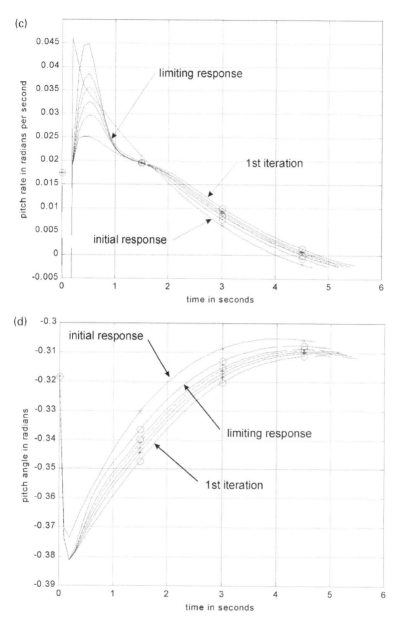

Figure 3.8. *Continued*

ninth-order 6-DoF inner-loop flight controller together with individual second-order controllers for each servoactuator. A trim routine was used to calculate the steady-state settings of the aircraft control surfaces required to achieve the desired flight conditions, with the state variables and controlled inputs for the flight control system taken to be the deviations from the trim point. In the present example, two

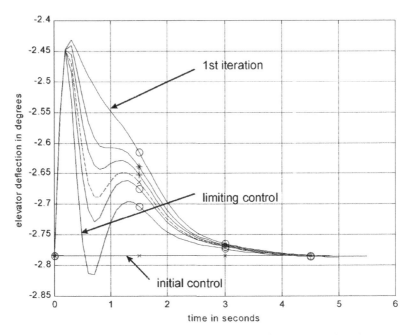

Figure 3.9. Elevator deflection on the zeroth to fifth and 60th iteration.

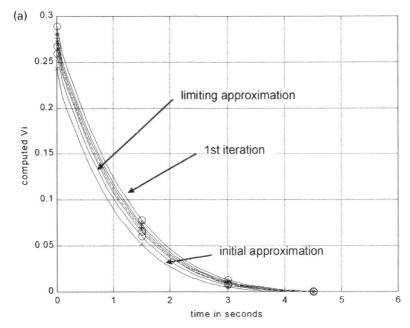

Figure 3.10. (a) Computed and (b) RBF approximation of the optimal cost functional on the zeroth to fifth and 60th iteration.

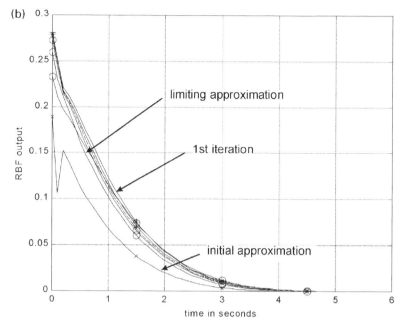

(b)

Figure 3.10. *Continued.*

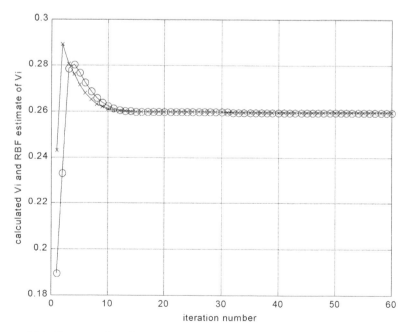

Figure 3.11. Cost-to-go based on the computed ("x"s) and RBF approximation ("o"s) of the optimal cost functional versus iteration number.

trim settings were calculated with the aircraft flying at 100 ft/s and 65 ft/s. The nine states and four inputs for this 6-DoF model are listed in Tables 3.4 and 3.5, respectively.

The simulated performance of the NAC^{TM} flight control system at each trim point is illustrated in Fig. 3.12. The uncompensated response of the aircraft at 100 ft/s and 65 ft/s to a simultaneous pitch, roll, and yaw command is illustrated in Figs. 3.12a and 3.12c, respectively. Clearly, the uncompensated aircraft does not handle well, as would be expected of a waverider flying at subsonic speeds. In particular, the yaw response badly lags the pilot's input while the aircraft wobbles badly in the roll axis, a fact that has been observed also in our flight tests. These difficulties are alleviated by the NAC^{TM} flight controller where the aircraft response closely follows the command in all three axes, with its handling qualities improving as the controller adapts, as illustrated in Figs 3.12b and 3.12d.

To validate the ability of the NAC^{TM} flight controller to reconfigure itself to compensate for in-flight aircraft damage and system failures, we simulated a damaged aircraft by moving its center of gravity from its normal 51% to 56%, 6 seconds into a simulated flight, thereby destabilizing the aircraft. The performance of the NAC^{TM} flight controller in response to this instantaneous destabilization at 100 ft/s is illustrated in Fig. 3.13. As expected, without compensation the aircraft goes unstable when its center of gravity is moved, while the compensated aircraft quickly recovers, after a short pitch rate spike, with a pitch, roll, and yaw response that is almost identical to the stable aircraft. The commanded elevator, aileron, and rudder inputs generated by the flight controller to achieve this response, however, differ significantly as indicated in Fig. 3.14. In particular, since the destabilization occurs in the longitudinal axis, the elevator command goes from slightly negative for the stable aircraft to positive for the unstable aircraft while the aileron command is increased.

TABLE 3.4. States of Linearized 6-DoF X-43A-LS Model

State	Symbol	Units	Trim at 100 ft/s	Trim at 65 ft/s
Roll rate	p	rad/s	0.0	0.0
Yaw rate	r	rad/s	0.0	0.0
Pitch rate	q	rad/s	0.0	0.0
Roll	ϕ	rad	0.0	0.0
Yaw	ψ	rad	0.0	0.0
Pitch	θ	rad	0.1673	0.3081
Vertical component of airspeed	w	ft/s (positive in down direction)	16.8	19.7111
Horizontal/forward component of airspeed	u	ft/s	99.4675	61.9393
Side component of airspeed	v	ft/s	0.0	0.0

TABLE 3.5. Input (Symbols, Units) of Linearized 6-DoF X-43A-LS Model

Control	Symbol	Units	Trim at 100 ft/s	Trim at 65 ft/s
Elevator deflection	de	deg	-2.8458	-7.0367
Aileron deflection	da	deg	0.0	0.0
Rudder deflection	dr	deg	0.0	0.0
Thrust	T	lb	-10.728	26.4303

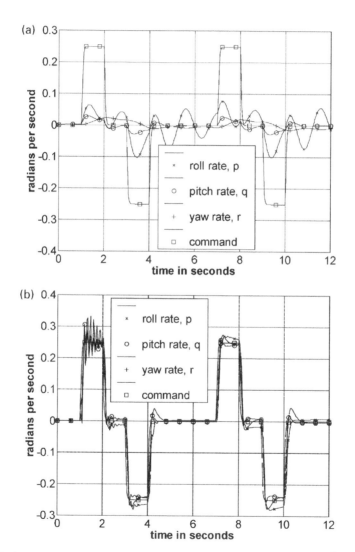

Figure 3.12. Performance of Neural Adaptive Flight Controller in LoFLYTE® simulation. (**a**) Uncompensated and (**b**) compensated response at 100 ft/s and 1500 ft; (**c**) uncompensated and (**d**) compensated response at 65 ft/s and 900 ft.

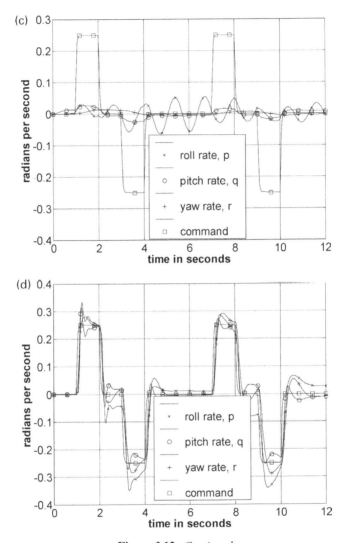

Figure 3.12. *Continued*

3.7 DESIGN FOR UNCERTAINTY WITH HARD CONSTRAINTS

The emphasis on *"design for uncertainty"* as a fundamental consideration in engineering design has led to an expanded emphasis on soft computing techniques in engineering design. In fact, however, many engineering problems have *"hard constraints."* For a *"soft constraint"* (size, weight, cost, etc.), one can usually find a few extra dollars in the budget to cover a "small deviation" from the constraint set, whereas for a *"hard constraint"* even the smallest deviation from the constraint

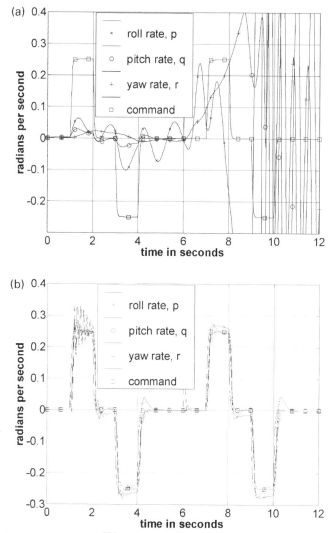

Figure 3.13. Recovery of NAC^TM from instantaneous destabilization 6 s into a simulated flight at 100 ft/s and 1500 ft. (**a**) Uncompensated and (**b**) compensated.

set will lead to a fundamental change in the characteristics of the system. This is the case, for example, in:

- *Control*, as we have seen, where even the smallest instability will eventually grow to catastrophic proportions
- *Signal processing*, where a response that precedes the excitation is not physically realizable

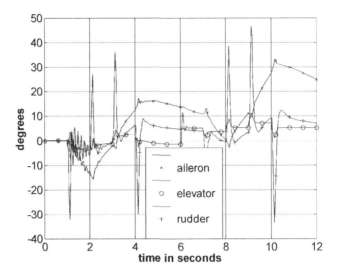

Figure 3.14. Aileron, elevator, and rudder inputs before and after destabilization.

- *Electromagnetics*, where a signal in a waveguide is dissipated if its wavelength exceeds a threshold
- *Electronics*, where an active system requires a completely different infrastructure (power supplies, etc.) than a passive system
- *Decision systems*, where a small change in utility can fundamentally change a quantized outcome (from one to zero, etc.)

Our goal in this chapter has been to demonstrate that one can deal with this challenging class of problems, where one must "design for uncertainty" under a "hard constraint" via a fusion of soft- and hard-computing techniques.

Although some authors have suggested that one can use pure soft-computing techniques to deal with these problems, with an external agent used to correct any deviations from the hard constraint set, this is somewhat ingenuous in that it assumes that the agent is not part of the system. For example, to improve the performance of some older aircraft, where the pilot is always in the loop, the designers allowed the flight control system to be marginally unstable, relying on the pilot to compensate for any instabilities. Although this opens up the constraint set, the allowed instabilities are still constrained by the pilot's reaction time, and, as such, one has simply traded off one constraint set for another. Indeed, experience with human–machine systems indicates that one is better served by treating the human-in-the-loop as part of the system and accepting the necessity of a fused soft/hard-computing solution. Moreover, in a modern fly-by-wire flight control system, the pilot provides commands to the control system, but does not react fast enough to be in-the-loop, once again requiring a fully automated flight control system with "hard stability constraints."

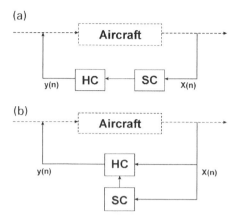

Figure 3.15. Soft/hard-computing fusion models for (**a**) the Adaptive Dynamic Programming and (**b**) the Neural Adaptive Control algorithms.

3.8 FUSION OF SOFT COMPUTING AND HARD COMPUTING

Soft-Computing/Hard-Computing Fusion Models for the Adaptive Dynamic Programming and Neural Adaptive Control algorithms described in this chapter are illustrated in Figs. 3.15a and 3.15b, respectively. The ADP algorithm uses an SC-HC architecture, while the NAC^{TM} algorithm uses a transposed SC+HC architecture (Chapter 1). For the ADP algorithm a soft-computing subsystem, used to learn the cost functional, is cascaded with a hard-computing subsystem used to implement the control law via the Hamilton–Jacobi–Bellman Equation. On the other hand, the primary NAC^{TM} controller is implemented with a hard-computing algorithm, with soft-computing methods used to fine-tune its parameters in a feedforward configuration. Note, in both cases we have included the aircraft in Fig. 3.15 with the flight controller in a feedback mode to emphasize that the feedback controller is composed of both soft- and hard-computing subsystems, independently of the aircraft, whose implementation may be completely unknown to the control system designer.

3.9 CONCLUSIONS

Adaptive control systems were used on both the F-111 and X-15 aircraft in the 1960s. As the need to deal with uncertainty became apparent, however, the industry adopted a more conservative approach, often using gain scheduled (robust) linear controllers, where one might once have employed a nonlinear adaptive controller. Our goal in the preceding has been to demonstrate that one can have the best of both worlds by fusing soft- and hard-computing techniques in an advanced adaptive flight control system. Indeed, the two approaches are highly synergistic, fusing into a powerful toolset for the control system designer.

In both the Adaptive Dynamic Program and Neural Adaptive Control algorithms, the underlying stability and convergence proofs require multiple pages of mathematical analysis to deal with the "hard stability constraint," and yet they are completely synergistic with the soft-computing-based learning algorithms used to deal with uncertainty. Moreover, one can often interchange the soft- and hard-computing techniques in these algorithms. Indeed, the algebraic learning algorithm used in the linear implementation of the ADP is a real-time implementation of the Newton–Raphson algorithm for solving the matrix Riccati Equation [32], which would normally fall under the hard-computing banner, while the radial basis function implementation of the ADP in the nonlinear case is typical soft-computing. Similarly, the integrals used to compute the control gains in the Neural Adaptive Control algorithm also define a neural network, as illustrated in reference 4.

Although we have chosen to illustrate the ADP and NAC^{TM} algorithms via their application in flight control, they have also been demonstrated in servoactuators [4], robotic joint control systems [4,33], and a hybrid electric vehicle [24] (where multiple NAC^{TM} controllers are used for directional and speed control, together with an ADP power system controller), while they are equally applicable to a wide variety of control systems where one must "design for uncertainty" with "hard constraints."

ACKNOWLEDGMENTS

This chapter is based on the theory and applications developed in references [1,4,11,25]. The author would like to thank his coauthors on those papers; Chadwick Cox and Dr. James Neidhoefer of the Accurate Automation Corporation, Dr. John Murray of the State University of New York at Stony Brook, and Dr. George Lendaris of Portland State University for their support in this work; and the U.S. National Science Foundation, the U.S. Navy, the U.S. Air Force, and NASA for their support of this work under a series of Small Business Innovative Research Contracts.

REFERENCES

1. J. J. Murray, C. J. Cox, G. G. Lendaris, and R. E. Saeks, "Adaptive Dynamic Programming," *IEEE Transactions on Systems, Man, and Cybernetics—Part C: Applications and Reviews* **32**, 140–153 (2002).

2. R. E. Bellman, *Dynamic Programming*, Princeton University Press, Princeton, NJ, 1957.

3. D. G. Luenberger, *Introduction to Dynamic Systems: Theory, Models, and Applications*, Wiley, New York, 1979.

4. J. C. Neidhoefer, C. J. Cox, and R. Saeks, "Development and Application of a Lyapunov Synthesis Based Neural Adaptive Controller," *IEEE Transactions on Systems, Man, and Cybernetics—Part C: Applications and Reviews* **33**, 125–136 (2003).

5. D. P. Bertsekas, *Dynamic Programming: Deterministic and Stochastic Models*, Prentice-Hall, Englewood Cliffs, NJ, 1987.

6. R. E. Saeks and C. J. Cox, "Adaptive Critic Control and Functional Link Networks," *Proceedings of the IEEE International Conference on Systems, Man, and Cybernetics*, San Diego, CA, 1998, pp. 1652–1657.

7. D. Prokhorov and L. Feldkamp, "Primitive Adaptive Critics," *Proceedings of the International Conference on Neural Networks*, Houston, TX, 1997, **4**, pp. 2263–2267.

8. P. J. Werbos, "Approximate Dynamic Programming for Real Time Control and Neural Modeling," in P. J. White and P. J. Sofge, eds., *Handbook of Intelligent Control*, Van Nostrand, New York, 1994, pp. 493–525.

9. L. Yang, R. Enns, Y. T. Wang, and J. Si, "Direct Neural Dynamic Programming," in D. Liu and P. Antsaklis, eds., *Contemporary Issues in Systems Stability and Control with Applications*, Birkhauser, Boston, 2003, Ch. 10, pp. 193–213.

10. R. Zaman, D. Prokhorov, and D. C. Wunsch II, "Adaptive Critic Design in Learning to Play Game of Go," *Proceedings of the International Conference on Neural Networks*, Houston, TX, 1997, **1**, pp. 1–4.

11. J. J. Murray, C. J. Cox, and R. Saeks, "The Adaptive Dynamic Programming Theorem," in D. Liu and P. Antsaklis, eds., *Contemporary Issues in Systems Stability and Control with Applications*, Birkhauser, Boston, 2003, Ch. 19, pp. 379–394.

12. S. Sastry and M. Bodson, *Adaptive Control: Stability, Convergence, and Robustness*, Prentice-Hall, Englewood Cliffs, NJ, 1989.

13. C. Cox, S. Stepniewski, C. Jorgensen, and R. Saeks, "On the Design of a Neural Network Autolander," *International Journal of Robust and Nonlinear Control* **9**, 1071–1096 (1999).

14. G. G. Lendaris, C. J. Cox, R. E. Saeks, and J. Murray, "A Radial Basis Function Implementation of the Adaptive Dynamic Programming Algorithm," *Proceedings of the 41st IEEE Midwest Symposium on Circuits and Systems*, Tulsa, OK, 2002, pp. II-338–II-341.

15. J. Dieudonne, *Foundations of Mathematical Analysis*, Academic Press, New York, 1960.

16. A. Halanay and V. Rasvan, *Applications of Lyapunov Methods in Stability*, Kluwer, Dordrecht, The Netherlands, 1993.

17. H. Seraji, "Decentralized Adaptive Control of Manipulators: Theory, Simulation, and Experimentation," *IEEE Transactions on Robotics and Automation* **5**, 183–201 (1989).

18. J.-J. E. Slotine and W. Li, "Adaptive Manipulator Control: A Case Study," *IEEE Transactions on Automation Control* **AC-33**, 995–1003 (1988).

19. G. Liu, V. Kadkivkamanthan, and S. Billings, "Variable Neural Network for Adaptive Control of Nonlinear Systems," *IEEE Transactions on Systems, Man, and Cybernetics—Part C: Applications and Reviews* **29**, 34–43 (1999).

20. R. M. Sanner and J. E. Slotine, "Gaussian Networks for Direct Adaptive Control," *Proceedings of the American Control Conference*, Boston, 1991, pp. 2153–2159.

21. S. N. Singh, W. Yim, and W. R. Wells, "Direct Adaptive and Neural Control of Wing-Rock Motion of Slender Delta Wings," *Journal of Guidance, Control and Dynamics* **18**, 25–30 (1995).

22. L.-X. Wang, "Stable Adaptive Fuzzy Controllers with Applications to Inverted Pendulum Tracking," *IEEE Transactions on Systems, Man, and Cybernetics—Part B: Cybernetics* **26**, 677–691 (1996).

23. B. Martensson, "The Order of Any Stabilizing Regulator Is Sufficient A Priori Information for Adaptive Stabilization," *Systems and Control Letters* **6**, 87–91 (1985).

24. R. E. Saeks, C. J. Cox, J. C. Neidhoefer, P. R. Mays, and J. J. Murray, "Adaptive Control of a Hybrid Electric Vehicle," *IEEE Transactions on Intelligent Transportation Systems* **3**, 213–234 (2002).

25. R. E. Saeks and C. J. Cox, "LoFLYTE®: A Neurocontrols Testbed," *Proceedings of the 35th AIAA Aerospace Sciences Meeting*, Reno, NV, 1997, Paper 97-0085.

26. R. E. Saeks, C. J. Cox, J. C. Neidhoefer, and G. G. Lendaris, "Neural Adaptive Control of LoFLYTE®," *Proceedings of the American Control Conference*, Arlington, VA, 2001, pp. 2913–2917.

27. C. Gibson, J. Neidhoefer, S. Cooper, and L. Carlton, "Development and Flight Test of the X-43A-LS Hypersonic Configuration UAV," *Proceedings of the 1st AIAA Unmanned Aerospace Vehicles, Systems, Technologies, and Operations Conference and Workshop*, San Jose, CA, 2002, Paper 2002-3462.

28. J. Sitz, "HYPER-X: Hypersonic Experimental Research Vehicle," *NASA Fact Sheet*, 1998, FS-1994-11-030.

29. C. Cox, C. Lewis, R. Saeks, and R. Pap, "Development of the LoFLYTE® Vehicle," *Proceeding of the 34th AIAA Aerospace Sciences Meeting*, Reno, NV, 1996, Paper 96-0813.

30. C. Gibson, J. Buckner, L. Carlton, C. Cox, M. Kocher, and C. Lewis, "The LoFLYTE® Program," *Proceedings of the AIAA 9th International Space Planes and Hypersonic Systems and Technologies Conference*, Norfolk, VA, 1999.

31. R. J. Pegg, C. E. Cockrell Jr., and D. E. Hahne, "Low-Speed Wind Tunnel Tests of Two Waverider Configuration Models," *Proceedings of the 6th AIAA International Aerospace Planes Hypersonics Technologies Conference*, Chattanooga, TN, 1995, Paper 95-6093.

32. W. Holley and S. Wei, "An Improvement in the MacFarlane–Potter Method for Solving the Algebraic Riccati Equation," *Proceedings of the Joint Automatic Control Conference*, Denver, CO, 1979, pp. 921–923.

33. C. Cox, M. Lothers, R. Pap, and C. Thomas, "A Neurocontroller for Robotics Applications," *Proceedings of the IEEE International Conference on Systems, Man, and Cybernetics*, Chicago, IL, 1992, pp. 712–716.

EDITOR'S INTRODUCTION TO CHAPTER 4

Switched reluctance motors (SRMs) have a simple and rugged construction that does not contain brushes, magnets, or rotor conductors. In addition, SRMs are more economical to manufacture than many other types of electric machines. These characteristics make the switched reluctance motor a potential rival for permanent magnet brushless DC motors as well as induction motors. Sensorless SRM motor drives—that is, drive systems *without* physical rotor angle or angular velocity sensors—have received wide attention in the power electronics and motion control literature [1].

To obtain satisfactory control performance with sensorless drives, a diverse set of angle estimation schemes have been developed and evaluated since the beginning of the 1990s [2]. Most of the accurate, noise-insensitive, and robust estimation methods are utilizing soft computing (SC), or the complementary fusion of soft computing and hard computing (HC). The motivation for the use of SC comes mainly from the necessity to handle considerable nonlinearities, time-variant characteristics, and uncertainties.

Chapter 4 of the present book, "Sensorless Control of Switched Reluctance Motors," is authored by Adrian David Cheok. It introduces an advanced angle estimation scheme for SRMs that is based on the fusion of SC and HC methodologies. First, a computationally efficient fuzzy logic model of the SRM was developed using the adaptive-network-based fuzzy inference system (ANFIS). Then, a robust fuzzy-logic-based phase selection method is created. To further improve the accuracy of those pure soft-computing approaches, complementary hard-computing algorithms are introduced to form a computationally intelligent hybrid system. At the

Computationally Intelligent Hybrid Systems. Edited by Seppo J. Ovaska
ISBN 0-471-47668-4 © 2005 the Institute of Electrical and Electronics Engineers, Inc.

end of the chapter, comprehensive simulations and experimental results are provided to illustrate the operation and performance of the entire switched reluctance motor drive.

It is important to point out that although HC methods based on the use of conventional observers could provide satisfactory angle estimates under certain operating conditions, their accuracy and convergence deteriorate under transient (load/speed) conditions and industrial environments with electromagnetic interferences (EMI) and noise.

The Sugeno-type fuzzy motor model that was created using the ANFIS has altogether 151 rules. Thus, its real-time implementation in a digital signal processor (DSP) environment is feasible. Optimal phase selection is an important step in the measurement of flux linkage and current. Those measured quantities should be as accurate as possible, because they are used directly as inputs to the angle estimator. Fuzzy logic is used to compute the *confidence* of estimation accuracy. With such confidence information available, the phase that provides the highest confidence is selected for computing the angle estimate. This angle estimate is finally lowpass filtered by a polynomial predictive filter that does not introduce harmful delay into the low-degree polynomial component (i.e., trend) of the estimated angle waveform [3]. In parallel with those SC and HC accuracy enhancement algorithms, there is also a simple HC algorithm that updates the value of phase resistance periodically. This is necessary because the resistance value is time varying. And it is a critical quantity in the integration of flux linkage. As a conclusion, HC methods relying on the available domain knowledge are used with optimized SC methods to develop a hybrid system for angle estimation and control of switched reluctance motors.

At the end of the chapter, extensive simulations and experimental results are presented. A wide range of operating conditions and modes were applied to the SRM:

1. Start-up from zero speed
2. Low current and low speed with constant load
3. High speed with constant load
4. Medium speed with step change in load

These tests confirm the high accuracy of the multistage angle estimation method. The absolute values of average estimation errors were below 0.5 degrees, and the maximum values were less than 3.0 degrees. It should be noted that the largest errors correspond to the test cases 1 and 4 with transient-like behavior.

Mese and Torrey developed a neural-network-based angle estimation scheme for SRMs and analyzed its performance with similar experiments as those of the present chapter [2]. They studied empirical error histograms and found out that the estimation error was typically bounded on $[-5, +5]$ degrees, while a significant part of the error was within the range $[-2, +2]$ degrees. The computational complexity of this neural network estimator was higher than that of the fuzzy-logic-based scheme.

It is demonstrated in this chapter that the proposed angle estimation scheme provides highly satisfactory behavior in a broad range of operating conditions. Also, the method is practical for DSP implementation. The applied fusion structures are cascades of SC and HC methodologies, as well as a master–slave-type SC-assisted HC (Chapter 1).

REFERENCES

1. B. K. Bose, ed., *Power Electronics and Variable Frequency Drives: Technology and Applications*, IEEE Press, Piscataway, NJ, 1997.

2. E. Mese and D. A. Torrey, "An Approach for Sensorless Position Estimation for Switched Reluctance Motors Using Artificial Neural Networks," *IEEE Transactions on Power Electronics* **17**, 66–75 (2002).

3. S. Väliviita, S. J. Ovaska, and O. Vainio, "Polynomial Predictive Filtering in Control Instrumentation: A Review," *IEEE Transactions on Industrial Electronics* **46**, 876–889 (1999).

CHAPTER 4

SENSORLESS CONTROL OF SWITCHED RELUCTANCE MOTORS

ADRIAN DAVID CHEOK

National University of Singapore, Singapore

4.1 INTRODUCTION

Due to its intrinsic simplicity and reliability, the switched reluctance motor (SRM) has recently become a promising candidate for variable-speed drive applications. However, the SRM has the disadvantage of position information requirement for high performance control. The traditional position sensors (or encoders) not only add complexity and cost to the system but also tend to reduce the reliability of the drive system. Therefore, over the past decade, various sensorless methods have been proposed to eliminate the position sensors. Some methods use diagnostic signals (such as injected motor winding current pulses) to derive rotor position information [1]. These methods have the disadvantages such as added cost and complexity of the motor and limited resolution for high-speed operation. Other methods use the actual motor excitation waveforms instead. These methods utilize either the state observer theory [2] or the magnetic characteristics of the SRM [3]. Observer-based rotor position estimation methods can achieve a high accuracy; however, they require a rather complex mathematical model of the motor to take the magnetic saturation into account [2]. Moreover, though the observer-based methods can provide an accurate position estimation under normal conditions, their accuracy and stability deteriorate under transient conditions or electromagnetically noisy environments.

Magnetization data of the motor, such as flux linkage and inductance, can also be used in sensorless position estimation, since they are functions of the rotor position. Computation and measurement of flux linkage is more direct and simple than that of inductance and hence is more preferred in sensorless position detection schemes [4]. A flux/current table has been traditionally used to derive rotor position from flux and current waveforms [5]. However, this method has the disadvantages such as

Computationally Intelligent Hybrid Systems. Edited by Seppo J. Ovaska
ISBN 0-471-47668-4 © 2005 the Institute of Electrical and Electronics Engineers, Inc.

large memory requirement and sensitivity to measurement noise and error in the input signals.

The above-mentioned methods use pure hard-computing (HC) techniques. However, many soft-computing (SC) methods have also been developed for this problem. For example, fuzzy logic systems that are nonlinear universal approximators [6] have been used to address the problem. They do not require complex mathematical models, nor do they require large memory lookup tables. Moreover, the width of the membership functions of the fuzzy sets can be considered as an allowable level of noise [7]; thus fuzzy logic systems are robust in nature. Hence, the use of fuzzy logic is well-suited for this application. A fuzzy-logic-based rotor position estimation method for an SRM drive has previously been described in references 8 and 9, which has shown high reliability and robustness against noise and error in the feedback signal. However, as stated in reference 8, the robustness is only achieved at the cost of the accuracy due to their inverse relationship with fuzzy modeling. Since the fuzzy model is not optimized, the number of the fuzzy rules is large to ensure a satisfactory estimation accuracy, and the obtained accuracy is worse when the current and flux linkage are low. Moreover, the fuzzy predictive filter used in that scheme needs to be trained during the initial starting of the scheme, which makes the estimation error high during the start-up of the motor.

Hence, although SC techniques have advantages, they can be improved by combining them with HC methods. In this research, a fused HC- and SC-based method is adopted for the sensorless rotor position estimation scheme and implemented for a real-time digital signal processor (DSP)-based SRM drive. Compared with the algorithm used in reference 8, this proposed estimation scheme uses an efficient (compact and accurate) fuzzy model of the motor, which is created using an adaptive neuro-fuzzy inference system (ANFIS). This fuzzy model has only 151 rules compared to nearly 1000 rules used in refernce 9 while maintaining a high accuracy. Moreover, an improved fuzzy optimal sensing phase selector is developed, which uses flux linkage and current as the inputs and *confidence* of the estimation accuracy as the output. With this optimal sensing phase selector, only the flux linkage and current of the optimal phase will be used for the angle estimation, which saves a lot of computation power while providing better accuracy. In addition, instead of using a fuzzy predictive filter, an HC-based delayless polynomial predictive filter is employed, which shows good error reduction capabilities.

Furthermore, another improvement has been made using real-time resistance estimation, which is an exact HC estimation method. As it was stated in reference 4, the main problem with flux-linkage-based methods is that they are not suitable for low-speed operation due to the inaccurate measurement of flux linkage. In the various flux-linkage-based methods [5], the winding resistance was assumed to be invariant during motor operation. However, in real motor operations, the winding temperature changes with time and different operation conditions, which consequently leads to considerable variation in the winding resistance. This variation will certainly cause errors in the calculated flux linkage and will, in turn, cause errors in the estimated rotor position. Therefore, to address this problem, an on-line resistance estimation algorithm is developed in this chapter to constantly track the actual winding resistance, which helps to further improve the estimation accuracy. The HC-based resistance estimation will be shown below to improve the fuzzy method's accuracy. Hence this confirms the advantage of fusing the SC and HC methods for mutual benefit.

In the first part of this chapter, the development of the fuzzy model based on the flux linkage characteristics of the SRM is detailed. In the second part, the proposed accuracy enhancement algorithms are described. Finally the simulation and experimental results are presented to demonstrate the effectiveness of the new hybrid algorithm in a real-time DSP-based SRM drive.

4.2 FUZZY LOGIC MODEL

Fuzzy logic models have been proven to be universal approximators of any continuous functions [10]. Therefore, it allows the nonlinear motor magnetization characteristics of the SRM to be modeled without any complex mathematical description of the motor. Compared with lookup tables, fuzzy logic models have the advantage of reduced memory requirement [11] and inherent robustness [12]. Moreover, compared with a complex HC-based mathematical models, a fuzzy logic model allows fast computation due to simple mathematical calculations used in fuzzy rules processing [13]. Thus it is suitable for real-time implementation.

In this section, the development of a fuzzy motor model is described, which includes the following steps:

- Measure the flux linkage characteristics of the SRM.
- Generate training data and verification data from the measured flux-linkage data and use ANFIS to create an efficient (in terms of low number of rules, while maintaining accuracy) fuzzy model.
- Validate the fuzzy model using verification data.

4.2.1 Measurement of Flux Linkage Characteristics

The accuracy of the magnetic characteristics measurement is critical for accurate sensorless rotor position estimation. Several methods of flux linkage measurement have been proposed for experimentally measuring the flux linkage [14,15]. The most popular measurement method is to keep the rotor in a fixed position while exciting the winding with a step voltage. Then the flux linkage can be obtained by integration using (4.1).

$$\psi(t) = \int_0^t [v(t) - i(t)R]\, dt + \psi_0 \tag{4.1}$$

where R is the winding resistance while ψ_0 is the flux linkage at time $t = 0$.

In the previously proposed methods, it was assumed that the winding resistance will not change significantly if a very short current pulse is applied to the phase windings. Thus winding resistance R was measured in advance and used in the integration as a constant value. However, with a high current repeatedly applied to the phase winding during the measurement tests, the winding temperature will vary, leading to variation in the winding resistance and, in turn, causing errors in the calculated flux linkage. The error in the flux linkage at time t caused by resistance variation can be written as

$$\Delta \psi(t) = -\Delta R \int_{t_0}^{t} i(t)\, dt \tag{4.2}$$

where ΔR is the resistance error and t_0 is the time when the current increases from 0 A.

As shown in (4.2), the error in the flux linkage is proportional to the resistance error and the integral of current. Therefore, to minimize the measurement error in the flux linkage, an improved flux linkage measurement scheme is developed, which employs real-time DSP calculations to constantly track the actual winding resistance during the measurement. Moreover, errors are further reduced by on-line removal of the sensor offset errors.

To perform on-line resistance measurement, a regulated DC current source is used to provide a short pulse of current in the test phase winding (the same waveforms of current are also used for integration together with the corresponding voltage across the phase winding). When the current reaches a constant value regulated by the DC current source, the phase winding resistance will be obtained with dividing voltage by current. Then the updated resistance value will be used in the next integration. An alternative method of on-line winding resistance estimation is also presented in the next section of this chapter, which will be used for the proposed sensorless rotor position estimation scheme.

As the current and voltage sensors normally have some offset errors in their output, which should be removed for better measurement accuracy, calibration of the sensors before the flux linkage measurement is necessary. This is done by reading 10,000 consecutive digital values from the ADC (analog-to-digital converter) channel, which is connected to the input signal (i.e., current or voltage) when the DC power supply is off. Then these values are averaged and the mean value is taken as the offset. After numerical removal of the offset, the current and voltage signals are then used for integration as well as resistance estimation.

A 1-hp, 8/6-pole four-phase SRM is used for the flux linkage data collection. During the measurement, a series of square current pulses were applied to the phase winding. The corresponding voltage, current, and flux linkage waveforms were captured, and typical waveforms for the aligned and unaligned rotor position are shown in Fig. 4.1.

It can be noted from Fig. 4.1 that when the current reaches constant value, the flux linkage will remain unchanged, which confirms that accurate resistance value is used during the integration. This confirms with the theoretical prediction that for a constant position and current, the flux linkage in the SRM must be constant, as under this condition the motor stator winding acts as a constant inductance.

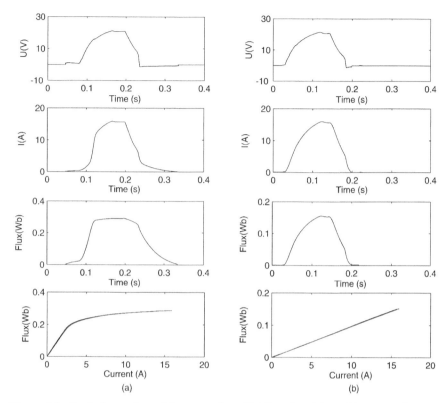

Figure 4.1. Typical waveforms (**a**) rotor angle $= 0°$ (aligned position); (**b**) rotor angle $= 30°$ (unaligned position).

Figure 4.2 shows the measured flux linkage versus current curves for rotor positions from $0°$ (unaligned angle, where the rotor pole is facing the antipole space) to $30°$ (aligned angle, where the rotor pole is fully aligned with the stator poles) in steps of $1°$.

4.2.2 Training and Validation of Fuzzy Model

Once the flux linkage data are available, a training scheme is used to create a fuzzy model based on the measured magnetization data. In reference 9, the table lookup scheme was used, where the fuzzy sets of the input and output domains were equally partitioned and the membership functions were fixed as triangular shape. The advantage of this training scheme is its simplicity, while its disadvantage is that the partition of the input/output space and the membership functions of the fuzzy sets must be specified in advance and no optimization on them is conducted during the training [16]. Hence, such a fuzzy model is inefficient: To obtain an accurate model, normally it is required that the number of fuzzy sets and fuzzy rules is

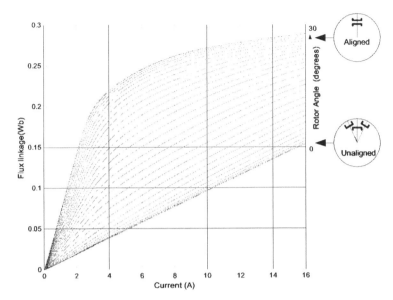

Figure 4.2. Flux linkage versus current curves for different rotor angles.

very large, which not only raises the memory needed for storing the fuzzy rules but also increases the calculation time.

Therefore, in this chapter an improved method is used to create an efficient and accurate fuzzy model. The method used in this chapter for training a fuzzy interference system (FIS) is a two-step procedure: The first step uses a clustering method for initial identification of FIS, and the second step uses an adaptive neuro-fuzzy inference system [17] for tuning and optimizing the initially identified FIS.

Several clustering methods for automatically extracting fuzzy rules for data classification and pattern recognition problems have been proposed. These methods include FCM (Fuzzy C-means clustering) [18], nearest-neighborhood clustering [19], mountain clustering [20], and subtractive clustering [21]. Subtractive clustering method was adopted in this work due to its efficient and robust computation for identifying fuzzy models.

With the subtractive clustering method, each data point is assumed as a potential cluster center, and a measure of the potential for each data point based on the density of surrounding data points is calculated. The algorithm selects the data point with the highest potential as the first cluster center and then deletes the potential of data points near the first cluster center. The algorithm then selects the data point with the highest remaining potential as the next cluster center and reduces the potential of data points near this new cluster center (similarly to deleting the potential of the data points near the first cluster, but in this case reducing the potential value). This process of acquiring new cluster centers and reducing the potential of surrounding data points repeats until the remaining potentials of all data points are below a threshold. The cluster information obtained by this method is used for determining the initial rules for identifying the FIS. Then, the linear least-squares estimation is used to determine the consequence for each rule. The result is an initial first-order Sugeno fuzzy model, which will be further optimized by the ANFIS.

ANFIS has proven to be an excellent function approximation tool [22]. Figure 4.3 shows a typical ANFIS structure with two inputs (x and y) and one output (f). ANFIS implements a first-order Sugeno-style fuzzy system:

Rule n: If x is A_n and y is B_n, then $f_n = p_n x + q_n y + r_n$

The first layer in the ANFIS structure is the fuzzification phase, and its outputs are membership values. The membership functions can be differentiable, such as Gaussian curve built-in membership functions:

$$\mu(x) = e^{-(x-c)^2/2\sigma^2} \tag{4.3}$$

where x is the input of the fuzzy system while c and σ are tunable parameters known as premise parameters.

The second layer performs the fuzzy AND operator to calculate the firing strength w of the rule. Then the third layer acts to normalize the firing strengths. The output of the fourth layer is comprised of a linear combination of the inputs multiplied by the normalized firing strength $\bar{w}$.

$$\bar{w}_1 f_1 = \bar{w}_1(px + qy + r) \tag{4.4}$$

where $\{p, q, r\}$ are known as consequent parameters.

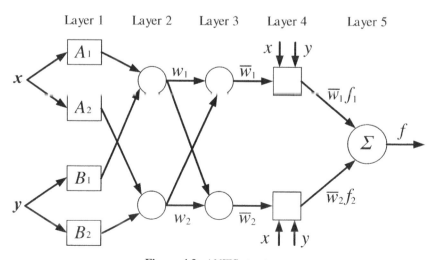

Figure 4.3. ANFIS structure.

The fifth layer is simple summation of the outputs of the fourth layer. The adjustment of modifiable parameters is a two-step process. First, while holding the premise parameters fixed, information is propagated forward in the network until layer four, where the parameters are identified by a least-squares estimator. Then in the backward pass, the parameters in layer two are modified using a gradient descent algorithm while the consequent parameters are held fixed. With ANFIS, the membership functions are iteratively adjusted and the resulted FIS corresponds to the minimum training error.

To create an efficient fuzzy model of the motor magnetization data with subtractive clustering and ANFIS, a set of training data was formed by sampling the measured flux linkage data. Then subtractive clustering method was used to generate an initial fuzzy inference system from the training data. The resultant Sugeno-type FIS has 151 rules, which was found to provide sufficient accuracy after optimization (note that the number of the fuzzy rules will vary according to different motor characteristics). Then the parameters of the initial FIS were trained by ANFIS using the hybrid method. To control the possibility for the model overfitting the training data, a validation data set was also used during the training. The validation data set was formed with sampled measured flux linkage data. The mapping surface of the resulted fuzzy model after optimization is shown in Fig. 4.4.

To verify the accuracy of the derived fuzzy motor model, its mapping behavior is compared with the original measured data. Figure 4.5 shows the error between the output angle of the fuzzy model and the actual angle for equal flux and current values. It can be noted that the modeling error is reasonably small (about $\pm 0.1°$)

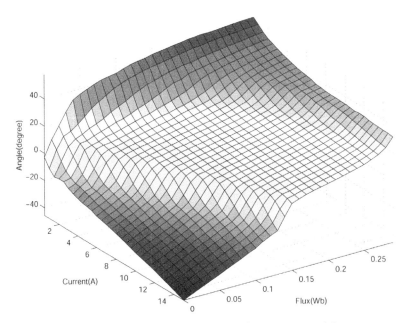

Figure 4.4. Mapping surface of the fuzzy motor model.

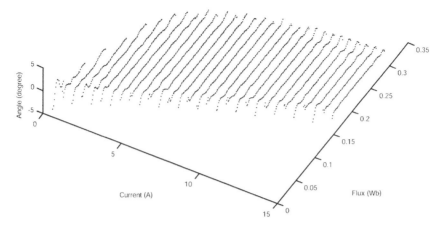

Figure 4.5. Modeling error of the created fuzzy motor model.

in most regions. However, the error is large when the rotor is at the aligned angle or at the unaligned angle or when the motor phase current is low. This is because, as it can be noted from Fig. 4.2, the angle curves are tightly bunched up in those regions. This causes large partial derivative values $\partial\theta/\partial\psi$ and $\partial\theta/\partial i$ in the angle versus current and flux linkage plane [8]. Thus, to accurately model such an inflection, a large number of fuzzy sets and fuzzy rules should be used. However, this would entail two obvious disadvantages:

1. Memory requirement increases.
2. Real-time computation power requirement becomes high.

Therefore, a better approach is to try to avoid using these regions for angle estimation. This is normally possible in practice because almost all practical control schemes for the SRM will produce overlapping current pulses in the motor phases (therefore more than one phase can be chosen for performing position estimation). Only in cases where very short (in time), nonoverlapping, and low-amplitude motor phase current pulses are used could these regions be unavoidable. However, this would be an inefficient nonpractical control scheme. Hence, a method for avoiding these regions for sensing in a practical drive will be detailed in the next section.

4.3 ACCURACY ENHANCEMENT ALGORITHMS

Accurate rotor position information is essential for high-performance control of SRMs because excitation of the motor phases needs to be synchronized with the rotor position. However, various sources of angle estimation errors exist in the real-time implementation of the sensorless rotor position estimation scheme. As shown above, the derived fuzzy model has errors due to the imperfect modeling. Therefore, the rotor angle estimated by the fuzzy model will have errors during actual operation. Moreover, winding resistance variation, measurement errors, and noise in the feedback signals, as well as the integration errors in the flux linkage, will also tend to deteriorate the estimation accuracy. For a detailed error sources and error analysis, please refer to reference 8. Thus the fuzzy modeling method alone is prone to errors and noise.

Therefore, to improve the estimation accuracy, three accuracy enhancement algorithms are added to the sensorless position estimation scheme, and these form a combination of IIC and SC methods. The first SC algorithm determines the optimal sensing phase with minimum estimation error. The second HC one constantly updates the resistance value, while the last one uses an HC-type predictive filter to further reduce error in the estimated angle. The three algorithms are detailed below.

4.3.1 Soft-Computing-Based Optimal Phase Selection

In the normal operation of the SRM, more than one phase may be simultaneously excited. Theoretically, the same position should be obtained by feeding the different current and flux-linkage values of each conducting phase into the fuzzy inference system. However, as we can see in Fig. 4.5, the modeling error is large in the edge regions where the rotor position is near the aligned or unaligned angle or when the motor phase current is low. Moreover, by both qualitative and quantitative error analysis, the angle estimation is more sensitive to errors in the input signals in these regions [9]. Hence it should be avoided to use these regions as the sensing region if possible. On the other hand, the error in the flux linkage will increase with current during integration [14]. Consequently, the region where the current is very high is also not suitable for angle estimation since the flux linkage is prone to errors. Therefore, each phase has a different *confidence* value according to their different sensing region. Based on the above discussion, the approximate confidence value of different sensing region can be deducted. The approximate optimal sensing region is shown in Fig. 4.6, where the confidence should be high, whereas for the rest of the regions the confidence should be much lower. Intuitively, these *bad* regions where the confidence is very low include:

- Region where i or ψ is *very low*
- Region where *angle* is *very small* (close to $0°$)
- Region where *angle* is *very large* (close to $30°$)
- Region where i is *very high*

In reference 9, a fuzzy inference system was used for calculating the different confidence values with the estimated angle and phase current of different phases. Then a weighted angle based on the confidence values of the four estimated angles was used as the final estimated angle. However, that means that all four

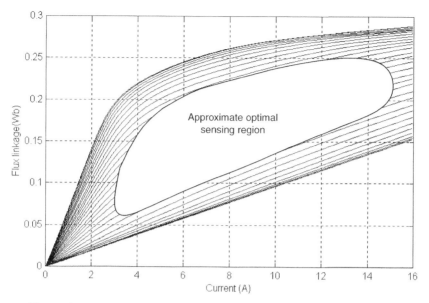

Figure 4.6. Approximate optimal sensing region of the magnetization curves.

phases need to be used for calculating the angle, which can cause significant computation load. Moreover, it was demonstrated that using the weighted value of the estimated angles of all four phases produces more errors in rotor position estimation than using the optimal phase only [5].

In this chapter, a new fuzzy inference system, of which the phase current and flux linkage are the two input variables, is created to calculate the confidence value of different sensing region based on the above heuristic knowledge. Mamdani's fuzzy inference method is used for the FIS because it is intuitive and well-suited to human input. Gaussian membership functions are used for both input and output fuzzy domains. Both flux and current domains are equally partitioned into six fuzzy sets, namely, *very low (VL)*, *low (L)*, *medium1 (M1)*, *medium2 (M2)*, *high (H)*, and *very high (VH)*. The *confidence* domain is normalized to [0,1] and partitioned into five fuzzy regions such as *very low (VL)*, *low (L)*, *medium (M)*, *high (H)*, and *very high (VH)*, which were tuned by the human experimentally to give a good modeling result. In total, 30 fuzzy if–then rules are designed by the human based on the above analysis about the optimal sensing regions in the flux linkage curves. A few sample rules are shown below:

- $R^{(1)}$: If i is *very low* or ψ is *very low*, then *confidence* is *very low*.
- $R^{(2)}$: If i is *low* and ψ is *low*, then *confidence* is *medium*.
- $R^{(3)}$: If i is *low* and ψ is *high*, then *confidence* is *very low*.
- $R^{(4)}$: If i is *very high* and ψ is *low*, then *confidence* is *very low*.
- $R^{(5)}$: If i is *medium1* and ψ is *medium1*, then *confidence* is *very high*.

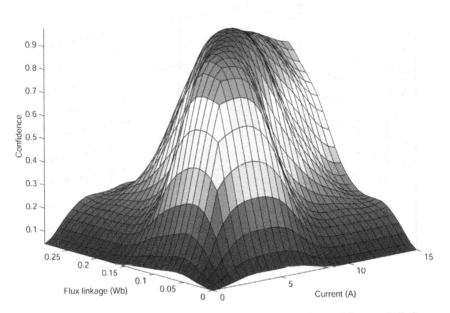

Figure 4.7. Mapping surface of the fuzzy inference system for confidence calculating.

The resulted mapping surface of this fuzzy model is shown in Fig. 4.7.

After the confidence values of different phases are calculated, the current and flux linkage values of the phase with highest confidence value (the optimal phase) will be fed to the motor fuzzy model to estimate the rotor position. In this way, only one phase is used for position estimation at any time, which helps to reduce the computation load.

4.3.2   Hard-Computing-Based On-Line Resistance Estimation

The winding resistance is normally assumed as a constant value during the motor operation in the various proposed sensorless schemes. However, in real time motor operation, the winding temperature changes with time and different operation conditions, which consequently leads to the variation in the winding resistance. As shown in (4.2), the error in the resistance value will cause error in the calculated flux linkage. As a result, the corresponding angle error at time t_n will be given by

$$\Delta\theta(t_n)_r = \Delta\psi(t_n)\frac{\partial\theta}{\partial\psi}\bigg|_{i(t_n),\psi(t_n)} = -\Delta R\int_{t_0}^{t_n}i(t)\,dt\cdot\frac{\partial\theta}{\partial\psi}\bigg|_{i(t_n),\psi(t_n)} \tag{4.5}$$

where $\Delta\theta(t_n)_r$ = the angle error due to error in the resistance, $i(t_n)$ = the actual motor phase current, $\psi(t_n)$ = the actual motor phase flux linkage, and t_0 is the time when the current begins to rise from 0 A.

It can be noted from (4.5) that the angle error is proportional to the resistance error, the integral of current, and the partial derivative of the rotor position function with respect to flux linkage at the point $(i(t_n), \psi(t_n))$. Resetting the phase flux to zero whenever the current reaches zero in each electrical cycle helps to reduce the error. However, as the electrical cycle becomes longer at low speed, the integration error will be notably large due to the long integration time and thus this will cause significant error in the estimated position. Therefore, it is desirable to track the resistance variation during the motor operation. Note from the above that in this case, due to the exact mathematical relationship linking resistance error in proportion to the angle error, it is required to know the exact value of the resistance, in order to reduce the resistance error effectively. Thus HC methods are called for to solve this problem, rather than SC methods. In this chapter, a simple on-line resistance estimation algorithm is presented. The method is described below.

As noted from the magnetic characteristics of the SRM, the phase flux linkage is always zero when the phase current is zero. Now if we assume that t_a is the time when the phase winding is about to be excited while t_b is the time when the phase current drops to zero, then since $i(t_b) = 0$, we have

$$\psi(t_b) = \int_{t_a}^{t_b} [v(t) - i(t)R(t)] \, dt = \int_{t_a}^{t_b} v(t) \, dt - R(t) \cdot \int_{t_a}^{t_b} i(t) \, dt = 0 \qquad (4.6)$$

Since the time from t_a to t_b is normally short, it is feasible to assume the phase winding resistance $R(t)$ during this period to be invariant. As a result, the resistance can be calculated using (4.7):

$$R = \int_{t_a}^{t_b} v(t) \, dt \div \int_{t_a}^{t_b} i(t) \, dt \qquad (4.7)$$

Therefore, the winding resistance can be updated whenever the phase current drops to zero, and the updated resistance value R will be used for the calculation of the flux linkage using (4.8):

$$\psi(t) = \int_{t_a}^{t} v(t) \, dt - R \cdot \int_{t_a}^{t} i(t) \, dt \qquad (4.8)$$

where t_a is the time when the phase current start to rise up from zero.

It can be expected that by this method the error caused by the resistance variation can be greatly reduced. Simulation results will be shown in the next section to verify the effectiveness of this method.

4.3.3 Polynomial Predictive Filtering

Besides the estimation error due to the imperfect modeling and resistance variation, the measurement noise in the voltage and current will cause additional errors.

However, since both the nonlinear voltage and current waveforms in the SRM comprise a wide frequency spectrum, it is difficult to remove the noise without amplitude error and phase delay of the primary signals. Therefore, it is more practical to smooth the estimated rotor position.

Conventional lowpass filters can be used to smooth the estimated rotor position; however, they will inevitably introduce harmful delay. Moreover, in real-time applications, additional delay in the output signal is caused by the data acquisition and signal processing. Therefore, a predictive filter with no phase delay would be desirable for real-time applications. A predictive filter is defined as an algorithm that estimates future values of the primary signal, while it simultaneously attenuates the noise components [23]. Several predictive algorithms have been proposed, such as linear prediction [24], polynomial prediction [25], neural-network-based prediction [26], and fuzzy prediction [11]. These methods have been reviewed in references 23 and 27. The selection of these prediction algorithms is usually based on the characteristics of the primary signal to be predicted and the noise component, as well as the implementation environment (available computing power and accuracy) [23].

A fuzzy predictor for angle error reduction was presented in reference 9. However, the predictor requires certain time to build up enough rules to make accurate predictions and provides no noise attenuation by itself. As we know, due to the rotor and load inertia, the mechanical time constant of the motor is normally much larger than the sampling time. Therefore, the motor speed can be regarded as a constant during a short time interval. As a result, the cumulative rotor angle can be accurately modeled as a first-degree polynomial within narrow time windows. In this case, a polynomial predictive filter is preferred due to its low computational complexity, simple design process, and good primary signal restoring ability [27].

In this chapter, a one-step-ahead ramp predictor, which is the simplest form of recursive linear smoothed Newton (RLSN) predictors [28], is adopted as the filtering method because it can offer good noise attenuation and fast computation while avoiding harmful delay. Its transfer function can be expressed as

$$H(z) = \frac{a + \dfrac{1}{N} - \dfrac{z^{-N}}{N}}{1 - (1 - a)z^{-1}} \tag{4.9}$$

where N is the length of a built-in moving averager, and a is a weighting factor in the recursive section. The selection of the two parameters N and a is a trade-off between noise attenuation and transient overshoot. With smaller N and large a, the overshoot during transient will be smaller but the signal-to-error ratio will be larger. In this chapter, N is selected as 16 and a is 0.1. The Bode plot of the filter is shown in Fig. 4.8.

As it can be noted from Fig. 4.8, the cutoff frequency of the filter is about 0.085 times the Nyquist frequency. Hence though this filter proves to be very effective for error reducing when the motor speed is smoothly changing, it is not applicable for

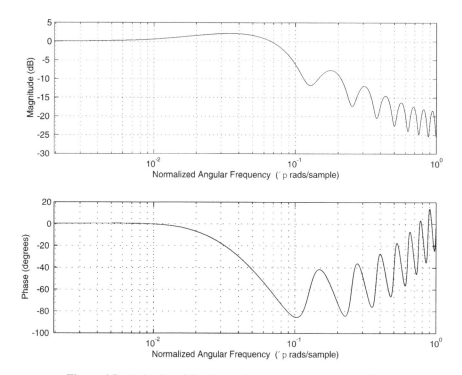

Figure 4.8. Bode plot of the designed one-step-ahead ramp predictor.

extreme conditions such as high-speed stalling when the speed signal suffers a sudden change. Thus to keep the angle estimation accuracy under all conditions, a decision block is used to make the best choice of the output angle based on the acceleration of the motor.

Acceleration can be calculated from the estimated angle. However, because only the qualitative acceleration (for example, high or low) is required for making a decision, an acceleration factor, instead of the actual acceleration value, is used for decision-making. The acceleration factor A_n is defined as

$$A_n = \frac{\theta_n - \theta_{n-2} - (\theta_{n-1} - \theta_{n-3})}{\Delta T} \tag{4.10}$$

where θ_n is the rotor angle at step n and ΔT is the sampling time.

By continuously calculating the acceleration factor, the decision block will output the angle before filtering when the absolute value of the acceleration factor is higher than a threshold value. After a certain time period, which allows the filter to settle down, the output angle will be the filtered angle again.

4.4 SIMULATION ALGORITHM AND RESULTS

In order to examine the performance of the proposed scheme, a Matlab®–Simulink® program was developed. The simulation algorithm includes a current chopping controller, a block to determine current waveforms by lookup table and flux by integration, a fuzzy inference system to estimate angle from flux and current signals, and all the above-mentioned accuracy enhancement algorithms.

As detailed above, with the phase current and flux linkage, the fuzzy inference system (fuzzy motor model) will produce four estimated rotor positions. Another fuzzy inference system is used to choose the output angle with the highest confidence value. Then the output angle passes through a predictive filter (RLSN predictor) to further reduce error. The following decision block will act during very high acceleration to output the angle before filtering instead of the filtered angle.

First, to verify the effectiveness of the on-line resistance estimator, the winding resistance is artificially increased from $1.35\,\Omega$ to $1.6\,\Omega$ in 1 s while the speed remains constant at 100 rpm. The simulation results are shown in Figs. 4.9 and 4.10. It can be noted in Fig. 4.9b that there still exists some error in the estimated resistance. This is due to the fast change in the winding resistance and the assumption that the resistance is constant during one integration cycle. To reduce this error, in the simulation, all four phases are used to estimate the winding resistance, assuming that the winding resistances of all four phases are equal. In this way, the estimated resistance updates more frequently and thus is more accurate. Figures 4.9c and 4.9d show the real flux linkage and the flux linkage calculated with the estimated resistance respectively. It can be noted from Fig. 4.9e that the error in the calculated flux linkage is very small. Figure 4.10 shows the position estimation result with and without on-line resistance estimation. It can be noted that the position estimation error with on-line resistance estimation is limited within $\pm0.5°$ while the error without on-line resistance estimation reaches $10°$ in this simulation.

However, it is worth emphasizing that in reality, the winding resistance will not suffer such a fast change (in the above example there was approximately 18.5% change in the resistance in 1 s). This is because for electric motors, the phase resistance change will be proportional to the thermal time constant of the phase windings [29] (temperature change being the main cause of resistance change), which is typically in the range of 30 min to 1 h depending on the motor rated power and size [29]. Thus for a typical rated speed of 3000 rpm there would be thousands of rotor phase cycles in one thermal time constant. Hence, it can be expected that the resistance estimation is accurate even with only one phase used for the estimation. Therefore in real-time implementation, to reduce the computation load, only one phase was used for resistance estimation.

Second, to examine the performance of the sensorless motor control scheme under all operating conditions, the motor speed is increased from 0 rpm to 4000 rpm in 0.25 s and then goes to zero suddenly. This speed signal is capable of simulating different motor operating conditions such as a motor starting from standstill, low and high motor speed, high acceleration, and high-speed stalling. Also the chopping mode operation and the single-pulse mode operation can be examined with the low motor speed range and the high-speed range, respectively.

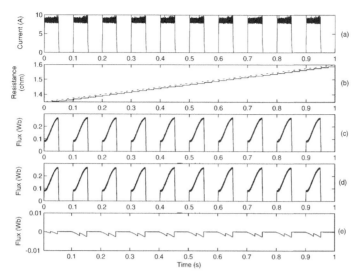

Figure 4.9. Resistance estimation in motor phase A. (**a**) Phase current. (**b**) Real resistance (dotted) and estimated resistance. (**c**) Real phase flux linkage. (**d**) Flux linkage calculated with the estimated resistance. (**e**) Error between the real flux linkage and the flux linkage calculated with the estimated resistance.

Figure 4.11 shows the simulated voltage, current, and flux waveforms of phase D (one of the four motor phases). It can be noted that due to the high acceleration, the motor begins to operate in the single-pulse mode in two revolutions. The angle error before and after the RLSN predictive filter as well as the final error after the decision block are shown in Fig. 4.12. It can be noted that the amplitude of the angle error before filtering can reach about $0.8°$; while after filtering, the error is reduced to about $0.2°$ except for a large overshoot that occurs when the motor suddenly stops. However, this overshoot is effectively removed by the decision block. Hence it can be seen that the proposed scheme achieves high robustness even under the extreme high speed stall condition.

4.5 HARDWARE AND SOFTWARE IMPLEMENTATION

4.5.1 Hardware Configuration

To evaluate the sensorless scheme, an experimental setup was built, which consists of the following units:

1. A desktop PC, Matlab® and Simulink®, as well as ControlDesk®, which is a complete experiment environment with virtual instrument panels, automation, and comprehensive management functions.
2. A dSPACE® 1003/1004 alpha combo DSP board.

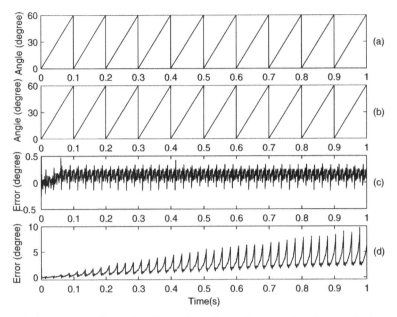

Figure 4.10. Rotor position estimation with on-line resistance estimation. (**a**) Real position. (**b**) Estimated position. (**c**) Angle estimation error with on-line resistance estimation. (**d**) Angle estimation error without on-line resistance estimation.

3. A 1-hp, 8/6-pole four-phase SRM and a resistance loaded DC generator.

4. A variable DC power supply and a four-phase IGBT DC–DC chopper.

5. Voltage sensors, current sensors, and a 12-bit absolute encoder. Note that in this setup, the voltage sensor is directly connected across the winding, therefore, the voltage drop and switching delay of the switching devices (IGBT) will have little effect on the calculation of the flux linkage (because it will be calculated using the actual voltage across the winding only).

6. A DS2201 Multi-I/O board, which features 20 12-bit ADC channels, eight 12-bit DAC channels, 16 parallel digital I/O lines, and six 16-bit pulse-width-modulated (PWM) outputs.

7. An interface circuits board that provides the interface between the DS2201 board and the measurement sensors as well as the DC chopper.

The actual hardware drive system is shown in Fig. 4.13.

4.5.2 Software Implementation

In all the algorithms implemented in this study, the fully unaligned rotor position is treated as $0°$ while the aligned rotor position is $30°$.

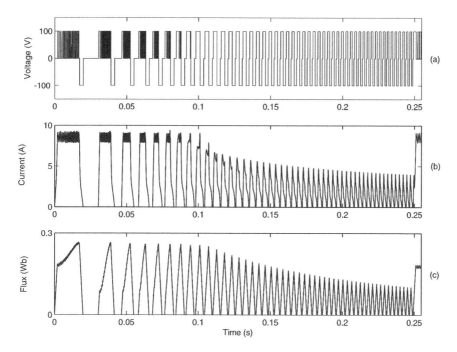

Figure 4.11. Simulated waveforms of motor phase D. (**a**) Phase voltage. (**b**) Phase current. (**c**) Phase flux linkage.

During standstill, no rotor position is available. To start up, two adjacent phases are energized simultaneously and used for rotor position estimation. A unique rotor position will be determined through comparing four possible positions. Then the absolute value of rotor position will be used for current hysteresis control.

The sensorless position estimation algorithm was developed with C and Matlab/ Simulink. To provide a good accuracy while allowing fast computation, the trapezoidal integration method is adopted in the algorithm. The overall execution time of the software is 158.1 μs and the sampling period is chosen to be 166.67 μs, which corresponds to a 6-kHz sampling frequency.

4.6 EXPERIMENTAL RESULTS

To evaluate the performance of the sensorless motor control scheme, a wide range of operating modes and conditions were applied to the SRM. Several distinct results are presented in the following subsections: start-up, low speed, high speed, and step change of speed. For each operating mode, voltage and current waveforms, as well as calculated flux linkage, are shown. The estimated rotor angle and the real rotor angle measured with the absolute encoder are compared and presented to show the effectiveness of the scheme.

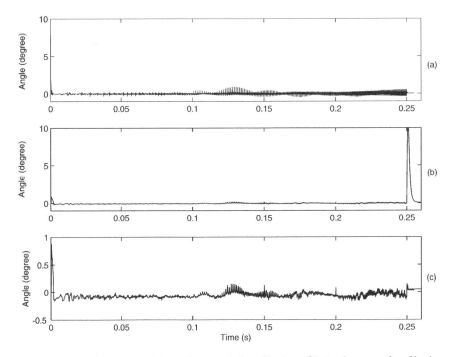

Figure 4.12. Position error. (**a**) Angle error before filtering. (**b**) Angle error after filtering. (**c**) Final error (please note the different vertical scale).

Note that in these experiments, a closed-loop control scheme for speed was not implemented (an open-loop control scheme was used). This was because the research results are focused on the performance of the sensorless rotor position estimation scheme, and thus the effect of our algorithm in isolation only is desirable for this study (without the effects of the closed-loop control). Thus, the turn-on angle, turn-off angle, DC link voltage, as well as current hysteresis reference are varied by the open-loop control method to adjust the motor speed as required in the experimental tests. Many closed-loop control schemes that use either a traditional control approach [30] or modern control approach [31] have been developed for SRMs.

4.6.1 Acceleration from Zero Speed

In this test, the motor is started up from zero speed to about 600 rpm in 0.3 s. The actual voltage, current, as well as the calculated flux linkage in phase A are shown in Fig. 4.14. The measured and estimated position as well as the estimation error are shown in Fig. 4.15.

It can be seen that at the beginning of the start-up, both the current and flux linkage in the conducting phase are small in value. As explained before, the position estimation is most error-prone when the current or flux linkage is small. Therefore,

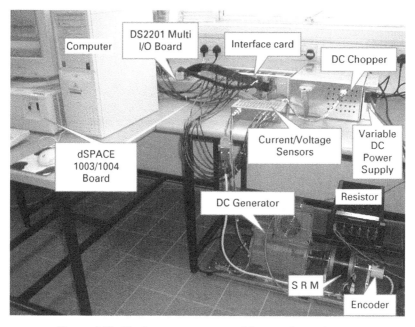

Figure 4.13. Hardware arrangement of the experimental setup.

the position estimation error is considerably large during the start-up. However, after 0.25 s, the error is much lower, with an average value of 0.23° and maximum value of 1.0°.

4.6.2 Low-Current Low-Speed Test

As was mentioned before, the sensorless position estimation tends to have error under low-speed operation if the resistance value is not accurate. Moreover, if at low speed the load placed on the shaft is also low, the phase current would be at a very low value during low-speed operation. We deliberately set this condition in order to have a low-speed, low-current experimental result. This is because, as pointed out before, the modeling error of the fuzzy motor model is large when the current is low. Therefore, such a low-current low-speed operation poses a very rigorous test for the proposed angle estimation scheme.

Because no closed-loop speed control was implemented to allow the motor to be running at very low speed with light load, both the DC link voltage and the current hysteresis level were manually adjusted. During this test, the DC link voltage was adjusted to about 5 V while the current hysteresis level was set to 2.5 A so that the SRM was running at about 50 rpm. As pointed out above, the modeling error of the fuzzy motor model is large when the current is low. Therefore, such a low current value poses a difficult test for the estimation scheme.

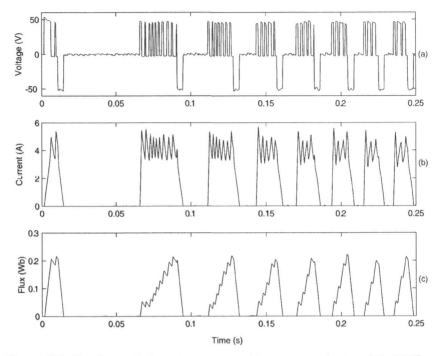

Figure 4.14. Waveforms of phase A at start-up with current regulated at 4 A. (**a**) Phase voltage. (**b**) Phase current. (**c**) Calculated phase flux linkage.

Figure 4.16 shows the waveforms of motor phase A. It can be seen from Fig. 4.17 that the estimated angle before the predictive filter has an maximum error of $1.17°$, while the error is about the same after filtering. This is because when the motor is running at low speed, the estimated error tends to have a large low-frequency component, which is below the cutoff frequency (about 250 Hz) of the predictive filter.

Figure 4.18 shows the power spectral density (dB) of the estimated position by the Welch method and the Hanning window. It can be noted from Fig. 4.18 that there is a large noise component around 50 Hz, which is within the passband of the predictive filter and thus will not be attenuated out. Therefore, the predictive filter is less effective in low-speed operation. Nevertheless, it is fair to say that the estimated position still has a good accuracy under low-current low-speed operation.

4.6.3 High-Speed Test

When the motor is running at high speeds, the turn-off angle will be reached before the hysteresis current level is exceeded. Thus the motor operates in single-pulse mode. Moreover, due to the short excitation time in the phase winding, the flux linkage will be much smaller than that of normal speed, which in turn will deteriorate the estimation accuracy. However, the predictive filter will work more

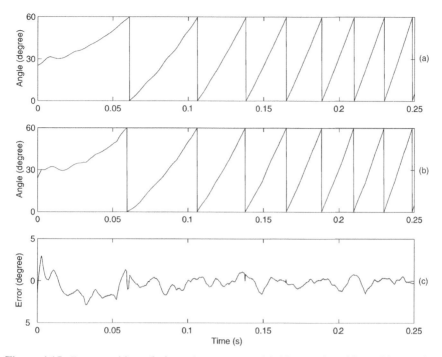

Figure 4.15. Rotor position of phase A at start-up. (**a**) Measured position with encoder. (**b**) Estimated position. (**c**) Angle error.

effectively as the estimation error will be above the cutoff frequency of the predictive filter. Figure 4.19 shows the phase voltage, current, and calculated flux linkage when the motor is running at 4100 rpm (high speed).

From Fig. 4.19, it can be noted that the amplitudes of phase current in every exciting cycle are not uniform. This is mainly due to the combination of the sampling rate of the DSP-controlled power electronic controller and the high motor speed, which means that there are less samples per cycle than at lower speeds. To be more precise, since the motor is running at 4100 rpm while the sampling rate is 6 kHz, the rotor rotates about 4.1° during every sampling period. This causes a large truncation error. Due to this error, the turn-on and turn-off angle of one phase in each exciting cycle have an error of up to 4.1°. Hence the excitation time is not uniform, which, in turn, causes the fluctuation in the current amplitude. The fluctuation of the current amplitude will lead to undesirable torque ripple. To reduce this effect, a faster DSP controller should be used to achieve a higher sampling rate (the sampling speed recommendable would depend on the highest speed of the motor).

Figure 4.20 shows the measured and estimated position, as well as the position estimation error before and after filtering. It can be noticed that, compared with the result of low speed, the maximum position estimation error before filtering

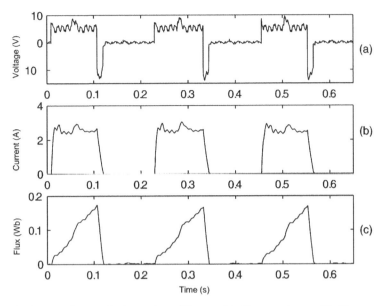

Figure 4.16. Waveforms of phase A at 50 rpm. (**a**) Phase voltage. (**b**) Phase current. (**c**) Calculated phase flux linkage.

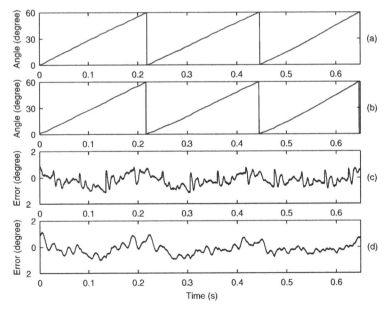

Figure 4.17. Rotor position of phase A at 50 rpm. (**a**) Measured position with encoder. (**b**) Estimated position. (**c**) Angle error before filtering. (**d**) Angle error after filtering.

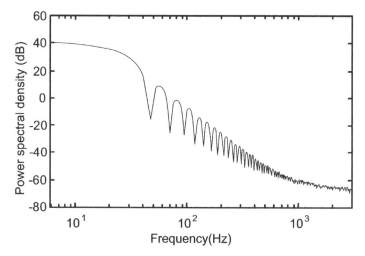

Figure 4.18. Power spectral density of the estimated angle signal at 50 rpm.

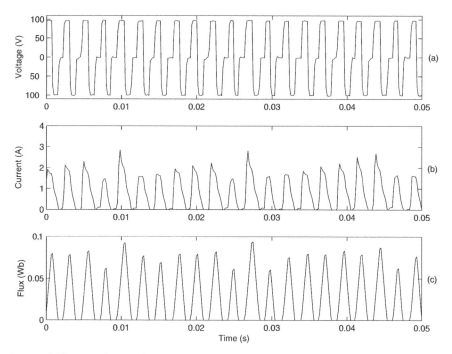

Figure 4.19. Waveforms of phase A at 4100 rpm. (**a**) Phase voltage. (**b**) Phase current. (**c**) Calculated phase flux linkage.

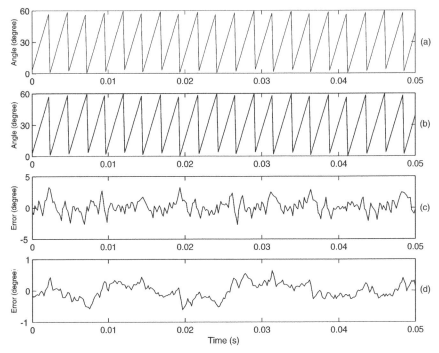

Figure 4.20. Rotor position of phase A at 4100 rpm. (**a**) Measured position with encoder. (**b**) Estimated position. (**c**) Angle error before filtering. (**d**) Angle error after filtering (please note the different vertical scale).

increases to 3.6°. However, the maximum error and the average error are effectively reduced to 0.63° and 0.04°, respectively, after filtering.

4.6.4 Test of Step Change of Load

In this test, the motor is running at 860 rpm in single-pulse mode when a step load is applied by switching a resistive load that is connected to a loading DC generator. Consequently, the motor speed decreases to 510 rpm in 0.1 s where it works in current chopping mode. The corresponding waveforms are shown in Fig. 4.21. It can be noted from Fig. 4.22 that the maximum position estimation error increases to about 1.18° during this transient stage. The estimation accuracy of the sensorless scheme is therefore verified under transient torque and speed operation.

For clarity and comparison, Table 4.1 shows the summary of the experimental results, where average and maximum absolute values of the position estimation errors are presented. The overall experimental results verify that the proposed scheme is able to provide very accurate and robust position information at both low and high speeds, low current and flux, start-up, as well as torque and speed transients.

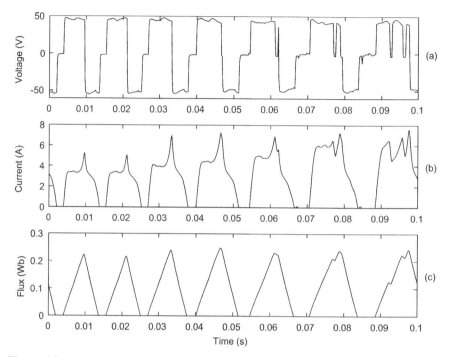

Figure 4.21. Waveforms of phase A of step load test. (**a**) Phase voltage. (**b**) Phase current. (**c**) Calculated phase flux linkage.

However, it can be noted that the position estimation error of the experimental results is significantly higher than that of the simulation results. This is due to the real-time implementation effects such as the low sampling frequency (6 kHz), sensor measurement error, integration error, and the measurement noise. For a thorough error analysis, please refer to reference 8.

4.7 FUSION OF SOFT COMPUTING AND HARD COMPUTING

As was detailed in Chapter 1 of this book, both soft computing (SC) and hard computing (HC) techniques are often successful for solving real-world control problems. In cases where problems could be solved by either or both methodologies, an important research challenge is to find advantages (in terms of performance, robustness, or lower complexity) for fusing SC methods together with HC methods, rather than using them alone. The application domain in which this chapter's study was made was for the sensorless speed control of switched reluctance motors (SRMs). This is because SRMs have highly nonlinear characteristics, and the conventional HC-type controller can often be detrimentally affected by modeling inaccuracies,

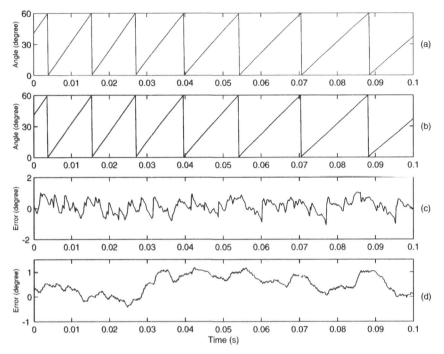

Figure 4.22. Rotor position of phase A of step load test. (**a**) Measured position with encoder. (**b**) Estimated position. (**c**) Angle error before filtering. (**d**) Angle error after filtering (please note the different vertical scale).

as well as noise (seen in the sensors due to imperfect grounding and decoupling, along with the presence of switching power electronic circuits).

It was seen that this chapter described a novel angle estimation scheme for a real-time digital signal processor (DSP)-based switched reluctance motor drive, where several advanced SC and HC techniques in combination are implemented to improve the estimation accuracy. First, an efficient fuzzy model of the motor was created using an adaptive neuro-fuzzy inference system (ANFIS) based on

TABLE 4.1. Summary of the Experimental Results at Different Motor Operating Conditions

Operation Mode	Average Position Estimation Error (degree)	Maximum Position Estimation Error (degree)
Low speed	$-0.15°$	$1.17°$
High speed	$0.04°$	$0.63°$
Start-up	$-0.45°$	$2.92°$
Transient load	$0.37°$	$1.18°$

accurately measured flux linkage data. Second, a fuzzy optimal sensing phase selector was developed based on the analysis of both modeling error and measurement error. However, these SC techniques were improved using exact HC estimation methods. Thus, a delayless polynomial predictive filter and an on-line phase winding resistance estimator were also implemented to further enhance the position estimation accuracy.

In Chapter 1 the theoretical basis for the fusion of SC and HC was analyzed and defined through structural categories and features of core fusion topologies. Various theoretical frameworks for the fusion of SC and HC were defined. Under this categorization, the work presented in this chapter falls under the SC-assisted HC master–slave-type structure (SC//HC). This type of structure is a type of symbiosis between a principal HC algorithm and an assisting SC algorithm, and is defined as a very high fusion grade structure.

To observe this, a high-level block diagram of the system is shown in Fig. 4.23. It can be seen that the HC part has an input of the motor measurements of voltage and current to calculate flux. This is corrected using an HC resistance estimation algorithm. The output of this is then fed to the SC optimal phase selection block, which in turn is fed into the SC motor model to estimate the angle. The angle is then fed into the HC predictive filter algorithm to output the angle in every iteration. The system corresponds to the general block diagram of (SC//HC)-type systems which was shown in Chapter 1.

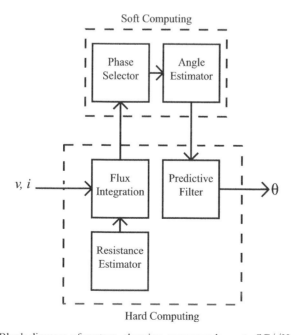

Figure 4.23. Block diagram of system, showing correspondence to SC//HC-type system.

4.8 CONCLUSION AND DISCUSSION

As mentioned above, in cases where problems could be solved by either SC or HC or both methodologies, an important research question is, What are the advantages for fusing SC methods together with HC methods, rather than using the HC method alone? Hence, in this chapter a discussion was presented on the advantages of using a fuzzy-logic-based method and, additionally, showed that it could be improved with HC-based additional algorithms, to produce a hybrid SC//HC method.

Thus, an improved fuzzy-logic-based sensorless rotor position estimation scheme with several accuracy enhancement algorithms was described. In this scheme, an optimized (efficient and accurate) fuzzy motor model based on accurately measured motor magnetization data is created to calculate the rotor position from the current and flux waveforms. An on-line HC resistance estimation algorithm is designed to track the resistance variation during the motor operation. An improved fuzzy-logic-based optimal phase selector and an HC predictive filter are also implemented to further improve the estimation accuracy.

Both simulation results and experimental results are presented to verify the effectiveness of the proposed scheme. It is demonstrated in this chapter that this scheme is capable of providing robust and accurate angle estimation under all operating speeds and conditions, including start-up, low speed, high speed, and transient load.

REFERENCES

1. G. Suresh, B. Fahimi, and M. Ehsani, "Improvement of the Accuracy and Speed Range in Sensorless Control of Switched Reluctance Motors," *Conference Proceedings of Applied Power Electronics Conference and Exposition*, Anaheim, CA, 1998, **2**, pp. 771–777.

2. Y. J. Zhan, C. C. Chan, and K. T. Chau, "A Novel Sliding Mode Observer for Indirect Position Sensing of Switched Reluctance Motor Drives," *IEEE Transactions on Industrial Electronics* **46**, 390–397 (1999).

3. B. Y. Ma, W. S. Feng, T. H. Liu, and C. G. Chen, "Design and Implementation of a Sensorless Switched Reluctance Drive System," *IEEE Transactions on Aerospace and Electronic Systems* **34**, 1193–1207 (1998).

4. W. F. Ray and I. H. Al-bahadly, "Sensorless Methods for Determining the Rotor Position of Switched Reluctance Motors," *5th European Conference on Power Electronics and Applications*, Brighton, UK, 1993, pp. 7–13.

5. G. Gallegos-Lopez, P. C. Kjaer, and T. J. E. Miller, "High-grade Position Estimation for SRM Drives Using Flux Linkage/Current Correction Model," *IEEE Transactions on Industry Applications* **35**, 859–869 (1999).

6. L. X. Wang, "Fuzzy Systems are Universal Approximators," *IEEE International Conference on Fuzzy Systems*, San Diego, CA, 1992, pp. 1163–1169.

7. P. J. Costa Branco and J. A. Dente, "An Experiment in Automatic Modelling an Electrical Drive System Using Fuzzy Logic," *IEEE Transactions on Systems, Man, and Cybernetics* **28**, 254–262 (1998).

8. A. D. Cheok and N. Ertugrul, "High Robustness and Reliability of Fuzzy Logic Based Position Estimation for Sensorless Switched Reluctance Motor Drives," *IEEE Transactions on Power Electronics* **15**, 319–334 (2000).

9. A. D. Cheok and N. Ertugrul, "Use of Fuzzy Logic for Modelling, Estimation, and Prediction in Switched Reluctance Motor Drives," *IEEE Transactions on Industrial Electronics* **46**, 1207–1223 (1999).

10. B. Kosko, "Fuzzy Systems as Universal Approximators," *IEEE Transactions on Computers* **43**, 1329–1333 (1994).

11. J. M. Sousa and M. Setnes, "Fuzzy Predictive Filters in Model Predictive Control," *IEEE Transactions on Industrial Electronics* **46**, 1225–1232 (1999).

12. E. H. Mamdani, "Twenty Years of Fuzzy Control: Experiences Gained and Lessons Learnt," *2nd IEEE International Conference on Fuzzy Systems*, San Francisco, CA, 1993, **1**, pp. 339–344.

13. B. K. Bose, "Expert System, Fuzzy Logic, and Neural Network Applications in Power Electronics and Motion Control," *Proceedings of the IEEE* **82**, 1303–1323 (1994).

14. P. W. Lee and C. Pollock, "Flux Linkage Estimation in Electrical Machines," *International Conference on Electric Machines*, Paris, France, Sept. 1994, pp. 463–467.

15. V. K. Sharma, S. S. Murthy, and B. Singh, "An Improved Method for the Determination of Saturation Characteristics of Switched Reluctance Motors," *IEEE Transactions on Instrumentation and Measurement* **48**, 995–1000 (1999).

16. L. X. Wang, *Adaptive Fuzzy Systems and Control: Design and Stability Analysis*, Prentice-Hall, Englewood Cliffs, NJ, 1994.

17. J. S. R. Jang, "ANFIS: Adaptive-Network-Based Fuzzy Inference System," *IEEE Transactions on Systems, Man, and Cybernetics* **23**, 665–684 (1993).

18. J. Bezdek, R. Hathaway, M. Sabin, and W. Tucker, "Convergence Theory for Fuzzy C-Means: Counter-Examples and Repairs," *IEEE Transactions on Systems, Man, and Cybernetics* **17**, 873–877 (1987).

19. L. X. Wang, "Training of Fuzzy Logic Systems Using Nearest Neighborhood Clustering," *IEEE International Conference on Fuzzy Systems*, San Francisco, CA, 1993, pp. 13–17.

20. R. Yager and D. Filev, "Generation of Fuzzy Rules by Mountain Clustering," *Journal of Intelligent and Fuzzy Systems* **2**, 209–219 (1994).

21. S. Chiu, "Fuzzy Model Identification Based on Cluster Estimation," *Journal of Intelligent and Fuzzy Systems* **2**, 267–278 (1994).

22. MATLAB, *Users Guide: Fuzzy Logic Toolbox*, 2nd ed., The MathWorks, Inc., Natic, MA, 1999.

23. S. Väliviita, S. J. Ovaska, and O. Vainio, "Polynomial Predictive Filtering in Control Instrumentation: A Review," *IEEE Transactions on Industrial Electronics* **46**, 876–888 (1999).

24. R. N. J. Veldhuis, *Restoration of Lost Samples in Digital Signals*, Prentice-Hall International, London, UK, 1990.

25. O. Vainio and S. J. Ovaska, "Multirate Polynomial Prediction with Unevenly Spaced Samples," *IEEE Transactions on Instrumentation and Measurement* **41**, 506–509 (1992).

26. R. Carotenuto, L. Franchina, and M. Coli, "Non-Linear System Process Prediction Using Neural Networks," *Proceedings of the IEEE International Conference on Neural Networks*, Washington, DC, June 1996, pp. 184–189.

27. S. J. Ovaska, "Predictive Signal Processing in Instrumentation and Measurement: A Tutorial Review," *IEEE Instrumentation and Measurement Technology Conference*, Ottawa, Canada, 1997, pp. 48–53.

28. S. J. Ovaska and O. Vainio, "Recursive Linear Smoothed Newton Predictors for Polynomial Extrapolation," *IEEE Transactions on Instrumentation and Measurement* **41**, 510–516 (1992).

29. M. G. Say, *The Performance and Design of Alternating Current Machines: Transformers, Three-phase Induction Motors and Synchronous Machines*, Pitman, London, 1958.

30. L. B. Amor, L. Dessaint, O. Akhrif, and G. Oliver, "Adaptive Feedback Linerization for Position Control of a Switched Reluctance Motor: Analysis and Simulation," *International Journal of Adaptive Control and Signal Processing* **7**, 117–136 (1993).

31. P. Tandon, A. V. Rajarathnam, and M. Ehsani, "Self-Tuning Control of a Switched Reluctance Motor Drive with Shaft Position Sensor," *Proceedings of the IEEE IAS Annual Meeting*, St. Louis, MO, 1996, **1**, pp. 101–108.

EDITOR'S INTRODUCTION TO CHAPTER 5

Linear H_∞ optimal control was an active topic of research and development during the 1980s, with principal research motivations focused on robustness. In engineering control applications, robustness is required to manage *system model uncertainty* and *varying operating conditions*. Grimble and Johnson [1] concisely define the objective of robust control synthesis:

> Robust control design is the search for controllers which can cope with a designer specified range of process dynamics and disturbance signals.

To achieve the desired robustness, an H_∞ controller design is optimized for worst-case conditions (bounds of uncertainty). This conservative approach usually limits the control performance while guaranteeing closed-loop stability in all expected situations.

Sliding mode control (SMC), another robust control technique, was first proposed in the early 1950s. Only recently, however, has it become popular in industrial applications due to its ability to provide robustness and good control performance for *nonlinear* systems [2]. A properly designed SMC system is insensitive to changing dynamics and external disturbances, as long as they remain within specified bounds. Like H_∞ control, it is common to choose such uncertainty bounds for SMC synthesis that are overly conservative to guarantee stability. From the practical point of view, the implementation of sliding mode controllers must address two limiting factors: (1) the need for high sampling rate and (2) the difficulty of ensuring the sliding condition in all cases.

Computationally Intelligent Hybrid Systems. Edited by Seppo J. Ovaska
ISBN 0-471-47668-4 © 2005 the Institute of Electrical and Electronics Engineers, Inc.

Surprisingly, many textbooks on robust control do not provide formal methods for estimating the bounds of modeling uncertainty. For this reason, it is usually possible to enhance the control performance of H_∞ and SMC systems by introducing complementary soft-computing (SC) methods to be fused with the primary hard-computing (HC) controller.

Chapter 5 of this book, "Estimation of Uncertainty Bounds for Linear and Nonlinear Robust Control," is authored by Gregory D. Buckner. It introduces a modified radial basis function network (RBFN, the 2-sigma network) for estimating stochastic uncertainty bounds associated with linear and nonlinear system models. The proposed method is applied to the design of both H_∞ controllers and SMC systems and is demonstrated experimentally on an active magnetic bearing (AMB) application.

Active magnetic bearings eliminate concerns with friction, lubrication, and wear that are typical with traditional bearings. In addition, active suspensions make it possible to effectively compensate vibrations caused by mechanical imperfections [3]. Despite those advantages, AMBs are unstable devices that require complicated controllers.

Due to associated modeling uncertainties and time-varying operating conditions, robust control techniques are obvious candidates for the control of active magnetic bearings.

Buckner first describes the nominal H_∞ control of an AMB test rig. To investigate the robustness and performance of the nominal H_∞ controller, he varied both the setpoint and setpoint frequency from their nominal values. As could be expected, the system remained stable as long as those variations stayed within the design specifications. However, the tracking behavior of the controlled system deteriorated away from its reference trajectory.

To alleviate this serious problem, two approaches for estimating the uncertainty bounds are presented. The first one is a parametric scheme that uses the recursive least-squares (RLS) algorithm, and the other one a nonparametric RBFN approach. Both of those enhancements to the basic H_∞ controller provided improved results: The tracking performance was superior to that of the nominal H_∞ controller when the setpoint and setpoint frequency were altered. Furthermore, the neural-network-based approach was clearly better than the parametric HC scheme.

Next the H_∞ controller was replaced by a sliding mode controller, and similar evaluations were carried out. One might expect that a nonlinear controller would provide even higher tracking performance, because AMB system dynamics are known to be highly nonlinear. This was indeed the case, but the price paid for this improvement was substantial chattering—that is, high-frequency oscillations at the controller output. To reduce the effects of chattering, a similar RBFN approach for estimating the uncertainty bounds between the AMB plant and its nonlinear model was introduced. The tracking performance remained high, and simultaneously the harmful effects of chattering were considerably reduced.

In conclusion, neural networks can enhance the performance of well-established robust control (hard computing) designs. This conclusion is based on the extensive simulations and experimental results that Buckner provides in his chapter. The primary fusion category is SC/HC (Chapter 1). Similar benefits have also been attained by other cooperative SC methods as reported by Kaynak et al. in their comprehensive review [2].

REFERENCES

1. M. J. Grimble and M. A. Johnson, "H_∞ Robust Control Design—A Tutorial Review," *Computing & Control Engineering Journal* **2**, 275–282 (1991).
2. O. Kaynak, K. Erbatur, and M. Ertugrul, "The Fusion of Computationally Intelligent Methodologies and Sliding-Mode Control—A Survey," *IEEE Transactions on Industrial Electronics* **48**, 4–17 (2001).
3. A. Charara, J. De Miras, and B. Caron, "Nonlinear Control of a Magnetic Levitation System without Premagnetization," *IEEE Transactions on Control Systems Technology* **4**, 513–523 (1996).

CHAPTER 5

ESTIMATION OF UNCERTAINTY BOUNDS FOR LINEAR AND NONLINEAR ROBUST CONTROL

GREGORY D. BUCKNER
North Carolina State University, Raleigh, North Carolina

5.1 INTRODUCTION

Robust control is a hard-computing design methodology focused on achieving guaranteed stability and performance for uncertain dynamic systems. Robust control synthesis requires an accurate mathematical model of the plant dynamics and bounds on the uncertainty associated with that model. Such uncertainties may result from parameter variations, undermodeled dynamics, or process disturbances. By specifying a nominal model and a hard bound on the uncertainty associated with that model, robust control aims to guarantee "robust stability" for the plant, which must lie within the set defined by the model plus the bound. Common linear approaches to robust control include H_∞ and μ synthesis [1], while nonlinear approaches include sliding mode control (SMC) [2,3].

Techniques for modeling dynamic systems are well established. Analytical approaches, which make use of physical principles (Newton's laws, Maxwell's equations, principles of thermodynamics, etc.) [4,5], and experimental approaches (modal analysis, system identification, etc.) [6] are both commonly used. System identification and parameter estimation approaches are also extensively documented [7], even "intelligent" techniques that incorporate neural networks (NNs) to retain and generalize adaptive information [8–10].

Despite this abundance of techniques for dynamic modeling and system identification, very few procedures exist for estimating the bounds of model uncertainty. For robust control synthesis it is customary to choose uncertainty bounds that are somewhat arbitrary and overly conservative to guarantee stability, usually at the

Computationally Intelligent Hybrid Systems. Edited by Seppo J. Ovaska
ISBN 0-471-47668-4 © 2005 the Institute of Electrical and Electronics Engineers, Inc.

expense of performance. In fact, many textbooks on the subject provide no formal procedures for estimating the modeling uncertainty so critical for robust control synthesis.

Recently, however, research has focused on improving the accuracy of uncertainty bounds associated with dynamic models. Specific approaches include stochastic embedding, which relies on the statistical properties of an identified model [11]; set membership, an identification procedure that estimates a set of feasible models which in turn provides the uncertainty quantification related to the nominal model [12–14]; and model error modeling, which identifies a system representing the error due to under-modeling [13,15,16].

This chapter presents a soft-computing variation of the model error modeling approach, with applications to robust control. Confidence interval networks (CINs) are used to estimate stochastic uncertainty bounds associated with linear and nonlinear dynamic models, and results are incorporated into standard robust control synthesis. This research couples the hard-computing features of H_∞ and sliding mode control with the soft-computing characteristics of intelligent system identification, and it realizes the combined advantages of both. Simulations and experimental demonstrations conducted on an active magnetic bearing test rig confirm these capabilities.

5.2   ROBUST CONTROL OF ACTIVE MAGNETIC BEARINGS

Robust control is well-suited to applications where guaranteed stability and performance are critical. One such application is the active magnetic bearing (AMB). AMBs provide noncontacting support of rotors, eliminating concerns with friction, wear, lubrication, and power consumption typical of conventional bearings. This technology has the potential to revolutionize high-speed rotating systems, such as the Combat Hybrid Power System (CHPS) flywheel alternator of Fig. 5.1. This flywheel alternator, developed at the University of Texas Center for Electromechanics, stores 25.0 MJ of energy at its peak operating speed of 20,000 rpm and delivers up to 5.0 MW of electrical power (350 kW continuous) to meet the needs of future combat systems [17,18]. Its 318 kg (700 lb) rotor is supported using an innovative "inside out" AMB topology in which the flywheel rotor is located outside the stationary bearing components.

Despite their advantages, AMBs are inherently unstable devices that require sophisticated real-time controllers. The modal characteristics and gyroscopic nature of high-speed rotors further complicate the control issues, and they have hindered large-scale commercial adoption of this technology. For this reason, the development of robust control algorithms for AMBs has been an active field of research in recent years. Much of this research has focused on fixed-gain controllers where few (if any) flexible vibration modes are encountered [16,19,20]. Although fixed-gain control can be effective for rigid rotors and limited speed ranges, the modeling uncertainties associated with more challenging applications (like the CHPS flywheel battery) severely restrict the effectiveness of this approach. To date, research

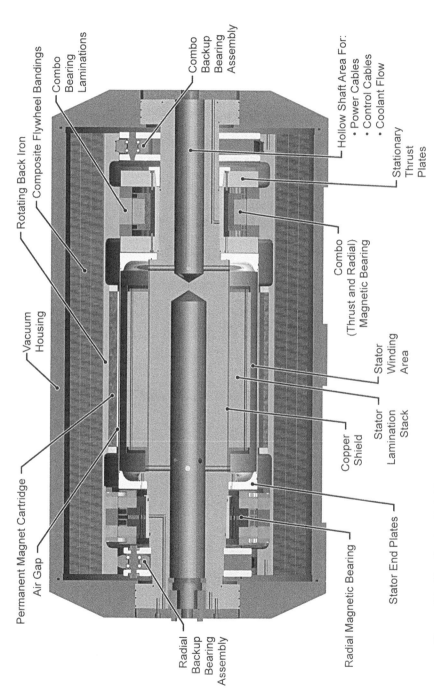

Figure 5.1. The Combat Hybrid Power System (CHPS) flywheel alternator, with "inside out" AMB topology [17,18].

focused on real-time estimation of modeling uncertainties with specific application to robust control synthesis has been limited. The following sections demonstrate standard hard-computing approaches to robust control of an AMB system, and they introduce unique benefits that soft computing can contribute to controller synthesis and performance.

5.2.1   Active Magnetic Bearing Test Rig

The AMB test rig used to experimentally demonstrate this fused approach to robust control is shown in Figs. 5.2 and 5.3. This single-input, single-output test rig is inherently unstable and highly nonlinear. However, because it eliminates complications associated with flexible modes and multivariable dynamics, it serves as an ideal platform for experimental validation. The control objective is to manipulate the coil current $i(t)$ so that the vertical position of the mass $y(t)$ tracks the desired trajectory $y_d(t)$. Nonlinear state equations for this system can be derived using magnetic circuit analysis and conservation of energy techniques [21]. Using measured system parameters (mass $= 67.0$ g, coil inductance $= 1.1$ mH, coil resistance $= 0.35$ Ω, nominal air gap $= 2.0$ mm), the system dynamics can be modeled:

$$\dot{x}_1 = x_2$$

$$\dot{x}_2 = -5.61 \times 10^{-6} \frac{u^2}{x_1^2} + 9.81 \tag{5.1}$$

where x_1 represents mover position (m), x_2 is mover velocity (m/s), and u is coil current (A).

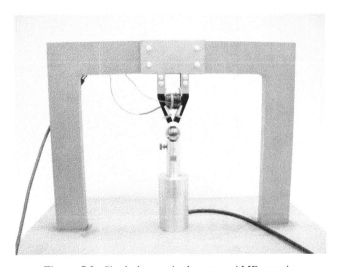

Figure 5.2. Single-input, single-output AMB test rig.

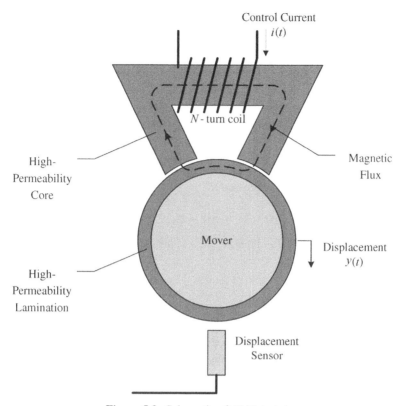

Figure 5.3. Schematic of AMB test rig.

5.3 NOMINAL H_∞ CONTROL OF THE AMB TEST RIG

Minimizing the adverse effects of modeling uncertainty, noise, and disturbances are fundamental goals of control synthesis. H_∞ control allows for bounds to be placed on each of these effects during controller synthesis to ensure admissible levels of these undesirable effects [1]. The synthesis objective is to specify a nominal linear model (G_0) and a bound (weighting function W_Δ) on the uncertainty between that model and the actual system. The H_∞ controller will then be guaranteed to stabilize the set of all plants bounded by the nominal model plus the uncertainty.

5.3.1 Parametric System Identification

To obtain a linear model for control design, (5.1) can be linearized about a nominal setpoint. Alternately, experimental system identification can be performed using measured data from the test rig. System inputs and outputs can be related using a linear ARX (autoregressive with exogenous input) model [7]:

$$y(t) + a_1 y(t-1) + a_2 y(t-2) + \cdots + a_n y(t-n)$$
$$= b_1 u(t-1) + b_2 u(t-2) + \cdots + b_m u(t-m) \tag{5.2}$$

There exists a least-squares optimal parameter vector

$$\boldsymbol{\theta} = [a_1, a_2, \ldots, a_n \quad b_1, b_2, \ldots, b_m]^T \tag{5.3}$$

that, when used in (5.2), will best predict the current system output $y(t)$ given a history of inputs and outputs expressed as

$$\varphi(t) = [-y(t-1), -y(t-2), \ldots, -y(t-n)$$
$$u(t-1), u(t-2), \ldots, u(t-m)]^T \tag{5.4}$$

Then (5.2) can be written

$$\hat{y}(t) = \varphi^T(t)\boldsymbol{\theta} \tag{5.5}$$

The ith recursive least-squares (RLS) estimate of the optimal system parameter vector $\hat{\boldsymbol{\theta}}_i$ can be determined using the algorithm [7]:

$$\hat{\boldsymbol{\theta}}_i = \hat{\boldsymbol{\theta}}_{i-1} + \mu_i \mathbf{R}_i^{-1} \psi(t, \hat{\boldsymbol{\theta}}_{i-1}) e(t, \hat{\boldsymbol{\theta}}_{i-1})$$
$$\psi(t, \hat{\boldsymbol{\theta}}_{i-1}) = \frac{\partial}{\partial \boldsymbol{\theta}} \hat{y}(t | \hat{\boldsymbol{\theta}}_{i-1})$$
$$e(t, \hat{\boldsymbol{\theta}}_{i-1}) = y(t) - \hat{y}(t | \hat{\boldsymbol{\theta}}_{i-1}) \tag{5.6}$$
$$\mathbf{R}_i = \mathbf{R}_{i-1} + \mu_i \left[\psi, (t, \hat{\boldsymbol{\theta}}_{i-1}) \psi^T(t, \hat{\boldsymbol{\theta}}_{i-1}) - \mathbf{R}_{i-1} \right]$$

The AMB plant (Figs. 5.2 and 5.3) is open-loop unstable; thus to perform system identification it must first be stabilized. A PID controller (which does not require a model to synthesize) was implemented using xPC Target, a real-time execution environment using PC-compatible processors from the MathWorks, Inc. (Natick, MA). Using gains of $K_p = 30,000$, $K_i = 500,000$, $K_d = 100$ and a fixed timestep of 0.6 ms, this controller enabled tracking of the square-wave reference trajectory:

$$x_{1d}(t) = 2.0 + 0.1 \text{sign}(\sin(20\pi t)) \tag{5.7}$$

To clarify the nomenclature, the reference trajectory (5.7) has a *setpoint* of 2.0 mm, a *setpoint amplitude* of 0.1 mm, and a *setpoint frequency* of 20π rad/sec (10.0 Hz).

Once stable tracking was achieved, the RLS algorithm (5.6) was implemented in real time. The parameter vector (5.3) was initialized to zero, $\mathbf{R}_0$ was initialized to

$1 \times 10^{-8} \cdot \mathbf{I}_4$ (where $\mathbf{I}_4$ is a four-dimensional identity matrix) and μ_i was fixed to 1.0×10^{-3}. Uniform random noise (variance $= 0.1$ A) was injected into the control signal to ensure persistent excitation. The real-time RLS algorithm converged to its optimum within 20 s, resulting in the discrete-time transfer function

$$\frac{Y(z)}{U(z)} = \frac{-4.041 \times 10^{-7} z - 1.019 \times 10^{-6}}{z^2 - 1.992 z + 0.980} \tag{5.8}$$

Because the model (5.8) is unstable (having poles at 0.88 and 1.11 in the z-plane), it is not possible to generate a stable simulation using the measured control input $u(t)$. It is, however, possible to validate the model using *k-step-ahead prediction* [7]. Figure 5.4 compares the measured output $y(t)$ to the 1- and 10-step-ahead modeled predictions $y_p(t)$ over the time interval 90.0–90.5 s. The prediction performance is noticeably reduced with the larger horizon (10 steps ahead), indicating the presence of modeling uncertainty. Thus uncertainty must be accounted for in the design of robust controllers.

5.3.2 Uncertainty Bound Specification

For H_∞ control synthesis, a representation of model uncertainty is required to bound the differences between the actual plant (which has an infinite number of states) and

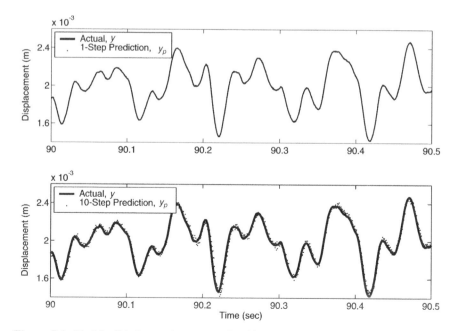

Figure 5.4. Model validation results: measured and *k-step-ahead* predicted rotor displacements.

the linear model used for control design (which has a small number of states). Even if system identification is used to estimate the model, there will still be dynamics present in the plant that cannot be fully captured. These unmodeled dynamics typically result in high-frequency uncertainties that are best modeled as *unstructured uncertainties* because they are difficult to express in highly structured parameterized forms [1].

Two common unstructured representations of modeling uncertainty, illustrated in (Fig. 5.5), are *additive uncertainty*:

$$G_{\Delta a}(s) = G_0(s) + W_a(s)\Delta_a(s)$$
$$\Delta_a(s) = |G(s) - G_0(s)|$$

(5.9)

and *multiplicative uncertainty*:

$$G_{\Delta m}(s) = G_0(s)(1 + W_m(s)\Delta_m(s))$$
$$\Delta_m(s) = \left|\frac{G(s) - G_0(s)}{G_0(s)}\right|$$

(5.10)

Here W_a and W_m (generalized by W_Δ) are weighting functions that describe the spatial and frequency characteristics of the uncertainty and define a neighborhood about the nominal model G_0 inside which the actual infinite-order plant resides [1]. For the AMB test rig, the additive case will be used to represent model uncertainty.

Typically, uncertainty weighting functions are chosen somewhat arbitrarily or through trial-and-error procedures that can result in overly conservative error bounds to guarantee stability. Textbooks on robust control provide general guidelines for specifying modeling uncertainty (W_Δ), tracking performance (W_p), and control input (W_{in}) as functions of frequency. For this application, all three weighting functions were constructed based on a priori knowledge of the test rig dynamics and trial-and-error adjustments (Fig. 5.6). The shape of the *nominal* uncertainty weighting function (a highpass filter) was selected based on the realistic assumption that unmodeled dynamics are more prevalent at high frequencies, and its magnitude

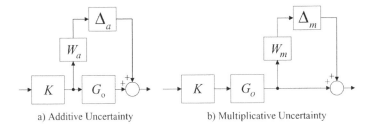

a) Additive Uncertainty   b) Multiplicative Uncertainty

Figure 5.5. Additive and multiplicative model uncertainty.

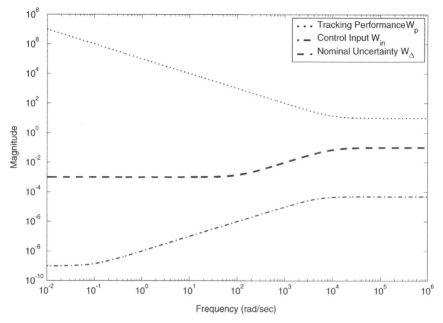

Figure 5.6. Weighting functions for nominal H_∞ controller synthesis.

was adjusted to ensure that $|W_\Delta(j\omega)| \geq \Delta_a(j\omega)$ for all frequencies. A *nominal H_∞* controller was designed using the MATLAB® Robust Control Toolbox from The MathWorks, Inc. (Natick, MA).

5.3.3 Nominal H_∞ Control: Experimental Results

The AMB test rig (Fig. 5.2) was used to experimentally validate the robust stability and performance of the nominal H_∞ controller. This controller was implemented using xPC Target at a fixed timestep of 0.6 ms. Figure 5.7 shows measured tracking responses for the reference trajectory of Eq. (5.7). Clearly, this nominal controller stabilized the plant dynamics and provided reasonable tracking performance, as quantified by the mean of square tracking errors (MSTE):

$$\text{MSTE} = \frac{\sum_{k=1}^{N}(x_{1d}(kT) - x_1(kT))^2}{N} \qquad (5.11)$$

Here T is the discrete sample time, 0.6 ms. The MSTE for the nominal setpoint $(2.0 \times 10^{-3}$ m, 10.0 Hz) was 3.31×10^{-8} m^2 ($N = 40,000$).

To investigate the robustness of this nominal H_∞ controller, the setpoint and frequency of (5.7) were varied from their nominal values (those used for system identification, $x_1 = 2.0$ mm and $f = 10.0$ Hz, respectively). Figures 5.7 and 5.8

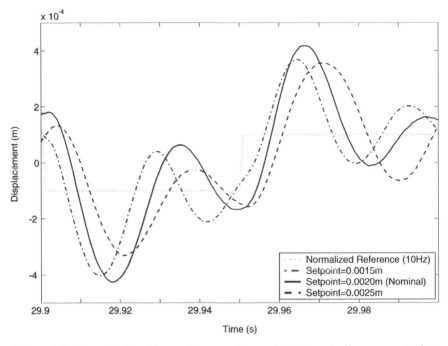

Figure 5.7. Normalized tracking performance for nominal H_∞ controller versus setpoint.

show that stability was maintained, but tracking performance deteriorated, away from the nominal reference trajectory. Table 5.1 quantifies these reductions in tracking performance.

5.4 ESTIMATING MODELING UNCERTAINTY FOR H_∞ CONTROL OF THE AMB TEST RIG

The nominal H_∞ controller utilized a somewhat arbitrary uncertainty weighting function for synthesis. The shape of this weighting function was specified based on the assumption that unmodeled dynamics are more prevalent at high frequencies, and its magnitude was specified with the benefit of extensive a priori information. Experimental results indicate that this weighting function was conservative enough (defined an adequately large neighborhood about the nominal model G_0 inside which the actual infinite-order plant resides) to provide robust stability for a reasonable range of reference setpoints and frequencies.

However, as the size of the set of stabilizable plants increases, tracking performance tends to decrease. Thus, it is advantageous to select uncertainty bounds that are accurate, but not overly conservative, for robust stability and improved performance. By using system identification to estimate the modeling error and construct

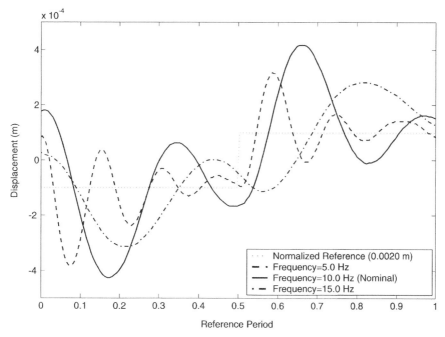

Figure 5.8. Normalized tracking performance for nominal H_∞ controller versus setpoint frequency.

an uncertainty weighting function, the plant should lie just inside the bound of stabilizable model sets, thus minimizing uncertainty bound conservativeness and optimizing controller performance. Two methods for estimating the uncertainty weighting function are presented here: a parametric approach based on the RLS equations (5.6) and a nonparametric approach based on neural networks.

TABLE 5.1. Tracking Performance (MSTE) for H_∞ Controllers Versus Setpoint ($\times 10^{-9}$)

Uncertainty Bound	Setpoint Frequency (Hz)	Setpoint (m)		
		0.0015	0.0020	0.0025
Nominal	5.0	10.654	4.729	7.026
	10.0	10.920	6.362	5.931
	15.0	12.438	7.572	7.340
MEM (99.9%)	5.0	2.347	2.288	2.565
	10.0	4.534	4.678	5.112
	15.0	6.646	6.944	7.951
CIN (99.9%)	5.0	2.034	2.113	2.333
	10.0	4.015	4.267	4.701
	15.0	5.920	6.384	7.046

5.4.1 Model Error Modeling

Classical approaches to model validation address the correlations between residuals and regressors [7,22]. A newer approach is to formulate a linear mapping from the inputs to the modeling errors. A direct extension of the parametric system identification approach used to identify the nominal model G_0 can be used to identify the modeling error between the actual nonlinear plant and the identified linear model. This process is called *model error modeling* (MEM) [22], and is illustrated in Fig. 5.9. Two modifications to the RLS algorithm (5.6) are necessary:

1. The signal to be predicted is the difference between the output of the plant and the nominal model, that is, $e(t) = y(t) - \hat{y}(t)$.
2. The system to be identified, the *model error model*, represents the unmodeled dynamics, and has input $u(t)$ and output $\hat{e}(t)$.

As before, the AMB test rig was made to track the reference trajectory (5.7) and identification of an error model was initiated. Iterative order selection indicated that a tenth-order ARX model adequately represented the error dynamics. Figure 5.10 shows the Bode plot of the identified error model with 99.9% confidence intervals. As outlined in Reinelt et al. [15], the nominal model (5.8) can be validated by adding the error confidence bounds on a frequency-by-frequency basis to the model. Since the nominal model lies inside the uncertainty region defined by these bounds, both the model and error confidence bounds are suitable for H_∞ control synthesis, as will be shown in Section 5.4.4.

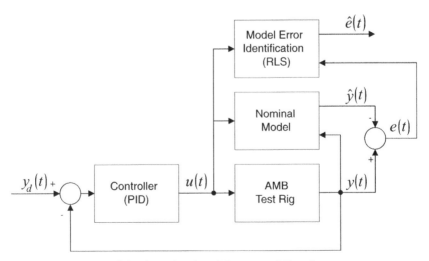

Figure 5.9. Control and model error modeling diagram.

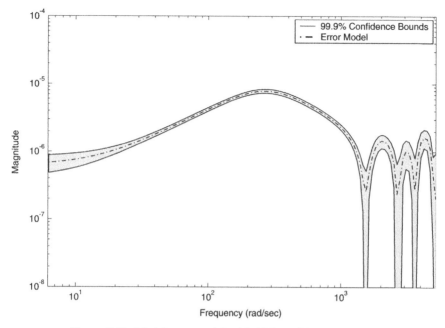

Figure 5.10. Model error model, with 99% confidence intervals.

5.4.2 Intelligent Model Error Identification

Intelligence, as defined by *Merriam-Webster's Collegiate Dictionary* [23], implies the ability to *respond* successfully to a new experience and *learn* or understand from previous experiences. For a system or process to be intelligent, it must possess two distinct characteristics:

1. The ability to successfully *adapt* (or respond) to changes in its environment (time-varying plant parameters, unmodeled plant dynamics, etc.) such that overall system performance is improved
2. The ability to *retain* (or learn) this adaptive information for future reference

Thus, an intelligent system is one that *adapts* and *retains* information related to previous adaptive experiences. Neural networks (NNs) are frequently used to provide this learning capability, although it is important to note that not all NN-based control systems satisfy this definition of intelligence. NNs are highly interconnected data processing elements typically used for function approximation and pattern recognition [24]. They are documented as being self-adapting "universal approximators" because of their ability to model any nonlinear function to any desired level of accuracy, given enough processing elements [25,26].

For this research application, intelligent model error identification can be viewed as a nonparametric regression problem in the frequency domain involving feedforward neural networks. One specific type of network, the Radial Basis Function Network (RBFN), is well suited to the task of real-time system identification for two reasons. First, the RBFN uses localized activation functions, and thus it learns information in a localized fashion [10]. As a result, parameter estimates obtained from a small region of the plant operating space do not adversely affect estimates from other regions. Second, the interconnection weights, which are self-adjusted during learning, are applied linearly on the output side of the network. This feature significantly simplifies the training process and reduces the computational requirements, making RBFNs well-suited for real-time implementation.

The goal of intelligent model error identification is to estimate the upper magnitude bound (99.9% confidence interval) of the error model frequency response function $|G_e(j\omega)| = |E(j\omega)|/|U(j\omega)|$. Stochastic estimates of this frequency response function (FRF) can be obtained from the fast Fourier transforms (FFTs) of prediction error $e(t)$ and control input $u(t)$. Note that there are plant nonlinearities and nondeterministic effects that result in frequency-dependent confidence intervals associated with $|G_e(j\omega)|$.

Figure 5.11 shows one nonparametric approach for estimating the model error FRF $|G_e(j\omega)|$ using sampled input–output data and a single RBFN. The RBFN provides a regression estimate of the model error magnitude $\hat{G}_e(\omega, \mathbf{w})$ that is conditioned on the input frequency ω and the N-element network weight vector $\mathbf{w}$. Using this approach, the estimated magnitude corresponding to

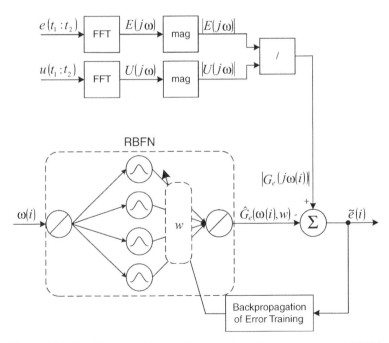

Figure 5.11. Intelligent model error identification using a nonrecurrent RBFN.

frequency ω is:

$$\hat{G}_e(\omega, \mathbf{w}) = \mathbf{w} \cdot e^{-((\omega - \mathbf{c})/\mathbf{s})^2} \tag{5.12}$$

where $\mathbf{c}$ represents the normalized basis function centers and s represents the basis function widths, both vectors with N elements. The RBFN (5.12) can be trained to minimize a cost function of prediction errors by adjusting the network weights $\mathbf{w}$. The standard quadratic error cost function for P input–output training patterns is

$$\tilde{e}(i) \equiv |G_e(j\omega(i))| - \hat{G}_e(\omega(i), \mathbf{w})$$

$$J(e) \equiv \frac{1}{2} \sum_{i=1}^{P} \tilde{e}(i)^2 \tag{5.13}$$

The optimal weight vector $\mathbf{w}$ could be determined using a closed-form, off-line approach (where complete batches of input–output data are available). For on-line implementation, a backpropagation of error approach is used to update the weights according to the negative error gradient [27]:

$$\mathbf{w}_{new} = \mathbf{w}_{old} - \eta \cdot \frac{\partial J(e(i))}{\partial \mathbf{w}}$$

$$\frac{\partial J(e(i))}{\partial \mathbf{w}} = -(|G_e(j\omega(i))| - \hat{G}_e(\omega(i), \mathbf{w})) \cdot e^{-((\omega - \mathbf{c})/\mathbf{s})^2} \tag{5.14}$$

The training gain η is selected to provide rapid, yet stable, convergence during training.

Because of the symmetric nature of the error cost function (5.13), a network trained using standard backpropagation (5.14) should converge to the average FRF magnitude. To illustrate this point, an RBFN was trained to identify the average error magnitude of the identified model (5.8) across the frequency range $0.0 - 1904.0\pi$ rad/s (1904.0π rad/s represents the Nyquist frequency for data collected at 0.6 ms). A simple network pruning approach indicated that 18 basis functions provided both estimation accuracy and computational efficiency. The centers of these basis functions $\mathbf{c}$ were distributed uniformly across the input domain ($0.0 - 1904.0\pi$ rad/s, every 112.0π rad/s), and all basis function widths $\mathbf{s}$ were set to 112.0π rad/s. The network weights $\mathbf{w}$ were initialized to zero. Input–output data collected from the AMB test rig was used to generate sequential 16,384-point FRFs of model error $G_e(j\omega)$. Using a training gain of $\eta = 0.001$, the error cost function $J(e)$ dropped from 1.76×10^{-6} to 5.96×10^{-7} in 100 training epochs, as a smooth approximation of the average FRF magnitude was achieved (Fig. 5.12).

Also plotted in Fig. 5.12 is the computed average magnitude across 100 FRFs. Note that the RBFN provides a much smoother estimate of this mean and requires far less computational resources to approximate it (only 18 network weights, as

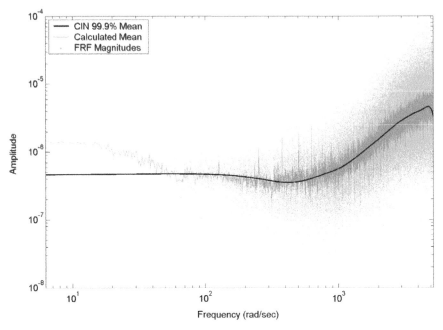

Figure 5.12. RBFN estimate of average model error magnitude.

opposed to an 819,200 element double precision array). The discrepancies at low frequencies (1.0–20.0 rad/s) between the calculated average magnitude and the RBFN estimate are accentuated by the logarithmic frequency scale. These low-frequency differences could be reduced with more radial basis functions and smaller activation widths. However, it is the high-frequency modeling error that is more critical for robust control synthesis, hence these discrepancies are acceptable.

If the standard quadratic error cost function (5.13) is replaced with an asymmetric, bilinear error cost function, the learning characteristics of the RBFN will be dramatically changed [16]. The quadratic cost function causes network outputs to converge to the statistical mean of the model error magnitudes because positive and negative errors are equally weighted. Using an asymmetric bilinear cost function, it is possible to weight positive and negative errors differently, enabling approximation of confidence intervals. Consider the asymmetric cost function described by

$$\tilde{e}(i) \equiv |G_e(j\omega(i))| - \hat{G}_e(\omega(i), \mathbf{w})$$

$$c_H(i) \equiv \begin{cases} a \cdot \tilde{e}(i) & \tilde{e}(i) \geq 0 \\ \tilde{e}(i) & \tilde{e}(i) < 0 \end{cases} \qquad (5.15)$$

$$J_H(\tilde{e}) \equiv \sum_{i=1}^{P} c_H(i)$$

As before, this network can be trained by updating the weights in the negative error gradient:

$$\mathbf{w}_{\text{new}} = \mathbf{w}_{\text{old}} - \eta \cdot \frac{\partial J_H(\tilde{e}(i))}{\partial \mathbf{w}}$$

$$\frac{\partial J_H(\tilde{e}(i))}{\partial \mathbf{w}} = -e^{-((\omega - \mathbf{c})/\mathbf{s})^2} \cdot \begin{cases} a & \tilde{e}(i) \geq 0 \\ 1 & \tilde{e}(i) < 0 \end{cases}$$

(5.16)

By selecting a unit cost constant ($a = 1$), positive and negative prediction errors will be evenly weighted, and an RBFN will converge to the statistical median of the training data (if the data are normally distributed, this will coincide with the mean) [16]. This occurs because each weight update depends not on the magnitude of error, but on its sign. Thus, each weight update is of a consistent magnitude, with a direction depending on the sign of the prediction error. Whenever the likelihood of positive prediction errors equals the likelihood of negative prediction errors, the weight update process will chatter back and forth about a stable equilibrium point. This point equals the median of the distributed training data.

By selecting a larger cost constant ($a > 1$), an RBFN trained using this error cost function will consistently overestimate the median of distributed training data. Similarly, if ($0 < a < 1$) an RBFN will underestimate the median of distributed training data. In fact, it is possible to select this cost constant so that an RBFN will approximate a desired confidence interval associated with randomly distributed training data, resulting in a confidence interval network (CIN) [16]. To estimate the 99.9% confidence interval, the cost constant a must be selected to equally weight 999 negative prediction errors and 1 positive prediction error; thus $a = 999$.

Recall the RBFN used to estimate the average error magnitude of the identified model (Fig. 5.12). A CIN was constructed by simply replacing the quadratic error cost function (5.13) with an asymmetric bilinear error cost function (5.15). This CIN was trained to approximate the upper uncertainty bound (99.9% confidence interval) between the identified model (5.8) and the actual plant (Fig. 5.1). As before, the 18 basis function centers $\mathbf{c}$ were distributed uniformly across the input domain ($0.0 - 1904.0\pi$ rad/s, every 112.0π rad/s), and all activation widths $\mathbf{s}$ were set to 112.0π rad/s. The network weights $\mathbf{w}$ were initialized to zero. Input-output data collected from the AMB test rig was again used to generate sequential 16,384-point FRFs of model error $G_e(j\omega)$. The error cost function $J_H(\tilde{e})$ dropped from 2.91 to 0.23 in 100 training epochs, resulting in a smooth approximation of the 99.9% confidence interval (Fig. 5.13).

One undesirable characteristic of the CIN weight update process was addressed by selecting a very small training gain ($\eta = 1.00 \times 10^{-9}$). Because the weight update algorithm is independent of prediction error magnitudes (it depends only on the sign of these errors), the weights exhibit a "chattering" characteristic as they approach their steady-state values. The amplitude of this weight chattering is directly proportional to the training gain, which must be initialized (or decremented during training) accordingly.

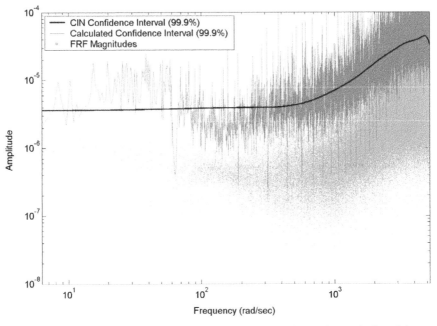

Figure 5.13. CIN estimate of uncertainty bound (99.9% confidence interval of model error magnitude).

5.4.3   Uncertainty Bound Specification

The additive uncertainty weighting function (W_Δ) required for H_∞ control synthesis can be derived directly from the identified confidence intervals of Figs. 5.10 and 5.13, instead of being constructed arbitrarily. To assess the robust control benefits associated with identified bounds, two additional H_∞ controllers were synthesized. The uncertainty weighting function for the first controller was a sixth-order transfer function derived using MATLAB®'s *fitsys* command. This enabled the identified bounds to be expressed in a low-order framework more suitable to H_∞ synthesis. To maintain a conservative bound, the *fitsys* transfer function was constructed so that its magnitude was not less than the 99.9% confidence interval identified using the MEM approach (Fig. 5.14). The order of this transfer function was determined heuristically to provide an optimal fit. Another uncertainty weighting function, a second-order transfer function, was constructed similarly from the 99.9% confidence interval obtained from the CIN (Fig. 5.14).

The performance and input weighting functions (W_p and W_{in}) were the same as those used for *nominal H_∞* synthesis, shown in Fig. 5.6. These two *identified* H_∞ controllers were designed using MATLAB®'s Robust Control Toolbox as before.

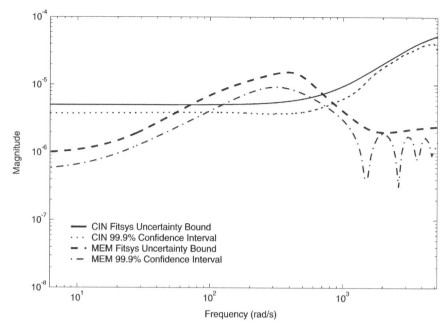

Figure 5.14. Uncertainty bounds derived from MEM and CIN confidence intervals.

5.4.4 Identified H_∞ Control: Experimental Results

The AMB test rig (Fig. 5.1) was used to compare the robust stability and performance of the *nominal* and *identified* H_∞ controllers. Figure 5.15 shows tracking responses for the reference trajectory defined by (5.7). This figure reveals that all three controllers stabilized the plant dynamics and provided reasonable tracking performance. However, the performance of the *identified* controllers is significantly better than the *nominal* controller, as quantified by MSTEs of Table 5.1.

To investigate the robustness of these *identified* H_∞ controllers, the setpoint and frequency of (5.7) were varied from their nominal values ($x_1 = 2.0$ mm and $f = 10.0$ Hz, respectively). As with the nominal controller, stability was maintained but tracking performance deteriorated away from the nominal reference trajectory. However, the tracking performance of the *identified* H_∞ controllers was far superior to that of the *nominal* H_∞ controller. Table 5.1 quantifies these significant improvements in tracking performance. For the 1.5-mm setpoint with a 5.0-Hz frequency, the performance of the intelligent H_∞ controller was 300% better than that of the nominal controller and was approximately the same (5% better) as that of the MEM controller. These results clearly illustrate the performance benefits that soft computing can provide to H_∞ control synthesis.

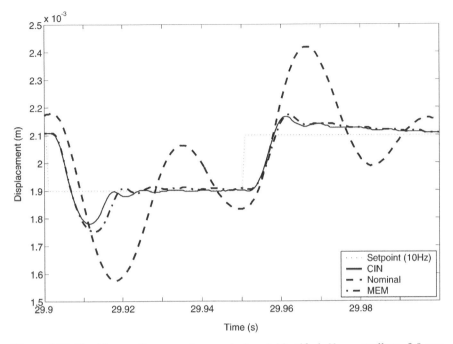

Figure 5.15. Tracking performance for nominal and identified H_∞ controllers: 2.0-mm setpoint, 10.0-Hz frequency.

5.5 NONLINEAR ROBUST CONTROL OF THE AMB TEST RIG

The previous sections illustrated the unique benefits that soft computing can provide to linear robust control synthesis. Similar benefits can be demonstrated for nonlinear robust controllers. Sliding mode control (SMC) is a variable-structure, robust control strategy for certain classes of nonlinear systems subject to modeling uncertainties [2,3]. Such uncertainties may be structured (parametric uncertainties and variations), unstructured (unmodeled dynamics), or may result from non-deterministic features of the plant. The SMC law is formulated using a Lyapunov approach that guarantees robustness despite the presence of bounded modeling uncertainties. The ultimate performance of SMC relates to the accuracy of these cumulative uncertainty bounds over the entire operating space. A straightforward SMC design example will be used to demonstrate the benefits of soft computing for bounding modeling uncertainty in control applications.

5.5.1 Nominal Sliding Mode Control of the AMB Test Rig

Consider the most general form of a nonlinear plant with full state measurement:

$$\dot{\mathbf{x}} = \mathbf{f}(\mathbf{x}, \mathbf{u})$$
$$\mathbf{y} = \mathbf{x}$$

(5.17)

Here $\mathbf{x}$ is the state vector, $\mathbf{u}$ is the input vector, $\mathbf{y}$ is the output vector, and $\mathbf{f}$ is a nonlinear vector function. The nonlinear state equations for the AMB test rig, which represent an approximation of the true plant dynamics, can be expressed in this form. For a nominal air gap of 2.7 mm:

$$\dot{x}_1 = \hat{f}_1(\mathbf{x}, u) = x_2$$

$$\dot{x}_2 = \hat{f}_2(\mathbf{x}, u) = -2.56 \times 10^{-6} \frac{u^2}{x_1^2} + 9.81$$

(5.18)

The control objective for this example is to track the harmonic reference trajectories:

$$x_{1d} = 0.0027 + 0.0005 \sin(10\,t)$$
$$x_{2d} = 0.005 \cos(10\,t)$$
$$\dot{x}_{2d} = -0.05 \sin(10\,t)$$

(5.19)

The first step in SMC design is to define a "sliding surface" in terms of tracking errors [3]:

$$S(t) \equiv \{\mathbf{x}: s(\mathbf{x}) = 0\}$$
$$s(\mathbf{x}) \equiv (x_{2d} - x_2) + \lambda(x_{1d} - x_1)$$

(5.20)

According to this definition, the control objective is to reach the sliding surface from arbitrary initial conditions and remain on the sliding surface for all time. Here λ is a positive constant that determines the bandwidth and reaching time to the sliding surface.

The SMC law is composed of two distinct terms: a stabilizing term u_S and a performance term u_P. The stabilizing term is defined so that $\dot{s}(\mathbf{x}) = 0$ and would provide perfect tracking in the absence of modeling uncertainties. The performance term provides robustness to modeling uncertainties through a switching action:

$$u = u_S + u_P$$
$$u_P \equiv -k \cdot \mathrm{sign}(s(\mathbf{x}))$$

(5.21)

The switching gain k makes the closed-loop system robust to bounded modeling uncertainties associated with the model $\hat{\mathbf{f}}(\mathbf{x}, \mathbf{u})$. For guaranteed stability, this gain must be larger than the modeling uncertainties at every point in the $(\mathbf{x}, \mathbf{u})$ domain:

$$k > |\mathbf{f}(\mathbf{x}, \mathbf{u}) - \hat{\mathbf{f}}(\mathbf{x}, \mathbf{u})|$$

(5.22)

Although conservative switching gains provide guaranteed robustness, they increase the amplitude of high-frequency switching. This may result in unacceptable tracking performance, with chattering at the plant output, and may dramatically increase the required control power.

Using the nonlinear state equations (5.18) and the sliding surface definition (5.20), the SMC law for the AMB test rig becomes

$$u = u_S + u_P$$

$$u_S = \sqrt{\frac{x_1^2(-\lambda(x_{2d} - x_2) - \dot{x}_{2d} + 9.81)}{2.56 \times 10^{-6}}} \tag{5.23}$$

$$u_P = -k \cdot \text{sign}((x_{2d} - x_2) + \lambda(x_{1d} - x_1))$$

For typical SMC synthesis problems, the bounds of modeling uncertainty across the $(\mathbf{x}, \mathbf{u})$ operating space are not known, making the specification of a switching gain somewhat arbitrary and frequently overconservative. For the AMB test rig, however, a priori experimental information reveals that the largest modeling uncertainty between the plant (Fig. 5.1) and model (5.18) is approximately 8.0 (m/s^2). Using this value for the switching gain and $\lambda = 1000$ for the bandwidth constant results in the *nominal* SMC law:

$$u = \sqrt{\frac{x_1^2(-1000(x_{2d} - x_2) - \dot{x}_{2d} + 9.81)}{-2.56 \cdot 10^{-6}}} - 8 \cdot \text{sign}((x_{2d} - x_2) + 1000(x_{1d} - x_1)) \tag{5.24}$$

5.5.2 Nominal SMC: Experimental Results

This nominal control law was implemented on the AMB test rig using an ACE 1102® real-time hardware kit from dSPACE, Inc. (Paderborn, Germany) with a fixed time step of 0.2 ms. The experimental results are presented in Fig. 5.16. Clearly, the tracking performance of this control approach is good, because the peak displacement tracking error $(x_{1d} - x_1)$ is less than 1.0 mm. This performance can be quantified using the mean of squared tracking errors (MSTE) from 0.94 s of experimental data:

$$\text{MSTE}_{\text{nominal}} = \frac{\sum_{k=1}^{4700} (x_{1d}(kT) - x_1(kT))^2}{4700} = 1.90 \times 10^{-9} \, \text{m}^2 \tag{5.25}$$

However, this satisfactory performance is achieved at the expense of extremely active control due to the performance term u_P. The conservative global switching gain needed to compensate for modeling uncertainties results in high-amplitude switching, which can be quantified using the mean of squared control inputs (MSCI):

$$\text{MSCI}_{\text{nominal}} = \frac{\sum_{k=1}^{4700} u(kT)^2}{4700} = 31.06 \, \text{A}^2 \tag{5.26}$$

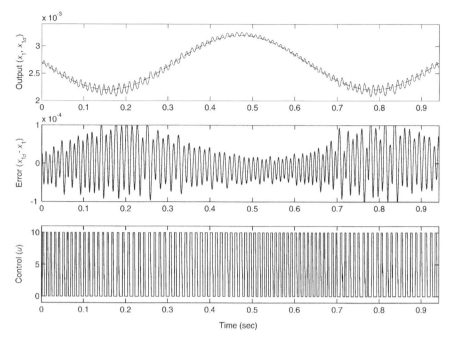

Figure 5.16. Experimental tracking performance and control activity for SMC with constant switching gain.

5.6 ESTIMATING MODEL UNCERTAINTY FOR SMC OF THE AMB TEST RIG

The *nominal* sliding mode controller utilized a constant switching gain for synthesis. Because this gain was selected based on a priori experimental information, it was conservative enough (defined an adequately large neighborhood about the nominal model $\hat{f}(x, u)$ inside which the actual infinite-order plant resides) to provide robust stability for a reasonable range of reference setpoints and frequencies.

However, as the size of the set of stabilizable plants increases, tracking performance tends to decrease and control activity tends to increase, as confirmed by the performance indices (5.25) and (5.26). Thus, it is advantageous to select a variable switching gain $k = k(x, u)$ that is accurate, but not overly conservative, for robust stability and improved performance. A soft-computing approach for estimating the uncertainty bound between the plant (Fig. 5.2) and model (5.18) is presented in the following sections.

5.6.1 Intelligent System Identification

In the context of this example, intelligent system identification is a multidimensional, nonlinear regression problem involving feedforward RBFNs. Intelligent system identification provides a nonparametric model $\hat{\mathbf{f}}(\mathbf{x}, \mathbf{u}, \mathbf{w})$ that is conditioned on the state vector $\mathbf{x}$, the input vector $\mathbf{u}$, and the RBFN weights $\mathbf{w}$. Generally, there will be unmodeled dynamics, time-varying parameters, and nondeterministic effects that result in spatially dependent confidence intervals associated with $\hat{\mathbf{f}}(\mathbf{x}, \mathbf{u}, \mathbf{w})$.

To facilitate SMC synthesis for the AMB test rig, intelligent system identification is needed to provide a nonparametric estimate of the acceleration dynamics $\hat{\dot{x}}_2(t) = \hat{f}_2(x_1, u, \mathbf{w})$. Figure 5.17 shows a nonrecurrent approach for estimating the plant dynamics $\hat{f}_2(x_1, u, \mathbf{w})$ using sampled input–output data and a single RBFN. Using this approach, the estimated dynamics corresponding to state x_1 and input u_1 are

$$\hat{f}_2(x_1, u_1, \mathbf{w}) = \sum_{t=1}^{T} \mathbf{w} \cdot e^{\ ((x_1(t)-\mathbf{c_x})^2+(u(t)-\mathbf{c_u})^2)/\mathbf{s}^2} \tag{5.27}$$

Here $\mathbf{c_x}$ and $\mathbf{c_u}$ represent the normalized (x_1, u) coordinates of the basis function centers and $\mathbf{s}$ represents the activation width vector. The RBFN (5.27) can be trained to minimize a cost function of prediction errors $e(t) = \dot{x}_2(t) - \hat{\dot{x}}_2(t)$ by adjusting the network weights $\mathbf{w}$. The standard quadratic error cost function for T input–output training patterns is

$$e(t) \equiv \dot{x}_2(t) - \hat{\dot{x}}_2(t) = \dot{x}_2(t) - \hat{f}_2(x_1, u, \mathbf{w})$$

$$J(e) \equiv \frac{1}{2} \sum_{t=1}^{T} e(t)^2 \tag{5.28}$$

For on-line implementation, the optimal weight vector $\mathbf{w}$ is again determined through backpropagation of error:

$$\mathbf{w}_{\text{new}} = \mathbf{w}_{\text{old}} - \eta \cdot \frac{\partial J(e)}{\partial \mathbf{w}}$$

$$\frac{\partial J(e)}{\partial \mathbf{w}} = -\sum_{t=1}^{T} (\dot{x}_2(t) - \hat{\dot{x}}_2(t)) \cdot e^{-((x_1(t)-\mathbf{c_x})^2+(u(t)-\mathbf{c_u})^2)/s^2} \tag{5.29}$$

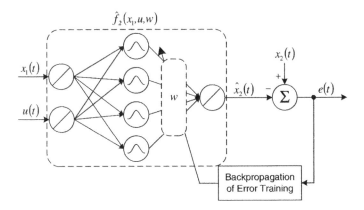

Figure 5.17. Intelligent system identification using a nonrecurrent RBFN.

As discussed in Section 5.4.2, the symmetric nature of the error cost function (5.28) causes network training to converge to the average plant dynamics $\bar{f}_2(x_1, u)$. To illustrate this point, an RBFN was trained to estimate *simulated* acceleration data from a nondeterministic plant:

$$\dot{x}_1 = x_2$$

$$\dot{x}_2 = -3.00 \cdot 10^{-6} \frac{(u + \xi)^2}{x_1^2} + 9.81 \tag{5.30}$$

Here $\xi(t)$ is stationary Gaussian noise with zero mean and unit variance. Simulated acceleration data are presented in the three-dimensional plot of Fig. 5.18, along with calculated 99% confidence intervals.

A simple network pruning approach indicated that 64 two-dimensional basis functions provided both estimation accuracy and computational efficiency. The 64 activation centers c_x and c_u were distributed uniformly across the normalized input domain. The activation widths s were set to 0.2 for each neuron. All RBFN weights w were initialized to zero. Using a training gain of $\eta = 0.01$, the error cost function $J(e)$ dropped from 110.91 to 12.87 in 200 training epochs, as nearly perfect approximation of the average plant dynamics was achieved (Fig. 5.19).

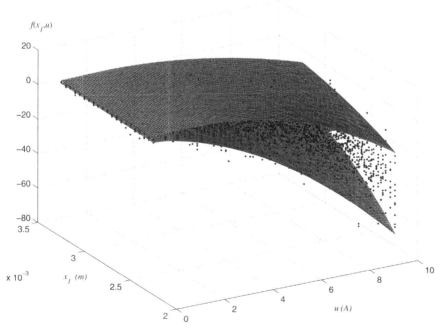

Figure 5.18. Acceleration data (points) for simulated plant (5.30), with computed 99% confidence intervals (mesh plots).

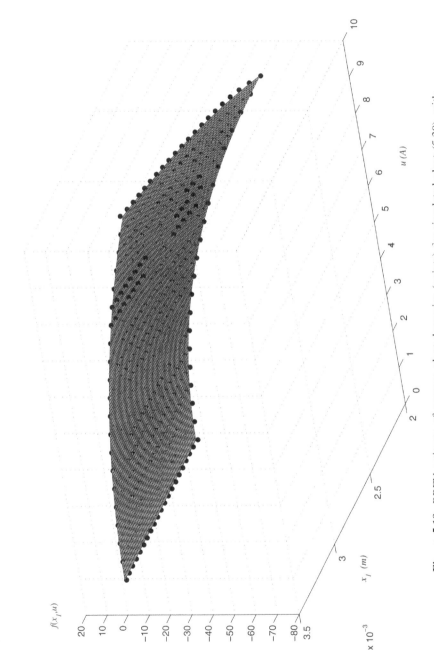

Figure 5.19. RBFN estimate of average plant dynamics (points) for simulated plant (5.30), with computed average (mesh).

5.6.2 Intelligent Model Error Identification

Estimating model uncertainty using RBFNs is similar to intelligent system identification, but first requires a nominal model $g(x_1, u)$ of the plant dynamics. The objective is to estimate the average differences between the model and the plant across the operating space (x_1, u). The RBFN implementation of Fig. 5.20, clearly a fusion of soft and hard computing, provides one means of accomplishing this objective. Using this approach, the estimated acceleration $\hat{\dot{x}}_2(t)$ corresponding to state $x_1(t)$ and input $u(t)$ is

$$\hat{\dot{x}}_2(t) = g(x_1, u) + \hat{f}_2(x_1, u, \mathbf{w}) = g(x_1, u) + \sum_{t=1}^{T} \mathbf{w} \cdot e^{-((x_1(t)-\mathbf{c_x})^2 + (u(t)-\mathbf{c_u})^2)/s^2} \quad (5.31)$$

To estimate the average error between the model (5.18) and simulated plant (5.30), an RBFN can be trained using a quadratic error cost function and backpropagation of error:

$$e(t) \equiv \dot{x}_2(t) - \hat{\dot{x}}_2(t) = \dot{x}_2(t) - g(x_1, u) - \hat{f}_2(x_1, u, \mathbf{w})$$

$$J(e) \equiv \frac{1}{2} \sum_{t=1}^{T} e(t)^2$$

$$\mathbf{w}_{\text{new}} = \mathbf{w}_{\text{old}} - \eta \cdot \frac{\partial J(e)}{\partial \mathbf{w}} \quad\quad (5.32)$$

$$\frac{\partial J(e)}{\partial \mathbf{w}} = -\sum_{t=1}^{T} (\dot{x}_2(t) - \hat{\dot{x}}_2(t)) \cdot e^{-((x_1(t)-\mathbf{c_x})^2 + (u(t)-\mathbf{c_u})^2)/s^2}$$

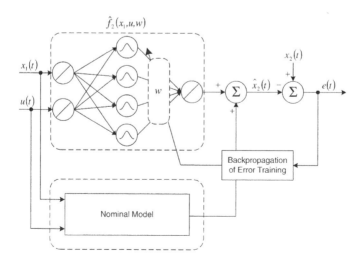

Figure 5.20. Intelligent model error identification using a nonrecurrent RBFN.

To illustrate this, an identical RBFN (64 normalized basis functions, centers uniformly distributed, activation widths set to 0.2, network weights initialized to zero) was trained to approximate the average model error. Using a training gain of $\eta = 0.0001$, the error cost function $J(e)$ dropped from 4.123 to 0.017 in 200 training epochs, resulting in a smooth, accurate estimation of average model error (Fig. 5.21).

A CIN is constructed by replacing the standard quadratic error cost function (5.28) with an asymmetric, bilinear error cost function, enabling approximation of specific confidence intervals associated with the model error $f_2(x_1, u) - g(x_1, u)$. This bilinear cost function has the same form as (5.15), but after incorporating nomenclature specific to this SMC synthesis example it becomes

$$e(t) \equiv \dot{x}_2(t) - \hat{\dot{x}}_2(t) = \dot{x}_2(t) - g(x_1, u) - \hat{f}_2(x_1, u, \mathbf{w})$$

$$c_H(t) \equiv \begin{cases} a \cdot e(t) & e(t) \geq 0 \\ e(t) & e(t) < 0 \end{cases} \tag{5.33}$$

$$J_H(e) = \sum_{t=1}^{T} c_H(t)$$

The weight update equations for this CIN are identical to those given by (5.16). Using these equations, two CINs were trained to approximate the upper and lower uncertainty bounds (99% confidence intervals) between the model (5.18) and simulated plant (5.30). Using identical network and training parameters (64 normalized basis functions, centers uniformly distributed, activation widths set to 0.2, network weights initialized to zero, and a training gain of $\eta = 0.1$), the upper-bound error cost function $J_H(e)$ dropped from 75.92 to 9.17 in 200 training epochs, while lower cost function $J_L(e)$ dropped from 80.69 to 13.53 in 200 training epochs.

Figure 5.22 shows the estimated upper and lower modeling uncertainty bounds, along with sampled modeling errors. Specifically, the mesh surfaces of Fig. 5.22 represent RBFN estimates of the upper and lower uncertainty bounds (99% confidence intervals) between the model (5.18) and simulated plant (5.30), learned without knowledge of the true plant dynamics. The data points in this figure represent sampled modeling errors, clearly revealing the nondeterministic nature of the simulated plant.

5.6.3 Intelligent SMC: Experimental Results

To experimentally demonstrate the benefits of fusing soft computing with nonlinear robust control synthesis, the SMC law (5.24) was augmented with a spatially dependent switching gain $k = k(x_1, u)$ derived from intelligent model error identification. Two CINs were trained using experimental data to approximate the upper and lower uncertainty bounds (99% confidence intervals) between the model (5.18) and the AMB test rig (Fig. 5.1). Input–output data were acquired using dSPACE® real-time hardware at a sampling frequency of 6666.6 Hz, and they were anti-aliased

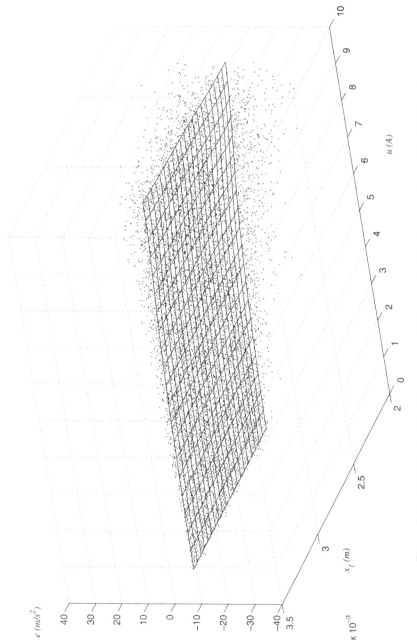

Figure 5.21. RBFN estimate of average model error (mesh) between the model (5.18) and simulated plant (5.30), with sampled modeling error (points).

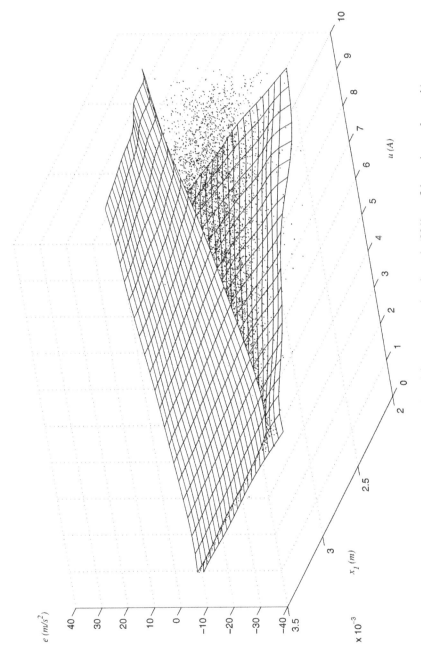

Figure 5.22. RBFN estimates of model error uncertainty bounds (99% confidence intervals, mesh) between the model (5.18) and simulated plant (5.30), with sampled modeling error (points).

using a first-order digital filter with a 1000.0-Hz cutoff frequency. Sixty-four basis functions were distributed uniformly across the normalized input domain (x_1, u). The activation widths were set to 0.3, and the network weights were initialized to 1.0 for the upper-bound network and -1.0 for the lower-bound network. To expedite convergence, training gains were initialized to $\eta = 10.0$, but were decremented 1% for each training epoch ($\eta_i = 0.99\eta_{i-1}$). The upper-bound error cost function $J_H(e)$ dropped from 2.23×10^{-5} to 7.34×10^{-7} in 150 training epochs, while the lower cost function $J_L(e)$ dropped from 1.60×10^{-5} to 1.08×10^{-6} in 150 training epochs.

A spatially dependent switching gain $k \equiv k(x_1, u)$ was defined from the cumulative uncertainty bound:

$$k(x_1, u) = \max \{|F_L(x_1, u)|, |F_H(x_1, u)|\} \tag{5.34}$$

Where $F_L(x_1, u)$ and $F_H(x_1, u)$ represent the lower and upper uncertainty bounds (99% confidence intervals) between the model (5.18) and experimental plant (Fig. 5.2), learned without knowledge of the true plant dynamics. This experimentally derived switching gain surface is shown in Fig. 5.23. Note that these bounds are tight near the center of the (x_1, u) operating space, indicating that the model is accurate in these regions. These bounds are typically higher in peripheral regions, primarily due to modeling errors.

The augmented SMC law is now

$$u = \sqrt{\frac{x_1^2(-\lambda(x_{2d} - x_2) - \dot{x}_{2d} + 9.81)}{-2.56 \times 10^{-6}}} - k(x_1, u) \cdot \text{sign}((x_{2d} - x_2))$$
$$+ 1000(x_{1d} - x_1)) \tag{5.35}$$

This intelligent control algorithm was implemented on the experimental test rig, with typical results presented in Fig. 5.24. The tracking performance is good, as the peak tracking error $(x_{1d} - x_1)$ remains less than 1.0 mm. It is even better than the constant-gain experiment, with a 34% reduction in MSTE (to 1.25×10^{-9} m^2). It is worth noting that this improved performance has been achieved with reduced control activity, a direct benefit of more accurate uncertainty bounds. Figure 5.24 clearly shows that switching excursions are minimal in regions where the model uncertainty is small. The result is a 19% reduction in MSCI compared to the fixed-gain demonstration (to 25.10 A^2).

5.7 FUSION OF SOFT COMPUTING AND HARD COMPUTING

The examples presented in this chapter clearly illustrate the benefits of fused soft-computing and hard-computing methodologies to robust control synthesis. Despite the significant differences in H_∞ and sliding mode control theory, the performance of both hard-computing methods depends heavily on accurate model uncertainty

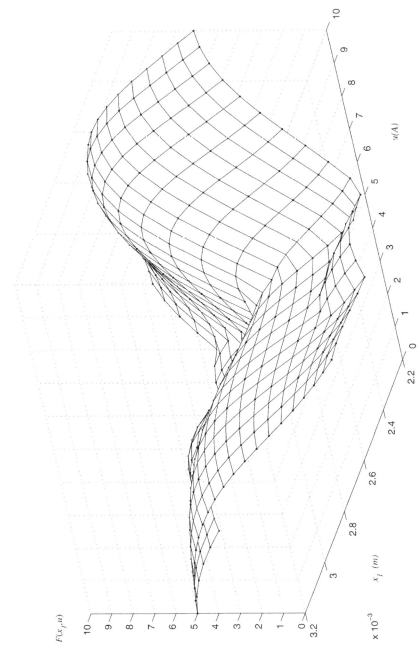

Figure 5.23. Cumulative uncertainty bound (99% confidence interval) between the model (5.18) and AMB test rig (Fig. 5.2).

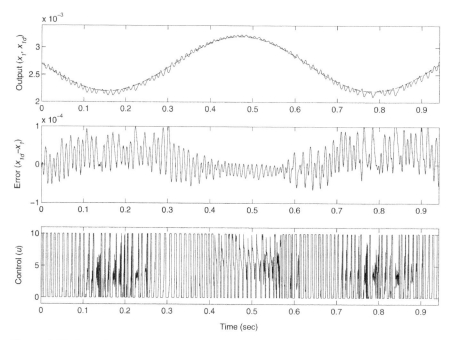

Figure 5.24. Experimental tracking performance and control activity for SMC with spatially dependent scheduled gain.

bounds. The control synthesis examples presented here show that excellent tracking performance can be achieved using low-order HC models in parallel with simple SC error models (Fig. 5.20). Thus, the primary fusion category of this approach is soft computing and hard computing in parallel (SC/HC), as defined in Chapter 1 of this text. Specifically, the SC estimation of uncertainty bounds, provided by CINs, complements the behavior and capabilities of HC control algorithms. The potential performance benefits to self-adapting controllers, in which SC uncertainty bounds are updated and HC controller gains are resynthesized on-line, are obvious and far-reaching.

Although HC techniques (like the model error modeling (MEM) approach [22]) have been developed for bounding model uncertainty, these require extensive intervention on the part of the control designer, have significant computational requirements, and are therefore difficult to implement in a self-adapting fashion. The fused approaches presented here directly address the principal requirements essential for widespread adoption of technology discussed in Chapter 1:

- Scalable results
- Practicality
- Little models or theory

Although the application considered in this chapter was a single-input, single-output AMB, research is currently underway at North Carolina State University to scale these results to a five-input, five-output flexible rotor AMB. It is expected that accurate, SC error models will enable the use of relatively low-order, HC rotor dynamic models and associated controllers.

5.8   CONCLUSION

A novel soft-computing approach has been demonstrated to estimate bounds of model uncertainty resulting from parameter variations, unmodeled dynamics, and nondeterministic processes in dynamic plants. This approach uses confidence interval networks, neural networks trained using asymmetric bilinear error cost functions, to estimate confidence intervals associated with nominal models for linear and nonlinear robust control synthesis. This research couples the hard-computing features of H_∞ and sliding mode control with the soft-computing characteristics of intelligent system identification, and it realizes the combined advantages of both. Simulations and experimental demonstrations conducted on an active magnetic bearing test rig confirm these capabilities.

ACKNOWLEDGMENTS

This work was supported by the National Science Foundation, grant ECS-0093101. The author would like to thank Dr. Paul Werbos (Control, Networks & Computational Intelligence Program Director, National Science Foundation) and Dr. Benito Fernandez (Department of Mechanical Engineering, The University of Texas at Austin) for their insightful suggestions and assistance in conducting this research.

REFERENCES

1. K. Zhou and J. Doyle, *Essentials of Robust Control*, Prentice-Hall, Upper Saddle River, NJ, 1998.
2. V. I. Utkin, *Sliding Modes in Control Optimization*, Springer-Verlag, Berlin, Germany, 1992.
3. J. E. Slotine and W. Li, *Applied Nonlinear Control*, Prentice-Hall, Englewood Cliffs, NJ, 1991.
4. D. C. Karnopp, D. L. Margolis, and R. C. Rosenberg, *System Dynamics: A Unified Approach*, Wiley-Interscience, New York, 1990.
5. L. Ljung and T. Glad, *Modeling of Dynamic Systems*, Prentice-Hall, Englewood Cliffs, NJ, 1994.
6. D. J. Ewins, *Modal Testing: Theory, Practice and Application*, 2nd ed., Research Studies Press, Philadelphia, 2000.
7. L. Ljung, *System Identification: Theory for the User*, Prentice-Hall, Englewood Cliffs, NJ, 1987.

8. K. S. Narendra and K. Parthasarathy, "Identification and Control of Dynamical Systems Using Neural Networks," *IEEE Transactions on Neural Networks* **1**, 4–27 (1990).

9. J. Sjöberg, H. Hjalmarsson, and L. Ljung, "Neural Networks in System Identification," *Proceedings of the IFAC System Identification Symposium*, Copenhagen, Denmark, July 1994, pp. 359–382.

10. D. A. White and D. A. Sofge, *Handbook of Intelligent Control: Neural, Fuzzy, and Adaptive Approaches*, Van Nostrand Reinhold, New York, 1992.

11. G. C. Goodwin and M. Salgado, "A Stochastic Embedding Approach for Quantifying Uncertainty in Estimation of Restricted Complexity Models," *International Journal of Adaptive Control and Signal Processing* **3**, 333–356 (1989).

12. B. Wahlberg and L. Ljung, "Hard Frequency-Domain Model Error Bounds from Least Squares Like Identification Techniques," *IEEE Transactions on Automatic Control* **37**, 900–912 (1992).

13. A. Garulli and W. Reinelt, "On Model Error Modeling in Set Membership Identification," *Proceedings of the IFAC System Identification Symposium*, Santa Barbara, CA, June 2000, pp. WeMD 1–3.

14. L. Giarre, M. Milanese, and M. Taragna, "H_∞ Identification and Model Quality Evaluation," *IEEE Transactions on Automatic Control* **42**, 188–199 (1997).

15. W. Reinelt, A. Garulli, and L. Ljung, "Comparing Different Approaches to Model Error Modeling in Robust Identification," *Automatica* **38**, 787–803 (2002).

16. G. D. Buckner, H. Zhang, and N. S. Gibson, "Confidence Interval Networks for Random Data Distributions," *IEEE Transactions on Neural Networks*, submitted.

17. M. A. Pichot, J. P. Kajs, B. R. Murphy, A. Ouroua, B. M. Rech, J. H. Beno, G. D. Buckner, and B. Palazzolo, "Active Magnetic Bearings for Energy Storage Systems for Combat Vehicles," *IEEE Transactions on Magnetics* **37**, 318–323 (2001).

18. G. D. Buckner, A. Palazzolo, J. Kajs, B. Murphy, and J. Beno, "Control System for Inside-Out Configuration Active Magnetic Bearings," *Proceedings of the 5th International Symposium on Magnetic Suspension Technology*, Santa Barbara, CA, Dec. 1999.

19. K. Nonami and T. Ito, "μ-Synthesis of Flexible Rotor-Magnetic Bearing Systems," *IEEE Transactions on Control Systems Technology* **4**, 503–512 (1996).

20. W. M. Cui and K. Nonami, "H_∞ Control of Flexible Rotor Magnetic Bearing Systems," *Proceedings of the 3rd International Symposium on Magnetic Bearings*, Alexandria, VA, 1992, pp. 505–512.

21. A. E. Fitzgerald, C. Kingsley Jr., and S. D. Umans, *Electric Machinery*, 5th ed., McGraw-Hill, New York, 1990.

22. L. Ljung, "Model Validation and Model Error Modeling," *Proceedings of the Åström Symposium on Control*, Lund, Sweden, Aug. 1999, pp. 15–42.

23. *Merriam-Webster's Collegiate Dictionary*, WWW page, 2003. Available from <http://www.merriam-webstercollegiate.com>.

24. S. Haykin, *Neural Networks: A Comprehensive Foundation*, Prentice-Hall, Englewood Cliffs, NJ, 1985.

25. G. Cybenko, "Approximations by Superpositions of Sigmoidal Functions," *Mathematics of Control, Signals, and Systems* **2**, 303–314 (1989).

26. K. Hornik, M. Stinchcombe, and H. White, "Multilayer Feedforward Networks are Universal Approximators," *Neural Networks* **2**, 359–366 (1989).

27. D. Rumelhart, G. Hinton, and R. Williams, "Learning Internal Representations by Error Propagation," in D. E. Rumelhart and J. L. McClelland, eds., *Parallel Distributed Processing: Explorations in the Microstructure of Cognition*, MIT Press, Cambridge, MA, 1986, pp. 318–362.

EDITOR'S INTRODUCTION TO CHAPTER 6

Tool wear monitoring plays an important role in metal-cutting manufacturing processes using tools with defined cutting edges (such as drilling, milling, and turning). If metal machining continues with a considerably worn tool, the quality of workpieces will first degrade, and eventually they will no longer be of any use. Automatic or semiautomatic tool wear monitoring systems should be able to provide master machinists information that allows them to make "optimal" decisions about tool replacement [1]. Such accurate and timely decisions are needed for maximizing the usage time of expensive machining tools as well as minimizing the amount of production waste—that is, machined parts that do not meet the quality specifications (e.g., geometric measures or surface requirements).

Accurate and reliable tool wear estimation is usually a difficult task, because the machining processes are nonlinear and time-varying, and the environmental conditions may change drastically in a workshop or factory. To overcome these difficulties, several schemes for wear monitoring of machining tools have been proposed in the literature. For example, Fish et al. introduced a hidden Markov models (HMMs)-based multilevel classification scheme of milling tool wear [1]; Li et al. used an adaptive neuro-fuzzy inference system (ANFIS) for on-line estimation of cutting forces in a metal turning process [2]; and Li et al. applied wavelet transforms and fuzzy logic to monitor wear conditions and tool breakage in drilling operations [3]. Advanced tool wear estimation schemes are based on the use of multiple methodologies—both soft computing (SC) and hard computing (HC).

Chapter 6 of the present book, "Indirect On-Line Tool Wear Monitoring," is authored by Bernhard Sick. It gives first a pragmatic introduction to the turning

Computationally Intelligent Hybrid Systems. Edited by Seppo J. Ovaska
ISBN 0-471-47668-4 © 2005 the Institute of Electrical and Electronics Engineers, Inc.

process and presents a generic framework of tool wear monitoring systems. Before proposing a hybrid approach for indirect wear estimation of turning tools, Chapter 6 provides an insightful discussion on the state-of-the-art tool wear monitoring techniques that use the complementary fusion of hard computing (physical models) and soft computing (empirical models). Finally, the new approach is carefully detailed, and its performance is verified by illustrative experiments.

Various neural-network-based approaches have been developed for tool wear estimation during the past decade. Altogether, 12 supervised and six unsupervised network paradigms are summarized in the overview part of Chapter 6. In almost all the reported hybrid schemes, the fusions of SC and HC are cascade connections with moderate fusion grade (Chapter 1).

The new hybrid approach for tool wear monitoring contains the following three functional levels:

1. Measurement preprocessing
2. Feature extraction
3. Wear estimation

Levels 1 and 2 are using pure hard-computing techniques, while level 3 is a time-delay neural network (TDNN) that takes feature vectors as its inputs and computes a flank wear estimate. The TDNN topology is preferred here, because its feed-forward structure with tapped delay lines provides the necessary dynamics without possible threat of instability. On the other hand, physical force models of machining processes with defined cutting edges are used in the preprocessing stage. The core motivation behind this fusion scheme is to combine analytical domain knowledge originating from simple physical models (HC) with empirical knowledge learned by dynamic neural networks (SC) using training examples that roughly describe the turning process. And the applied fusion structures are HC-SC or SC-HC (Chapter 1).

In the experimental part, Sick demonstrates the operation and performance of the developed methods by five experiments. Also, the alternative use of a multilayer perceptron (MLP) instead of the TDNN was studied in these experiments:

1. Average values of unnormalized force signals as inputs to MLP
2. Five cutting conditions as additional inputs to MLP
3. Unnormalized force signals as inputs to TDNN
4. Normalized force signals as inputs to MLP
5. Normalized force signals as inputs to TDNN

When comparing the identification rates and maximum estimation errors for a test data, it can be concluded that the time-delay neural network with normalized force signals (experiment 5) provided the best identification rates and lowest values of maximum estimation errors.

Neither pure HC approaches nor pure SC approaches would likely be able to estimate the flank wear of a tool (i.e., the most important wear parameter) with the same precision and reliability as the proposed computationally intelligent hybrid system.

Thus, it can be emphasized once again that before soft-computing methods are taken in applications use, it is recommended to utilize carefully the available domain knowledge. Moreover, to be able to compensate for common uncertainties of physical and analytical models, the use of soft-computing techniques should definitely be considered as a viable extension.

REFERENCES

1. R. K. Fish, M. Ostendorf, G. D. Bernard, and D. A. Castanon, "Multilevel Classification of Milling Tool Wear with Confidence Estimation," *IEEE Transactions on Pattern Analysis and Machine Intelligence* **25**, 75–85 (2003).

2. X. Li, A. Djordjevich, and P. K. Venuvinod, "Current-Sensor-Based Feed Cutting Force Intelligent Estimation and Tool Wear Condition Monitoring," *IEEE Transactions on Industrial Electronics* **47**, 697–702 (2000).

3. X. Li, S. K. Tso, and J. Wang, "Real-Time Tool Condition Monitoring Using Wavelet Transforms and Fuzzy Techniques," *IEEE Transactions on Systems, Man, and Cybernetics—Part C: Applications and Reviews* **30**, 352–357 (2000).

CHAPTER 6

INDIRECT ON-LINE TOOL WEAR MONITORING

BERNHARD SICK

Micro-Hybrid Electronics GmbH, Hermsdorf, Germany

6.1 INTRODUCTION

Metal-cutting manufacturing processes like drilling, milling, or turning can be optimized significantly utilizing flexible and reliable tool wear monitoring systems. The most important tasks in this context are:

- Fast detection of collisions—that is, unintended contacts between the tool or the tool holder and the workpiece or components of the machine tool
- Identification of tool fracture (breakage)—for example, outbreaks at brittle cutting edges
- Estimation or classification of tool wear caused by abrasion, erosion, or other influences

While collision and tool fracture are sudden and mostly unexpected events that require immediate reactions, the development of wear is slowly proceeding until the end of the tool's lifetime, when outbreaks at the cutting edges occur. This chapter focuses on the determination of wear, the most difficult of the three tasks.

The importance of tool wear monitoring is implied by the possible economic advantages. By replacing worn tools in time, it is possible to avoid the production of waste. Additionally, tool costs can be reduced significantly with a precise exploitation of a tool's lifetime. With an accurate estimation of a current tool wear state, it might even be possible to (a) adjust the tool position in order to meet geometric specifications and (b) control the tool wear rate in order to guarantee a desired surface quality of the workpiece.

Computationally Intelligent Hybrid Systems. Edited by Seppo J. Ovaska
ISBN 0-471-47668-4 © 2005 the Institute of Electrical and Electronics Engineers, Inc.

Today's approaches in the area of tool wear monitoring usually measure different process parameters which are *indirectly* correlated with tool wear (such as force, acoustic emission, temperature, or vibration signals) [1]. These signals are measured *on-line*—that is, during a cutting process. The process itself is influenced by various cutting conditions such as tool geometry or work material and also by many kinds of disturbances (see Fig. 6.1).

Very often, either analytical models based on physical laws (that describe the process behavior during cutting) or empirical models (such as neural networks or fuzzy systems) based on experimentally obtained observations of the process behavior are used to model the nonlinear dependencies between features (extracted from the measured signals) and cutting conditions on the one hand and tool wear on the other hand. That is, wear models are built using either hard- or soft-computing techniques. Initially, the focus of international research was put on the former group of techniques. The latter group is investigated intensively during about one decade. However, particularly due to insufficient generalization capabilities (e.g., the use is restricted to a specific machine tool or a specific combination of work material and tool coating, only a small range of cutting conditions is allowed, or time-consuming "teach-in" cycles are needed) or a lack of precision, even promising methods are not marketable up to now.

Why is tool wear monitoring such a difficult task? An answer is provided by reference 2: "Firstly, many machining processes are non-linear time-variant systems, which makes them difficult to model, and secondly, the signals obtained from sensors are dependent on a number of other factors, such as machining

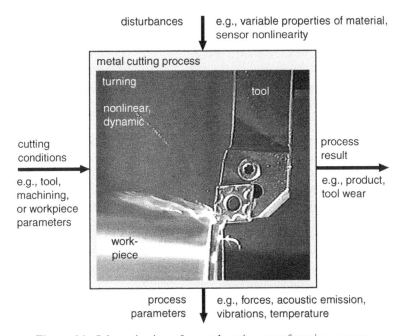

Figure 6.1. Schematic view of a metal-cutting manufacturing process.

conditions . . . ." Apart from the complexity of the process and the large number of machining conditions (i.e., cutting conditions), there are also many disturbing influences [3]: "Signals from sensors in machine tools are disturbed for many reasons: outbreaks at cutting edges, chatter (i.e., self-excited vibrations), variances of the tool geometry or of the properties of the work material, sensor nonlinearity, noise of digitizers, crosstalk effects between sensor channels, etc." In reference 4 it is stated that ". . . time series data obtained from the sensors are usually noise laden due to non-homogeneities in the workpiece material and electric interference during the signal transmission through cables and instrumentation . . . ."

Here, we present a new and efficient method for on-line, indirect tool wear estimation in turning that fuses a physical model (*HC: hard-computing part*) with a neural network model (*SC: soft-computing part*) in order to improve the results of the estimation significantly. The main ideas of this approach are not restricted to turning processes, but could also be applied to many other process monitoring tasks in a more or less straightforward way.

The *physical model* establishes a nonlinear, static relationship between cutting conditions and certain process parameters and allows a normalization of the measured signals in order to separate signal changes caused by cutting conditions from signal changes caused by tool wear. This technique deals with "sharp" knowledge originating from an *analytical* understanding of the physics of metal cutting. The *neural network model* establishes a nonlinear, dynamic relationship between the normalized signals and the wear state of the tool in order to obtain a continuous estimate of a certain wear parameter. That technique uses "fuzzy" (uncertain) knowledge originating from *empirical* observations of the cutting process. It will be shown that this *cascaded combination* of hard- and soft-computing techniques (HC-SC; cf. Chapter 1) provides significantly better results than either a pure hard-computing or a pure soft-computing approach. Also, various other approaches that fuse physical and neural network models for on-line, indirect tool wear monitoring in turning will be investigated.

The remainder of this chapter is structured as follows:

- Section 6.2 gives more information about the turning process and presents a generic architecture of tool wear monitoring systems that is used to categorize existing tool wear monitoring approaches.
- Section 6.3 deals with the state of the art in on-line, indirect tool wear monitoring in turning. The focus of this section is on a review of approaches that also combine physical and neural network models.
- Section 6.4 describes the new, hybrid approach, which was briefly introduced above, in greater detail.
- Results of several experiments demonstrating the advantages of this approach are given in Section 6.5.
- Section 6.6 relates the fusion technique used here to the structural categories identified in Chapter 1.
- Section 6.7 summarizes the most important results and points out some useful suggestions for the solution of comparable problems.

6.2   PROBLEM DESCRIPTION AND MONITORING ARCHITECTURE

In this section, the turning process is described in more detail and a generic architecture for tool wear monitoring systems is introduced. A detailed description of metal-cutting manufacturing processes can be found in [5,6], for instance. Some of the most important terms used here are informally described in Figs. 6.2 and 6.3.

A turning process is influenced by *cutting conditions* such as feed rate, workpiece material, or tool geometry. Table 6.1 summarizes the most important of these conditions together with the corresponding variables and their values in the cutting experiments that have been available for our investigations (see Fig.6.2, as well).

The main result of a turning process is, of course, the machined workpiece with its geometry, surface roughness, and so on. Another process result, however, is tool wear. Tool wear is caused by abrasion, erosion, diffusion, or various other influences. *Wear parameters* are used to describe the wear at the major flank, the minor flank, or the rake face of a tool. The most important wear parameters (from the viewpoint of monitoring) are the width of flank wear land at the major flank (VB; see Fig. 6.3) and the crater depth at the rake face (KT) [7]. According to reference 1, tool wear monitoring systems aim to do the following:

1. Estimate the current values of one or several wear parameters.
2. Classify the wear state of the tool (usually defined by means of one or several of these wear parameters).
3. Estimate the tool's lifetime directly.

In the first and the second cases, an appropriate tool change policy can be established easily. An adaptive control of cutting conditions is possible in the first case only.

Most tool wear monitoring systems (apart from a few sensorless approaches) use signals of *process parameters* to assess the tool state. The most important process parameters are cutting forces in three orthogonal directions (main cutting force, feed force, and thrust force), acoustic emission, and vibrations. Cutting forces during a cylindrical turning process are shown in Fig. 6.2; vibrations of the tool or the tool holder can also be measured in the same three orthogonal directions. Acoustic emission is a substrate-borne, high-frequency sound (in metal-cutting up to several megahertz) in contrast to audible (airborne) sound. These indirect monitoring parameters are correlated with tool wear. Usually, several process parameters are measured in indirect and continuous (on-line) tool wear monitoring systems. The information from different sensors (and additional domain-specific information provided by the user of the machine tool or by database systems, for example) has to be combined in order to get an accurate estimate of the tool state. The general advantages of sensor fusion can be summarized as follows [8]: "The main advantages are an increased confidence (due to statistical advantages), reduced ambiguity and, therefore, a robust operational performance and an improved precision. In some

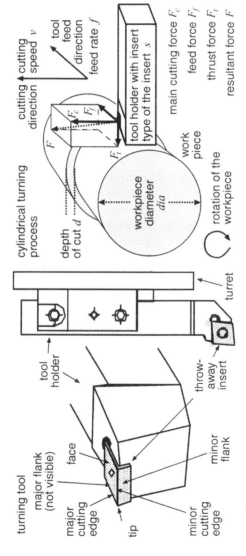

Figure 6.2. Turning tool, cutting conditions, and process parameters (cylindrical turning process).

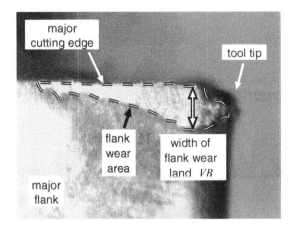

Figure 6.3. Wear parameters of an insert.

applications an extended temporal and spatial coverage and an increased dimensionality (e.g., measuring different spectral bands) are also important." In general, a sensor fusion system consists of several levels.

A generic architecture which can be used to categorize tool wear monitoring systems is described in reference 1 (see Fig. 6.4). Sensor fusion techniques may be applied at any level of this architecture. Additional information provided by a database system or user inputs may also be considered. Different *disturbances*

TABLE 6.1. Nomenclature and Variation of Cutting Conditions

	Machining Parameters	
Depth of cut	d	0.8–4.0 mm
Feed rate	f	0.15–0.5 mm/rev
Cutting speed	v	200–340 m/min
	Tool Parameters	
Type of the insert	s	CPX (aluminium oxide on hard metal),
(coating and substrate)		CL4 (titanium nitride on hard metal),
		PS5 (titanium nitride on cermet)
Clearance angle	α	6°
Rake angle	γ	−6°
Cutting edge inclination angle	λ	−6°
Cutting edge angle	κ	95°
Tool included angle	ε	80°
Corner radius	r_ε	0.8 mm
	Workpiece Parameters	
Work material	*wm*	Steel Ck45
Workpiece diameter	*dia*	22–101 mm
	Other Parameters	
Coolant	*coo*	None

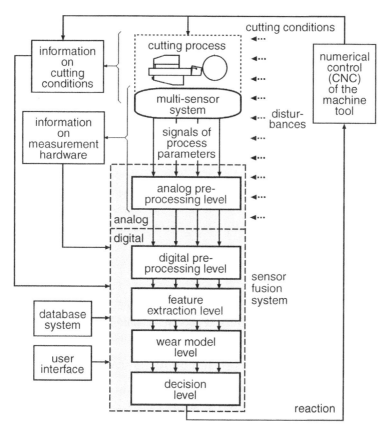

Figure 6.4. Generic architecture of a tool wear monitoring system.

were already mentioned above. The five levels of this architecture can be characterized as follows:

- *Analog preprocessing* deals with the preparation of raw data before digitization.
  Signals of one sensor can be used to align the signals of another sensor, for
  instance (e.g., in order to eliminate undesired temperature influences).
- At the *digital preprocessing* level the information contents of the digitized data
  are increased using, for example, digital filters or secondary information on the
  behavior of analog or digital hardware or on influences of cutting conditions on
  certain sensor signals. Examples are the linearization of a characteristic curve
  of a sensor or the alignment of a sensor signal by means of a process model that
  describes the influence of cutting conditions.
- The *feature extraction* condenses the remaining information in a few wear-
  sensitive values that can be used as inputs of a wear model at the following level.

- A *wear model* establishes a relationship between wear-sensitive features and a decision on the tool state (e.g., a wear estimate or class). The publications that will be investigated here use either neural network or physical models for this task.
- Based on an output of the wear model, the monitoring system introduces appropriate measures (reactions) at the *decision* level. Some methods applied at this level take the output of the model level as a preliminary result and combine several of these preliminary results to come to a final conclusion.

It can be noticed that most of the systems do not use methods at each level (see reference 1 for more details).

6.3 STATE OF THE ART

Describing the state of the art, this section focuses on approaches that combine physical models (HC) with neural network models (SC) for indirect, on-line tool wear monitoring in turning. It turns out that there exist a few approaches only. On the other hand, there are many methods that use either physical or neural models. The disadvantages of these pure HC and pure SC techniques are pointed out first.

6.3.1 Monitoring Techniques Based on Analytical Models

In this section, the disadvantages of techniques that are exclusively based on physical models are pointed out. *Sensorless* techniques aim to describe the dependencies between cutting conditions on the one hand and the tool's lifetime or wear on the other hand without considering any process parameters. *Sensor-based* approaches use additional information on the current values of process parameters. First, some of the most important of these pure HC approaches are described. Subsequently, the disadvantages of a pure physical approach are summarized. Some more references to related publications can be found in reference 9.

Examples for Sensorless Methods. A well-known approach for the estimation of a tool's lifetime is Taylor's tool life equation (see, e.g., reference 7). This equation establishes a rough relationship between the cutting speed v (see Table 6.1) and the lifetime T of the tool as follows:

$$v \cdot T^{-\frac{1}{k}} = C \tag{6.1}$$

where C and k are constants that have to be determined experimentally. Two additional cutting conditions (feed rate f and depth of cut d) are considered in the extended Taylor equation

$$v = C \cdot f^E \cdot d^F \cdot T^G \cdot (VB_{\max})^H \tag{6.2}$$

mentioned in reference 10. The constants C, E, F, G, and H have to be determined experimentally; VB_{max} is the width of flank wear land (major flank) at the end of the lifetime. Often, a value of $VB_{max} = 0.5$ mm is considered useful (cf. the recommendations of the International Organization for Standardization [7]).

A physical model of the cutting process that uses the cutting conditions v, f, d, and γ (rake angle) as inputs and the tool wear (wear land) as an output is described in reference 11. The vertical cutting force and the tool temperature are internal variables of this model. The internal variables need not be measured. The dependencies between inputs and internal variables on the one hand and between internal variables and the output of the model on the other hand are defined by means of a set of equations, some of them being first-order differential equations. Putting all these equations together, the overall model is nonlinear. It considers abrasion wear as well as diffusion wear. A linearized version of the model allows the prediction of tool life. However, constants of the model have to be determined experimentally, and the approach is applicable to steel turning with carbide tools only.

Examples for Sensor-Based Methods. A technique that monitors the tool wear through measurements of the cutting force is introduced in [12]. It is mentioned that changes in cutting conditions will have two effects: A *direct effect* causes an immediate change in the cutting force when a cutting condition is changed—for example, whenever the feed rate f is increased. Furthermore, an increasing f has a significant impact on the wear rate which raises, too. This is called an *indirect effect*. The approach aims to separate direct from indirect effects. The cutting force is estimated by means of a physical model. Cutting conditions like f, d, and v are the inputs of this model and flank wear is the internal state. Again, the overall model is nonlinear and partly described by first order differential equations. The unknown coefficients of the model are estimated on-line by means of a recursive least-squares algorithm. For that, the estimated cutting force has to be compared to the actually measured cutting force. Using the estimation error, coefficients which are related to direct effects are determined in a first step. Subsequently, the remaining coefficients related to indirect effects are computed. With this on-line parameter estimation, flank wear could be tracked during cutting. Results are, however, not presented.

In reference 13 a dynamic state model of tool wear is proposed, too. This physical model uses the cutting force as an output and f as an input. Flank wear (caused by abrasion or diffusion) and crater wear as well as the tool-work temperature on the flank and the maximum tool-chip interface temperature are the internal variables. Coefficients of the model are adopted from a large number of investigations published earlier. A linearized version can be used to develop an adaptive observer for tool wear estimation.

A physical model "that allows the calculation of the absolute wear rates of tool materials from basic physical property data" is presented in reference 14. The model considers abrasive wear (dominant at low cutting temperatures) as well as dissolution wear (dominant at high cutting temperatures). The abrasive wear rate and the dissolution wear rate, respectively, are defined as functions of v. Some of the parameters in the given formulas depend on the cutting temperature that is monitored in-process using the chip-tool thermocouple technique.

Ultrasound waves for tool wear monitoring in turning are used in reference 15. A physical model describes the dependencies between a change in the tool geometry caused by tool wear and a "change in the acoustic behavior of ultrasound waves inside the body of the cutting tools." The main idea of this approach is that an increase of tool wear changes the orientation of a reflecting surface. Therefore, the areas and the orientation of reflecting surfaces are used as input parameters of a physical model that considers the propagation and reflection of the ultrasound waves. Changes of the acoustic properties of the tool material due to an increase in the tool temperature during cutting are eliminated by means of a reference signal.

Disadvantages of Pure Physical Approaches. As a summary, it can be noticed that the experience with pure physical wear models is very poor: Reference 16, for example, states in a comparison with other models: "The cutting process is inherently very complex. The complete understanding of the physics of the process is practically difficult. For this reason analytical models fail to accurately describe the cutting process." Two fundamental disadvantages can be given:

1. Constants of the models have to be determined experimentally again and again for particular combinations of cutting conditions (e.g., tool and work materials).
2. Some models are based on input signals that cannot be measured or that can be measured with greatest efforts only (e.g., the temperature at the cutting edge).

Many other investigations come to comparable conclusions. Therefore, an application of pure physical wear models to tool wear monitoring seems to be impractical.

6.3.2 Monitoring Techniques Based on Neural Networks

In this section, disadvantages of techniques that are exclusively based on neural network models will be pointed out. A comprehensive review of 138 publications dealing with on-line and indirect tool wear monitoring in turning by means of neural networks (NN) is set out in reference 1. Table 6.2 shows the network paradigms that are used in these publications in a descending order according to their frequency in the two categories of supervised and unsupervised paradigms. MLPs are used in about 70% of the publications.

In the following, a few pure SC approaches using neural networks will be described. Additional examples are cited in reference 1. Subsequently, disadvantages of a pure neural approach will be summarized.

TABLE 6.2. Network Paradigms Used for Tool Wear Monitoring

	Supervised Network Paradigms
MLP	Multilayer Perceptron
RNN	Recurrent Neural Network (*Group of paradigms*)
NFS-S	Supervised Neuro-Fuzzy System (*Group of paradigms*)
TDNN	Time-Delay Neural Network
SLP	Single-Layer Perceptron
RBF	Radial Basis Function Network
CPROP	Counterpropagation Network
CNNN	Condensed Nearest-Neighbor Network
WNN	Wavelet Neural Network
CSOM	Classifying Self-Organizing Map
LRF	Localized Receptive Fields Network
LVQ	Learning Vector Quantization
	Unsupervised Network Paradigms
ART	Adaptive Resonance Theory (*Group of paradigms*)
KFM	Kohonen Feature Map
SCBC	Single-Category-Based Classifier
CL	Competitive Learning (*Group of paradigms*)
NFS-U	Unsupervised Neuro-Fuzzy System (*Group of paradigms*)
NEM	Nonparametric Empirical Modeling

Examples for Neural Network Approaches. The majority of the 138 publications evaluated in reference 1 uses a neural network at the wear model level in order to estimate or to classify tool wear with the network's output. Inputs of such a network are characteristic features extracted from signals of process parameters and (sometimes) the current values of cutting conditions. A typical example for this approach is described in reference 17. There, the paradigms MLP, CSOM, FuzzyARTMAP (a fuzzy variant of ART), and NEFCLASS (neuro-fuzzy classifiers) are compared. In this comparison, MLP outperforms the other network paradigms.

An alternative approach is described in references 18 and 19: The cutting process is considered to be a nonlinear, dynamic system that can be modeled by means of a hierarchical combination of static (MLP) and dynamic (RNN) neural networks. This system is characterized as "a state space representation of the turning process" [19]. Outputs of the system are either forces or force ratios, and inputs are different cutting conditions. Wear parameters (such as flank, nose, crater, or notch wear) are internal states of this system and ". . . the neural networks act as a nonlinear observer for estimating wear components (nonobservable states), using cutting forces (observable outputs), and cutting conditions (inputs)" [18]. Basically, this approach can be regarded as a finite-state machine (FSM) with a Moore-type output function.

Another method that considers the current values of cutting conditions is proposed in reference 20. There, the computation of some of the features is based on an empirical model of the cutting process. The spindle revolutions and the spindle motor current are measured at the main drive, and the speed in feed direction and the motor current are measured at the two feed drives. The cutting process is modeled by means of dynamic first- and second-order systems that use the spindle revolutions or the speed in a feed direction as inputs and the corresponding motor current as an output. Internal parameters of this system, like temporal constants or amplification factors, are estimated by means of a recursive least-squares algorithm. These parameters are sensitive to tool wear and used, together with some other features, as inputs of a neuro-fuzzy model that estimates the wear state. The advantage of this method is that the influence of v and f in the features is more or less eliminated. Nevertheless, the influence of other cutting conditions such as d or tool geometry remains and is not considered appropriately.

It seems to be an obvious solution to use dynamic systems for the supervision of a dynamic process like a cutting process. However, only a few publications suggest the use of dynamic network paradigms. An important reason for the abdication of dynamic models is that many researchers avoid the financial and temporal effort that is necessary to obtain data to set up a dynamic model. Another possible reason is that stability problems arise in many solutions based on recurrent systems. In reference 16, for example, recurrent networks are used at the decision level. Due to stability problems, the output of these networks and the difference of two subsequent values in a feedback connection have to be limited.

Disadvantages of Pure Neural Network Approaches. As a summary, it can be noticed that the experience with pure neural network wear models is very poor, too. Process-specific information and temporal information are not used in an appropriate way [1]. Process-specific information includes any information on cutting conditions—that is, information on their current values and their influence on the measured process parameters. Temporal information includes any kind of information related to a time series (e.g., the consecutive values of a signal, its trend in a certain time window, etc.).

It is well known that process parameters are influenced by cutting conditions. However, process-specific information is not used in about 39% of the publications. Forty-six percent of the publications use cutting conditions as additional input features—that is, as inputs of a neural network at the wear model level. If networks with or without cutting conditions as inputs are compared, very often only minor improvements or even deteriorations of the results can be noticed. Obviously, the networks are not able to model the dependencies between cutting conditions and process parameters in an appropriate way. An additional problem is a possible overfitting effect: With cutting conditions used as additional inputs, the number of weights within the network increases significantly. The number of available training patterns, on the other hand, is usually strictly limited.

The temporal development of process parameters is usually not considered in an appropriate way and is very often even neglected. Many of the publications that use temporal information recognize problems—for example, with recurrent networks (e.g., stability problems) or with the current lifetime used as an input feature (e.g., overfitting effects). Only a few publications investigate possible reasons for these problems. However, it should be emphasized that the use of temporal information only makes sense if the cutting conditions remain constant (which is, of course, not close to reality) or if the influence of varying cutting conditions can be detected in order to separate signal changes caused by cutting conditions from signal changes caused by wear. A detailed discussion of the problems mentioned can be found in reference 1.

6.3.3 Monitoring Techniques Based on Fusion of Physical and Neural Network Models

In this section, we provide an overview of methods that combine physical and neural models for indirect, on-line tool wear monitoring in turning. The approaches are categorized using the generic architecture (see Fig. 6.4) and their specific disadvantages are outlined.

Physical and Neural Network Models at Wear Model Level. A combination of a neural network (RBF) and a physical model is used in references 21 and 22 for a continuous wear estimation. The dependencies between cutting conditions, wear parameters, and force signals are modeled by means of a nonlinear, discrete, and dynamic system. Cutting conditions are the inputs, force signals are the outputs, and wear parameters are the internal states of this system.

The system can be characterized as a finite-state machine (FSM) with an output function. The state transition function of this Moore-type FSM (see Fig. 6.5) is nonlinear and dynamic, and the output function is nonlinear and static. The state transition function is implemented by means of an RBF network. This network is trained off-line with learning patterns that have been obtained by simulation or cutting experiments. For this purpose, a modified recursive least-squares algorithm (RLS) is used. The output function is realized by a very simple physical model (see, e.g., reference 23). Model parameters (constants of the cutting process) have to be determined experimentally. It is assumed that the input values of the system can be determined exactly. The values of states and outputs, however, are assumed to be superimposed by white noise describing measurement errors. The wear parameter

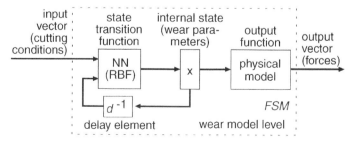

Figure 6.5. State space representation of the machining process.

that has to be determined is an internal state of the system. For system identification, a state estimator on the basis of a nonlinear filter is introduced [24]. In references 24–26, the method is derived step by step and tested with simulated data (obtained by means of physical models, see above) before it is used with real data in references 21 and 22. Results (estimates of the width of wear land and the crater depth) are presented in a graphical form that makes an assessment difficult. According to what the authors themselves state, the prediction of the crater depth is quite poor [22]. During the initial phase of a tool's lifetime, the system produces large errors such that an output limiter has to be introduced [21,26].

It can be stated that this approach suffers from the same stability problems as many other approaches based on recurrent networks. Moreover, it is not understandable why the relationships between wear parameters and forces are described by a static model.

In reference 10, a so-called cutting variable is estimated by means of a neural network (MLP or CNNN). Using Taylor's tool-life equation, specific formulas are defined that use this cutting variable in order to compute two estimates for the width of wear land and the remaining cutting length (see Fig. 6.6). The remaining cutting length can be interpreted as the length of cut for which the tool can be used further on under the assumption of constant values of cutting conditions (e.g., f or v) and a "normal" (i.e., average) wear behavior. Unfortunately, the article does not provide experimental results for the estimation of these parameters. The network that estimates the cutting variable cannot consider variable cutting conditions appropriately.

The approach mentioned in reference 27 is closely related to the techniques described so far, even if physical and neural network models are not combined with the objective of tool wear or lifetime estimation (see Fig. 6.7). The approach intends to predict and compensate for (a) static dimensional deviations of the workpiece and the machine tool caused by cutting forces and (b) dynamic deviations caused by tool wear (a displacement of the cutting edge). By means of an adaptive control of d, the method is supposed to reach the desired workpiece dimensions within low tolerances. A neural network is used at the model level in order to predict the flank wear at the minor flank and, therefore, to determine the displacement of the cutting edge. A physical model at the model level computes the current deformation of the workpiece and the machine tool using estimates of the cutting forces as inputs. Both estimates are combined at the decision level. The same approach is described in reference 28. It can be assumed that this approach suffers from the same problems as many other neural network approaches using cutting conditions as additional inputs.

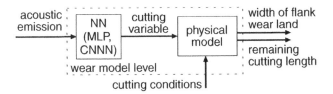

Figure 6.6. Estimation of flank wear and remaining cutting length.

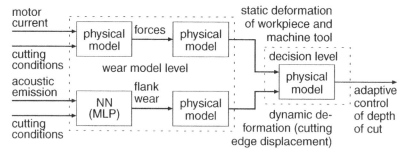

Figure 6.7. Adaptive control of the cutting process.

Physical Models at Wear Model Level and Neural Network Models at Decision Level. Complex dependencies between measured process parameters (forces in main and feed direction, acoustic emission, and temperature), cutting conditions (e.g., f, γ, and d), and a wear parameter are described by means of several physical models in reference 29. These models compute wear estimates that are used as inputs of an MLP network. The network produces a final estimate at the decision level (see Fig. 6.8). The same idea is mentioned in reference 30, where the networks at the decision level are compared to a least-squares regression technique and a group method of data handling (GMDH) approach. GMDH is a set of algorithms for different problems such as process identification, pattern recognition, or forecasting.

Obviously the physical models are not able to consider the influence of cutting conditions sufficiently, because the cutting conditions are used as additional inputs of the MLP network, too. Basically, this approach suffers from the same problems as the pure physical approaches cited above.

Neural Network Models at Wear Model Level and Physical Models at Decision Level. An interesting approach combines several methods within an expert system at the decision level (see Fig. 6.9): Reference 31 uses the ideas of a plausibility check (by means of Taylor's tool-life equation), a consideration of

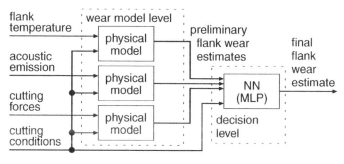

Figure 6.8. Fusion of results of several physical models with an MLP.

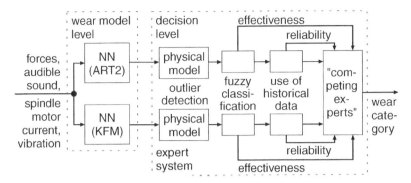

Figure 6.9. Expert system at the decision level.

past outputs of networks at the wear model level (ART2 and KFM, respectively), and a neural network ensemble (fusing the outputs of ART2 and KFM) for wear classification. The technique is described as follows [31]: "After feature extraction, the feature vector is presented to the neural networks which give their predictions based solely on sensory information. Tool life knowledge based on Taylor's equation predictions is then applied in order to eliminate most classifications that fall outside a confidence band around the empirical formulae prediction. Both neural networks are tested for tool wear evolution coherence and finally combined to give the final tool wear level prediction." The neural network ensemble technique (which is basically a "competing experts" approach) works as follows [31]: "If the ANNs agree on the state of the tool, or one reports an *unknown* state, a solution is possible, otherwise tool state will be resolved from a reliability perspective."

The plausibility check based on Taylor's tool life equation is also used in reference 2 in order to "remove illogical classifications by the neural networks." The same idea is mentioned (but not investigated) in reference 32. In this approach, the current values of cutting conditions are not considered in an appropriate way. Again, the networks at the wear model level cannot separate signal changes caused by cutting conditions from signal changes caused by wear.

6.4 NEW SOLUTION

In this section, we will explain our new, hybrid approach in more detail. Additional information can be found in references 33–35, for instance. Here, only the techniques applied at the digital preprocessing level and the wear model level are considered in order to focus on the fusion of HC and SC techniques.

6.4.1 Solution Outline

In order to overcome the two main drawbacks of pure neural network approaches (poor consideration of process-specific information and poor consideration of temporal information), the dependencies between cutting conditions and process parameters, on the one hand, and between process parameters, and tool wear, on the other hand, are described by two separate models. Figure 6.10 outlines this novel approach:

- At the *digital pre-processing level*, three physical process models are used to compute so-called correction factors. These factors describe the influence of variable cutting conditions on force signals (main cutting force F_c, feed force F_f, and thrust force F_t) with respect to fundamental (fixed) values of the cutting conditions. The correction factors are used to normalize the measured force signals—that is, to eliminate the influence of variable cutting conditions as far as possible.

- Techniques that can be applied at the *feature extraction level* are not investigated in this chapter (as well as techniques used at the analog preprocessing or the decision level; see Fig. 6.4). In order to demonstrate the advantages of the proposed methods, only the average values of the normalized force signals in a short time window are used here.

- At the *wear model level*, a dynamic but nonrecurrent neural network model continuously estimates the current value of the wear parameter "width of flank wear land," *VB*. For this task, a neural network (TDNN: time-delay neural network) uses the average values of the normalized force signals as inputs.

The physical force model at the digital preprocessing level and the dynamic neural network at the wear model level are described in the following two subsections.

6.4.2 Physical Force Model at Digital Preprocessing Level

The correction factors C_{F_c}, C_{F_f}, and C_{F_t} are derived from physical models of machining processes with defined cutting edges developed by Kienzle, Victor, and many other researchers during several decades (see, e.g., references 5 and 6).

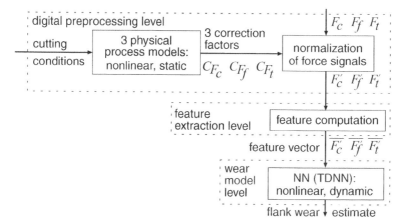

Figure 6.10. Outline of the new, hybrid approach.

These models also consider some cutting conditions (γ, λ, κ, and α, for instance) that are not varied in the cutting experiments that have been available for our investigations (see Table 6.1). Therefore, the correction factors are restricted to the parameters varied here, but they could easily be extended in order to consider the additional cutting conditions mentioned above.

The factors C_{F_c}, C_{F_f}, and C_{F_t} for the main cutting force, the feed force, and the thrust force, respectively, are defined as follows:

$$C_{F_c} \stackrel{\text{def}}{=} f_A \cdot f_h \cdot f_{s,v} \tag{6.3}$$

with

$$f_A \stackrel{\text{def}}{=} \frac{d \cdot f \cdot \sin 95°}{3 \text{ mm}^2}$$

$$f_h \stackrel{\text{def}}{=} \left(\frac{1 \text{ mm}}{\sin 95° \cdot f} \right)^{0.25} \tag{6.4}$$

$$f_{s,v} \stackrel{\text{def}}{=} \max \left\{ 0.85, \left(\frac{100 \text{ m/min}}{v} \right)^{0.1} \right\}$$

$$C_{F_f} \stackrel{\text{def}}{=} g_A \cdot g_h \cdot g_v \tag{6.5}$$

with

$$g_A \stackrel{\text{def}}{=} \frac{d \cdot f \cdot \sin 95°}{3 \text{ mm}^2}$$

$$g_h \stackrel{\text{def}}{=} \left(\frac{1 \text{ mm}}{\sin 95° \cdot f} \right)^{0.73} \tag{6.6}$$

$$g_v \stackrel{\text{def}}{=} \left(\frac{100 \text{ m/min}}{v} \right)^{0.35}$$

$$C_{F_t} \stackrel{\text{def}}{=} h_A \cdot h_h \tag{6.7}$$

with

$$h_A \stackrel{\text{def}}{=} \frac{d \cdot f \cdot \sin 95°}{3 \text{ mm}^2}$$

$$h_h \stackrel{\text{def}}{=} \left(\frac{1 \text{ mm}}{\sin 95° \cdot f} \right)^{0.34} \tag{6.8}$$

A detailed discussion of the meaning of various factors can be found in reference 36. The factor $f_{s,v}$, for example, describes the influence of s and v on the main cutting force with respect to a reference tool material and a fundamental value of the cutting speed (see Fig. 6.11). The factors f_A, g_A, and h_A describe the influence of

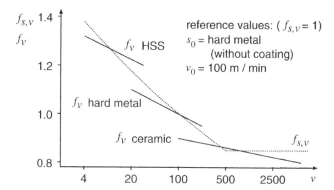

Figure 6.11. Influence of tool material and cutting speed on the main cutting force.

the undeformed chip thickness A on the force signals. The factors are normalized with respect to an undeformed chip thickness of $3\,\text{mm}^2$. Constants, such as $\sin 95°$ or 0.73 in g_h, depend on cutting conditions that are not varied here (see Table 6.1). It should also be mentioned that the different tool coatings used here are not distinguished by the model. Moreover, the model does not consider the workpiece parameter *dia*.

The normalization procedure (see Fig. 6.10) is given by

$$F'_c = \frac{F_c}{C_{F_c}}, \quad F'_f = \frac{F_f}{C_{F_f}}, \quad F'_t = \frac{F_t}{C_{F_t}} \tag{6.9}$$

The normalized process parameters can now be transferred to the feature extraction level. At this level, different features in the time, frequency, joint time-frequency, statistical, or cepstral domain could be computed. For the purpose of this chapter, it is sufficient to consider very simple features: the average of the force signals in a short time interval (denoted by $\bar{F}'_c$, $\bar{F}'_f$, and $\bar{F}'_t$).

6.4.3 Dynamic Neural Network at Wear Model Level

In this section, time-delay neural networks (TDNN) are introduced. Multilayer perceptrons (MLP) and multilayer perceptrons with a sliding input window (MLP-sw) can be seen as special cases of TDNN.

There are three types of neurons in a TDNN: input neurons, hidden neurons, and output neurons (see Fig. 6.12). These types of neurons are grouped in the following layers: input (I), one or more hidden (H_j, $j \in \{1, \ldots, m\}$), and output (O). The variables i, h_j, and o represent the number of neurons in these layers.

The activation function of the neurons in I is the identity. The other neurons use a nonlinear activation function like the hyperbolic tangent or the logistic sigmoid activation function. The layers are fully connected layer-by-layer.

Tapped delay lines are used for the feedforward connections (see Fig. 6.13). Tapped delay lines are shift registers where the output values form a weighted

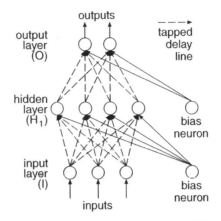

Figure 6.12. Time-delay neural network (TDNN).

sum like the output of an FIR (finite impulse response) filter [37]. The unit delay operator is denoted by q^{-1}, that is, $q^{-1}(f(t)) = f(t-1)$. The inputs of a neuron consist of the outputs of previous n neurons ($n \in \{i, h_1, \ldots, h_m\}$) not only during the current time step t, but during some previous time steps as well (usually a time sequence without gaps which is identical for all connections between two layers of neurons—for example, $t, t-1, \ldots, t-(l-1)$ with $l \in \{l_1, \ldots, l_{m+1}\}$). The value $l_{j'}$ ($j' \in \{1, \ldots, m+1\}$) describes the number of weights in a tapped delay line (number of delay elements plus 1) between the layers I, H_j, and O, respectively. The output (activation) of a neuron k is consequently given by

$$y_k(t) = A\left(w_k^{\text{bias}} + \sum_{a=1}^{n}\sum_{b=0}^{l-1} y_a(t-b) \cdot w_{a,k,b}\right) \tag{6.10}$$

where $y_k(t)$ is the output of neuron k at time t, $w_{a,k,b}$ is the weight of a connection between neuron a in layer x and neuron k in layer $x+1$ with time delay b

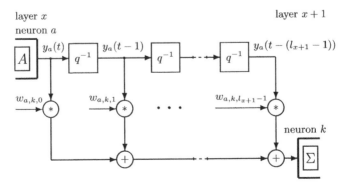

Figure 6.13. Tapped delay line (FIR filter).

(see Fig. 6.13), and A is a nonlinear, sigmoid activation function. The bias w_k^{bias} of the neuron k is usually implemented as a weight of a connection between a neuron with constant output "1" and the neuron k.

All in all, $i \xrightarrow{l_1} h_1 \xrightarrow{l_2} \cdots \xrightarrow{l_m} h_m \xrightarrow{l_{m+1}} o$ is a unique notation for the structure of a TDNN. The network can be trained with temporal backpropagation or temporal RPROP (resilient propagation), for example (see, e.g., references 37 and 38). TDNN [39], also called FIR networks [37], have been developed originally for speech recognition. One important feature of TDNN is their ability for a time-invariant recognition of pattern sequences in time series. TDNN is a nonrecurrent, dynamic network paradigm that only uses local time information. That is, input information remains only for a certain, limited time window (receptive window) in the network. Therefore, stability problems do not exist [40]. The length of the receptive window is $1 + (\sum_{j'=1}^{m+1} l_{j'} - 1)$.

An MLP is the degenerated static version of this network paradigm [41]. It can be derived from the generic model in the following way: $\forall j' \in \{1, \ldots, m+1\} : l_{j'} = 1$. In an MLP-sw there are only delay elements between I and H_1: $\forall j' \in \{2, \ldots, m+1\} : l_{j'} = 1$.

6.5 EXPERIMENTAL RESULTS

To assess the generalization capability of a trained network, results for learning (training) patterns are compared to results for unknown test patterns (extrapolation). In order to demonstrate the ability to reproduce the result of a training starting with randomly initialized weights (50,000 epochs with Temporal RPROP), each experiment has been repeated 25 times. The most important assessment criterion is the mean average error μ_ϕ (where "mean" refers to the 25 repetitions and "average" refers to the set of test patterns in one experiment) given by

$$\mu_\phi = \frac{1}{R} \sum_{r=1}^{R} \underbrace{\left(\frac{1}{P} \sum_{p=1}^{P} |t_p - y_{p,r}| \right)}_{\mu_r} \tag{6.11}$$

where R is the number of repetitions in one experiment (i.e., $R = 25$), P is the number of test patterns, t_p is the "target" output value for a specific pattern p (i.e., the measured wear), $y_{p,r}$ is the output of the network for p in repetition r (i.e., the estimated wear), and μ_r is the average error in r. Additionally, the standard deviation of the average errors divided by the mean average error σ_ϕ/μ_ϕ, the minimum $\min_\phi$, the maximum $\max_\phi$, and the median med_ϕ of the 25 average errors have been determined.

Additional criteria are the identification rates for test patterns with a given acceptable maximum error i_x in %, where x ranges from 10 μm to 300 μm (i.e., the percentage of test patterns that can be determined with an error that is less than a given maximum error), and the mean and the standard deviation of the maximum errors for test patterns in an experiment with 25 repetitions (denoted by μ_{max} and σ_{max}/μ_{max}). These criteria are computed using a wear criterion of 0.5 mm; that is, patterns with $VB > 0.5$ mm are not evaluated. The reason for this measure is that a worn insert with $VB > 0.5$ mm would have been changed in a "normal" cutting process (see, e.g., reference 7).

In the following experiments the numbers of learning and test patterns have been 769 and 225, respectively. It must be noticed that the test patterns belong to three chipping experiments with combinations of cutting conditions lying in an area of the parameter space that is covered quite well with chipping experiments. For the available data, this measure turned out to be necessary as a result of the uneven and sparse distribution of condition combinations in the condition space. The trained networks are better suited to predict tool wear for this area of the parameter space; therefore, results for test patterns are better than results for training patterns. However, the relative improvements in the experiments are obvious and the conclusions are valid.

In order to demonstrate the advantages of the techniques introduced in Section 6.5, five experiments are carried out (results are given in Tables 6.3 and 6.4):

- Experiment **1** uses average values of force signals that are not normalized as inputs of an MLP.
- In experiment **2**, five cutting conditions (see above) are taken as additional inputs (the tool type is coded at three input neurons).
- Experiment **3** uses force signals that are not normalized as inputs of an TDNN in order to consider the temporal development of these force signals.
- In experiment **4**, the force signals are normalized and used as inputs of an MLP.
- Experiment **5** combines the two techniques by considering the temporal development of normalized force signals with a TDNN.

Comparing the results of the experiments **1** and **2**, it can be stated that μ_ϕ for learning patterns is improved significantly. However, μ_ϕ for test patterns increases slightly, and the raise of σ_ϕ/μ_ϕ for learning and for test patterns is remarkable: It cannot be guaranteed that a good result obtained in one repetition of the experiment can be repeated in another repetition. Additional results given in reference 36 show that overfitting effects occur in experiment **2**. Experiment **2** emphasizes the problems of a pure neural network approach using cutting conditions as additional inputs.

If the results of experiment **3** are compared to the results of experiment **1**, it can be noticed that in this case μ_ϕ is reduced for training and for test patterns. However, σ_ϕ/μ_ϕ raises for learning and for test patterns, and μ_{max} for test patterns is higher than in experiment **1**. In experiment **3**, it is very difficult for the TDNN to separate signal changes caused by cutting conditions from signal changes caused by tool wear.

In experiment **4**, the preprocessing technique based on a physical model is applied for the first time. Compared to experiment **1**, the reduction of σ_ϕ/μ_ϕ for learning and for test patterns is remarkable. Moreover, the decrease of μ_{max} and

TABLE 6.3. Average Estimation Errors for Learning and Test Data

Experiment	1		2		3		4		5	
					Neural Network Configuration					
Paradigm	MLP		MLP		TDNN		MLP		TDNN	
Inputs										
$\bar{F}_c, \bar{F}_f, \bar{F}_t$	$\checkmark$									
$\bar{F}'_c, \bar{F}'_f, \bar{F}'_t$			$\checkmark$		$\checkmark$		$\checkmark$		$\checkmark$	
d, v, f, dia, s			$\checkmark$							
Structure	$3 \xrightarrow{1} 12 \xrightarrow{1} 1$		$10 \xrightarrow{1} 12 \xrightarrow{1} 1$		$3 \xrightarrow{2} 12 \xrightarrow{2} 1$		$3 \xrightarrow{1} 12 \xrightarrow{1} 1$		$3 \xrightarrow{2} 12 \xrightarrow{2} 1$	
			Evaluation for Learning (L) and Test (T) Data							
Errors	L	T	L	T	L	T	L	T	L	T
μ_ϕ in μm	99.4	70.0	33.9	71.7	82.0	64.3	95.3	54.1	79.5	43.7
σ_ϕ/μ_ϕ in %	2.8	4.3	7.0	8.7	6.1	6.9	1.7	2.3	2.2	2.2
$\min_\phi$ in μm	95.5	66.7	30.0	61.1	72.9	55.8	92.6	51.9	75.5	41.5
$\max_\phi$ in μm	104.4	77.0	39.2	82.4	89.8	70.9	97.3	55.5	83.1	45.4
med_ϕ in μm	98.2	69.6	33.6	72.4	81.2	64.8	96.5	54.8	78.6	43.8

TABLE 6.4. Identification Rates and Maximum Estimation Errors for Test Data (Using the Wear Criterion $VB_{max} \leq 0.5$ mm)

	Identification Rates				
Experiment	1	2	3	4	5
Maximum error of . . .					
10 μm: i_{10} in %	11.6	9.7	12.3	9.7	19.0
25 μm: i_{25} in %	26.9	25.8	30.1	30.7	36.4
50 μm: i_{50} in %	55.5	56.7	60.9	68.1	78.0
75 μm: i_{75} in %	82.3	76.5	82.6	88.6	92.7
100 μm: i_{100} in %	92.9	90.0	93.8	95.1	97.1
200 μm: i_{200} in %	99.9	99.3	99.8	100.0	100.0
300 μm: i_{300} in %	100.0	100.0	100.0	100.0	100.0
Evaluation of Maximum Estimation Errors					
μ_{max} in μm	185.1	219.7	198.0	143.6	131.9
σ_{max}/μ_{max} in %	10.3	14.4	11.3	1.4	3.6

σ_{max}/μ_{max} for test patterns is significant, too. All in all, the results are better than in experiment **1** and more reliable, too.

The results of experiment **4** can be improved once more in experiment **5**: μ_ϕ is improved for learning and for test patterns, whereas σ_ϕ/μ_ϕ does not change significantly in both cases. Therefore, it can be stated that the normalization of force signals by means of a physical model together with the use of temporal information by means of a neural model yields the best results.

It has to be mentioned that the conclusions drawn here are not only supported by the small number of experiments which can be given. Detailed results of an enormous number of additional experiments can be found in references 3, 17, 33, and 36, for instance. With additional techniques (optimization of the neural network structure and the number of delay elements, new features and automatic feature selection, etc.), it has been possible to reduce μ_ϕ to 73.1 μm for learning patterns and to 37.7 μm for test patterns, respectively. That is, compared to experiment **1** the error for test patterns could be reduced by about 50%.

Figure 6.14 shows two examples of tool wear estimation for test patterns. The first result (top) is obtained with an MLP in experiment **1**, and the second is achieved with a TDNN using the same inputs as in experiment **5**, but with a slightly different network structure ($3 \overset{2}{\rightarrow} 12 \overset{3}{\rightarrow} 1$). It can be stated that the wear estimation is precise when the wear is relatively low. At the end of the lifetime, when outbreaks at the cutting edges occur, the detection of a high degree of wear is still reliable.

6.6 FUSION OF SOFT COMPUTING AND HARD COMPUTING

In the tool wear monitoring concept described here, the two main functional blocks—that is, the HC part (physical process model) and the SC part (dynamic

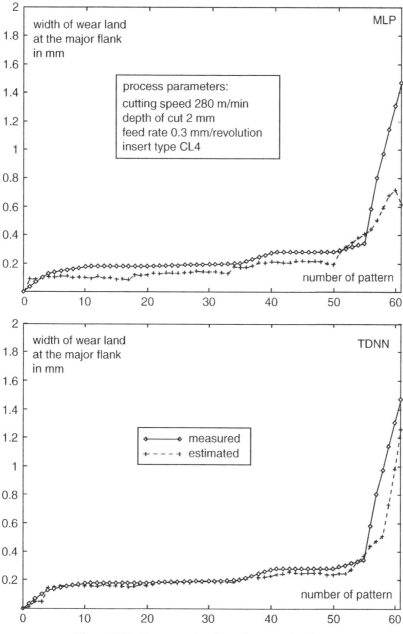

Figure 6.14. Two examples for tool wear estimation.

neural network)—are arranged in a sequential order (see Figs. 6.4 and 6.10). There-fore, the fusion category (cf. Chapter 1) can clearly be identified as being a *cascaded combination* of HC and SC techniques (type: HC-SC). This configuration has a moderate fusion grade. The HC part can be assigned to the digital preprocessing level of the generic monitoring architecture, whereas the SC part belongs to the wear model level.

A closer look to related monitoring approaches analyzed in Section 6.3.3 shows that in the area of tool wear monitoring a cascaded combination is the favored way of fusing HC and SC techniques. Typical examples are shown in Fig. 6.6 (SC-HC), 6.8 (HC-SC), or 6.9 (SC-HC-SC).

The central motivation behind our fusion approach was to combine *analytical knowledge* originating from a simplistic physical model of the process at hand (HC) with *empirical knowledge* learned by dynamic neural networks using examples which roughly describe this process (SC). Neither a pure HC approach nor a pure SC approach are able to model the complex process behavior with the same accuracy as the new, hybrid technique.

In our system, HC and SC techniques are fused in a *cooperative sense*. The result of the preprocessing step that uses an HC technique can be seen as a signal of an abstract sensor that is subsequently transformed into a wear estimate by means of an SC method. As in our case, this type of fusion often contains one component that is highly application-specific (here: the physical process model).

6.7   SUMMARY AND CONCLUSIONS

In this chapter the advantages of a new, hybrid technique for on-line, indirect tool wear monitoring in turning were set out. This technique fuses a physical model describing the influence of cutting conditions on measured force signals (HC part) with a neural network model describing the relationship between normalized force signals and the wear state of the tool (SC part). It was shown that the consideration of process parameters, cutting conditions, and wear in *one* model (either physical or neural) is extremely difficult and that the existing hybrid approaches are not adequate.

The physical process model that is proposed here avoids the open problem of finding a precise analytical relationship between cutting conditions and process parameters on the one hand and tool wear on the other hand. The model is valid under the assumption of applying new tools. Therefore, it can be used to normalize the measured force signals—that is, to eliminate the influence of changing cutting conditions as far as possible. The model can be adapted to new technologies (e.g., the use of new tool coatings and higher cutting velocities). It can also be applied to other process monitoring tasks, for example, in order to define dynamic thresholds for a collision detection.

The neural model focuses on the task of finding a relationship between normalized force signals and wear. Neural networks with a small number of inputs and weights can be used and, therefore, the problem of overfitting can be avoided even if a large number of cutting conditions is considered. A dynamic but nonrecurrent network paradigm captures the temporal development of normalized process parameters without suffering from stability problems. It also should be emphasized that the two models can be developed separately. Additional, more general advantages of a hybrid system are given in reference 31: improved performance, faster configuration and easy maintenance, reduced requirements for personnel, and increased productivity.

What are the conclusions and the suggestions that follow from these investigations? First of all, it should be mentioned that most of the following remarks can be transferred to other machining processes using tools with defined cutting edges (e.g., drilling or milling) or even to many other process monitoring tasks.

In our opinion, information on the observed or controlled cutting process and/or the measurement hardware (sensors, filters, converters, etc.) should be used at a very early level of the sensor fusion process (i.e., at the digital preprocessing level). For example, information on characteristic curves of sensors could be used to align a sensor signal with respect to the behavior of a specific sensor. Physical process models could also be developed for other process parameters—for example, to eliminate signal contributions caused by chatter, chip lamination, or fundamental resonant frequencies of particular tool–workpiece combinations. Future research should also focus on the improvement of the physical process models for force signals.

In our opinion, dynamic but nonrecurrent neural networks should be preferred at the model level—for example, TDNN or other network paradigms like ATNN (adaptive time-delay neural networks) or TDRBF (time-delay radial basis function networks). If it is necessary to consider global temporal information, dynamic network paradigms that combine feedback connections with delay elements in feedforward direction should be used—for example, NARX (nonlinear autoregressive model with exogenous inputs) or IIR (infinite impulse response) networks.

In most cases the way proposed to construct a monitoring system will yield a cascaded combination of HC and SC techniques (HC-SC, cf. Chapter 1).

Finally, the following statement given in reference 42 shall be mentioned: "Whereas some researchers in the ... community see neural networks as a panacea for solving all realistic ... problems, another school rejects the neural-network paradigm altogether in favour of well-established conventional schemes with a sound theoretical basis. Much of promising research using neural networks for modelling, prediction and control, however, realises the value of, and the need for, both paradigms, and exploits their mutual complementarity to address realistic problem situations." In our opinion, a similar but more general conclusion can be drawn for the fusion of HC and SC techniques.

REFERENCES

1. B. Sick, "On-line and Indirect Tool Wear Monitoring in Turning with Artificial Neural Networks: A Review of More than a Decade of Research," *Mechanical Systems and Signal Processing* **16**, 487–546 (2002).

2. R. G. Silva, R. L. Reuben, K. J. Baker, and S. J. Wilcox, "Tool Wear Monitoring of Turning Operations by Neural Network and Expert System Classification of a Feature Set Generated from Multiple Sensors," *Mechanical Systems and Signal Processing* **12**, 319–332 (1998).

3. W. Maydl and B. Sick, "Recurrent and Non-Recurrent Dynamic Network Paradigms: A Case Study," *Proceedings of the International Joint Conference on Neural Networks,* Como, Italy, 2000, **6**, pp. 73–78.

4. S. Pittner, S. V. Kamarthi, and Q. Gao, "Wavelet Networks for Sensor Signal Classification in Flank Wear Assessment," *Journal of Intelligent Manufacturing* **9**, 315–322 (1998).

5. G. Boothroyd and W. A. Knight, *Fundamentals of Machining and Machine Tools,* 2nd ed., Dekker, New York, 1989.

6. M. C. Shaw, *Metal Cutting Principles,* Clarendon Press, Oxford, UK, 1984.

7. ISO (International Organization for Standardization), *Tool-Life Testing with Single-Point Turning Tools (ISO 3685),* 2nd ed., ISO, 1993.

8. B. Sick, "Chances and Risks of Sensor Fusion with Neural Networks: An Application Example," *Proceedings of the 8th International Conference on Artificial Neural Networks,* Skövde, Sweden, 1998, **2**, pp. 713–718.

9. B. Sick, "Fusion of Soft and Hard Computing Techniques in Indirect, Online Tool Wear Monitoring," *IEEE Transactions on Systems, Man, and Cybernetics—Part C: Applications and Reviews* **32**, 80–91 (2002).

10. D. Barschdorff, U. Wahner, G. Wöstenkühler, G. Warnecke, and M. Müller, "Mustererkennungsverfahren zur prozessbegleitenden Verschleissüberwachung beim Drehen," *Tagungsband Meßsignalverarbeitung und Diagnosemittel zur Prozeß- und Qualitätssicherung,* Langen, Germany, 1995, pp. 115–124.

11. Y. Koren and E. Lenz, "Mathematical Model for the Flank Wear While Turning Steel with Carbide Tools," *CIRP Proceedings on Manufacturing Systems* **1**, 127–139 (1972).

12. Y. Koren, A. G. Ulsoy, and K. Danai, "Tool Wear and Breakage Detection Using a Process Model," *Annals of the CIRP* **35**, 283–288 (1986).

13. K. Danai and A. G. Ulsoy, "A Dynamic State Model for On-line Tool Wear Estimation in Turning," *Journal of Engineering for Industry* **109**, 396–399 (1987).

14. B. M. Kramer, "A Comprehensive Tool Wear Model," *Annals of the CIRP* **35**, 67–70 (1986).

15. N. H. Abu-Zahra and G. Yu, "Analytical Model for Tool Wear Monitoring in Turning Operations Using Ultrasound Waves," *International Journal of Machine Tools and Manufacture* **40**, 1619–1635 (2000).

16. S. V. Kamarthi, "On-line Tool Wear Estimation in Turning Through Sensor Data Fusion and Neural Networks," Doctoral Dissertation, Pennsylvania State University, Department of Industrial and Manufacturing Engineering, University Park, 1994.

17. B. Sick, A. Sicheneder, and H.-J. Lindinger, "A Comparative Evaluation of Different Neural Network Paradigms for Tool Wear Classification in Turning," *Proceedings of the 3rd International Workshop on Neural Networks in Applications,* Magdeburg, Germany, 1998, pp. 139–146.

18. A. Ghasempoor, J. Jeswiet, and T. N. Moore, "Real Time Implementation of On-line Tool Condition Monitoring in Turning," *International Journal of Machine Tools and Manufacture* **39**, 1883–1902 (1999).

19. A. Ghasempoor, T. N. Moore, and J. Jeswiet, "On-line Wear Estimation Using Neural Networks," *Proceedings of the Institution of Mechanical Engineers—Part B* **212**, 105–112 (1998).

20. W. Adam, I. Suwalski, and J. Krüger, "Werkzeugüberwachung für CNC-Drehmaschinen mit Fuzzy-Logik," Final Report of a DFG Research Project, Fraunhofer Institut für Produktionsanlagen und Konstruktionstechnik (IPK), Berlin, Germany, 1996.

21. S. Elanayar and Y. C. Shin, "Robust Tool Wear Estimation with Radial Basis Function Neural Networks," *Journal of Dynamic Systems, Measurement, and Control* **117**, 459–467 (1995).

22. S. V. T. Elanayar and Y. C. Shin, "Design and Implementation of Tool Wear Monitoring with Radial Basis Function Neural Networks," *Proceedings of the American Control Conference*, Seattle, WA, 1995, pp. 1722–1726.

23. S. Elanayar and Y. C. Shin, "Modeling of Tool Forces for Worn Tools: Flank Wear Effects," *Journal of Manufacturing Science and Engineering* **118**, 359–366 (1996).

24. S. V. T. Elanayar and Y. C. Shin, "Radial Basis Function Neural Network for Approximation and Estimation of Nonlinear Stochastic Dynamic Systems," *IEEE Transactions on Neural Networks* **5**, 594–603 (1994).

25. S. Elanayar and Y. C. Shin, "Tool Wear Estimation in Turning Operations Based on Radial Basis Functions," in C. H. Dagli, S. R. T. Kumara, and Y. C. Shin, eds., *Intelligent Engineering Systems through Artificial Neural Networks*, ASME Press, New York, 1991, pp. 685–692.

26. S. Elanayar and Y. C. Shin, "Robust Tool Wear Estimation via Radial Basis Function Neural Networks," *Proceedings of the ASME Winter Annual Meeting on Neural Networks in Manufacturing and Robotics*, Anaheim, CA, 1992, **PED-57**, pp. 37–51.

27. G. Warnecke and R. Kluge, "Control of Tolerances in Turning by Predictive Control with Neural Networks," *Journal of Intelligent Manufacturing* **9**, 281–287 (1998).

28. R. Kluge, "Prädiktive modellbasierte Regelung von Zerspanprozessen," Doctoral Dissertation, Universität Kaiserslautern, Fachbereich Maschinenbau und Verfahrenstechnik, Kaiserslautern, Germany, 1999.

29. G. Chryssolouris, M. Domroese, and P. Beaulieu, "Sensor Synthesis for Control of Manufacturing Processes," *Journal of Engineering for Industry* **114**, 158–174 (1992).

30. G. Chryssolouris and M. Domroese, "Sensor Integration for Tool Wear Estimation in Machining," *Proceedings of the ASME Winter Annual Meeting on Sensors and Controls for Manufacturing*, Chicago, 1988, **PED-33**, pp. 115–123.

31. R. G. Silva, "Cutting Tool Condition Monitoring of the Turning Process Using Artificial Intelligence," Doctoral Dissertation, University of Glamorgan, School of Technology, Glamorgan, UK, 1997.

32. R. G. Silva, K. J. Baker, S. J. Wilcox, and R. L. Reuben, "The Adaptability of a Tool Wear Monitoring System Under Changing Cutting Conditions," *Mechanical Systems and Signal Processing* **14**, 287–298 (2000).

33. B. Sick, "Wear Estimation for Turning Tools with Process-Specific Pre-Processing for Time-Delay Neural Networks," in C. H. Dagli, M. Akay, O. Ersoy, B. R. Fernández, and A. Smith, eds., *Intelligent Engineering Systems through Artificial Neural Networks*, ASME Press, New York, 1997, **7**, pp. 791–796.

34. B. Sick, "On-line Tool Wear Classification in Turning with Time-Delay Neural Networks and Process-Specific Pre-Processing," *Proceedings of the International Joint Conference on Neural Networks*, Anchorage, AK, 1998, pp. 84–89.

35. B. Sick, "On-line Tool Wear Monitoring in Turning Using Neural Networks," *Neural Computing & Applications* **7**, 356–366 (1998).

36. B. Sick, *Signalinterpretation mit Neuronalen Netzen unter Nutzung von modellbasiertem Nebenwissen am Beispiel der Verschleißüberwachung von Werkzeugen in CNC-Drehmaschinen*, VDI-Verlag, Düsseldorf, Germany, 2000.

37. E. A. Wan, "Finite Impulse Response Neural Networks with Applications in Time Series Prediction," Doctoral Dissertation, Stanford University, Department of Electrical Engineering, Stanford, CA, 1993.

38. M. Riedmiller, "RPROP—Description and Implementation Details," Technical Report, Universität Karlsruhe, Institut für Logik, Komplexität und Deduktionssysteme, Karlsruhe, Germany, 1994.

39. A. Waibel, T. Hanazawa, G. Hinton, K. Shikano, and K. J. Lang, "Phoneme Recognition Using Time-Delay Neural Networks", *IEEE Transactions on Acoustics, Speech, and Signal Processing* **37**, 328–339 (1989).

40. S. Haykin, *Neural Networks—A Comprehensive Foundation*, Macmillan College Publishing Company, New York, 1994.

41. R. Rojas, *Neural Networks—A Systematic Introduction*, Springer-Verlag, Berlin, Germany, 1996.

42. M. Agarwal, "Combining Neural and Conventional Paradigms for Modelling, Prediction and Control," *International Journal of Systems Science* **28**, 65–81 (1997).

EDITOR'S INTRODUCTION TO CHAPTER 7

Although undergraduate power systems and power electronics study programs do not contain much about signal processing (SP) and soft computing (SC), the field of electric power engineering is a vital user of these principal technologies. At the graduate level, some advanced courses on applied signal processing and SC have recently been adapted to the specific needs of power engineers. On the other hand, the research in electric power applications with advanced signal processing and SC techniques has been active for more than a decade [1–3]. It is notable that the IEEE Power Engineering Society created a videotape tutorial on "Artificial Neural Networks with Applications to Power Systems" (M. El-Sharkawi and D. Niebur, eds.) in 1996, at the time when SC was just gradually emerging to industrial products. However, because the practicing power engineers typically do not have an extensive SP or SC background, only rudimentary algorithms with considerable limitations are used in many practical cases. Furthermore, specialists from the signal processing and SC fields do not usually understand the particular needs of the electric power area; therefore, tailoring of general-purpose algorithms to specific power applications is not as common as it should be. Prudent tailoring could lead to competitive solutions that are both efficient and robust, and their implementation complexity would be lower.

Computationally Intelligent Hybrid Systems. Edited by Seppo J. Ovaska
ISBN 0-471-47668-4 © 2005 the Institute of Electrical and Electronics Engineers, Inc.

But what are those specific needs of electric power engineering? The field is broad and has a great variety of fundamental characteristics; however, the following items are universal in many SP-related applications:

- Signals are narrow-band in nature (50/60-Hz fundamental sinusoid).
- Disturbances include odd harmonics of the fundamental frequency.
- Filtering tasks are delay-constrained.

Chapter 7 of the present book, "Predictive Filtering Methods for Power Systems Applications," is authored by Seppo J. Ovaska. It provides an explanatory presentation on the use of *tailored* SP and SC methods in zero-crossings detection of corrupted current or voltage waveforms, as well as in generating an accurate current reference for active power filters. Also in the electric power field, new products are increasingly more "intelligent" than their predecessors [4]. In this context, we refer to Fogel's practical definition of the common term [5]:

Intelligence can be defined in terms of the capability of a system to adapt its behavior to meet its goals in a range of environments.

Accurate zero-crossings detectors and current reference generators need to be *adaptive* signal processing systems due to the inherent frequency variation. Moreover, the proposed adaptive systems are *pre-optimized* using evolutionary computation (EC) to meet their goals in a specific operation environment. According to the above definition, both of the considered SP systems are therefore intelligent— or more precisely, "computationally intelligent."

Evolutionary computation offers opportunities for solving challenging optimization problems. The use of EC is nowadays within the reach of every engineer, because of the available low-cost computers with 2- to 3-GHz clock rates. Many optimization tasks that were earlier "nonsolvable" could now be successfully revisited.

Chapter 7 proposes the use of evolutionary computation (genetic algorithm and evolutionary programming) in the design of computationally efficient adaptive filters for narrow-band applications. Thus the applied fusion structure is SC=HC (Chapter 1). The evolutionary algorithms are needed to complement the hard-computing (HC)-type design and tuning process of predictive filters. In these case examples, the use of EC has no value of its own, but there is a *true demand* for a hybrid design and adaptation scheme. Generally speaking, the selection between individual HC and SC algorithms is application-driven, and the available domain knowledge should be utilized effectively before taking SC in use [3]. In the SC literature, however, there are too many examples where real-world problems are solved using pure SC techniques, although there would exist well-proven HC solutions to the same problems. To minimize this kind of research and development work with only a marginal value, closer cooperation between power systems, SC, and signal processing specialists is definitely encouraged. Also, the fusion of SC and HC offers substantial innovation opportunities. To unleash the development potential, careful re-thinking and adaptation of the power systems and power electronics curricula are required. It is good to remember that also in engineering education the whole is often more than a sum of its parts.

REFERENCES

1. Y. Dote and S. J. Ovaska, "Industrial Applications of Soft Computing: A Review," *Proceedings of the IEEE* **89**, 1243–1265 (2001).
2. S. Väliviita, "Predictive Filtering Methods for Motor Drive Instrumentation," Doctoral Dissertation, Helsinki University of Technology, Institute of Intelligent Power Electronics, Espoo, Finland, 1998.
3. R. L. King, "Artificial Neural Networks and Computational Intelligence," *IEEE Computer Applications in Power* **11**, 14–16 and 18–25 (1998).
4. M. El-Hawary, ed., *Electric Power Applications of Fuzzy Systems*, IEEE Press, Piscataway, NJ, 1998.
5. D. B. Fogel, *Evolutionary Computation: Toward a New Philosophy of Machine Intelligence*, IEEE Press, Piscataway, NJ, 2000.

CHAPTER 7

PREDICTIVE FILTERING METHODS FOR POWER SYSTEMS APPLICATIONS

SEPPO J. OVASKA

Helsinki University of Technology, Espoo, Finland

7.1 INTRODUCTION

Predictive lowpass and bandpass filters have important applications in delay-constrained signal processing, particularly in the area of control instrumentation. There are numerous such applications, for example, in the fields of electric power systems and industrial electronics, where distorted line voltages or currents should be filtered *without delaying* the fundamental 50/60-Hz component. Conventional analog or digital filters are not appropriate for these applications, because they all introduce harmful delay into filtered primary signals.

Vainio and Ovaska proposed the use of predictive finite impulse response (FIR) filters for zero-crossings detection with thyristor or triac power converters [1]. That application requires precise zero-crossings information for synchronizing the operation of power switches in the main circuit. Väliviita and Ovaska introduced a delayless method to generate current references for active power filters [2]. The phase accuracy of the compensating current affects directly the harmonics reduction capability of such a power filter. Therefore, they used a predictive filtering scheme, based on the Widrow–Hoff least mean-square (LMS) adaptation algorithm. Furthermore, Dawson and Klaffke presented a delayless, frequency-adaptive filter that can be used to acquire time-varying narrow-band signal components in the presence of considerable input disturbances [3]. Their method is applicable to delay-constrained signal acquisition and sampling synchronization, needed frequently in power systems instrumentation.

But what could be the most suitable signal processing algorithm for such applications? We can try to answer this interesting question by referring synergistically to

Computationally Intelligent Hybrid Systems. Edited by Seppo J. Ovaska
ISBN 0-471-47668-4 © 2005 the Institute of Electrical and Electronics Engineers, Inc.

the "no free lunch" (NFL) theorems that Wolpert and Macready discussed in the context of optimization algorithms [4]. They proved that improved performance for any optimization algorithm indicates a match between the structure of the algorithm and the structure of the problem. Stimulated by this work, D. B. Fogel pointed out that "whenever a new algorithm is presented as being well-suited for a problem, it should be asked why it is well-suited and for which problems it will not be appropriate" [5]. Thus, a general-purpose algorithm is never the most suitable one for a specific problem, and the most suitable algorithm for a specific problem is not a general-purpose one. Intuitively thinking, it could be possible to develop similar NFL theorems also for delayless signal restoration; this task is, however, beyond the scope of our present chapter. Nevertheless, if we apply such intuition freely to the electric power applications discussed above, we can identify the following structural characteristics of the underlying signal restoration problem:

1. There exists only one principal signal component at a time.
2. No phase delay at the instantaneous fundamental frequency is allowed.
3. The fundamental frequency is varying slightly around the nominal frequency.
4. Frequency variation is slow.
5. Harmonic frequencies should not disturb the adaptation process.
6. Computational efficiency is required for microcontroller or field programmable gate array (FPGA) implementations.

These structural characteristics of the problem can now be turned to structural characteristics of the digital filtering algorithm that could be the most suitable one for this application:

1. Bandpass filter for the principal signal component
2. Delayless filtering method
3. Adaptation capability within the required frequency tolerance
4. Low adaptation gain factor
5. No more than two degrees of freedom in adaptation (capability to track the amplitude and phase of the fundamental component only)
6. Implementation with a small number of multiplications

An adaptive LMS-FIR filter is probably the first algorithm that comes to the mind of an instrumentation design engineer when he starts to look at this particular problem. LMS-FIRs can be designed to behave as forward-predictors of time-varying input signals. And with noisy narrow-band inputs, they will typically converge to some kind of lowpass or bandpass responses. Moreover, the LMS algorithm is computationally efficient compared to most other adaptive filters. But such an LMS-FIR is definitely a general-purpose solution; therefore, it is not likely that it would be the most suitable solution for the present problem.

On the evolution path toward the ultimate solution, Vainio and Ovaska proposed recently a harmonics-resistant adaptive FIR filter with general parameter (GP) adaptation for line-frequency signal processing [6]. That computationally efficient and robust adaptation algorithm was further developed in reference 7, where the novel multiplicative general parameter (MGP) algorithm was introduced.

This chapter is organized as follows. The multiplicative general parameter method is first presented, and the motivation for filter tap cross-connection optimization is discussed. A detailed introduction to the genetic algorithm that is tailored for the cross-connection optimization problem is then given. An evolutionary programming-based procedure for designing multiplierless basis filters for MGP-FIR systems, as well as an efficient evolutionary programming algorithm, is described. Illustrative design examples show the usefulness of the proposed techniques in delay-constrained zero-crossings detection and current reference generation applications. The role of fusion or symbiosis of SC and HC methodologies (Chapter 1) in the above filter design applications is also explored. Finally, possible directions for further research are discussed with conclusions of this work.

7.2 MULTIPLICATIVE GENERAL-PARAMETER FILTERING

The considered filtering scheme has low computational burden, it provides effective attenuation of disturbances without phase shifting the fundamental line frequency component, and finally it offers robust adaptation around the nominal frequency. Therefore, it overcomes the obvious amplitude/phase accuracy limitations of fixed filters [1], considerable memory requirements of lookup-table-based filtering systems [8], and the poor attenuation capability of harmonic frequencies with fully adaptive filters [9].

All this is achieved by using a new tuning scheme for FIR filters that is based on multiplicative general parameters. These MGP-FIR filters have only two adaptive coefficients, which make it possible to track the small variations of the line frequency and, at the same time, provide sufficient attenuation for the (odd) harmonics that are commonly distorting both line currents and voltages in industrial environments. Our MGP algorithm is a computationally efficient modification of the rather unknown general parameter method introduced by Ashimov and Syzdykov for system identification in 1981 [10], and it was analyzed recently in the context of signal processing by Vainio and Ovaska [6].

In a typical MGP-FIR implementation, the filter output is computed as

$$y(n) = g_1(n) \overbrace{\sum_{k \in A} h(k)x(n-k)}^{\text{Subfilter \#1}} + g_2(n) \overbrace{\sum_{k \in B} h(k)x(n-k)}^{\text{Subfilter \#2}} \qquad (7.1)$$

where $g_1(n)$ and $g_2(n)$ are the multiplicative general parameters, $h(k), k \in \{0,1,\ldots, N-1\}$, are the fixed-basis filter coefficients, and A and B are integer sets containing the tap indexes of the two FIR subfilters; $A \cup B = \{0,1,\ldots,N-1\}$ and $A \cap B = \emptyset$. Thus, the coefficients of the composite filter are $\theta(k) = g_1(n)h(k)$ for $k \in A$, and $\theta(k) = g_2(n)h(k)$ for $k \in B$. Figure 7.1 illustrates the MGP-FIR filter of Eq. (7.1). In a p-step-ahead prediction configuration used later in this chapter, the multiplicative

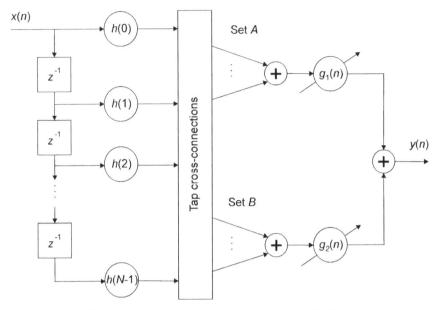

Figure 7.1. Multiplicative general-parameter FIR filter.

general parameters are updated according to the following equations:

$$g_1(n+1) = g_1(n) + \mu[x(n) - y(n-p)] \overbrace{\sum_{k \in A} h(k)x(n-k)}^{\text{Subfilter \#1}} \tag{7.2}$$

$$g_2(n+1) = g_2(n) + \mu[x(n) - y(n-p)] \overbrace{\sum_{k \in B} h(k)x(n-k)}^{\text{Subfilter \#2}} \tag{7.3}$$

where μ is the adaptation gain factor, $0 < \mu < 1$. The fixed-basis FIR filter is typically designed according to the nominal signal characteristics [1]. Here, the basis filter should have a unity gain on the nominal line frequency (50/60 Hz), along with a positive phase shift in accordance with the required prediction property. Therefore, the basis filter is a forward predictor of the nominal frequency with a prediction step p. Such predictive filters are often designed analytically to minimize the white noise gain, given by

$$\text{NG} = \sum_{k=0}^{N-1} [h(k)]^2 \tag{7.4}$$

while satisfying the forward prediction constraint:

$$x(n+p) = \sum_{k=0}^{N-1} h(k)x(n-k) \tag{7.5}$$

for a sinusoidal signal of the nominal line frequency. This straightforward optimization is carried out conveniently using the well-known method of Lagrange multipliers, and it leads to bandpass-type frequency responses [1].

At the nominal input frequency, $g_1(n) = g_2(n) = 1$, and thus $\theta(k) = 1 \cdot h(k), k \in A \cup B$. When the line frequency deviates from its nominal value, both of the multiplicative general parameters adapt in order to minimize the prediction error for the instantaneous fundamental frequency. The white noise gain of the overall filter is also affected, because the composite filter coefficients are formed as a product of the subfilter coefficients and the corresponding multiplicative general parameter.

Our MGP algorithm has certain advantageous properties in the present applications, compared, for example, with the standard LMS adaptive algorithm [9] or any of its more robust, leaky modifications [11]. Since there are only two degrees of freedom available in adaptation, the MGP-FIR filter tracks successfully the fundamental signal component, and adaptation is largely insensitive to the harmonic components. The popular LMS algorithms, having usually more degrees of freedom, react consistently to all correlating signal components and adjust the filter to pass also the harmonics [9], which in this case is undesirable. Also, adaptive notch filter algorithms [12] are typically disturbed by strong harmonics.

In the basic MGP-FIR algorithm of reference 7, the N-length basis FIR filter is simply halved, that is, $A = \{0, 1, \ldots, N/2 - 1\}$ and $B = \{N/2, N/2 + 1, \ldots, N - 1\}$. And both of these $N/2$-length subfilters have their own multiplicative general parameter. Because the individual subfilter outputs are used also in approximating the instantaneous gradient of the prediction error surface [see Eqs. (7.2) and (7.3)], it could be beneficial to form the subfilters more freely, leading possibly to sparse impulse responses.

To optimize the contents of sets A and B for certain signal specifications, we have to solve a discrete optimization problem that is highly nonlinear. The full size of the search space to be explored is 2^{N-1} candidates. With a moderate filter length of 30, there exist over 5×10^8 candidate solutions, and with a lengthy basis filter of 60 taps, the number of solution candidates is more than 6×10^{17}. Therefore, it is not feasible to apply an exhaustive search algorithm for this set optimization problem even with moderate filter lengths. Without the existence of evolutionary computation, a core methodology of SC, our set optimization problem would likely remain beyond the interest of practicing engineers.

7.3 GENETIC ALGORITHM FOR OPTIMIZING FILTER TAP CROSS-CONNECTIONS

Evolutionary systems are becoming increasingly popular among researchers and engineers, as the clock rates of low-cost personal computers have well exceeded the gigahertz level. Due to robustness of typical evolution processes, it is straightforward to develop computational evolutionary systems even without much prior knowledge of the field. Genetic algorithm (GA), a core constituent of evolutionary computation [5], is an efficient method for complex optimization problems. There are actually three principal lines of investigation in simulated evolution: evolution strategies, evolutionary programming, and genetic algorithms [13]. Each of these techniques has its strengths and appropriate applications, and they all share the following characteristics: They are population-based search algorithms, impose random variation in the search process, and apply selection operation for creating improved populations. Simulated evolution has its roots in the 1950s; during the lengthy time, similar ideas and algorithms have been independently invented numerous times [14].

Genetic algorithm is a particularly useful and flexible method for discrete optimization. Each option is coded as a binary sequence with the survival of the sequence determined by its fitness to achieve the desired goal. Components from the surviving sequences are then combined and perturbed by mutations to create the new generation of options, with the fittest of the new generation surviving to define the next generation until a satisfactory sequence that optimizes the fitness criteria is obtained [15]. Though computationally intensive, genetic algorithm is perfectly suited for difficult problems where there is no derivative information available to aid the optimization process, and one would otherwise use some inefficient exhaustive search technique. With current computing platforms, like the 3-GHz Pentium® 4 and Matlab® 6, GAs are often able to provide competitive or nearly optimal solutions in a practical computing time. In this context, we define the vague "practical computing time" to be no more than 10–20 min. Genetic algorithms have been used successfully for solving various optimization problems in the field of power systems [16–18].

Below is a description of the genetic algorithm that was developed and fine-tuned for optimizing the contents of tap sets A and B (see also Fig. 7.2 for a flow diagram):

1. Create an initial random population of N_P candidate solutions. Each candidate solution is coded as a binary sequence, or chromosome, of length N. The chromosome contains one gene for each filter tap, and the gene positions identify the corresponding tap index. When some gene has the value 1, it means that the corresponding tap index belongs to set A, and with the gene value 0, the tap index belongs to set B. The leftmost gene position corresponds to the tap index $k = 0$, and the rightmost one to $k = N - 1$. Figure 7.3 shows an example of this simple chromosome encoding with $N = 8$.

2. Evaluate the fitness of each chromosome in the population, and sort the population in the order of decreasing fitness scores. The application-specific fitness issue is discussed further below.

3. Select the $N_P/2$ fittest chromosomes from the sorted population for reproduction, and discard the others.

4. Form $N_P/4$ pairs of parent chromosomes for crossover. These couples are selected in the order of their fitness scores; that is, the two fittest chromosomes form one pair, the two next fittest chromosomes form another pair, and so on. Thus, there is considerable elitist determinism in this pairing process.

5. Create two offspring involving two parent chromosomes. A random crossover point is selected between the first and last genes of the parent chromosomes.

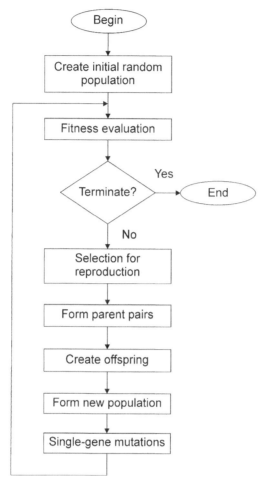

Figure 7.2. Genetic algorithm for solving the tap cross-connection optimization problem.

PARENT$_{\#1}$ passes its genes to the left of the crossover point to OFFSPRING$_{\#1}$. In a like manner, PARENT$_{\#2}$ passes its genes to the right of the crossover point to OFFSPRING$_{\#1}$. OFFSPRING$_{\#2}$ is constructed similarly from the remaining gene strings. This process is repeated for all the parent couples. Figure 7.4 illustrates the reproduction process with $N = 8$.

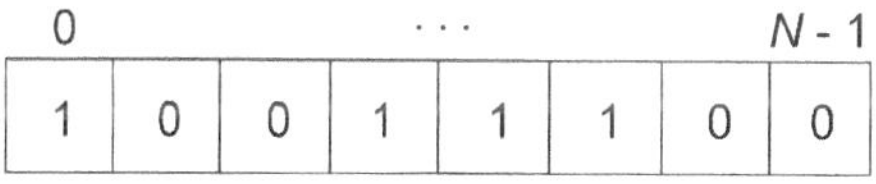

0				$\cdots$			$N - 1$
1	0	0	1	1	1	0	0

Figure 7.3. Chromosome encoding with $N = 8$; $A = \{0,3,4,5\}$, and $B = \{1,2,6,7\}$.

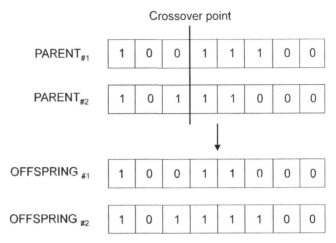

Figure 7.4. Crossover operator is applied to two parents; a crossover point is selected randomly and the two strings that follow the point are exchanged.

6. Unite the $N_P/2$ parents and $N_P/2$ offspring to form a new population of N_P chromosomes.

7. Apply possible single-gene mutation, $1 \rightarrow 0$ or $0 \rightarrow 1$, to the chromosomes in the new population. The mutation probability of each chromosome is m_p, and the specific gene to be mutated is selected randomly. However, the fittest parent chromosome is never mutated, and thus elitism is used also in this stage. Because the selection and pairing actions of Steps 3 and 4 are largely deterministic, the role of probabilistic mutation is emphasized here, and its probability should be considerably higher than in typical GA implementations. In this way, we can maintain the diversity of our population. The population diversity is in a key role, because the theory of evolutionary computation suggests that evolution cannot continue to search effectively after a population has converged [5].

8. Go to Step 2 and repeat this loop until the termination conditions are achieved. These termination conditions are application-dependent, and they will be detailed below.

Our efficient genetic algorithm has only two application-specific parameters, size of the population N_P and mutation probability m_p. In the following computational experiments, we used three different values of N_P—20, 40, and 80—depending on the length of the basis FIR filter ($N = 12$, 22, and 40, respectively). As an empirical rule of thumb, the population size should preferably be at least twice the filter length. We computed typically 50 generations in our GA runs. To ensure that the obtained best solution is at least close to the global optimum, a few overnight verification runs with several thousands of generations were performed. It turned out that less than 50 generations was adequate in most of the cases for finding a competitive solution. Furthermore, an appropriate mutation probability was found to be 0.5–0.7, which kept the average fitness score well separated from the maximum fitness.

7.4 DESIGN OF MULTIPLIERLESS BASIS FILTERS BY EVOLUTIONARY PROGRAMMING

In addition to the arithmetic operations needed in the fixed subfilters, the MGP-adaptive part [see Eqs. (7.1)–(7.3)] requires only three additions and five multiplications. If we had general fixed- or floating-point coefficients with $N = 40$, the number of arithmetic operations would increase by 40 multiplications and 39 additions, since, unlike in linear-phase FIR filters, coefficient symmetry cannot be exploited in these predictive filters. Such a large number of multiplications is a critical problem in FPGA and other hardware implementations, and it may be burdensome for microcontrollers without a parallel multiply-accumulate (MAC) instruction. Therefore, we decided to develop an alternative class of MGP-FIR filters with totally multiplierless subfilters; only coefficient values $\{-1, 0, +1\}$ are allowed. This would mean that the number of required multiplications remains always 5 and does not depend on the filter length N—only the number of additions $(=N + 2)$ will increase with the filter length. Next, we are going to introduce an efficient evolutionary programming algorithm for optimizing the discrete coefficient values of subfilters 1 and 2.

Evolutionary programming was originally developed by L. J. Fogel for creating artificial (computational) intelligence at the beginning of the 1960s [14], but in the mid-1980s it became an important tool for solving combinatorial optimization problems. Nevertheless, evolutionary programming is still less known than genetic algorithms that are already used routinely in various engineering applications [15]. It should be pointed out that there is simply no single evolutionary programming algorithm (EPA) only, but the basic algorithm, discussed, for example, by D. B. Fogel in reference 5 and Bäck in reference 13, is usually modified according to the specific characteristics and requirements of a particular problem. In evolutionary programming, N_P parents generate always N_P offspring; both the parents and offspring are included in the selection and can thus be part of the next generation. Evolutionary programming is used increasingly for solving demanding optimization problems also in the field of electric power systems [19–21].

Our EPA, to be introduced below, was tailored specifically to the nonlinear MGP-FIR optimization problem with strictly constrained coefficient values. In typical evolutionary programming algorithms, the elements in the population are real-valued and they are perturbed by real-valued random variables. In our case, however, the perturbing random variables are bi-valued, either $\{0, +1\}$, $\{-1, +1\}$, or $\{-1, 0\}$, due to the specific characteristics of this particular application.

Below is a description of the evolutionary programming algorithm that was developed for optimizing the coefficients of subfilter #1 and subfilter #2 in

Eq. (7.1); see also Fig. 7.5 for a flow chart:

1. Create an initial random population of N_P candidate solutions. Each candidate is a pair of two N-length vectors: one vector for subfilter 1 and the other for subfilter 2. The vector elements correspond to subfilter coefficients, and they may have values $\{-1, 0, +1\}$. When some element of subfilter 1 has a value ∓ 1, then the corresponding element in subfilter 2 is equal to 0, and vice versa. The total number of nonzero coefficients in all candidate solutions must always be equal to N.

2. Perform single-element mutations, either $-1 \rightarrow 0/+1$, $0 \rightarrow \mp 1$, or $+1 \rightarrow -1/0$, for each solution pair in the population. The specific element of subfilter 1 to be mutated is first selected randomly. After the selected element of subfilter 1 is mutated from $\mp 1 \rightarrow 0$ or $0 \rightarrow \mp 1$ (with equal probabilities), the corresponding element of subfilter 2 is also mutated, $0 \rightarrow \mp 1$, $-1 \rightarrow 0$, or $+1 \rightarrow 0$, to keep the number of nonzero coefficients equal to N. On the other hand, if an element of subfilter 1 is mutated from $-1 \rightarrow +1$ or $+1 \rightarrow -1$, no elements in subfilter 2 are mutated. At the end of this random perturbation step, we include the mutated vector pairs to the original population; therefore, the size of the enhanced population is $N_P + N_P = 2N_P$.

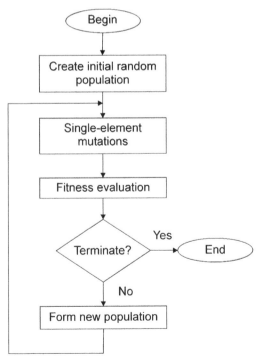

Figure 7.5. Evolutionary programming algorithm for solving the optimization problem of multiplierless basis filters.

3. Evaluate the fitness of all candidate solutions in the enhanced population, and sort the population in the order of decreasing fitness scores. The application-specific fitness issue is discussed further below.

4. Select the N_P fittest solutions from the sorted population to the new population and discard the N_P poorest ones. Thus, the selection process has built-in elitism.

5. Go to Step 2 and repeat this loop until the termination conditions are achieved. These termination conditions are application-dependent, and they will be detailed below.

Our evolutionary programming algorithm has only one application-specific parameter, size of the population N_P. In the following computational experiments, we used $N_P = 40$; this is a good compromise between population diversity and computation time. We computed typically less than 400 generations in our EPA runs. To ensure that the obtained best solution is at least close to the global optimum, a few verification runs with up to 2000 generations were performed. It turned out that 50–200 generations was adequate in most of the cases for finding a competitive pair of subfilter coefficient sets with FIR filter lengths 12, 22, and 40. An empirical observation was made that the number of generations needed for convergence roughly doubles when the filter length N doubles. This is understandable, because the population size remained always the same.

7.5 PREDICTIVE FILTERS FOR ZERO-CROSSINGS DETECTOR

To next illustrate the behavior and characteristics of the new GA-based cross-connection optimization scheme, we designed several MGP-FIRs for delayless line voltage or current restoration. All those filters are intended for zero-crossings (ZC) detectors. Accurate and robust detection of zero crossings is important in power and industrial electronics, particularly in power converters, where precise line synchronization requires reliable zero-crossing information. In industrial environments, line voltages and currents are usually corrupted by commutation notches, harmonics, ringing, and other disturbances that may lead to inaccurate firing synchronization. Details of the considered ZC detection approach can be found in references 1 and 9. Table 7.1 lists the six test cases that will be discussed below, and Appendix 7.1 contains the coefficients of those sinusoid-predictive FIR filters corresponding to test cases 1, 2, and 3. They were computed using the formulae of references 1 and 8.

7.5.1 Single 60-Hz Sinusoid Corrupted by Noise

In the first group of simulations, we wanted to compare the characteristics of MGP-FIRs that are based on 50-Hz sinusoid-predictive FIR filters to MGP-FIRs based on simple unity-coefficient averagers. The unity-coefficient basis filters were included in these experiments, because they do not need any multiplications and are, therefore, particularly attractive for FPGA and microcontroller implementations. In addition, their design task is trivial, compared to the Lagrange multipliers-based

TABLE 7.1. Summary of Test Cases

Case Number	Type of Basis FIR Filter	NG
1	Sinusoid-predictive filter, 50 Hz, $N = 12$	0.2504
2	Sinusoid-predictive filter, 50 Hz, $N = 22$	0.1469
3	Sinusoid-predictive filter, 50 Hz, $N = 40$	0.0524
4	Unity-coefficient filter, $N = 12$	0.0833
5	Unity-coefficient filter, $N = 22$	0.0455
6	Unity-coefficient filter, $N = 40$	0.0250

optimization of sinusoid-predictive filters. However, their prediction capability depends fully on the two adaptive parameters.

After determining the test cases (Table 7.1), we set the optimization objectives and defined the procedure for computing the fitness scores of candidate solutions. Here, the fitness is computed by simulating each MGP-FIR candidate with a 60-Hz test signal of length 400 samples corrupted by uniformly distributed noise of relative amplitude $\pm 4\%$. The applied sampling period is 600 μs, corresponding to the sampling rate of 1.67 kHz. This moderate sampling rate would typically be increased by linear interpolation in a practical ZC detector. Figure 7.6 illustrates the multistage structure of the complete ZC detection method [1]. And Fig. 7.7 shows a typical input waveform of such a zero-crossings detector, as well as the corresponding MGP-FIR output with accurately placed zero-crossings. It should be noted that a fixed sinusoid-predictive filter, designed for 50-Hz signals, does not work at all with 60-Hz signals.

The wide-band noise component in the test signal is needed to guarantee the necessary persistence of excitation during the optimization process. Both of the multiplicative general parameters, $g_1(n)$ and $g_2(n)$, were initialized to zero in the beginning of each simulation run. Furthermore, the fitness function F to be maximized was defined as

$$F = \frac{1}{NG \cdot \underbrace{\sum_{n=1}^{400} n \cdot |e(n)|}_{\text{ITAE}}} \tag{7.6}$$

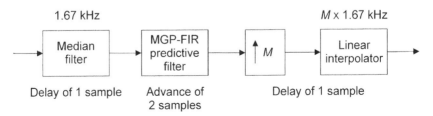

Figure 7.6. Block diagram of the multistage filter system for zero-crossings detectors [1]; the total delay of the system is $1 - 2 + 1 = 0$ samples at the fundamental frequency.

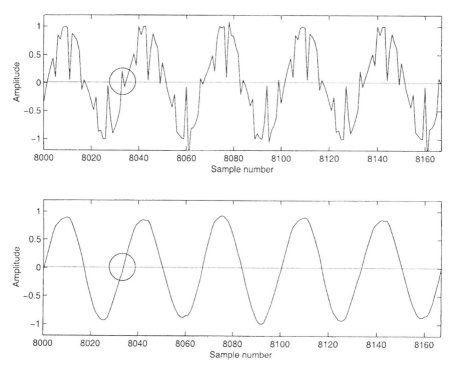

Figure 7.7. Corrupted input signal (**upper**) and filtered output with accurately placed zero crossings (**lower**).

where $e(n)$ is the observed prediction error, $x(n) - y(n - 2)$, in the filter output, and NG is the white noise gain at the end of the entire simulation cycle. Thus, we are designing two-step-ahead predictive filters in this example. Our principal objective is to minimize the white noise gain of the converged MGP-FIR filter. The converged tap index sets A and B could then be frozen and used in a real application. However, it is not enough to have the NG term alone in F, because such filters tend to have oscillatory convergence or even unstable behavior. By including the additional sigma term in the fitness function, we can guide the optimal solution toward an acceptable convergence behavior. The sigma term corresponds to the integral of time absolute error (ITAE) function, used frequently in control engineering for designing well-behaving responses.

Extensive GA runs were performed with all the six basis filters of Table 7.1. Table 7.2 contains a summary of typical optimization results. We can see that the best fitness increases consistently as the length of the basis filter increases (test cases 1, 2, 3, and 4, 5, 6). This is natural, because longer filters may obtain lower NG values, and NG has a central role in the fitness function of Eq. (7.6). With filter lengths 12 and 22, both the sinusoid-predictive basis filters and unity-coefficient basis filters lead to similar performance measures. Nevertheless, it should be remembered that the unity-coefficient alternatives are computationally more

TABLE 7.2. GA Optimization Results with 60-Hz Noisy Sinusoid

Case Number	Best Fitness	NG	Converged Chromosome
1	0.0024	0.2086	100000111111
2	0.0038	0.1330	0000000011111110001111
3	0.0058	0.0842	00011100000000000111 11100000001111111111
4	0.0020	0.2436	111111000000
5	0.0039	0.1374	0000011111111111111000
6	0.0079	0.0641	1111110000000000001 1111111111110000000

efficient to implement. When the filter length is increased to 40, the unity-coefficient basis filter offers considerably higher fitness value as well as better NG than the sinusoid-predictive counterpart does. Optimization results with other low-frequency sinusoids resembled those of Table 7.2. Figure 7.8 illustrates typical results of the GA maximizing the fitness score in the test case 3. It should be noted that although the mutation probability was set as high as 0.7, the converged average and lowest fitness scores are still quite close to the best fitness. This indicates that the coefficient sensitivity of the optimized basis filter is good. The corresponding prediction error

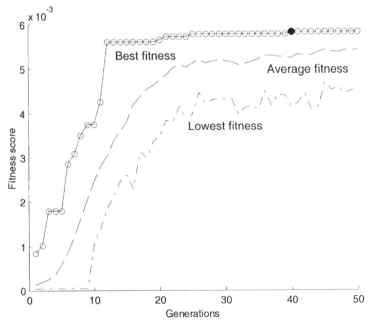

Figure 7.8. GA maximizing the fitness score; sinusoid-predictive basis FIR filter with $N = 40$.

with the best chromosome of Eq. (7.7) is plotted in Fig. 7.9.

$$[0001110000000000011111100000001111111111]_{BEST} \Rightarrow$$
$$A = \{3,4,5,17,18,19,20,21,22,30,31,32,33,34,35,36,37,38,39\} \qquad (7.7)$$
$$B = \{0,1,2,6,7,8,9,10,11,12,13,14,15,16,23,24,25,26,27,28,29\}$$

Our structurally optimized MGP-FIR is converging in about 75 samples from zero initial values of the multiplicative general parameters. The residual prediction error is due to the additive $\pm 4\%$ noise component in the input signal. At this point, based on Table 7.2, one might argue that there is no actual need to use sinusoid-predictive basis filters in adaptive MGP-FIR algorithms, because the unity-coefficient basis filters lead to implementations that are more effective.

7.5.2 Sequence of 49-, 50-, and 51-Hz Sinusoids Corrupted by Noise

In practical electric power applications, however, the line frequency is always slightly time-varying as discussed in the introduction of this chapter. Therefore, it would be important to optimize the index sets A and B not for any single frequency but simultaneously for multiple frequencies within the specified frequency tolerance. In the following experiments, we assumed the nominal 50-Hz line frequency with a tolerance of $\pm 2\%$; that is typical in Western European countries.

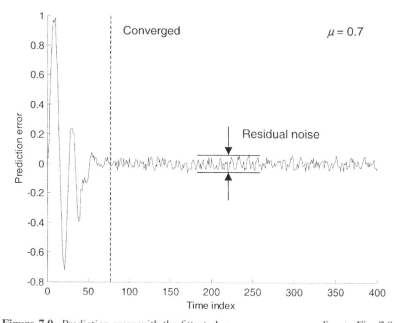

Figure 7.9. Prediction error with the fittest chromosome corresponding to Fig. 7.8.

To design optimal MGP-FIR structures for the narrow frequency band, we first created a test signal of length 900, containing three cascaded blocks of 300 samples—one block for each sinusoid sequence of 49, 50, and 51 Hz. The additive noise component was the same as used in the earlier tests with the single 60-Hz sinusoid. We also modified the fitness function to match the multiple-frequency problem:

$$F = \frac{1}{\max(NG_{49\,Hz}, NG_{50\,Hz}, NG_{51\,Hz}) \cdot ITAE} \tag{7.8a}$$

$$ITAE = \sum_{n=1}^{300} n \cdot |e(n)| + \sum_{n=301}^{600} (n - 300) \cdot |e(n)| + \sum_{n=601}^{900} (n - 600) \cdot |e(n)| \tag{7.8b}$$

Here, we use the maximum of the NG values at the end of each sinusoid sequence together with the stabilizing ITAE term for computing the fitness score.

Again, extensive genetic algorithm runs were performed with all the basis filters of Table 7.1. Table 7.3 gives a summary of typical optimization results. With filter lengths 12 and 40, the sinusoid-predictive basis filters lead to better performance measures than the unity-coefficient basis filters. Thus, the unity-coefficient option seems to be more sensitive to discontinuous frequency switching, and sinusoid-predictive basis filters are clearly advantageous for designing robust MGP-FIRs for zero-crossings detectors.

The reason for this obvious sensitivity problem is related to Eqs. (7.2) and (7.3). In these adaptation formulae, the prediction error term, $x(n) - y(n - p)$, is first multiplied by the adaptation gain, μ, and then by the output of subfilter 1 or subfilter 2. With practical sinusoid-predictive basis filters, both of the optimized subfilters are of bandpass nature, and their gain maximums are placed near the nominal line frequency. On the other hand, with unity-coefficient basis filters the subfilter magnitude responses are usually peaky and of lowpass nature. In addition, the largest

TABLE 7.3. GA Optimization Results with 49/50/51-Hz Noisy Sinusoids

Case Number	Best Fitness	NG 49 Hz	NG 50 Hz	NG 51 Hz	Converged Chromosome
1	0.0012	0.2520	0.2508	0.2522	100101001110
2	0.0020	0.1501	0.1471	0.1506	100001101101100100000010
3	0.0042	0.0491	0.0534	0.0563	01111100000000001111 1110000000011111111110
4	0.00078	0.3222	0.3173	0.3099	000000111111
5	0.0020	0.1182	0.1248	0.1306	111111110000000000000011
6	0.0029	0.0701	0.0677	0.0753	11111110000000000000 0011111111111111111110

gain is at the zero frequency (DC). This DC gain may be considerably higher than the gain at the nominal line frequency. Figure 7.10 shows the magnitude responses of optimized subfilters for the test cases 3 and 6 (see Table 7.3). When the input signal switches from one sinusoid sequence to another with an *amplitude disconti-nuity*, the switching transient excites those high-gain frequencies temporarily, and it leads to remarkable increase in the composite adaptation gain. That, unavoidably, produces oscillations and increases the ITAE component in the fitness function. To keep the oscillations tolerable, MGP-FIRs with unity-coefficient basis filters do not have as many degrees of freedom available for effective noise gain minimiz-ation as MGP-FIRs with sinusoid-predictive basis filters. Figure 7.11 illustrates the time-domain responses of two optimized subfilters—subfilter 2 of case 3 and subfil-ter 2 of case 6—around the frequency switching point of $50 \rightarrow 51$ Hz (time index 601). Here, the unity-coefficient-based MGP-FIR has a temporary down shift of the DC level, while the sinusoid-predictive-based counterpart behaves more consist-ently. It should be noted that the triple-frequency test sequence was designed to contain considerable amplitude discontinuities at the switching points, because, in this way, we may find robust adaptive filters that recover quickly also from deep commutation notches.

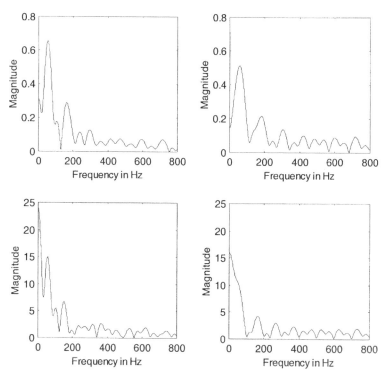

Figure 7.10. Magnitude responses of optimized subfilters 1 (**left**) and 2 (**right**) in test cases 3 (**upper**) and 6 (**lower**).

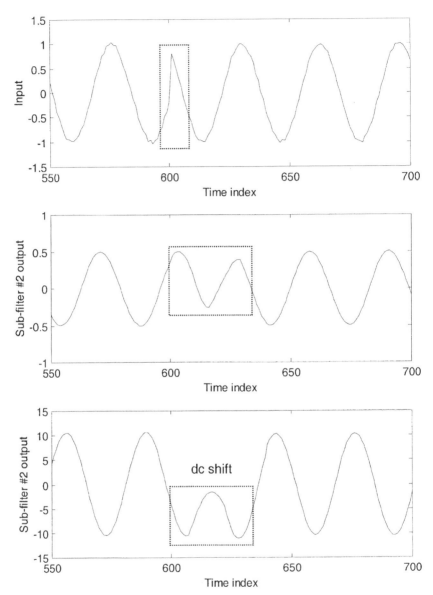

Figure 7.11. Input stepping from 50 to 51 Hz with discontinuous amplitude (**top**), and corresponding responses of two subfilters in test cases 3 (**middle**) and 6 (**bottom**).

But why does the test case 5 have lower NG values than those of the case 2? This is because the sinusoid-predictive basis filter of the test case 2 has two forced zeros, at DC (possible measurement bias) and 150 Hz (third harmonic), which were included as application-specific constraints in the Lagrange multipliers-based optimization process [8]. These fixed notches are highly desirable with *stand-alone* FIR filters, but they limit the adaptability of the corresponding MGP-FIR. Without such forced zeros, also the 22-length sinusoid-predictive basis filter would naturally offer better performance measures than the unity-coefficient counterpart would. Results with other multiple (low-) frequency test signals were similar to those of Table 7.3. Figure 7.12 illustrates the results of the GA maximizing the fitness score in the test case 5. Here it can be observed that the coefficient sensitivity of this basis filter is likely higher than that in the case of Fig. 7.8, because now the converged average and lowest fitness scores are more separated from the best fitness. The same mutation probability of 0.7 was used also in these simulations. In addition, Fig. 7.13 shows the corresponding prediction error with the best chromosome. This optimized MGP-FIR is converging in less than 60 samples. The convergence of the MGPs, $g_1(n)$ and $g_2(n)$, is depicted in Fig. 7.14. It should be noted that the values of converged multiplicative general parameters change only a little when the frequency steps from 49 to 51 Hz. On the other hand, the initial transients after each step-like frequency change are substantial. These transients are mainly due to amplitude discontinuities in the input waveform when switching from one sinusoid sequence to another. However, in practical electric power systems, the fundamental frequency is always changing smoothly and slowly, although some of the disturbances may be rather abrupt.

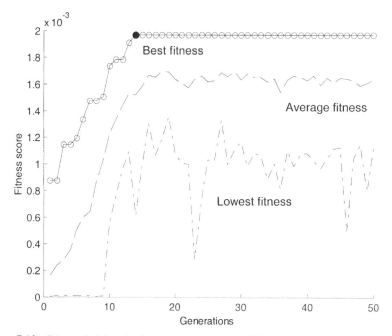

Figure 7.12. GA maximizing the fitness score; unity-coefficient basis FIR filter with $N = 22$.

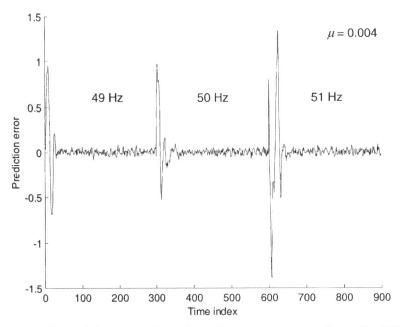

Figure 7.13. Prediction error with the fittest chromosome corresponding to Fig. 7.12.

7.5.3 Discussion of Zero-Crossings Detection Application

We introduced a genetic algorithm-based procedure for structural optimization of multiplicative general parameter FIR filters. These computationally efficient reduced-rank adaptive filters are robust and suitable for predictive configurations. The innovative design process of such filters has three independent stages: Lagrange multipliers-based optimization of the sinusoid-predictive basis filter, genetic algorithm-based search of basis FIR tap cross-connections, and, finally, the online MGP-adaptation phase guided by variations in signal statistics.

Concluding remarks on the simulation experiments of Sections 7.5.1 and 7.5.2 are given below:

- All the tested basis filters worked well with single (low-) frequency test signals.
- Tap cross-connection optimization is more effective with longer filters.
- With short sinusoid-predictive basis filters, the trivial halving of tap indexes is often a satisfactory choice.
- Sinusoid-predictive basis filters are preferable in applications with time-varying frequencies and considerable transient-like discontinuities.
- The robustness of sinusoid-predictive basis filters was not visible with single-frequency test signals.

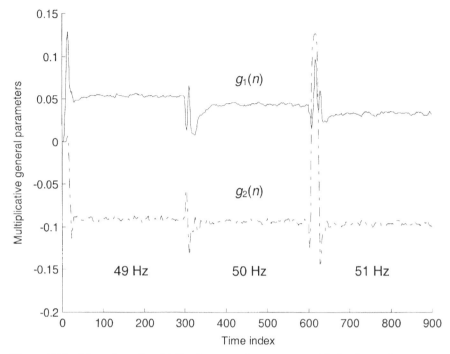

Figure 7.14. Adaptation of multiplicative general parameters with the fittest chromosome corresponding to Fig. 7.12.

- Unity-coefficient basis filters are attractive with single-frequency signals and with signals that contain only moderate transient-like discontinuities.
- Unity-coefficient basis filters are of particular interest, if the implementation platform cannot handle the required multiplications of sinusoid-predictive basis filters.

7.6 PREDICTIVE FILTERS FOR CURRENT REFERENCE GENERATORS

There is a growing global interest in electric power quality, both at electricity distribution and at consumer levels. This is due to the excessive use of nonlinear power electronics devices as well as power plant equipment capable of injecting considerable harmonic distortion into the power network [22]. As an example, three-phase six-pulse AC/DC converters, used widely in industry applications, distort the input current by fifth, seventh, ninth, and so on, order odd harmonics. On the other hand, simple single-phase AC/DC full-wave rectifiers, existing in various consumer electronics equipment, corrupt the line current by third, fifth, seventh, and so on, order harmonics. Thus, the distortion generation problem has spread all over the electricity distribution network. While the distortion effect of a single low-power converter is practically negligible, the cumulative effect of numerous nonlinear loads is certainly disturbing. Limiting this harmonic distortion is required to reduce the understandable risk of equipment damage, harmful malfunctioning, and extra energy losses; these would lead to various safety troubles and considerable monetary losses.

For solving harmonic distortion problems in electric power networks, there are generally two principal options: Develop and use only such converter topologies that do not produce excessive harmonics [23], or construct active or passive power filters to reduce the existing distortion level [24]. Both of these approaches are dynamic fields of research and development. Active power filters (APF) are typically used for attenuating current harmonics in supply networks at the low- to medium-voltage distribution level. A comprehensive review on APF technologies was presented by El-Habrouk et al. in reference 24, where the key aspects of active power filters are carefully outlined. The effective current injection method is used in many active power filters for reducing the harmonic distortion [22]. In such a straightforward scheme, distorted current waveforms are restored by injecting equal-but-opposite compensating harmonic currents to the corrupted load current. Therefore, current reference generation has a fundamental role in current injection-type active filters; a delayless bandstop filter with some frequency-adaptation capability is needed. To design such a filter is not a trivial task. Väliviita and Ovaska introduced a predictive digital signal processing method for generating current references in current injection-type active power filters [2]. Their method is suitable both for 50/60-Hz electricity distribution networks, as well as for emerging applications with truly altering frequencies. However, that hybrid method can be considered as *multiplication-intensive*, and thus it is not attractive for hardware implementations. Besides, it shares the harmful weight-drift problem of the standard LMS algorithm [11].

A simplified MGP-FIR-based current reference generator is depicted in Fig. 7.15. Here, the MGP-FIR behaves as a delayless bandpass filter of the fundamental

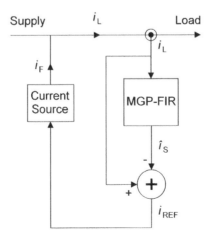

Figure 7.15. MGP-FIR-based current reference generator for shunt-type active power filters.

current component. When this estimated fundamental component, $\hat{i}_S$, is subtracted from the actual load current, i_L, we obtain an estimate, i_{REF}, of the harmonics and other existing disturbances. This reference current is then inverted and amplified in the current source, leading to i_F, and finally injected into the line current. The output impedance of the current source must be large enough so that it can be regarded as a real current source [22]. Details of such current sources are beyond the scope of our chapter, and interested readers are directed to the thorough APF reviews of references 24 and 25.

The filtering problems of ZC detection and current reference generation might first appear equal. However, in ZC detection applications we are only interested in locating the fundamental ZC points accurately, while the overall output waveform is not of principal interest. On the other hand, in current reference generation for active power filters, both the amplitude purity and phase accuracy of the reconstructed fundamental sinusoid are of crucial importance.

To illustrate the behavior and characteristics of the new evolutionary programming-based subfilter optimization scheme, we designed several bandpass-type MGP-FIRs for reconstructing the fundamental current component of 50 Hz $\pm 2\%$. All the designed filters are two-step-ahead predictive filters of the fundamental current frequency. In this example case, one prediction step is reserved for compensating both measurement (i.e., sensor and data acquisition) and computation delays, and the other step is needed for a possible up-sampling interpolator [2] that could be necessary in applications with high pulse-width modulation (PWM) switching rates at the output stage. Thus, the prediction step p in Eqs. (7.2) and (7.3) is an application-specific parameter. We consider again three filter lengths N, namely 12, 22, and 40. However, in current reference generators with no up-sampling, even longer filters could be beneficial.

7.6.1 Sequence of 49-, 50-, and 51-Hz Noisy Sinusoids

To design appropriate MGP-FIRs for the required frequency tolerance, we created again a test signal of length 900, containing three blocks of 300 samples—one block for each sinusoid sequence of 49, 50, and 51 Hz. The sinusoids were corrupted by uniformly distributed noise of relative amplitude $\pm 4\%$ to guarantee the persistence of excitation during the optimization process. Both of the multiplicative general parameters were initialized to zero in the beginning of every simulation run. Each test signal block has the form

$$x(n) = \sin(\omega_F n) + \varepsilon(n) \tag{7.9}$$

where ω_F corresponds to the fundamental frequency and $\varepsilon(n)$ represents the additive noise sequence. The sampling period that was applied throughout the following simulations was 600 μs.

From our earlier work with fixed sinusoid-predictive FIR filters [1,8], we know that when such predictive filters are designed by minimizing the white noise gain, the resulting filter response will have a bandpass nature. Therefore, we first decided just to minimize the white noise gain of our MGP-FIR. In this case, the instantaneous white noise gain of the adaptive filter is defined as

$$\text{NG}(n) = \sum_{k \in A} [g_1(n)h(k)]^2 + \sum_{k \in B} [g_2(n)h(k)]^2 \tag{7.10}$$

However, it was soon observed that it is not enough to have the NG terms alone in the fitness function of the evolutionary programming algorithm, because such filters tend to have highly oscillatory convergence. This resembles the phenomenon with the genetic algorithm-based optimization of filter tap cross-connections, discussed above. Thus, we decided to use the dual-objective fitness function of Eq. (7.8) also in this case (but scaled by 1000). Nevertheless, with initial random populations, it frequently happened that some candidate solution had a noise gain very close to zero—considerably below the value that would be possible for the corresponding sinusoid-predictive FIR filter of length N. This naturally caused a high fitness score, although the particular solution would not be of any practical use. To avoid this erroneous condition, we included a simple test in the basic NG calculation of Eq. (7.10): if the instantaneous NG is below the minimum possible NG, then $\text{NG} = 10$. After this constraining modification, the evolutionary process advanced consistently from the very beginning.

Extensive EPA runs were performed with all three filter lengths, and Table 7.4 lists the optimization results (marked with $+$). The three columns $\text{NG} \cdot \cdot_{\text{OPT}}$ contain the white noise gains of optimal sinusoid-predictive FIR filters that were designed for the particular frequency using the conventional method of Lagrange multipliers [1]. These reference values are the strict low limits of the noise gains that could be achieved by any kind of two-step-ahead sinusoid-predictive FIR filter of length N, including the MGP-FIR. In addition, the columns $\text{NG} \cdot \cdot$ show the white noise gains of converged MGP-FIRs at the end of each sub-sequence (49/50/51 Hz). Also, the corresponding fitness values and applied adaptation gains are provided. It can be seen that the fitness value is increasing with the length of the filter. This is natural, because longer filters have more degrees of freedom for both controlling the convergence behavior and minimizing the noise gain. Table 7.5 shows the optimized coefficients of subfilters 1 and 2. The fourth case, marked with $*$, will be discussed later. Figure 7.16 illustrates the results of the EPA maximizing the fitness

TABLE 7.4. Optimal Noise Gains and Converged Noise Gains

N	NG49_{OPT}	NG50_{OPT}	NG51_{OPT}	NG49	NG50	NG51	Fitness	μ
12^+	0.2565	0.2504	0.2441	0.2821	0.2775	0.2758	0.9939	0.004
22^+	0.0929	0.0949	0.0971	0.1018	0.1013	0.1035	2.3645	0.004
40^+	0.0513	0.0524	0.0535	0.0568	0.0572	0.0577	3.9852	0.0005
40^*	0.0513	0.0524	0.0535	0.0702	0.0671	0.0684	4.8164	0.0005

$^+$NG-optimized filter.
*Harmonics-optimized filter.

TABLE 7.5. EPA-Optimized Coefficients of Subfilters

N	Subfilter 1	Subfilter 2
12^+	11111000−1−1−1−1	0000011−10000
22^+	−1000000001111111110000	0−1−1−1−1−11110000000001111
40^+	−1−1−100000111111111111	0001111100000000000
	00000−1−1−1−1−1−1	−1−1−111000000000000111
	−1−1−1−1−1−1−1000	
40^*	1111010000−1−1−1−1	0000101−1−1−1−1000000000−1
	−1−1−1−1−1−10	−11111111000000−11−11−11
	0000000011111000000	

+NG-optimized filter.
*Harmonics-optimized filter.

---

score F with $N = 40$. Also here the coefficient sensitivity of subfilters 1 and 2 is good, because even the converged lowest fitness is close to the best fitness score. It should be remembered that in the EPA, one or two coefficient values are always mutated to other discrete values, $\{-1, 0, +1\}$. In addition, Fig. 7.17 shows the corresponding prediction error $e(n)$ with the fittest pair of subfilters. The convergence of the multiplicative general parameters, $g_1(n)$ and $g_2(n)$, is depicted in Fig. 7.18. In this case, the converged value of $g_2(n)$ changes much

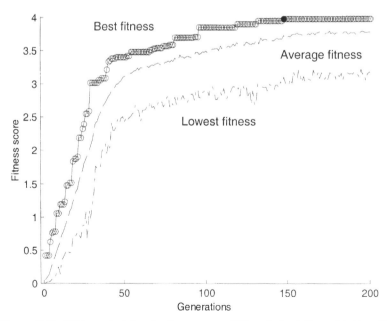

Figure 7.16. EPA maximizing the fitness score; NG-optimized filter with $N = 40$.

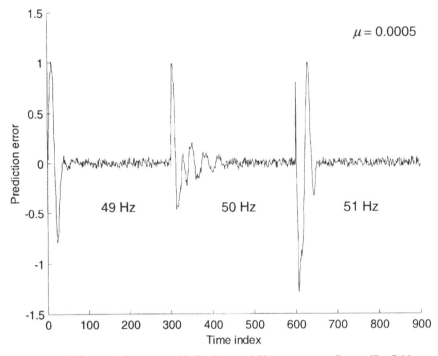

Figure 7.17. Prediction error with the fittest subfilters corresponding to Fig. 7.16.

more than the value of $g_1(n)$ when the frequency steps from 49 to 51 Hz. Moreover, $g_1(n)$ has an extensive transient after the latter frequency step, $50 \rightarrow 51$ Hz, when the value of $g_2(n)$ crosses the zero level twice. Such a zero-crossing means that the subfilter 2 becomes momentarily disconnected. In Section 7.5.2, we discussed the noticeable frequency-switching problem of unity-coefficient-based MGP-FIRs; that problem is less severe with MGP-FIRs that have basis filters with possible coefficient values of $\{-1, 0, +1\}$. Here, the availability of negative unity coefficients makes it easier to provide tolerable transient responses as well as adequate noise gains simultaneously. Nevertheless, the adaptation gain values of Table 7.4 should only be taken as *maximum* practical values, while the actual μ in a specific application must be selected according to the practical variation rate of the fundamental frequency. In large power distribution networks with several cooperative power plants, the fundamental frequency is varying very slowly, typically no more than 0.1 Hz/s, but this variation may be much faster in a weak local network that is supplied by a stand-alone diesel generator.

All the above simulation results are highly encouraging, and we decided to evaluate the performance of the 40-length MGP-FIR with artificial current signals of 49/50/51 Hz corrupted by strong third- to thirteenth-order odd harmonics.

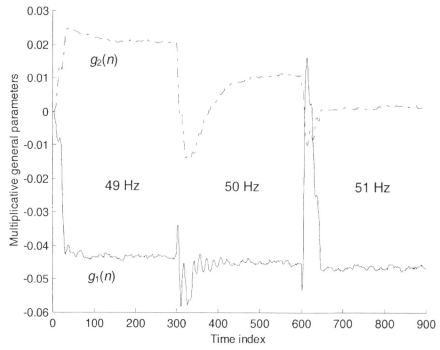

Figure 7.18. Adaptation of multiplicative general parameters with the fittest subfilters corresponding to Fig. 7.16.

7.6.2 Sequence of 49-, 50-, and 51-Hz Noisy Sinusoids Corrupted by Harmonics

Before proceeding to the evaluation phase with artificial current signals, we designed another set of subfilters for the case $N = 40$ (marked with * in Tables 7.4 and 7.5). Now, the aim was to concentrate explicitly on the attenuation of odd harmonics instead of just relying on the impact of white noise gain minimization. This was done by including harmonic frequencies into the test signal $x(n)$ specified above. The amplitude of third- to thirteenth-order odd harmonic components was 10% of the fundamental sinusoid, and the noise level was reduced to $\pm 2\%$. In addition, the error term $e(n)$ in the fitness function of Eq. (7.8) was modified to be

$$e(n) = x_F(n) - y(n-2) \tag{7.11}$$

where $x_F(n)$ is the pure fundamental component. Thus, we demanded the output of our MGP-FIR to be a two-step-ahead predicted version of the fundamental sinusoid only. Figure 7.19 illustrates the EPA maximizing the fitness score with the modified error term. Now the converged lowest fitness is considerably more separated from the best and average fitness scores than in the NG-optimized case of Fig. 7.16.

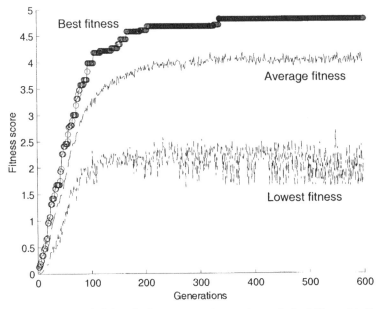

Figure 7.19. EPA maximizing the fitness score; harmonics-optimized filter with $N = 40$.

This new error term leads also to inherent increase in white noise gains, as shown in Table 7.4. The obvious reason behind this increase is that the filter needs some degrees of freedom for minimizing the gains at the specified harmonic frequencies, and, because the filter length remains the same, those degrees of freedom must be taken away from NG minimization.

7.6.3 Artificial Current Signal Corrupted by Odd Harmonics

Next, we constructed three artificial current signals that contain third- to thirteenth-order harmonics and no wide-band noise:

$$x(n) = \sin(\omega_F n) + \sum_{m \in \{3,5,7,9,11,13\}} 0.15 \cdot \sin(m\omega_F n) \tag{7.12}$$

where ω_F corresponds to the three fundamental frequencies, 49/50/51 Hz, within the specified frequency tolerance of interest. These test signals are meant for illustration purposes only, and they do not resemble the current waveform of any real-world AC/DC converter. The amplitudes of harmonic frequencies were set equal to make it easier to compare the attenuation capabilities within the whole harmonics range. It was calculated that the total harmonic distortion (THD) of our test signal is 36.7%. Figure 7.20 shows the distorted input signal of 49 Hz. This severely corrupted waveform is more like a square wave than a fundamental sinusoid.

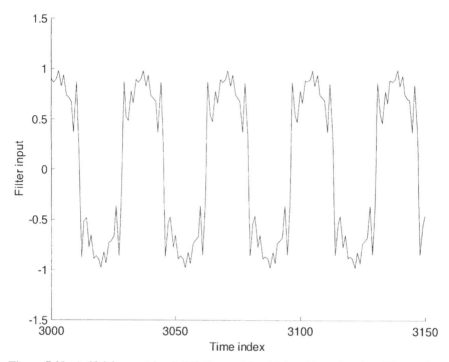

Figure 7.20. Artificial current signal of 49 Hz containing third- to thirteenth-order odd harmonics.

When the signal of Fig. 7.20 was fed to the NG-optimized MGP-FIR with $N = 40$, the multiplicative general parameters adapted as shown in Fig. 7.21. Adaptation converged around 200 samples; after that, the parameters had only slight periodical oscillation. This oscillation is typical for reduced-rank adaptive systems, because such a filter cannot track all the correlating signal components. Figure 7.22 shows an instantaneous magnitude response of the NG-optimized MGP-FIR, and Fig. 7.23 depicts the corresponding phase delay. Because the harmonic frequencies were not considered explicitly in the optimization procedure, the filter of Fig. 7.22 has an undesired gain peak just on the third harmonic. On the other hand, Fig. 7.24 illustrates an instantaneous magnitude response of the harmonics-optimized filter. Now the third harmonic has a gain minimum with about 29% lowered magnitude value, while the "don't care" frequencies around it have clearly more gain than in the case of Fig. 7.22. It can be concluded that the converged filters are, indeed, two-step-ahead predictive bandpass filters of 49-Hz sinusoids. Within an extended frequency range of 45 to 55 Hz, the prediction step changes quite linearly 0.5 sampling periods/Hz (see Fig. 7.23). Thus, an adaptive predictive filter is definitely needed for maintaining high phase accuracy with time-varying line frequencies. Figure 7.25 shows the amplitude spectrum of the odd harmonics at the NG-optimized filter output. The total harmonic distortion at the output is 5.3%, which is 31.4% units lower than the input THD.

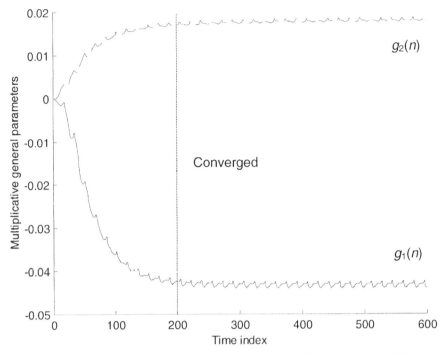

Figure 7.21. Adaptation of multiplicative general parameters with the test signal of Fig. 7.20; NG-optimized filter.

The harmonics-optimized filter behaves better than the NG-optimized one with the same artificial current signal. This could be expected by comparing the harmonics attenuation characteristics in Figs. 7.22 and 7.24. Table 7.6 shows a comparison of harmonic contents in the harmonics-optimized filter's output at all the three frequencies. Here, the output THD at 49 Hz is 3.66%, which is 1.64% units lower than in the case of NG-optimized MGP-FIR. The greatest improvement over the NG-optimized filter is at the third harmonic, where the output amplitude is reduced from 0.045 (Fig. 7.25) to 0.021 (Table 7.6)—that is, about 53%. The MGP-FIR-based current reference generator can provide highly similar phase and amplitude behavior throughout the specified frequency range of 49–51 Hz. Figure 7.26 depicts a half-cycle of the harmonics-optimized MGP-FIR output overlapped by a pure sinusoid of 49 Hz. It should be noticed that the phase accuracy of the filtered signal is excellent; this makes it feasible to use high up-sampling at the filter output, if the primary sampling rate is too low for some practical APF application.

7.6.4 Discussion of Current Reference Generation Application

We introduced an evolutionary programming-based method for designing robust and computationally efficient adaptive bandpass filters. These predictive filters were optimized for generating current references in active power filters. The accuracy

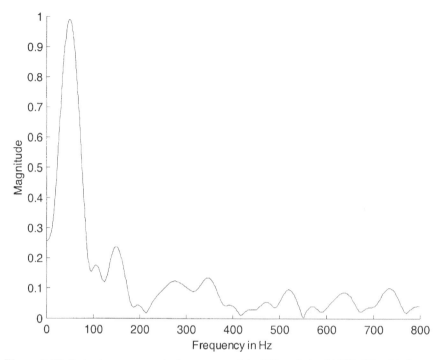

Figure 7.22. Instantaneous magnitude response of the NG-optimized MGP-FIR with the test signal of Fig. 7.20.

(phase/amplitude) of the reference current is crucial in current injection type systems, because it directly affects the harmonics reduction ability of the APF. Our digital filtering approach has the following advantages: selective bandpass response, efficient attenuation of specific harmonic components, capability to handle typical frequency alteration, small number of multiplications, and structural simplicity. Besides, practically no prior knowledge of the electricity distribution network and its loading characteristics is needed for designing the current reference generator. In an illustrative example, the total harmonic distortion of an artificial current waveform was reduced from 36.7% to less than 3.7% within the line frequency range of 49–51 Hz.

7.7 FUSION OF SOFT COMPUTING AND HARD COMPUTING

Some academic researchers may see the emerging soft computing (SC) as a collection of methods that are practical for all signal restoration problems and optimization tasks, whereas another school, particularly practicing engineers, rejects SC altogether in favor of more conventional hard computing (HC) [26]. In the present chapter, we have, instead, used a methodological fusion approach; HC-type adaptive filters are parameterized and structurally optimized by genetic and evolutionary programming algorithms that belong to the field of soft computing. The considered application

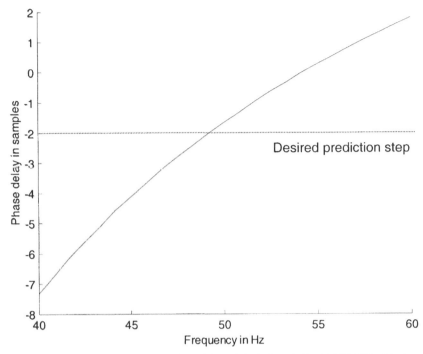

Figure 7.23. Zoomed instantaneous phase delay of the NG-optimized MGP-FIR with the test signal of Fig. 7.20.

examples show clearly that by combining individual methodologies with different characteristic features, it is possible to obtain efficient solutions that would not be achievable with a single method or only one class of methodologies. MGP-based adaptive filtering succeeds particularly well in the delay-constrained 50/60-Hz signal restoration problems, while computational evolutionary systems show their competence in discrete optimization tasks. Our methodological fusion approach can be classified as *SC-designed hard computing* (Chapter 1). The fusion grade of this symbiosis is high, because the evolutionary systems manipulate directly the internal structure and coefficients of the adaptive FIR filter. This kind of complementary fusion thinking is emerging among researchers and practicing engineers, and it can potentially lead to efficient combinations of HC and SC methodologies—both on the algorithm level and on the system level [27].

7.8 CONCLUSION

We introduced two evolutionary computation-based methods for assisting in the design of robust and computationally efficient adaptive bandpass filters. These predictive filters were optimized for zero-crossings detection in power converters, as

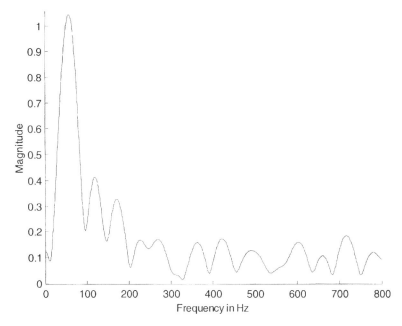

Figure 7.24. Instantaneous magnitude response of the harmonics-optimized MGP-FIR with the test signal of Fig. 7.20.

well as for generating current references in active power filters. Our novel filtering approaches offer the following desired characteristics:

- Selective bandpass response
- Effective attenuation of specific harmonic components
- Capability to handle typical frequency alteration
- Small number of multiplications
- Structural simplicity

TABLE 7.6. Comparison of Harmonic Contents in Filters' Input and Output

Harmonic Number	Input 49/50/51 Hz	Output 49 Hz	Output 50 Hz	Output 51 Hz
First	1	1	1	1
Third	0.15	0.021	0.013	0.018
Fifth	0.15	0.021	0.016	0.0092
Seventh	0.15	0.012	0.014	0.012
Ninth	0.15	0.016	0.0074	0.0042
Eleventh	0.15	0.0053	0.0091	0.011
Thirteenth	0.15	0.0054	0.0073	0.0061
THD %	36.7	3.66	2.85	2.70

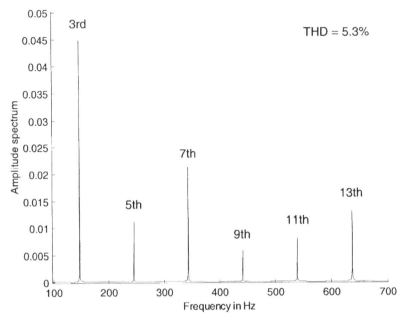

Figure 7.25. Amplitude spectrum of harmonic frequencies at the NG-optimized filter output.

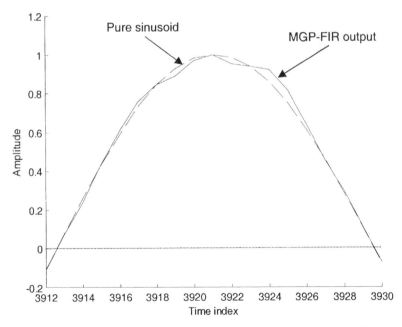

Figure 7.26. Half-cycle of the harmonics-optimized filter output overlapped by a pure sinusoid of 49 Hz.

Besides, practically no prior knowledge of the electricity distribution network is needed for designing these predictive instrumentation filters. The proposed scheme is a fusion of the HC-type multiplicative general parameter method and evolutionary computation that, on the other hand, is a core constituent of SC.

Our future research will concentrate on applying the efficient MGP-FIR algorithm also for polynomial-predictive filters [28] and radial basis function (RBF)-type neural network models [29] in industrial electronics applications. In addition, different variants of evolutionary programming and genetic algorithms will be evaluated with the present filter tap cross-connection and coefficient optimization problems.

ACKNOWLEDGMENTS

This work was supported by the Academy of Finland under Grants 80100 and 203436. The author wishes to thank Drs. Randy L. Haupt and Tamal Bose (Electrical and Computer Engineering, Utah State University) for providing the visiting scientist positions that made it possible to carry out the research work and complete this manuscript in the summers of 2002 and 2003, respectively. Numerous discussions with Dr. Olli Vainio (Information Technology, Tampere University of Technology) were very useful in conducting this research.

REFERENCES

6. O. Vainio and S. J. Ovaska, "Noise Reduction in Zero Crossing Detection by Predictive Digital Filtering," *IEEE Transactions on Industrial Electronics* **42**, 58–62 (1995).

7. S. Väliviita and S. J. Ovaska, "Delayless Method to Generate Current Reference for Active Filters," *IEEE Transactions on Industrial Electronics* **45**, 559–567 (1998).

8. F. P. Dawson and L. Klaffke, "Variable-Sample-Rate Delayless Frequency-Adaptive Digital Filter for Synchronized Signal Acquisition and Sampling," *IEEE Transactions on Industrial Electronics* **46**, 889–896 (1999).

9. D. H. Wolpert and W. G. Macready, "No Free Lunch Theorems for Optimization," *IEEE Transactions on Evolutionary Computation* **1**, 67–82 (1997).

10. D. B. Fogel, *Evolutionary Computation: Toward a New Philosophy of Machine Intelligence*, IEEE Press, Piscataway, NJ, 2000.

11. O. Vainio and S. J. Ovaska, "Harmonics-Resistant Adaptive Algorithm for Line-Frequency Signal Processing," *IEEE Transactions on Industrial Electronics* **49**, 702–706 (2002).

12. O. Vainio and S. J. Ovaska, "Adaptive Lowpass Filters for Zero-Crossing Detectors," *Proceedings of the 28th Annual International Conference of the IEEE Industrial Electronics Society*, Seville, Spain, Nov. 2002, pp. 1483–1486.

13. O. Vainio and S. J. Ovaska, "Digital Filtering for Robust 50/60 Hz Zero Crossing Detectors," *IEEE Transactions on Instrumentation and Measurement* **45**, 426–430 (1996).

14. O. Vainio, S. Väliviita, and S. J. Ovaska. "Multistage Adaptive Filters for In-Phase Processing of Line-Frequency Signals," *Proceedings of the IEEE Instrumentation and Measurement Technology Conference*, Ottawa, Canada, May 1997, pp. 428–433.

15. A. A. Ashimov and D. J. Syzdykov, "Identification of High Dimensional System by the General Parameter Method," *Preprints of the 8th IFAC World Congress*, Kyoto, Japan, 1981, pp. 32–37.

16. V. H. Nascimento and A. H. Sayed, "Unbiased and Stable Leakage-Based Adaptive Filters," *IEEE Transactions on Signal Processing* **47**, 3261–3276 (1999).

17. A. Nehorai, "A Minimal Parameter Adaptive Notch Filter with Constrained Poles and Zeros," *IEEE Transactions on Acoustics, Speech, and Signal Processing* **33**, 983–996 (1985).

18. T. Bäck, *Evolutionary Algorithms in Theory and Practice*, Oxford University Press, New York, 1996.

19. D. B. Fogel, ed., *Evolutionary Computation: The Fossil Record*, IEEE Press, Piscataway, NJ, 1998.

20. R. L. Haupt and S. E. Haupt, *Practical Genetic Algorithms*, Wiley, New York, 1998.

21. Y.-M. Chen, "Passive Filter Design Using Genetic Algorithms," *IEEE Transactions on Industrial Electronics* **50**, 202–207 (2003).

22. Y. L. Abdel-Magid and M. A. Abido, "Optimal Multiobjective Design of Robust Power System Stabilizers Using Genetic Algorithms," *IEEE Transactions on Power Systems* **18**, 1125–1132 (2003).

23. M. Bettayeb and U. Qidwai, "A Hybrid Least Squares-GA-Based Algorithm for Harmonic Estimation," *IEEE Transactions on Power Delivery* **18**, 377–382 (2003).

24. M. A. Abido and Y. L. Abdel-Magid, "Optimal Design of Power System Stabilizers Using Evolutionary Programming," *IEEE Transactions on Energy Conversion* **17**, 429–436 (2002).

25. H.-T. Yang, C.-M. Huang, and C.-L. Huang, "Identification of ARMAX Model for Short Term Load Forecasting: An Evolutionary Programming Approach," *IEEE Transactions on Power Systems* **11**, 403–408 (1996).

26. J. T. Ma and L. L. Lai, "Evolutionary Programming Approach to Reactive Power Planning," *IEE Proceedings—Generation, Transmission and Distribution* **143**, 365–370 (1996).

27. A. H. Samra, and A. Teshome, "Current Injection Method to Eliminate Harmonics," *IEEE Industry Applications Magazine* **1**, 28–33 (1995).

28. V. Grigore, "Topological Issues in Single-Phase Power Factor Correction," Doctoral Dissertation, Helsinki University of Technology, Institute of Intelligent Power Electronics, Espoo, Finland, 2001.

29. M. El-Habrouk, M. K. Darwish, and P. Mehta, "Active Power Filters: A Review," *IEE Proceedings—Electric Power Applications* **147**, 403–413 (2000).

30. B. Singh, K. Al-Haddad, and A. Chandra, "A Review of Active Filters for Power Quality Improvement," *IEEE Transactions on Industrial Electronics* **46**, 960–971 (1999).

31. M. Agarwal, "Combining Neural and Conventional Paradigms for Modeling, Prediction, and Control," *Proceedings of the 4th IEEE Conference on Control Applications*, Albany, NY, Sept. 1995, pp. 566–571.

32. S. J. Ovaska and H. F. VanLandingham, "Guest Editorial: Special Issue on Fusion of Soft Computing and Hard Computing in Industrial Applications," *IEEE Transactions on Systems, Man, and Cybernetics—Part C: Applications and Reviews* **32**, 69–71 (2002).

33. S. Väliviita, S. J. Ovaska, and O. Vainio, "Polynomial Predictive Filtering in Control Instrumentation: A Review," *IEEE Transactions on Industrial Electronics* **46**, 876–889 (1999).

34. D. F. Akhmetov, Y. Dote, and S. J. Ovaska, "Fuzzy-Neural Network with General Parameter Adaptation for Modeling of Nonlinear Time-Series," *IEEE Transactions on Neural Networks* **12**, 148–152 (2001), errata published in *IEEE Transactions on Neural Networks* **12**, 443 (2001).

APPENDIX 7.1: COEFFICIENTS OF 50-Hz SINUSOID-PREDICTIVE FIR FILTERS

Index	$N = 12$	$N = 22$	$N = 40$
0	0.225439	0.157780	0.0464414
1	0.200691	0.130349	0.0409146
2	0.168833	0.106669	0.0339384
3	0.130994	0.0867828	0.0257599
4	0.0885146	0.0689376	0.0166689
5	0.0428996	0.0504137	0.00698736
6	− 0.00423519	0.0286629	− 0.00294171
7	− 0.0512199	0.0023971	− 0.0127666
8	− 0.0963902	− 0.0277255	− 0.0221392
9	− 0.138146	− 0.0590387	− 0.0307275
10	− 0.175007	− 0.0874607	− 0.0382273
11	− 0.205669	− 0.108564	− 0.0443728
12	—	− 0.118798	− 0.0489464
13	—	− 0.116485	− 0.0517861
14	—	− 0.102294	− 0.0527912
15	—	− 0.0790288	− 0.0519262
16	—	− 0.0508153	− 0.0492217
17	—	− 0.0219269	− 0.0447734
18	—	0.00438650	− 0.0387390
19	—	0.0267068	− 0.0313323
20	—	0.0456490	− 0.0228156
21	—	0.0634021	− 0.0134907
22	—	—	− 0.00368786
23	—	—	0.00624563
24	—	—	0.0159579
25	—	—	0.0251048
26	—	—	0.0333625
27	—	—	0.0404381

(continued)

Index	$N = 12$	$N = 22$	$N = 40$
28	—	—	0.0460812
29	—	—	0.0500919
30	—	—	0.0523281
31	—	—	0.0527105
32	—	—	0.0512257
33	—	—	0.0479261
34	—	—	0.0429287
35	—	—	0.0364106
36	—	—	0.0286026
37	—	—	0.0197813
38	—	—	0.0102593
39	—	—	0.000373813

EDITOR'S INTRODUCTION TO CHAPTER 8

Computer security is an important and timely issue. In the summer of 2003, many records of intrusion and "worm" activity were unfortunately broken again. Those hostile attacks affected millions of people around the world, and they cost huge amounts of money.

The development of real-time intrusion detection systems (IDSs) started at the beginning of the 1990s [1]. Such systems aim at detecting both attempted and successful break-ins. Nonetheless, the detection coverage of current intrusion detection systems is still rather poor. The main detection approaches can be divided into two categories [2]:

1. *Misuse Detection*: This recognizes an attack on the basis of known attack signatures.
2. *Anomaly Detection*: This infers that a hacker attack is taking place by recognizing deviations from the normal behavior of a computer system.

Hence, misuse (or signature) detection can detect known attack types only, while anomaly detection searches for possible unknown attacks. It should be noted, however, that an IDS is not an alternative to the protection procedures and mechanisms, but rather a complementary technique.

Intrusion detection is a challenging area of research and development. An efficient IDS offers low probabilities of false-negative detections (undetected attacks) and false-positive detections (false alarms) [2]. In addition, it should be able to learn new attack patterns and update the signature database correspondingly. On the other hand, the next leap in computer/network security management will be a built-in ability to automatically create and implement reconfiguration and repair plans [3].

Computationally Intelligent Hybrid Systems. Edited by Seppo J. Ovaska
ISBN 0-471-47668-4 © 2005 the Institute of Electrical and Electronics Engineers, Inc.

Those demanding requirements and features call for the use of all available techniques—both soft computing (SC) and conventional hard computing (HC), as well as their complementary fusions. By considerably increasing the level of machine IQ, autonomous, learning, and robust intrusion detection systems that require minimal input from system administrators may likely be developed in the future.

Chapter 8 of the present book, "Intrusion Detection for Computer Security," is authored by Sung-Bae Cho and Sang-Jun Han. First, an overview on the use of soft-computing methods in intrusion detection is given. Considerable global activity on the research of neural networks, fuzzy logic, genetic algorithms, immune networks, and Bayesian probabilistic inference is reported. After this motivating overview, Cho and Han propose a multistage procedure for anomaly detection using the fusion of soft computing and hard computing:

- Data reduction using self-organizing maps (SOM)
- Modeling of normal behaviors using multiple hidden Markov models (HMM) with different measures
- Anomaly detection by fuzzy logic (FL)

Thus, their IDS contains two fusion borders: SOM-HMM (SC-HC) and HMM-FL (HC-SC). In such cascade configurations, the fusion grade is moderate (Chapter 1).

Because the audit databases to be analyzed by the IDS are usually very large, it is necessary to first reduce the amount of raw data. Self-organizing maps are used for clustering the input patterns topologically. The optimal selection of SOM's dimensions in the IDS application is discussed with a few examples. This selection is a compromise between the degree of map usage and its quantization error. It was found out that sizes 5×5 and 6×6 are both appropriate.

Separate HMMs for each user were found to be more effective than a single model, because the multimodel scheme provided lower rates of false alarms. There exists simply no single pattern for normal behavior. The lengths of input sequences for the hidden Markov models were 30, and the number of states was 10. These specific numbers were obtained heuristically.

The role of fuzzy logic is to perform model fusion—that is, to combine the individual submodels of each user. Those models are based on the distinct measures of system calls, file access, and their combination. The applied fuzzy rule set was determined by trial and error.

Finally, the performance of the new IDS was evaluated by an audit database collected from the behavior and actions of three students during a period of one week, when they were using the university's workstation network. Encouraging results were obtained with the somewhat restricted data: The detection rate of intrusion attacks (user-to-root intrusions) was 100%, while the false-positive error rate was slightly above 1%.

In commercial intrusion detection systems, conventional hard-computing techniques—for example, symbolic artificial intelligence (AI) and pattern recognition—are applied to misuse/anomaly detection. However, as the detection problem is complex and dynamically evolving, it is apparent that soft-computing methods would effectively complement the capabilities of hard computing. Therefore, the field of intrusion detection in computers and computer networks is a highly potential niche for computationally intelligent hybrid systems.

REFERENCES

1. R. A. Kemmerer and G. Vigna, "Intrusion Detection: A Brief History and Overview," *IEEE Computer* **35**, 27–30 (Apr. 2002).

2. S. Kent, "On the Trail of Intrusions into Information Systems," *IEEE Spectrum* **37**, 52–56 (Dec. 2000).

3. R. Barruffi, M. Milano, and R. Montanari, "Planning for Security Management," *IEEE Intelligent Systems* **16**, 74–80 (Jan./Feb. 2001).

CHAPTER 8

INTRUSION DETECTION FOR COMPUTER SECURITY

SUNG-BAE CHO and SANG-JUN HAN
Yonsei University, Seoul, Korea

8.1 INTRODUCTION

Due to worldwide proliferation and rapid progress in computer networking, faster and more diversified services have become a reality. As the reliance on computers becomes greater, the security of critical computers becomes more important. According to a report from the computer security response team coordination center (CERT/CC), the number of security incidents in 2002 has increased to four times more than that in 2000 as shown in Fig. 8.1. Altogether 76,404 incidents were reported in the first and second quarters of 2003 [1]. The high availability of hacking tools due to the proliferation of the Internet causes attacks simply out of curiosity.

As the damage from security incidents goes up, the security mechanism of computer systems becomes very important. However, building perfectly secure systems is not practical at present because usually perfect systems are overly expensive and commercial systems must be competitive. There is no bug-free software and nobody seems to make the effort to try to develop a perfect program [2]. Even if a totally secure system existed, it would be vulnerable to insiders' abuse. Thus, several additional security tools and equipment become essential to computer systems. Intrusion detection system (IDS) is one of the promising tools for computer security.

An IDS is software to detect attacks exploiting illegal uses or misuses, and modification of important data, by analyzing audit trails such as system call traces, system logs, activation time, network packets, and so on [3]. It informs the administrator of security alerts and takes reactions automatically if necessary.

In general, intrusion detection techniques can be divided into two groups: misuse detection and anomaly detection [4]. Misuse detection uses knowledge about known

Computationally Intelligent Hybrid Systems. Edited by Seppo J. Ovaska
ISBN 0-471-47668-4 © 2005 the Institute of Electrical and Electronics Engineers, Inc.

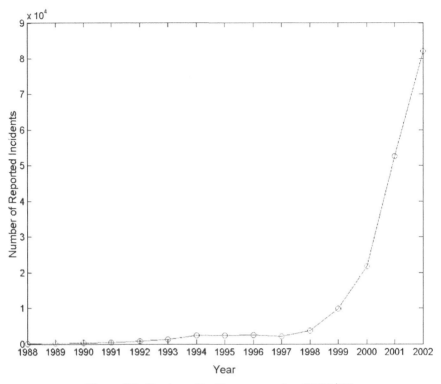

Figure 8.1. Number of incidents reported to CERT/CC.

attacks and attempts to match current behavior against the attack patterns. It has the advantage that known attacks can be detected economically and reliably with low false-positive error. The shortcoming is that it cannot detect unknown attacks. To remedy the problem of detecting unknown attacks, anomaly detection attempts to detect intrusions by noting significant deviation from normal behaviors. It has low false-negative error rate where attacks are considered as normal behaviors because the behaviors deviating from normal behavior are considered as intrusions. However, it suffers from high false-positive error rate, because unseen normal behaviors are considered as attacks as well.

Figure 8.2 shows a model of typical IDS. The monitored system can consist of one or multiple computer machines or one or multiple computer networks. It provides information needed to identify attacks, called audit data, such as command history, system call traces, and network packet dump. If it uses a host audit trail as an information source, it is host-based IDS, and if it uses network audit data such as network packets and simple network manipulation protocol (SNMP) information, it is network-based IDS. Sensors collect audit data and construct features by transforming audit data into suitable format for IDS. The type of output of sensor is dependent on the detection technique of IDS. It can be a sequence of

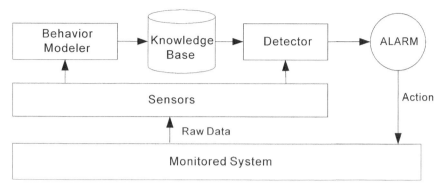

Figure 8.2. A typical intrusion detection system.

some events, set of numerical values, or portion of network packets. Behavior modeler builds a knowledge base about behavior of the monitored system. A misuse detector builds a knowledge base about attacks, whereas an anomaly detector builds that about normal behavior. The knowledge base can be implemented as a neural network, collection of audit trails, and set of rules according to the applied detection technique. The process of building knowledge base can be automatic or manual with domain experts. In case of neural network, knowledge base is constructed automatically using training data, and the administrator has to write detection rules manually if IDS is based on rule sets. Detector identifies attacks using the knowledge base and makes alarms. It detects misuse by identifying behaviors that are similar to predefined attacks or anomaly by identifying behaviors deviating from normal patterns. If necessary, IDS may take some actions actively to prevent the recurrence of an attack and additional damage. Cutting network connections, shutdown of vulnerable services, and modifying configurations are typical reactions against the attacks.

In this chapter, we will first review the current state of the art on intrusion detection using soft-computing techniques. Next, we introduce a study on intrusion detection that integrates soft computing (SC) and hard computing (HC) for the performance improvement.

8.2 RELATED WORKS

Most of the early commercial products and studies on intrusion detection applied HC methods such as rule-based analysis and pattern matching techniques to intrusion detection. They detect intrusions by identifying behaviors that match the predefined characteristics of attack (misuse detection) or deviate from the predefined normal behaviors (anomaly detection). If-then rules [5], state transition diagrams [6], numerical values from statistics [7], audit trails database [8], and colored Petri nets [9] have been used to represent user's or program's behavior, and the alarm is raised when new behavior conforms a detection rule and produces an evaluation value that exceeds the predefined threshold or cannot be found in the database. Table 8.1 summarizes the studies on intrusion detection using conventional hard computing techniques [6,7,9–14].

The main disadvantage of the pure HC approach is inflexibility. It can easily miss a malicious attack that slightly varies from defined attack patterns or normal behaviors that slightly deviate from normal behavior. It is due to the poor generalization ability. It leads to a large maintenance effort of systems, because it requires frequent updates of the knowledge about the characteristics of attacks or normal behavior. If the administrator neglects continuous updates like writing rules or diagrams that detect novel attacks and inserting new audit trails to the database, the performance of intrusion detection systems may rapidly retrograde. To remedy these shortcomings, many intrusion detection systems have attempted to incorporate SC techniques due to the merits of SC, such as tolerance for imprecision and partial truth for improving performance and saving the maintenance effort.

8.2.1 Neural Computing

Neural computing methodologies such as multilayer perceptrons (MLP) and self-organizing maps (SOM) have been applied to intrusion detection because they can provide the capability of generalizing attack behaviors from limited, noisy, and incomplete data. Generalization gives the potential to detect intrusions that are unseen—that is, not exactly matched and different from predefined patterns of previous attack behaviors. It helps to improve the robustness of intrusion detection systems.

The Hyperview of CS Telecom is a representative IDS using neural network [15]. It consists of two modules: neural network and expert system. The neural network in Hyperview uses temporal sequence of audit data as inputs and 60 types of audit data: CPU usage, memory usage, and so on. Ghosh et al. and Lippmann et al. have tested neural network techniques with real computer audit data generated by DARPA

TABLE 8.1. Representative Studies on Intrusion Detection

Organization	Name	Type		Technique				
		AD	MD	RB	PM	ES	STA	ST
AT&T	ComputerWatch [10]	X				X		
USAF	Haystack [11]	X						X
Purdue University	IDIOT [9]		X	X				
SRI International	NIDES [7]	X	X			X		X
SRI International	EMERALD [12]	X	X		X			X
UC Davis	NSM [13]	X	X		X			X
UC Davis	GrIDS [14]	X				X		
UCSB	STAT [6]		X				X	

AD, anomaly detection; MD, misuse detection.
RB, rule base; PM, pattern matching; ES, expert system; STA, state transition analysis; ST, statistics.

IDEVAL (intrusion detection evaluation) program. Ghosh et al. at Reliable Software Technologies Corporation have exploited some variations of neural network: the feedforward backpropagation and the recurrent Elman network for classifying system call sequences [16] and compared them with an HC approach of equality matching proposed by Forrest et al. (see reference 17 for details). The system call traces generated during program execution are used as inputs of neural network. The Elman networks showed the best performance among three methods in their experiment: 77% detection rate with no false alarms. Their results indicate that the generalization ability of neural network can significantly improve the perform-ance of detection system. Lippmann and Cunningham at MIT Lincoln Laboratory have applied a neural network to a keyword-based detection system [18]. They have used MLP to improve a simple baseline keyword intrusion detection technique. The keywords frequency from transcripts for Telnet sessions is used as input of neural network, and discriminative keywords are weighted through training. Their experimental results showed that a neural network can improve the overall perform-ance, like false alarm rate and detection rate, and detect novel attacks not included in training data as well as known attacks. It produced a good performance of 80% detection rate, with one false alarm per day. However, their experiment was against user-to-root attacks only.

Giacinto et al. have used an ensemble of MLPs to improve the reliability of IDS [19]. Three MLPs trained with distinct feature sets were used, and their results are combined by ensemble techniques. They extract three feature sets based on expert knowledge and learn each feature set using an MLP. In experiments, they showed that ensemble techniques produce performance superior to that of individual MLPs.

Girardin has applied an SOM to support the network administrator by visualizing network traffic [20]. SOM projects the network events to a space without any prior knowledge. The user is able to analyze network activity intuitionally by using the visual map metaphor. González and Dasgupta at the University of Memphis have compared anomaly detection techniques using SOM with an immune system approach using MLP [21]. They use SOM to cluster normal samples and detect attacks by identifying samples far from normal clusters. Their experimental results show that SOM is better, while the MLP networks have the advantage that they are less sensitive to changes on the threshold.

It was found from the results of many studies that the generalization ability of neural computing can enhance the accuracy of intrusion detection. However, the dis-advantage of the neural computing approach is that training neural networks requires heavy computational load, and it is practically impossible to figure out the explicit relationship between inputs and outputs because neural networks are black boxes.

8.2.2 Genetic Computing

Genetic algorithm (GA) is an attractive class of computational models that mimic natural evolution to solve problems in a wide variety of domains. A GA emulates biological evolution theories to solve demanding optimization problems. In common with all other evolutionary algorithms, a GA performs a search of a multidimensional space containing a hypersurface known as the fitness surface. A particular parameter set defines a point on a hyperplane onto which the surface is projected, with the height of the surface above the hyperplane reflecting the relative merit of the problem solution represented by the parameter set. GA can be used to find effective intrusion detection rules automatically. In the intrusion detection domain, the hyperplane can be defined as the space of all possible detection rules. In general, the hyperplane is extremely large. In other words, there are so many possible rules. Thus exhaustive searching is by no means feasible, and writing an effective detection rule requires a domain expert's knowledge. The height of a specific point on hypersurface can be measured by detection performance using intrusion detection systems. Through evolving detection rules, the intrusion detection system can attain the ability to detect novel attacks without domain specific knowledge or administrator's efforts like writing a new rule set by inspecting log files. These characteristics may provide active and automatic detection and self-repairing features. Figure 8.3 shows the process of rule generation with GA. Training data that contain labeled attacks are used as input of GA. GA searches effective detection rules with training data, and the most effective rules are inserted into the rule base. A detector identifies attacks matching input data with the constructed rule base.

Dasgupta and González have also employed genetic computing to intrusion detection. In reference 22, they proposed detection methods that generate detection and response rules by evolutionary algorithms. They monitored the system's behavior at multiple levels: packet, process, and system levels. The feature vectors are produced, and they consist of evaluation values from each level. The detection rules are encoded into a binary string that contains the threshold of each level and expected responses such as informing administrator and blocking a particular Internet protocol (IP) address. The basic GA has the disadvantage called genetic drift, which results in loss of diversity and gene convergence in finite populations even without selective pressure. Therefore, it needs multiple runs to generate different rules, because intrusion detection is a multimodal problem: The detection system needs not one rule but several detection rules instead. Thus, they employ the niching technique to get multiple rules through a single run. It has been developed to reduce the loss from genetic drift. It maintains population diversity and broadens the GA's parallel search capability. In reference 23, they use GA for generating

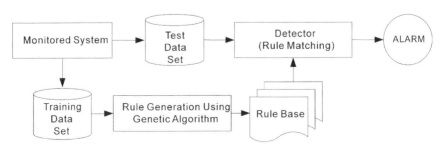

Figure 8.3. Process of rule generation using GA.

negative selection rules in an artificial immune system [24]. The idea of using the principles of the biological immune system in computer security has been progressed by many research groups. A negative selection algorithm inspired by natural immunological mechanism has been successfully applied to detect intrusions. It distinguishes non-self (unauthorized users, viruses, and intrusions) from self (legitimate users and normal program). In their approach, GA attempts to evolve the rules that distinguish non-self instances. Their experimental results against second-week data of 1999 DARPA IDEVAL data demonstrate that the approach is feasible with 87.5% detection rate and 1% false alarm rate.

Crosbie and Spafford of Purdue University COAST Laboratory have proposed a potential solution that uses genetic programming (GP) [25]. They use GP to learn abnormal behaviors from the network monitoring results. Because the feature values of their network monitoring results have multiple data types—time, integer, and Boolean—a type safety problem occurs between operands and operators in a GP parse tree. For example, adding a Boolean type to an integer type would be prohibited. Therefore, they evolve separately three child trees that deal with different aspects of behavior: connection timing (time), port number (integer), and privileged port (Boolean). A root tree that combines those child trees is also evolved separately. They show the potential of their approach through simple experiments with the data set which are collected by themselves. They make three GP parse trees by running the evolution three times using the training data with slightly different parameters guiding the evolution and test them with their test data set that contains three types of anomaly.

8.2.3 Fuzzy Logic

Fuzzy logic can readily be used to combine multiple inputs from different systems. In the intrusion detection domain, fuzzy logic can be used to combine multiple alarms from individual intrusion detectors. Fuzzy techniques can eliminate the problem of determining an appropriate threshold with fuzzy sets and membership functions. It is difficult to determine proper threshold because attacks cannot be defined distinctly. In terms of the fuzzy logic, output value of each detector is a fuzzy variable and the fuzzy sets are possible values of a fuzzy variable that has a linguistic name like normal, suspicious, or dangerous. Fuzzy membership function provides the degree of membership in fuzzy sets as shown in Fig. 8.4. Unlike in traditional bi-valued logic, a particular value can be a member of one or more fuzzy sets. For example, if a detector produces an alarm of level 3, it is a member of normal behavior to 0.6 degree and a member of suspicious behavior to 0.3 degree, while it is only in normal behavior using traditional bi-valued logic. Fuzzy clustering analysis can be used to adjust the fuzzy membership functions in automatic manner.

Dickerson et al. have exploited these merits of fuzzy systems [26]. Five fuzzy sets—LOW, MED-LOW, MED, MED-HIGH, and HIGH—in each detector are defined, and they use the fuzzy C-means clustering algorithm to quantify the membership functions of each detector. Fuzzy rules that determine attack by combining

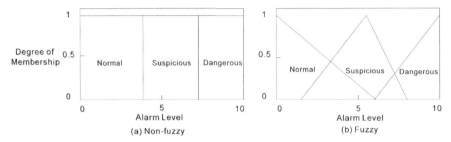

Figure 8.4. An example of fuzzy membership function for intrusion detection.

multiple detectors are defined with domain expert's knowledge. Figure 8.5 shows an overview of their method. They have developed three intrusion scenarios: host and port scanning, denial of service, and unauthorized servers. They have also developed the fuzzy rule sets for these three intrusion scenarios. The fuzzy system is tested using the data sets that were collected by themselves for two weeks that contain several anomalies—for example, installing a backdoor on an uncommon port as well as connecting and transferring some files to the backdoor. Their system correctly detects the installed backdoor, while the false-positive error rate is very high. To solve this problem, they have modified the fuzzy membership functions by hand, and the false-positive error rate has dropped to approximately 1.5% from 8%.

Gomez and Dasgupta have evolved fuzzy rules for intrusion detection using GA [27]. They encode fuzzy rules that classify patterns of system's behavior in normal and abnormal into the chromosome and evaluated the fitness using the length, sensitivity, and specificity of the rule. Evolved rules produce the results comparable to those reported in the literature against the KDD-Cup '99 data set, which is the subset

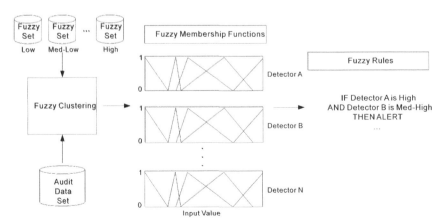

Figure 8.5. The scheme of combining multiple detectors using FL.

of 1998 DARPA IDEVAL data that is pre-processed by Columbia University and distributed as a part of the UCI KDD Archive [28].

8.2.4 Probabilistic Reasoning

Bayesian probabilistic inference is one of the famous models for inference and representation of the environment with insufficient information. Bayesian network (BN) is a graphical model that encodes probabilistic relationships among dependent set of variables. In the intrusion detection domain, BN is considered for developing a cooperative architecture. For mode accurate detection, it is required to integrate different types of IDS. BN can be used to infer intrusion probability by observing information from multiple detectors. However, it is hard to build the structure of BN and to calculate its probability distribution. Moreover, there is no absolute solution for learning BN.

Gowadia et al. have used BN to represent intrusion scenario in their agent-based IDS [29]. Their system consists of system-monitoring agents and intrusion-monitoring agents. Each system-monitoring agent produces suspicious events, attacks, or system and network parameter values by monitoring the computer system. All outputs of a system-monitoring agent are associated with nodes of BN and produce output variables to the intrusion-monitoring agent. The intrusion-monitoring agents are distributed over networks, and they receive the information from other agents and infer the probability of intrusion occurrence with them. BN provides not only an intuitive representation of an intrusion scenario but also an effective inference method of the probabilities of intrusion. They have developed a proof-of-concept prototype of their system, and it is expected that the distributed agents and BN provide the fault-tolerant data processing and flexible intrusion detection in the future study.

Barbara et al. have used a naïve Bayes classifier to overcome limitations of their anomaly detection system [30]. They have successfully applied association rules mining techniques to anomaly detection. However, recognizable attacks and normal behaviors of their system are limited to known instances. Through experiments against 1998 and 1999 DARPA data sets, they showed that a naïve Bayes classifier can give the ability of detecting the novel attacks to their system.

8.3 INTRUSION DETECTION WITH HYBRID TECHNIQUES

We are here concerned with the intrusion detection technique that fuses soft computing and hard computing. Soft-computing techniques are used to remedy drawbacks of conventional detection techniques based on hard computing. Hidden Markov model (HMM), a well-known probabilistic reasoning method, is useful to model the sequence of observed symbols of which the construction mechanism cannot be known. It has successfully applied to learning normal behavior for anomaly detection [31,32]. While HMM produces better performance in modeling normal behavior than other methods, it has two main drawbacks [31]. First it requires a very long time for modeling normal behavior because training an HMM requires heavy computational cost. Thus, efficient data reduction technique is necessary to save time required to train HMM. The second is the problem of determining a threshold: how much attacks deviate from normal behavior. It is uncertain and there is no clear solution. To remedy these drawbacks, we develop a novel IDS based on anomaly detection using HMM exploiting two soft-computing techniques. Among the principal constituents of soft computing, we have incorporated neural network and fuzzy logic into the hybrid IDS based on HMM.

8.3.1 Overview

In anomaly detection, normal behavior models are required to determine whether current behavior is an anomaly or not. HMM is used as a modeling tool, and it tests two different modeling strategies: single model without user discrimination, and separate models for individual users. First of all, we should decide the target activities to monitor for the system. Because there is typically a large amount of raw audit data to analyze, it is required to effectively reduce the data and extract information from them. In this chapter, we extract the measures of audit data from Sun Microsystems' Basic Security Module (BSM) [33], and we reduce them using a self-organizing map (SOM) that is a neural network for clustering input patterns into fixed vectors topologically. The reduced data can be used to model normal behaviors for intrusion detection. To select the distinctive measures from a BSM record, we evaluate the effect of the measures by investigating the performance to detect intrusions.

We should also be able to appropriately determine whether current behavior is normal or not. In this chapter, we implement three models based on HMM with different measures. The problem is how to decide if the present behavior is abnormal from the three information sources that are inherently imprecise and uncertain. Fuzzy logic is used to make the final decision from the three sources of information to improve the performance and reliability of the system.

Our intrusion detection system is composed of a preprocessing module that is in charge of data filtering and data reduction, along with an anomaly detection module that is responsible for the normal behavior modeling and anomaly detection, as shown in Fig. 8.6. Normal behaviors are modeled into profile database through HMM learning.

8.3.2 Preprocessing with Self-Organizing Map

BSM collects data whenever an event occurs, and then it makes a record and appends it to the tail of audit data. Therefore, audit data consist of a series of audit records as time goes on. However, because these data are too huge to process in real time, we have to extract useful information from BSM. Although much information is available to detect intrusion, it cannot guarantee a high detection rate because important information may be hidden.

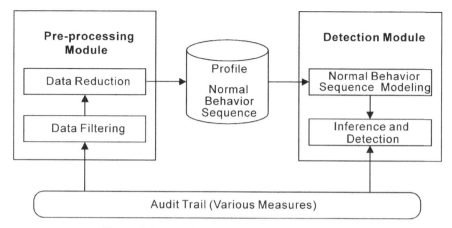

Figure 8.6. Overview of intrusion detection system.

Extracting effective measures is very important since they determine the performance of IDS. Measures widely used in IDS include CPU time, I/O access time, file access, system call, network activity, login/logout, and so on. To select the optimal measures in IDS, we have extracted several statistics from the BSM audit data based on the well-known attacks and investigate the effect of each measure by testing the performance of it. Table 8.2 summarizes the measures used in this chapter.

Typical audit data, composed of all events, may amount to hundreds of megabytes per day, which cannot be easily dealt with in real time. Many measures can be useful in statistical analysis, but they need to be transformed into lower-dimensional data for modeling techniques like HMM. Reducing the size of measures means that $x_1, x_2, \ldots, x_n$ are converted into $x'_1, x'_2, \ldots, x'_k$, where k is much smaller than n. In this chapter, the measure size is reduced based on the locality of user action. The ranges of the measures are observed, and the measures mainly used in the system are stored to find the value of a measure for current action. As a result of mapping the measures, we can reduce the data.

In order to select a set of features that are invariant with respect to some basic transformation groups of the input measures, we can consider several vector quantization and clustering techniques such as the k-means algorithm and SOM. Unlike batch algorithms, SOM has several merits that organize the map automatically according to the input pattern and preserve the topology of input space. We

TABLE 8.2. Measures Extracted from the BSM to Detect Intrusions

Category	Measures
System call	ID, return value, return status
Process	ID, IPC ID, IPC permission, exit value, exit status
File access	Access mode, path, file system, file name, argument length

choose the SOM to exploit the characteristics of topology preservation to trace the
sequence of observation symbols later in HMM.

SOM is an unsupervised learning neural network using Euclidean distance to
compute the distance between input and reference vectors [34]. The learning algorithm of SOM is as follows. Here, $i(x)$ is the best matching neuron to the input vector,
ε_i means neighborhood function that defines the region of influence that the input
vector has on the SOM, and η is learning rate.

1. Initialize the reference vectors $w_j(n)$, $n = 0$.
2. Compute the distance and select the minimum value

$$i(x) = \arg\min \|x(n) - w_j(n)\|$$

3. Update the reference vectors $w_j(n + 1) = w_j(n) + \eta(n)\varepsilon_{i(x)}(n,j)(x(n) - w_j(n))$.
4. Repeat steps 2 to 3 until the stop condition satisfies.

Several measures can be extracted from one audit record of BSM that includes an
event, and the information is normalized for the input of SOM. The normalization
depends on the measures, and it rescales them between 0 and 1. After training the
entire map, the weight vectors of the map define the centers of clusters covering
the input space and the point density function of these centers tends to approximate
the probability density function of the original input space. From the trained SOM,
we can get one representative value—that is, the index of the best matching
neuron—with the input event composed of many measures: One record is converted
into one representative. This reduced information can be used for modeling
techniques like HMM.

8.3.3 Behavior Modeling with Hidden Markov Models

Several techniques such as rule-based systems, statistical methods, and neural networks have been used to model the normal behaviors for intrusion detection
system. Neural networks seem to be a good candidate for our problem, but
they usually lack the modeling capability of temporal sequences, and some
researchers attempt to remedy it by utilizing recurrent networks. In terms of modeling a large number of temporal sequences, HMM can be the alternative because
it has been widely used for speech recognition [35]. Speech recognition and intrusion detection using temporal audit sequences can be formulated as the same
problem from the point of temporal data processing. In the data sources used, a
speech signal and an audit event are sequentially ordered, and they are needed
for modeling the temporal data not only for recognizing spoken words but also
for detecting intrusions. Therefore, HMM could be useful in solving both of
those problems.

An HMM is a doubly stochastic process with an underlying stochastic process
that is not observable, but can only be observed through another set of stochastic

processes that produce the sequence of observed symbols [35]. This model can be considered as a graph with N nodes called states and edges representing transitions between those states. Each state node contains an initial state distribution and observation probability at which a given symbol is to be observed. An edge maintains a transition probability with which a state transition from one state to another state is made. Figure 8.7 shows a left-to-right HMM with three states.

Given an input sequence $O = O_1, O_2, \ldots, O_T$, HMM can model it with its own probability parameters using the Markov process, although the state transition process cannot be seen outside. Once a model is built, the probability with which a given sequence is generated from the model can be evaluated. A model λ is described as $\lambda = (A, B, \pi)$ using its characteristic parameters as follows:

$T =$ length of the observation sequence
$N =$ number of states in the model
$M =$ number of observation symbols
$Q = \{q_1, q_2, \ldots, q_N\}$, states
$V = \{v_1, v_2, \ldots, v_M\}$, discrete set of possible symbol observations
$A = \{a_{ij} | a_{ij} = \Pr(q_j \text{ at } t+1)\}$, state transition probability distribution
$B = \{b_j(k) | b_j(k) = \Pr(v_k \text{ at } t | q_j \text{ at } t)\}$, observation symbol probability distribution
$\pi = \{\pi_i \mid \pi_i = \Pr(q_i \text{ at } t = 1)\}$, initial state distribution

Suppose, for example, that a sequence *aba* is observed in a model λ in Fig 8.7 and that the initial state is 1; then the probability with which the given sequence is generated via state sequence $1-2-3$ is calculated as follows:

$$\Pr(O = aba, q_1 = 1, q_2 = 2, q_3 = 3|\lambda)$$
$$= \pi_1 \cdot b_1(a) \cdot a_{12} \cdot b_2(b) \cdot a_{23} \cdot b_3(a)$$
$$= 1 \times 1/2 \times 1/3 \times 1/2 \times 1/2 \times 1/2$$
$$= 1/48$$

The probability with which the sequence is generated from the model can be calculated by summing the probabilities for all the possible state transitions. In practice, a more efficient method, known as forward–backward procedure, is used [35].

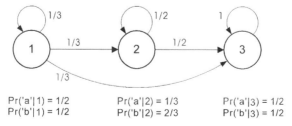

$\Pr(\text{'a'}|1) = 1/2$ $\Pr(\text{'a'}|2) = 1/3$ $\Pr(\text{'a'}|3) = 1/2$
$\Pr(\text{'b'}|1) = 1/2$ $\Pr(\text{'b'}|2) = 2/3$ $\Pr(\text{'b'}|3) = 1/2$

Figure 8.7. An example of left-to-right HMM.

1. *Anomaly Recognition.* Anomaly recognition matches current behavior against the normal behavior models and calculates the probability with which it is generated out of each model. Forward–backward procedure or Viterbi algorithm can be used for this purpose [35]. Each probability is passed to the determination module that decides whether it is normal or not with a threshold.

Forward–backward procedure calculates the probability $\Pr(O|\lambda)$, with which input sequence O is generated with model λ using forward and backward variables. Forward variable α denotes the probability at which a partial sequence $O_1, O_2, \ldots, O_t$ is observed and stays at state q_i.

$$\alpha_t(i) = \Pr(O_1, O_2, \ldots, O_t, i_t = q_i \mid \lambda) \tag{8.1}$$

According to this definition, $\alpha_t(i)$ is the probability with which all the symbols in input sequence are observed in order and the final state is i. Summing up $\alpha_t(i)$ for all i yields the value $\Pr(O|\lambda)$. Backward variable $\beta_t(i)$ is defined as follows. It can be calculated using a process similar to that for α.

$$\beta_t(i) = \Pr(O_{t+1}, O_{t+2}, \ldots, O_T, i_t = q_i \mid \lambda) \tag{8.2}$$

2. *Normal Behavior Modeling.* Determining HMM parameters is to adjust $\lambda = (A, B, \pi)$ to maximize the probability $\Pr(O|\lambda)$. Because no analytic solution is known for it, generally an iterative method called Baum–Welch reestimation is used [35]. This requires two more variables: $\xi_t(i,j)$ is defined as the probability with which it stays at state q_i at time t and stays at state q_j at time $t+1$.

$$\begin{aligned}
\xi_t(i,j) &= \Pr(i_t = q_i, i_{t+1} = q_j \mid O, \lambda) \\
&= \frac{\alpha_t(i)a_{ij}b_j(O_{t+1})\beta_{t+1}(j)}{\Pr(O \mid \lambda)}
\end{aligned} \tag{8.3}$$

And $\gamma_t(i)$ is the probability with which it stays at state q_i at time t.

$$\gamma_t(i) = \sum_{j=1}^{N} \xi_t(i,j) \tag{8.4}$$

Summing up the two variables over time t respectively, we can get the probability with which state i transits to state j and the expectation that it stays at state i. Given the above variables calculated, a new model $\bar{\lambda} = (\bar{A}, \bar{B}, \bar{\pi})$ can be adjusted using the following equations:

$$\bar{\pi}_i = \text{expected frequency (number of times) in state } i \text{ at time } (t = 1)$$
$$= \gamma_1(i)$$

$$\bar{a}_{ij} = \frac{\text{expected number of transitions from state } i \text{ to state } j}{\text{expected number of transitions from state } i}$$

$$= \frac{\sum_{t=1}^{T-1} \xi_t(i,j)}{\sum_{t=1}^{T-1} \gamma_t(i)} \tag{8.5}$$

$$\bar{b}_j(k) = \frac{\text{expected number of times in state } j \text{ and observing symbol } v_k}{\text{expected number of times in state } j}$$

$$= \frac{\sum_{\substack{t=1 \\ s.t.O_t=v_k}}^{T} \gamma_t(j)}{\sum_{t=1}^{T} \gamma_t(j)}$$

After $\bar{\lambda}$ is adjusted from sequence O, $\Pr(O \mid \bar{\lambda})$ is compared against $\Pr(O \mid \lambda)$. If $\Pr(O \mid \lambda)$ is greater than $\Pr(O \mid \bar{\lambda})$, it implies that a critical point in likelihood has been reached, thereby finishing the reestimation. Otherwise, $\Pr(O \mid \lambda)$ is substituted by $\Pr(O \mid \bar{\lambda})$ and reestimation continues.

8.3.4 Multiple Models Fusion by Fuzzy Logic

The HMM can provide a good probabilistic representation of temporal sequences, but the modeling performance must be dependent on the characteristics of input distributions. The BSM that collects audit data for our IDS provides us with many different input symbols as measures according to the usage patterns of the system. The measures are neither statistically independent nor unimodally distributed, and an HMM of a finite size cannot cover all kinds of measure and generalizes poorly.

The basic idea of the multiple models is to develop n independently trained models with different measures, and to decide if the current input sequence is abnormal by obtaining and fusing the outputs from the different models. There are many ways for the information fusion such as neural networks and parameterized classifiers, but in this problem, fuzzy logic is advantageous, because the outputs of the individual models are uncertain and imprecise, and human experts can have some intuition or knowledge on the characteristics of the models [36]. Figure 8.8 is a schematic diagram of the proposed fusion scheme.

A fuzzy inference system provides a computing framework based on the concepts of fuzzy sets, fuzzy if-then rules, and fuzzy reasoning [36]. The basic

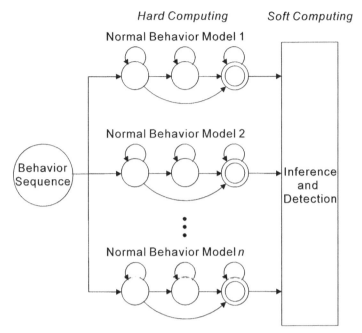

Figure 8.8. The scheme of fusing multiple HMM models.

structure consists of a fuzzy rule-base, reasoning mechanism, and defuzzification mechanism. A fuzzy rule base is a set of fuzzy rules that are expressed as follows:

Rule 1: If $(x_1$ is $A_1^1)$ and $(x_2$ is $A_2^1)$ and ... and $(x_n$ is $A_n^1)$, then y is B^1.
Rule 2: If $(x_1$ is $A_1^2)$ and $(x_2$ is $A_2^2)$ and ... and $(x_n$ is $A_n^2)$, then y is B^2.
Rule m: If $(x_1$ is $A_1^m)$ and $(x_2$ is $A_2^m)$ and ... and $(x_n$ is $A_n^m)$, then y is B^m.

Here, x_j $(1 \leq j \leq n)$ are input variables, y is output variable, and A_j^i and B^i $(1 \leq i \leq m)$ are fuzzy sets that are characterized by membership functions. In this chapter, the numbers of input and output variables are three and one, respectively.

In order to facilitate the design of the detection module, we have to select fuzzy sets for input and output parameters. The selection of more effective fuzzy sets could be performed with more investigation, but it is beyond the scope of this chapter. We just adopt the following fuzzy sets for them:

Input: HMM evaluation values $(M1, M2, \ldots, Mn)$ from different models $\in [0, -\infty)$
Input Fuzzy Set: $I = \{$Low, Medium, High$\}$
Output: Normality $(S) \in [0, 1]$
Output Fuzzy Set: $O = \{$Normal, Abnormal$\}$

The exact partitioning of input/output spaces depends on membership functions, and triangular shapes specify the membership function in this chapter. For fuzzy inference we use the correlation minimum method, which truncates the consequent fuzzy region at the truth of the premise, and the centroid defuzzification method is adopted to yield the expected value of the solution fuzzy region [36]. The fuzzy rules were devised according to the models in consideration.

8.4 EXPERIMENTAL RESULTS

We have used data obtained from three graduate students for one week. In order to collect the realistic data, we did not give any restriction on the time period, but they mainly used text editor, compiler, and their own programs. A total of 60,000 data have been collected; 30,000 of these are used for training and another 30,000 are used for testing. Seventeen cases of u2r (user-to-root) intrusion, one of the most typical intrusions, are included in each user's test data set. An unprivileged user acquires super user privilege by exploiting a subtle temporary file creation and race condition bug.

In anomaly detection, it is natural that false-positive error is higher than misuse detection. If false-positive error is high, the IDS may not be practical because users may be warned frequently from the intrusion detection system, although their action is not illegal. Therefore, we should regard false-positive error as critical error. Actually, we investigate an ROC (Receiver Operating Characteristics) curve in the experiment that presents the variation according to the change of false-positive error. An ROC curve is one of the most popular methods to visualize the performance of IDS, and it depicts the changes in attack detection rate and false-positive error rate as a modifiable parameter is changed. The evaluation threshold is used as a modifiable parameter. A desirable intrusion detection system must show a high detection rate at low false-positive error rate. In an ROC curve, the upper left curve is more desirable.

8.4.1 Preprocessing

In general, a large SOM is better than a small one in classifying samples, but it is not certain when the locality of input pattern is high. In the preprocessing step, we have attempted to find the effective map size of SOM, as well as the effective measures to improve the performance of the IDS based on HMM, by investigating the change of ROC curve for each measure.

1. *Effect of Map Size*. Applying SOM requires us to consider the map size. There is no answer to which map size of SOM is the best for intrusion detection. In order to solve this problem, we consider two factors: quantization error and map usage. The map size of low quantization error and high map usage is desirable for our SOM.

Figure 8.9 shows the variation of reference vectors with the different map sizes of SOM. In the figure, dark area means that one reference vector is distant from the

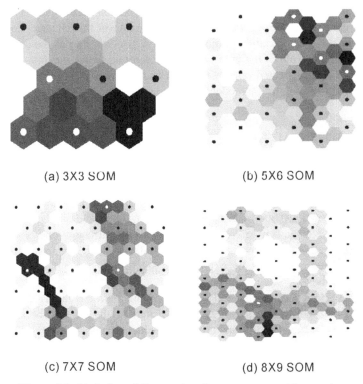

(a) 3X3 SOM   (b) 5X6 SOM

(c) 7X7 SOM   (d) 8X9 SOM

Figure 8.9. Variation of distance in reference vectors with map size.

other. The larger the map size becomes, the closer the distance among reference vectors is, which also indicates that the locality cannot disappear in spite of large map size of SOM. Also, as can be seen in Fig. 8.10, the larger the map size the smaller the quantization error, but the probability of usage gets lower. In addition, the gradient of error curve is lax when the map size is larger than 25. We can also see that the probability of usage is above 50% when the map size is smaller than 50. Therefore, we can select the useful map size between 25 and 50.

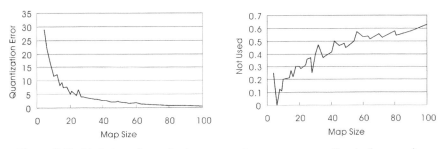

Figure 8.10. Variation of quantization error and map usage according to the map size.

2. *Usefulness of Measures.* We extract three measures from the data related to system call (ID, return value, and return status), process (ID, interprocess communication (IPC) ID, IPC permission, exit value, and exit status), and file access (access mode, path, argument length, and file system). We have also taken into account the combinations of the three measures, resulting in seven sets of different measures in total.

First of all, we reduce their size based on the locality, convert them into a representative form via SOM, and make a sequence so that it can be used for modeling normal behaviors with HMM. Several map sizes such as 5×5, 6×6, and 7×7 are considered for the experiment. The HMM used has 10 states and a different number of symbols according to the map size of SOM. The number of states is determined by a thorough investigation with experiments.

Figure 8.11 shows the ROC curves with respect to the map size of SOM. In case of map size of 25 (5×5), such measures as system call and combination of process and file access are useful. Moreover, file access can be helpful to detect the intrusion well in the map size of 36 (6×6). As can be seen in the 7×7 map, the larger map does not guarantee the performance improvement; actually, it happens to be worse than the smaller maps. In sum, we have obtained the following three sets of measures with different map sizes of SOM:

- The measure based on system call (5×5 SOM)
- The measure based on file access (6×6 SOM)
- Combination of the measures based on system call and file access (6×6 SOM)

8.4.2 Modeling and Intrusion Detection

Effectiveness of HMM for Intrusion Detection. At first, single HMM is used to model all the users. Effective HMM parameters that show superior performance are obtained through experiments: The length of input sequence is 30 and the number of states is 10. Figure 8.12 shows the change of the sequence evaluation values over time when an intrusion occurs. An attack was started at time 12 and ended at time 30. The sequence evaluation value around time 15 gets lower radically due to the abnormal behavior and this low state lasts by around time 22, which implies that the system has a potential to effectively detect the intrusion.

Evaluation with Different Modeling Strategies. This experiment is conducted with a separate model for each user. Table 8.3 shows the intrusion detection rate and false-positive error rate for each model. Here, the threshold is determined with the training data. The evaluation value is always below zero because the natural logarithm is taken. Separate modeling has produced lower false-positive error rates than single modeling in two of three cases.

We have obtained low evaluation values when a user's behavior is evaluated with other users' models. Table 8.4 shows the number of sequences whose evaluation values are low: less than -50. The low evaluation value indicates that the evaluated

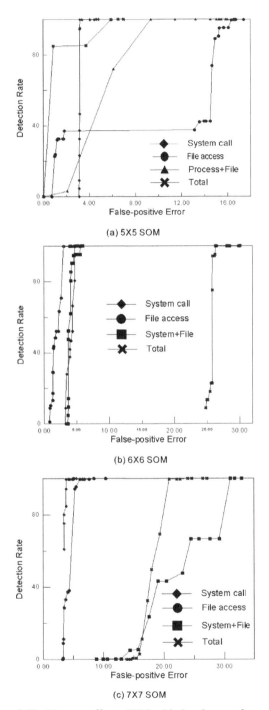

Figure 8.11. Measure effect of IDS with the change of map size.

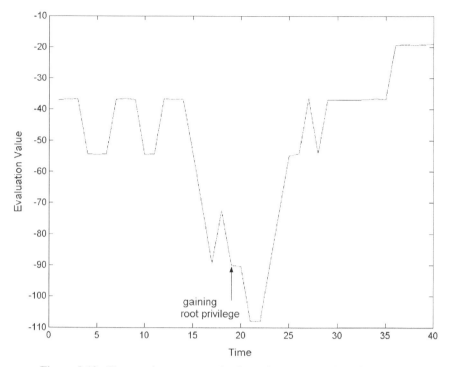

Figure 8.12. Change of sequence evaluation values when an intrusion occurs.

user's behavior deviates from the referenced user's behavior. Lower evaluation values were produced when evaluated user and referenced user are different. This shows that the proposed technique is effective in modeling the user's normal behaviors and can also be used for detecting intrusions from sniffed user accounts, which is also a very crucial attack for IDS. In the case where user 2 was evaluated with the same user profile, the number of low evaluation values (User 2/User 2 cell) was clearly larger than those of similar cases. It is because the test data of user 2 contains unseen behavior

TABLE 8.3. The Anomaly Detection Rate for Separate User Modeling

	Single Modeling	Individual User Modeling		
		User 1	User 2	User 3
Mean	−14.74	−15.54	−4.72	−4.25
Standard deviation	10.42	5.88	8.42	12.34
Threshold	−32.45	−26.21	−31.35	−36.92
Detection rate	100%	100%	100%	100%
False-positive error rate	2.95%	4.31%	1.73%	1.96%

TABLE 8.4. The Number of Sequences Whose Evaluation Values Are Less than −50 When Different User's Model is Used

Referenced User	Evaluated User		
	User 1	User 2	User 3
User 1	0	366	55
User 2	566	315	336
User 3	475	346	0

in the training data. Nevertheless, it is smaller than the number generated when different referenced user is attempted (User 1/User 2 and User 3/User 2 cells).

Improvement with Models Fusion. From the experimental results on the usefulness of measures, we have developed three HMM models based on the measure of system call, the measure of file access, and the combination of them, and we have combined them using the fuzzy inference system in Section 8.3. We have devised the following seven rules for intrusion detection based on the in-depth investigation on the characteristics of the three models and attack patterns:

Rule 1: If ($M1$ is Low), then (S is Abnormal).

Rule 2: If ($M2$ is Low), then (S is Abnormal).

Rule 3: If ($M1$ is High) and ($M2$ is Middle), then (S is Normal).

Rule 4: If ($M1$ is Low) and ($M2$ is Low) and ($M3$ is Low), then (S is Abnormal).

Rule 5: If ($M1$ is Middle) and ($M2$ is Middle) and ($M3$ is Middle), then (S is Normal).

Rule 6: If ($M1$ is High), then (S is Normal).

Rule 7: If ($M1$ is Middle) and ($M2$ is High), then (S is Normal).

$M1$: the output of HMM with the measure based on system call.

$M2$: the output of HMM with the measure based on file access.

$M3$: the output of HMM with the measure based on system call and file access.

We have used the best result from each model because the threshold for each model differs from each other. The false-positive error rate has improved compared to its primitive models as shown in Table 8.5. It is clearly better than the error rate of separate modeling. This result indicates that considering various aspects of audit event is truly important for effective intrusion detection. It also indicates that fuzzy logic is suitable for fusing multiple HMM models because the evaluation values in HMM from imprecise and uncertain information sources and the fuzzy logic provide a model for the modes of reasoning that are approximate rather than exact.

TABLE 8.5. The Performance of Multiple Models Fusion by Fuzzy Logic

	Single Modeling	Fuzzy Logic Fusion
Detection rate	100%	100%
False-positive error rate	2.95%	1.18%

8.5 FUSION OF SOFT COMPUTING AND HARD COMPUTING

In this chapter, two SC techniques (SOM and FL) and one HC technique (HMM) are fused together. These SC and HC techniques are fused in a cascade fashion and act as a preprocessor and a postprocessor of each other (Fig. 8.13). The structural category of fusing SC and HC is related to the SC-HC- and HC-SC-type fusion (Chapter 1). At the first stage, data reduction using SC and behavior modeling using HC form a cascade. SOM reduces the audit data as a preprocessor and then HMM evaluates its abnormality. SOM and HMM are fused in the way of SC-HC. SOM helps out HMM to consider various aspects of audit events.

At the next stage, the outputs of HC techniques are used for the inputs of SC technique. Fuzzy logic combines the results of HMM and makes the final decision. It is the HC-SC-type fusion. FL can improve the performance and reliability of the system with domain-specific knowledge because the outputs of HMM are inherently imprecise and uncertain. Our system can be viewed as a function that evaluates the normality of the given audit event sequence n. It can be expressed by the following equation:

$$\text{Normality}(n) = f_{FL}(\theta_{FL}; f_{HMM}(\theta_{HMM}; f_{SOM}(\theta_{SOM}; n))) \tag{8.6}$$

where n is an audit event sequence and $f_{FL}(\cdot;\cdot)$, $f_{HMM}(\cdot;\cdot)$, and $f_{SOM}(\cdot;\cdot)$ are algorithms of FL, HMM, and SOM respectively. θ_{FL}, θ_{HMM}, and θ_{SOM} are the corresponding system parameters.

Figure 8.14 illustrates the function of each technique in terms of the general framework. SOM acts as a good preprocessor that reduces dimensionality of problem space. We can solve the problem more easily by using the reduced data. Multiple

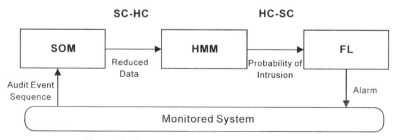

Figure 8.13. The scheme of fusing SC and HC.

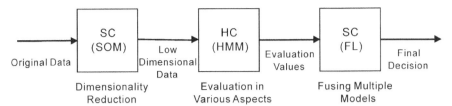

Figure 8.14. The functions of each technique.

HMMs provide the basis of decision. They produce several evaluation values in various aspects. FL is a decision-maker. It makes the final decision by fusing the intermediate decisions with domain knowledge. This approach can be used to solve the problem whose input data have too high dimensionality and complexity to be modeled with conventional modeling techniques.

We can extend this system to the hybrid detection systems that fuse host-based and network-based IDS as another possible application of this framework (Fig. 8.15). To detect various types of intrusion including both network-based and host-based intrusion, one needs to observe the user's behavior in various aspects. We could build the multiple detectors that use different types of audit data collected from host-based and network-based sources. One detector consists of a preprocessor to reduce the dimensionality and a modeler that models normal behavior and evaluates the probability of intrusion. Data fusion techniques such as rule base, voting, and FL can also be used for making the final decision by fusing the outputs from multiple detectors. In references 37 and 38, rule-base and voting techniques for fusing multiple detectors are implemented and tested.

8.6 CONCLUDING REMARKS

Conventional HC techniques such as rule base, expert system, and pattern matching have been applied for solving several problems in intrusion detection. Although they provide basic functions that are needed to detect intrusions, they have the limitations of inflexibility and large maintenance effort. To remedy these drawbacks of conventional IDS, SC techniques are employed. The complementary fusion of SC and HC techniques can give automatic, flexible, and robust features to IDS.

We have introduced a novel intrusion detection system that reduces raw audit data using SOM, models user's normal behaviors using HMM, and detects anomalies by combining several models with fuzzy logic. Experimental results indicate that this system can effectively detect the intrusions. It can be concluded that provided with the sufficient normal behaviors, the fusion of SC, like neural network and fuzzy logic, and HC, like HMM, can be used as an effective intrusion detection technique. In future studies, we will devise more sophisticated techniques of integrating SC and HC including an automatic rule acquisition for the fuzzy inference system, as well as evaluate our system with more realistic data sets.

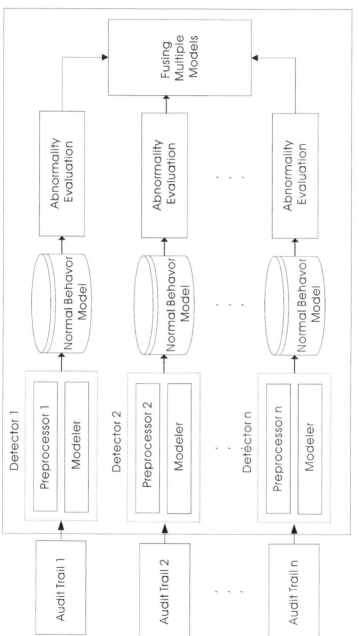

Figure 8.15. The extended hybrid detection system.

ACKNOWLEDGMENTS

This research was supported by the University IT Research Center Project.

REFERENCES

1. CERT Coordination Center, "CERT/CC Statistics 1988–2003," WWW page, 2003. Available from < http://www.cert.org/stats/ > .

2. B. P. Miller, D. Koski, C. P. Lee, L. Maganty, R. Murthy, A. Natarajan, and J. Steidl, "Fuzz Revisited: A Re-Examination of the Reliability of UNIX Utilities and Services," Technical Report, University of Wisconsin, Computer Sciences Department, Madison, 1995.

3. H. S. Vaccaro and G. E. Liepins, "Detection of Anomalous Computer Session Activity," *Proceedings of the IEEE Symposium on Research in Security and Privacy*, Oakland, CA, May 1989, pp. 280–289.

4. S. Axelsson, "Intrusion Detection Systems: A Survey and Taxonomy," Technical Report 99-15, Chalmers University, Department of Computer Engineering, Gothenburg, Sweden, 2000.

5. S. R. Snapp and S. E. Smaha, "Signature Analysis Model Definition and Formalism," *Proceedings of the 4th Workshop on Computer Security Incident Handling*, Denver, CO, 1992.

6. K. Ilgun, R. A. Kemmerer, and P. A. Porras, "State Transition Analysis: A Rule-based Intrusion Detection Approach," *IEEE Transaction on Software Engineering* **21**, 181–199 (1995).

7. T. F. Lunt, A. Tamaru, F. Gilham, R. Jagannathan, C. Jalali, and P. G. Neuman, "A Real-time Intrusion-Detection Expert System (IDES)," Technical Report Project 6784, SRI International, Computer Science Laboratory, Menlo Park, CA, 1992.

8. S. A. Hofmeyr, A. Somayaji, and S. Forrest, "Intrusion Detection Using Sequences of System Calls," *Journal of Computer Security* **6**, 51–180 (1998).

9. S. Kumar and E. Spafford, "An Application of Pattern Matching in Intrusion Detection," Technical Report 94-013, Purdue University, Department of Computer Sciences, West Lafayette, IN, 1994.

10. C. Dowell and P. Ramsetdt, "The Computer Watch Data Reduction Tool," *Proceedings of the 13th National Computer Security Conference*, Washington, DC, Oct. 1990, pp. 99–108.

11. S. Smaha, "Haystack: An Intrusion Detection System," *Proceedings of the 4th Aerospace Computer Security Applications Conference*, Orlando, FL, Oct. 1988, pp. 37–44.

12. P. A. Porras and P. G. Neumann, "EMERALD: Event Monitoring Enabling Responses to Anomalous Live Disturbances," *Proceedings of the 20th National Information Systems Security Conference*, Baltimore, MD, Oct. 1997, pp. 353–365.

13. T. Heberlein, G. Dias, K. Levitt, B. Mukherjee, J. Wood, and D. Wolber, "A Network Security Monitor," *Proceedings of the IEEE Symposium on Research in Security and Privacy*, Los Alamitos, CA, May 1990, pp. 296–304.

14. S. Staniford-Chen, S. Cheung, R. Crawford, M. Dilger, J. Frank, J. Hoagland, K Levitt, C. Wee, R. Yip, and D. Zerkle, "GrIDS—A Graph Based Intrusion Detection System for Large Networks," *Proceedings of the 19th National Information Systems Security Conference*, Oct. 1996, pp. 361–370.

15. H. Debar, M. Becker, and D. Siboni, "A Neural Network Component for an Intrusion Detection System," *Proceedings of the IEEE Symposium on Research in Security and Privacy*, Oakland, CA, May 1992, pp. 240–250.

16. A. K. Ghosh, A. Schwatzbard, and M. Shatz, "Learning Program Behavior Profiles for Intrusion Detection," *Proceedings of the 1st USENIX Workshop on Intrusion Detection and Network Monitoring*, Santa Clara, CA, Apr. 1999, pp. 51–62.

17. MIT Lincoln Laboratory, "DARPA Intrusion Detection Evaluation," WWW page. Available from < http://www.ll.mit.edu/IST/ideval/index.html > .

18. R. Lippmann and S. Cunningham, "Improving Intrusion Detection Performance Using Keyword Selection and Neural Networks," *Computer Networks* **34**, 594–603 (2000).

19. G. Giacinto, F. Roli, and L. Didaci, "Fusion of Multiple Classifiers for Intrusion Detection in Computer Networks," *Pattern Recognition Letters* **24**, 1795–1803 (2003).

20. L. Girardin, "An Eye on Network Intruder-Administrator Shootouts," *Proceedings of the 1st USENIX Workshop on Intrusion Detection and Network Monitoring*, Santa Clara, CA, Apr. 1999, pp. 19–28.

21. F. González and D. Dasgupta, "Neuro-Immune and Self-Organizing Map Approaches to Anomaly Detection: a Comparison," *Proceedings of the 1st International Conference on Artificial Immune Systems*, Canterbury, UK, Sept. 2002, pp. 203–211.

22. D. Dasgupta and F. González, "An Intelligent Decision Support System for Intrusion Detection and Response," *Proceedings of the International Workshop on Mathematical Methods, Models and Architectures for Computer Networks Security*, St. Petersburg, Russia, May 2001.

23. D. Dasgupta and F. González, "An Immunity-Based Technique to Characterize Intrusions in Computer Networks," *IEEE Transactions on Evolutionary Computation* **6**, 1081–1088 (2002).

24. S. Forrest, S. Hofmeyr, and A. Somayaji, "Computer Immunology," *Communications of the ACM* **40**(10), 88–96 (1997).

25. M. Crosbie and E. H. Spafford, "Applying Genetic Programming to Intrusion Detection," in E. V. Siegel and J. R. Koza, eds., *Working Notes for the AAAI Symposium on Genetic Programming*, AAAI Press, Cambridge, MA, 1995, pp. 1–8.

26. J. E. Dickerson, J. Juslin, O. Koukousoula, and J. A. Dickerson, "Fuzzy Intrusion Detection," *Proceedings of the 9th International Fuzzy System Association World Congress and the 20th North American Fuzzy Information Processing Society International Conference*, Vancouver, Canada, July 2001, pp. 1506–1510.

27. J. Gomez and D. Dasgupta, "Evolving Fuzzy Rules for Intrusion Detection," *Proceedings of the Information Assurance Workshop*, West Point, NY, June 2002.

28. The UCI KDD Archive, "KDD Cup 1999 Data," WWW page. Available from < http://kdd.ics.uci.edu/databases/kddcup99/kddcup99.html > .

29. V. Gowadia, C. Farkas, and M. Valtorta, "Agent Based Intrusion Detection with Soft Evidence," *Proceedings of the 14th International Resource Management Association International Conference*, Philadelphia, May 2003.

30. D. Barbara, N. Wu, and S. Jajodia, "Detecting Novel Network Intrusions Using Bayes Estimators," *Proceedings of the 1st Society for Industrial and Applied Mathematics International Conference on Data Mining*, Chicago, Apr. 2001.

31. C. Warrender, S. Forrest, and B. Pearlmutter, "Detecting Intrusions Using System Calls: Alternative Data Models," *Proceedings of the IEEE Symposium on Security and Privacy*, Oakland, CA, May 1999, pp. 133–145.

32. T. Lane, "Hidden Markov Models for Human/Computer Interface Modeling," *Proceedings of the 16th International Joint Conference on Artificial Intelligence Workshop on Learning about Users*, Stockholm, Sweden, 1999, pp. 35–44.

33. Sun Microsystems, *SunSHIELD Basic Security Module Guide*, Palo Alto, CA, 1998.

34. T. Kohonen, *Self-Organizing Maps*, Springer, Berlin, 1995.

35. L. R. Rabiner, "A Tutorial on Hidden Markov Models and Selected Applications in Speech Recognition," *Proceedings of the IEEE* **77**, 257–286 (1989).

36. J.-S. R. Jang, C.-T. Sun, and E. Mizutani, *Neuro-Fuzzy and Soft Computing*, Prentice-Hall, Upper Saddle River, NJ, 1997.

37. S.-J. Han and S.-B. Cho, "Detecting Intrusion with Rule-Based Integration of Multiple Models," *Computers & Security*, to appear.

38. S.-B. Cho and S.-J. Han, "Two Sophisticated Techniques to Improve HMM-based Intrusion Detection System," *Proceedings of the 6th International Symposium on Recent Advances in Intrusion Detection*, Pittsburgh, PA, 2003, pp. 207–219.

EDITOR'S INTRODUCTION TO CHAPTER 9

Computer–user interaction has not evolved much since the introduction of the first graphical user interfaces in the early 1980s. At that time, the mouse was also launched, and it was quickly accepted as a standard pointing device to complement the keyboard. Some attempts toward visual animation in guiding the use of a specific program or operating system have been made just recently. Those trials, however, have not obtained any established role among users; most users simply deactivate such gimmicks. Also, the use of spoken language in giving commands to the computer has not penetrated into everyday use of personal workstations.

Therefore, it is justified to say that the field of human–computer interaction is a truly demanding and highly subjective area, where possible breakthroughs are still somewhere in the future. This statement is obviously excluding those special applications where the use of a keyboard and mouse is either impractical or impossible.

In face-to-face human–human communication, there are always two complementary channels of interaction [1]:

1. Explicit message channel—that is, verbal information
2. Implicit message channel—that is, paralanguage and nonverbal information

The present human–computer interfaces use only the first channel, concentrating on the linguistic part of the communication process. On the other hand, the second channel, related to emotions and "body language," is not utilized at all. While psychologists are working in the area of implicit messages, most engineers have their

Computationally Intelligent Hybrid Systems. Edited by Seppo J. Ovaska
ISBN 0-471-47668-4   © 2005 the Institute of Electrical and Electronics Engineers, Inc.

interests in the explicit part only. Yet, one of the main difficulties that humans experience in communicating with each other is not so much a function of the language they use but rather a series of psychological and sociological factors acting on them [2].

Cowie et al. [1] give a comprehensive introduction to the use of emotion recognition in human–computer interaction. Concurrent speech signal analysis and face image analysis are suggested for effective and reliable emotion detection. They emphasize that "Hybrid systems have a particular attraction in that they link two types of elements that are prominent in reactions to emotion—articulate verbal descriptions and explanations and responses that are felt rather than articulated."

Chapter 9 of the present book, "Emotion Generating Method on Human–Computer Interfaces," is authored by Kazuya Mera and Takumi Ichimura. They introduce a systematical method to analyze the computer user's emotions from the contents of typed text. First, the proposed system estimates pleasure or displeasure from a single sentence or paragraph. Next, the initial rough pleasure/displeasure emotion state is refined into 20 specific classes of emotion. Finally, they consider the visual expression of recognized emotions. In this way, the remote human–human communication process that is facilitated by computers is enhanced and made more comfortable. Such an approach is related to the aims of Kansei information processing (KIP) [3], where the Japanese word "kansei" has the following meanings: emotion, feeling, sense, sensibility, sentiment, or susceptibility. One of the goals of the Japanese KIP project (1992–1995) was to realize human-friendly partner systems for future information environments.

The novel method of Mera and Ichimura estimates and analyzes emotions, as well as expresses the results numerically by using fuzzy systems theory and a neural network. This emotion-oriented human–computer interface uses the advantageous fusion of soft computing (SC) and hard computing (HC). Here, the principal fusion category is SC//HC (Chapter 1). In addition, the cascade structure HC-SC is applied. To utilize SC in such a Kansei communication system is natural, because emotion estimation and analysis contain difficulties related to imprecision, uncertainty, and partial truth.

Also an efficient method for representing emotions with facial expressions is proposed. Extracted emotions are fed into a multilayer neural network that selects the most suitable facial image from the available database. Both rudimentary (artificial) and complex (real) face information was used. It is, however, the editor's opinion that only such emotion-based user interfaces that use real face information have a chance to become popular. On the other hand, those simple artificial faces suffer the problem (rejection) of present help systems with elementary animation.

The developed techniques were applied into an e-mail software, JavaFaceMail, and a chat system, JavaFaceChat, with encouraging results. In JavaFaceMail, the emotions are estimated directly from the contents of the text message, and one facial expression corresponding to the recognized emotional state is generated and sent to the recipient of the e-mail. The new chat system also generates similar facial expressions. In addition, it continuously analyzes the emotions of each on-line user, and it invites two users with highly similar emotions to a private chat room.

As a final remark, the complementary fusion of SC and HC is a highly potential technique for developing emotion-based user interfaces.

REFERENCES

1. R. Cowie, E. Douglas-Cowie, N. Tsapatsoulis, G. Votsis, S. Kollias, W. Fellenz, and J. G. Taylor, "Emotion Recognition in Human-Computer Interaction," *IEEE Signal Processing Magazine* **18**, 32–80 (Jan. 2001).

2. M. J. Misshauk, *Management Theory and Practice*, Little, Brown, Boston, 1979.

3. S. Inokuchi, "Non-Verbal Interaction for Kansei Communication," *Proceedings of the IEEE International Conference on Systems, Man, and Cybernetics*, Tokyo, Japan, Oct. 1999, **4**, pp. 311–316.

CHAPTER 9

EMOTION GENERATING METHOD ON HUMAN–COMPUTER INTERFACES

KAZUYA MERA and TAKUMI ICHIMURA
Hiroshima City University, Hiroshima, Japan

9.1 INTRODUCTION

The computer is utilized in many aspects of our life, and the range of its influence varies from the business fields to the personal communication tools. Especially, since the cellular phone has been developed as a miniaturized communication tool, we can enjoy mobile communication anywhere at any time through the Internet. As the hardware develops, the functions they are equipped with are becoming more advanced. In spite of the development of many outstanding functions, there are many situations where we cannot use to them without confusion, bother, or difficulty.

The scientific and engineering technologies have not always dealt with human behavior explicitly. Probably, the reason for this is that humans who use these technologies do not necessarily have any standard behavior, because individuals have different feelings and they make their decisions by based on their feelings. One of the research fields in engineering attempts to achieve a smooth communication between humans and machines. It is natural that we wish to develop techniques for understanding human feelings and to embed human's functional behaviors in the machine.

Therefore, we are pursuing an interface tool for natural interactive communication. In order to achieve natural communication, developing an interactive communication tool that estimates the variations of the human mind is expected [1]. Ekman classified body actions related to communication: verbal information, paralanguage, and nonverbal information. Verbal information is expressed in the format of strings, which are extracted from sentences, utterances, and so on.

Computationally Intelligent Hybrid Systems. Edited by Seppo J. Ovaska
ISBN 0-471-47668-4 © 2005 the Institute of Electrical and Electronics Engineers, Inc.

Paralanguage is expressed by rhythm, intonation, and so on. Nonverbal information is expressed by facial expressions, gestures, blinks, and so on [2]. It is especially well known that the role of nonverbal information in communication and conversation is important. Mehrabian reported that "an affection reaches to the companion by verbal information (the weight is 7%), paralanguage (the weight is 38%), and nonverbal information (the weight is 55%) in a conversation [3]" from the view of psychology.

Various methods are proposed for perceiving the emotions from nonverbal information. However, people sometimes use facial expressions, which differ from their real emotions. For example, a person smiles even if he/she is displeased. In this situation, if the former system recognizes the user's emotion as happy from the smile, the system never obtains the confidence of the user because such misunderstandings often cause serious problems. Picard proposed a method to recognize eight types of emotional states (anger, hate, grief, platonic love, romantic love, joy, reverence, and no emotion) from the features of the subject's physiological data [4]. The method considers five types of physiological signals such as electromyogram, blood-volume pressure, heart rate, skin conductivity, and respiration. The method is not misled by counterfeit facial expression. However, we aim to recognize the user's emotions from human communication. People cannot detect the other's physiological data numerically. They regard, rather, the content of utterances, personal taste information, and so on. Therefore, a method to analyze the user's emotions based on not only nonverbal information but also verbal information is required.

We propose a method to analyze the user's emotion concerning the contents of utterances [5]. First, the system extracts pleasure/displeasure from an event [6]. Next, the pleasure/displeasure is classified in 20 types of complicated emotions [7]. We also have to consider how to express the extracted emotions [8,9]. We aim for smooth human–computer communication like human-to-human communication. Although the method is only enough to express the system's own emotions making it a pet of the user and attached, it is not enough for the user to feel a natural interaction with the computer interface.

Our method applies the idea of the "fusion of soft computing (SC) and hard computing (HC)." In our method, we use HC techniques to parse input sentences and to calculate emotion value (EV) based on favorite values (FV). However, HC is inadequate to express the subtleties of emotions. Therefore, our method includes two types of SC techniques: the "limitation of fuzzy linguistic truth value" and the "parallel sand grass type neural network." The former technique is used to calculate the modifier's effect for the preference degree of the object. The latter technique is used to generate a facial image to express the estimated emotions.

Some applications are introduced in this chapter. We applied the above method to mail software and a chat system. The mail software (JavaFaceMail [8]) calculates the emotions from the content of the mail, generates one facial expression image of the sender, and sends the mail with the facial image. The chat system (JavaFaceChat [10]) also generates a facial expression image like JavaFaceMail. Furthermore, it analyzes the variances of emotions for each user, and it invites two users to a new closed chat room when their tendencies of variances are alike.

9.2 EMOTION GENERATING CALCULATIONS METHOD

We present the Emotion Generating Calculations (EGC) method, which extracts emotions from the utterances [5]. This method is constructed by focusing on the similarities between the grammar structures and the semantic structures within the case frame representation. The input of our model is the sentence of the user's utterance. Figure 9.1 is the flow of procedure in our EGC method.

At first, the user's utterances are transcribed into the case frame representation based on the result of morphing and parsing for each utterance, because the input form of our proposed method is case frame representation.

Next, the system calculates pleasure/displeasure and its strength for an event described by case frame representation. In the psychological field, "unpleasure" is often used as the opposite of "pleasure." However, we use "displeasure," because an explicit intention about "unhappy" should be indicated and "unpleasure" often indicates neutral emotion (neither "happy" nor "unhappy.") We define three important elements for each type of event, which are classified by Okada [11]. The system constructs the synthetic vector based on the degree of element's impression about likes/dislikes (favorite value: FV). Each term element mainly means subject, object, and predicate. The method also calculates the degree of extracted emotion (emotion value: EV) using FVs for their terms. The negatives and the noun phrases are also considered in these calculations [12].

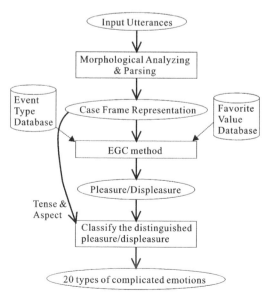

Figure 9.1. Procedure of the EGC method.

Then, the system classifies the pleasure/displeasure into 20 complicated emotions based on the "Emotion Eliciting Condition Theory [13]." The theory requires judging such conditions as follows; "feeling for another," "prospect and confirmation," and "approval/disapproval."

This method calculates the emotions not from the viewpoint of the computer system (agent) but from the viewpoint of the user. It enables an adequate facial expression in order to sympathize the user's emotion and to avoid the utterance that the agent causes displeasure.

9.2.1 Favorite Value Database

The elements' impression degrees about likes/dislikes (FV) are used to calculate pleasure/displeasure for an event in our method. We give positive numbers to some objects when the user likes them, and we assign negative numbers to the other objects that the user dislikes. The FV is predefined a real number in the range $[-1.0, 1.0]$.

There are two types of FVs, personal FV and default FV. Personal FV is stored in a personal database for each person who the agent knows well, and it shows the degree of like/dislike to an object from the person's viewpoint. On the other hand, default FV shows the common degree of like/dislike to an object that the agent feels. Generally, it is generated based on the agent's own taste information according to the result of some questionnaires. Both personal and default FVs are stored in each user's FV database. An object's FV is retrieved by the following procedure (Fig. 9.2):

- Retrieve the object in personal FV database.
- Retrieve the upper concept's FV in default value database.
- Retrieve further upper concept's FV in default value database.
- Retrieve the object or the upper concept in default FV database.
- Give the object the value 0 as the FV when there is no information in any database.

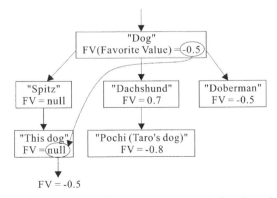

Figure 9.2. Retrieving further upper concept's favorite value.

Default Favorite Value. Default FVs are predefined based on a corpus in the field to which the system is applied. The object (noun), event core (verb), and attribute (adjective) have FVs. At first, we predefined the attributes' FVs based on a present-day adjective using a dictionary [14]. In this chapter, there is a list of adjective images, and the positive/negative image and its degrees of 1010 adjectives are listed in the range $[-3, +3]$. However, some of the adjectives have both images. For example, when the word "cool" is used about temperature, it means "not so cold but comfortable." On the other hand, when the word is used about eagerness, it means "not eager, lack of will." We did not deal with such words because identifying the difference in meaning is very difficult. Next, we predefined the favorite degree of the event cores. In the EGC method, pleasure/displeasure is extracted based on approach/avoidance of a likable/dislikable object. Then, we gave the verbs that relate to "gain" and "lose" positive numbers and negative numbers, respectively.

The FVs of the objects were gained from a web-based questionnaire sheet; based on that information, we constructed FV databases. The web site shows some nouns with an input frame for FV. The subjects input a real number in the range $[-1.0, 1.0]$ for each word. We adopted the average of all subjects' answer values (men: 10, women: 10) as the objects' default FVs. Because there are countless objects in the world, we limited the objects that have default FV into the words that frequently appear in the dialogue about the field where our method is applied.

Favorite Value Learning Method. The EGC method needs objects' FVs obtained from a web-based questionnaire sheet. However, predefining a common user's FV database is very different among people. Even for the same person, preferences for objects can change easily. Then, people generally guess a user's taste information in the dialogue. We propose some FV learning methods to learn the user's taste information from the dialogue using grammatical knowledge and already-known FVs [15,16].

The first method is the "direct expression about like/dislike." When we guess a person's taste information, we pay attention to the words "like" and "dislike." These words are used to tell one's impression about something. In this method, when the sentence's nominative is the person and its predicate is like/dislike, the word in object frame is regarded as liked/disliked for the person. Some adjectives also have good/bad impression. These impressions are identified using "standard good/bad impression of adjectives table [14]." Then, the adjectives that have good/bad impressions are interpreted the same as "like" and "dislike." For example, when the agent hears the sentence "I like an apple," the agent recognizes the user's taste about apple is "like," and when the sentence is "My sister is shameless," the agent can guess that the user does not like his/her sister, because the word "shameless" has a bad impression.

The second method is "favorite value changing situations" [15,16]. FV naturally increases when an object does something useful or favorite to the agent. It decreases, on the other hand, when an object does something harmful or unfavorable. Current FV for a predicate of an event is assigned a predetermined numerical value. In this approach, FV for an object is calculated based on the situations, which will influence its FV, from the agent's knowledge structure. Such situations are called "favorite value changing situations" and are defined with the following three rules:

1. Condition: events
2. Situation: situations represented by condition
3. FV change: increase or decrease

An example situation indicates that the agent dislikes a person who dates two people at the same time. The situation in which a person P1 is dating with two persons causes FV for P1 to decrease.

Condition: (date ((Subj P1)(Obj-M P2))) and (date ((Obj-M P1)(Goal P3)))

Situation: P1 is dating with two persons at the same time

Favorite value change: FV for P1 decreases

9.2.2   Calculation Pleasure/Displeasure for an Event

Arnold defined "emotions" as tendencies of activation about approach/avoidance of good/bad object [17]. We assumed the following conditions to extract pleasure based on Arnold's definition. The conditions for extracting displeasure are the opposite of pleasure's conditions:

1. Favorite agent gains a benefit/detestable agent suffers a loss.
2. The condition of favorite/detestable agent becomes better/worse.
3. Favorite/detestable agent gets good/bad evaluation.
4. Favorite/detestable agent has a favorite/detestable attribute.

Based on these conditions, we pay attention to three elements (subject, object, and action) in the target event for calculating pleasure/displeasure. We assume an emotional space as three-dimensional space and the degree of FV for the element as the axis. Then, we construct a synthetic vector among the FVs of the three elements as shown in Fig. 9.3. Therefore, we distinguish pleasure/displeasure by judging in which area the synthetic vector exists. Furthermore, we calculate the degree of pleasure/displeasure from the length of this vector.

Table 9.1 is a list indicating the sign of each axis and the generated pleasure/displeasure. When the vector is on the axis, the event does not raise any emotion. When

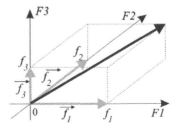

Figure 9.3. Synthetic vector for calculating pleasure/displeasure.

TABLE 9.1. Distinguish Pleasure/Displeasure Using the Sign of Each Axis

Area	$F1$	$F2$	$F3$	Emotion
I	+	+	+	Pleasure
II	−	+	+	Displeasure
III	−	−	+	Pleasure
IV	+	−	+	Displeasure
V	+	+	−	Displeasure
VI	−	+	−	Pleasure
VII	−	−	−	Displeasure
VIII	+	−	−	Pleasure

we calculate the synthetic vectors of the events that do not have third elements, we supply a dummy FV: β as f_2 element. We defined β as $+0.5$ because it does not affect our method.

We define three elements for each case frame type based on Okada's classification [11] as shown in Table 9.2. In this table, $V(S,{}^{*})$ is the type of event (verb),

TABLE 9.2. Each Axis for Each Case Frame Event Type

Type	Axis $F1$	$F2$	$F3$
V(S)	f_S	β	f_P
A(S, C)			
A(S, OF, C)			
A(S, OT, C)			
A(S, OM, C)			
A(S, OS, C)			
N(S)			
V(S, OF)	f_S	$f_{OT}-f_{OF}$	f_P
V(S, OT)			
V(S, OM)	f_S	f_{OM}	f_P
V(S, OS)	f_S-f_{OS}	β	f_P
V(S, O)	f_S	f_O	f_P
	f_O	β	f_P
V(S, O, OF)	f_O	$f_{OT}-f_{OF}$	f_P
V(S, O, OT)			
V(S, O, OM)	f_O	f_{OM}	f_P
V(S, O, I)	f_O	$|f_I|$	f_P
V(S, O, OC)	f_O	β	f_{OC}
A(S, O, C)	f_O	β	f_P

A(S,*) is the type of attribute (adjective), and N(S) is the type of "is-a" relationship (noun).

f_S: FV of Subject

f_O: FV of Object

f_{OF}: FV of Object—From

f_{OT}: FV of Object—To

f_{OM}: FV of Object—Mutual

f_{OS}: FV of Object—Source

f_{OC}: FV of Object –Content

f_P: FV of Predicate

f_I: FV of Implement

9.2.3   Favorite Value of Modified Element

The elements in the event have FVs. However, their words often appear with a modifier or aspect. For example, the nouns are modified as noun phrases or noun clauses, and the verb and adjective are modified by adverbs, tenses, and aspects. These modifications influence their FVs. The judge of like/dislike is changeable with a modifier as "apple" and "rotten apple." We propose calculation methods of the FV with modification [12].

When a predicate has a negative aspect, we reverse the sign of the FV of the predicate because the meaning of the predicate becomes opposite. There are not only negative aspects but also various aspects in dialogue, however, we do not take care of these aspects because they have no influence to distinguish likes/dislikes.

The FV of the noun phrase is defined as a product of the FV of the modifier and that of the modified word [Eq. (9.1)], because the modified word is giving information about the owner, attribute, and so on, by the modifier. When the modifier is a pronoun and the content of the pronoun can be guessed, we calculate the FV by supplying the omitted word. Furthermore, when the modified word is a proper noun, we deal with the FV of the modified word as the value of the whole noun phrase [Eq. (9.2)], because the concept of a proper noun is unlimited by the modifier.

$$\text{FV of Noun Phrase} = \text{FV of modifier} \times \text{FV of the modified word} \qquad (9.1)$$

$$\text{FV of Noun Phrase} = \text{FV of the proper noun} \qquad (9.2)$$

We apply the "limitation of fuzzy linguistic truth value [18]" method for evaluating the FV of noun clause, because the HC technique is too strict to calculate such an ambiguous modifier's effect. The "limitation of fuzzy truth value" is explained as follows:

First, we consider about

$$((x) \text{ is } A) \text{ is } \tau$$

as a fuzzy predicate with the "linguistic truth value." "A" is a fuzzy set on the universal set "U", and "x" is a variable fixed into an element in "U". When we fix a variable "x" into an element "*e*" in a group "U,"

$$((e) \text{ is } A) \text{ is } \tau$$

becomes a kind of fuzzy proposition and only one truth value is obtained as shown in Fig. 9.2. The truth value of the proposition $(((e) \text{ is } A) \text{ is } \tau)$ is described as $\mu_A(e)$. When we define $\mu_A(e)$ as "a", the fuzzy proposition "$((e) \text{ is } A) \text{ is } \tau$" changes into a new fuzzy proposition as

$$(a) \text{ is } \tau$$

Therefore, the truth value of the proposition becomes $\mu_\tau(a)$, and the truth value of the proposition "$((e) \text{ is } A) \text{ is } \tau$" is given as follows:

$$\mu_\tau(a) = \mu_\tau(\mu_A(e))$$

The impression (FV) of the modified word is enhanced/deflated by its action or attribute described in the modifier clause. The impression of the modifier clause is calculated by using the EGC method. The Emotion Value (EV) indicates pleasure/displeasure and its degree for the modifier clause. When the impressions of the modified word and the context of the modifier clause are the same (both good and bad), it enhances the FV of the modified word. On the other hand, when the impressions of the modified word and the context of the modifier clause are different, it deflates the FV of the modified word.

We propose a transition function for modifier clause as shown in Fig. 9.4 based on an idea that "the objects which do not have concrete evaluation are more effective about the FV." We have to adjust the maximum value of the effect not to over 1.0. We define the maximum effect to the FV as EV_{mdc}/α and α as 2.0, because the maximum of the EV is $\sqrt{3}$, where EV_{mdc} means the "EV of modifier clause."

9.2.4 Experimental Result

We extracted some responses of the users from the conversation log and adopted the EGC method to them. We calculated pleasure/displeasure from the speaker's view-

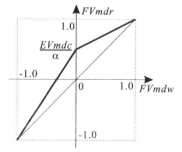

Figure 9.4. Transition function for modifier clause.

TABLE 9.3. Number of the Example Generated Emotion (EGC/Human)

	Event Type											
	I	II	III	IV	V	VI	VII	VIII	IX	X	XI	XII
Number of the emotion	19/31	0/0	11/11	3/3	4/4	17/27	0/1	0/2	0/0	1/1	0/0	0/0

point. Then, the EGC method calculated the same pleasure/displeasure with human feeling from 80 utterances as shown in Table 9.3.

We found two types of problems regarding the EGC method from the experimental result. At first, generating negative emotion against an unpopular person depends on the individual. Although the EGC method always detects negative emotion toward an unpopular person, some people occasionally feel sorry for the unlucky person even they do not like him/her. There were 11 counterexamples in the experiment. We found that it depends on the interest to the individual. In order to realize this, we have to consider the objects' parameter not only FV but also the other attributes like interest.

The next problem is about the aspect like "have to." The expression with this aspect "have to" often implies a duty like "Although the speaker *does not want to* do something, he/she *has to* do it." Then, we consider that the speaker will generate displeasure for the forced event. The EGC method should be developed to be able to consider the effects of aspects, not only "have to" but also "cannot," "take trouble to," and so on.

9.2.5 Complicated Emotion Allocating Method

Ortony proposed the theory of the cognitive structure of emotions, which views emotions as valid reactions to events, agents, and their actions, as well as objects [19,20]. The theory specifies a total of 22 emotion types. Elliott has used the extended and adapted 24-emotion-type version of the "Emotion Eliciting Condition Theory" as shown in Table 9.4. The descriptions of 24 emotion types are extended in order to refer the situation as an event [13].

This "Emotion Eliciting Condition Theory" requires pleasure/displeasure about an event and some information about the situation of the event (that is, affection of another, prospect, confirmation, approval, and attraction). We appraise pleasure/displeasure by the EGC result and extract situation information from the grammatical features aspect in the utterance. However, detecting the concepts for the likes/dislikes needs personal taste information, one's own experiences, perceptions, and so on. Then, we selected 20 types of emotions except "liking," "disliking," "love," and "hate."

TABLE 9.4. "Emotion Eliciting Condition Theory" by Elliott

Group	Specification	Types (Name)
Well-being	Appraisal of a situation as an event	Pleased about an event (joy)
		Displeased about an event (distress)
Fortunes of others	Presumed value of a situation as an event affecting another	Pleased about an event desirable for another (happy for)
		Pleased about an event undesirable for another (gloating)
		Displeased about an event desirable for another (resentment)
		Displeased about an event undesirable for another (sorry for)
Prospect-based	Appraisal of a situation as a prospective event	Pleased about a prospective desirable event (hope)
		Displeased about a prospective undesirable event (fear)
Confirmation	Appraisal of a situation as confirming or unconfirming an expectation	Pleased about an unconfirmed undesirable event (relief)
		Pleased about a confirmed desirable event (satisfaction)
		Displeased about a confirmed undesirable event (fears confirmed)
		Displeased about an unconfirmed desirable event (disappointment)
Attribution	Appraisal of a situation as an accountable act of some agent	Approving of one's own action (pride)
		Approving of another's action (admiration)
		Disapproving of one's own action (shame)
		Disapproving of another's action (reproach)
Attraction	Appraisal of a situation as containing an attractive or unattractive object	Finding an appealing object (liking)
		Finding an unappealing object (disliking)
Well-being/Attribution	Compound emotions	Admiration + Joy → Gratitude
		Reproach + Distress → Anger
		Pride + Joy → Gratification
		Shame + Distress → Remorse
Attraction/Attribution	Compound emotion extensions	Admiration + Liking → Love
		Reproach + Disliking → Hate

We propose the methods to evaluate the emotion-eliciting conditions (fortunes of others, prospect, confirmation, well-being, and attribution) by using the grammatical features in the utterance [7].

Fortunes of the Others. The emotions that belong to a group of "fortunes of others" are elicited from the emotion that the other affects. There are "happy for," "gloating," "resentment," and "sorry for" in this group.

The EGC method calculates pleasure/displeasure concerning the event from the user's viewpoint using FVs. The FVs that have been defined are based on the user's preference. However, some emotions like "sorry for" and "happy for" are aroused based on the other's emotions. Elliott gave the conditions for the emotions about "fortunes of others" as follows:

Happy for: pleased about *an event desirable for another*

Gloating: pleased about *an event undesirable for another*

Resentment: displeased about *an event desirable for another*

Sorry for: displeased about *an event undesirable for another*

In order to appraise a factor that an event is desirable/undesirable for a person in the conditions, we assumed the condition as that the event pleases/displeases the person. However, different reactions (pleased/displeased) have happened in the same type events. Therefore, we translated these conditions as follows: (1) When the user likes the individual that is pleased about an event, the user feels happy for him/her, and (2) when the user dislikes the individual that is pleased about an event, the user gloats over his/her misfortune. In order to confirm the translation, the adequacies of the translated conditions for generating these emotions are investigated by questionnaire. As the result, it was found that the person's preference and the event's impression for the person are important factors for these emotions.

Therefore, the method has to judge that the person is favorable/hateful for the user and the event is desirable/undesirable from the person's viewpoint. The EGC is used for appraising these conditions. First, it is detected whether an individual is favorite or hateful from the user's viewpoint. The FV for the target person is used for checking it, because the user's preference is already set by the FVs. When the FV is positive, the user likes the person. On the other hand, when the FV is negative, the user dislikes the person.

Next, it is detected that an event is pleasure/displeasure for the other person. The EGC method can calculate pleasure/displeasure from the user's viewpoint based on the user's FVs. Then, if we use not the user's FVs but the other person's FVs, the obtained EV (emotion value) indicates the emotion from the person's viewpoint. Therefore, we use "FVs from the other's viewpoint" for the EGC, and we consider the output EV as the emotion of "the other" about the event. When the value is positive, the event pleases the individual. On the other hand, when the value is negative, the event displeases the individual. The personal database of FV is managed in the same way as that of the user's one. The retrieving process of FV is the same as

TABLE 9.5. Generated Emotions for the Preference of an Individual and His/Her Emotion in the Event

	EV (A)		
A (user)	Pleasure	0	Displeasure
Like	Happy for "A"	0	Sorry for "A"
0	0	0	0
Dislike	Resentment	0	Gloating

shown in Section 9.2.1. When the individual's FV database does not exist, default database is adopted.

Table 9.5 shows a relationship among the preference of an individual, emotion for the event from the individual's viewpoint, and generated emotion. In this table, "A" means an individual without the user. We describe the FV of "A" from the user's viewpoint as "A (user)," and we describe the FV of "B" from C's viewpoint as "B (C)." The EV of the event is described in the same way, for example, "EV (A)" means the EV of the event from A's viewpoint.

Figure 9.5 is the procedure to extract the emotion of "fortunes of others." At first, EV of the event is calculated using FV database of an individual "A". This value means the emotion for the event from the viewpoint of "A". When the EV is not 0—that is, "A" feels pleasure/displeasure for the event—the FV of "A" is checked from the FV database of the user. It shows how the user feels against "A". Then, an emotion in this group is extracted based on EV (A) and A (user). When "A" does not feel any pleasure/displeasure for the event, or when the user does not take care of "A", any emotions from the event are not extracted.

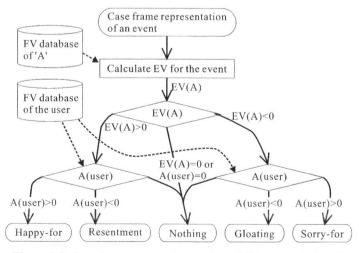

Figure 9.5. Procedure to extract the emotion of "Fortunes of others."

Prospect-Based Emotions. There are "hope" and "fear" in a group of "Prospect-based." The condition for the emotion is "pleased/displeased about a *prospective* desirable/undesirable event." We can already check that the event is desirable/undesirable using the EGC result. However, we have to give a method to check whether the event is prospective or not. Although we generally use reasoning to predict the future event, we do not always make a complete reasoning. When we cannot reason for the event, we occasionally refer to the grammatical features. Therefore, we also extract the information about "prospects" from the aspect in the case frame representation. When there is an aspect of "inference (will)" and "intention (be going to)," the event means a future event.

When we adopt the EGC to the prospective event and when its EV is positive/ negative, we consider the agent affects "hope/fear" based on "Emotion Eliciting Condition Theory." The event that will happen in the future is taken into account in the "prospective event list" in order to confirm that the prospective event has happened or not.

Figure 9.6 is the procedure to extract the "Prospect-based" emotions. At first, we check whether the aspect that means "inference" or "intention" in the event case frame exists or not. When the event has the appropriate aspect, the content of the event is prospective and the event accumulates in the prospective event list. Next, the EV of the prospect event is calculated by EGC from the user's viewpoint. Therefore, when the value is positive (i.e., the user feels pleasure for the event), the user arouses "hope." On the other hand, when the value is negative (i.e., the user feels displeasure for the event), the user arouses "fear."

Confirmation. There are "satisfaction," "relief," "fears confirmed," and "disappointment" in a group of "Confirmation." The conditions for the emotions are as follows:

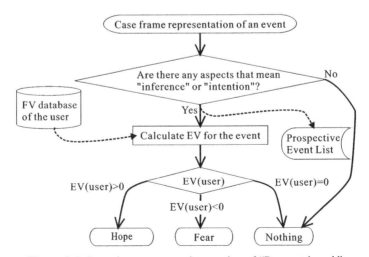

Figure 9.6. Procedure to extract the emotion of "Prospect-based."

Relief: pleased about an unconfirmed undesirable event

Satisfaction: pleased about a confirmed desirable event

Fears confirmed: displeased about a confirmed undesirable event

Disappointment: displeased about an unconfirmed desirable event

We can check that the event is desirable/undesirable by using the EGC method. However, we have to give a method to check whether the event is confirmed or not.

To recognize that an event is *confirmed*, the event has to be prospected in advance and it has to happen actually. To recognize that an event is *unconfirmed*, the event has to be prospected in advance and it has to be confirmed that the event will not happen any more. In order to check the conditions, we consider "whether the event is prospected or not" and "the event is confirmed/unconfirmed/unknown." Prospected events have already been taken into account in the prospective event list. Now, we propose a confirmation method for the prospected event as follows.

First, we inspect the event with the past aspect in order to confirm realization of the prospective events. When there is the same content event as the one that was shown before, we consider that "we had predicted the event and it happened." The effect of the negative aspect is shown in Table 9.6.

Next, we extract four emotions such as "satisfaction," "relief," "fears confirmed," and "disappointment" using the result of confirmation and the EGC output based on the conditions for the emotions. Table 9.7 shows the relationship among the result of confirmation, the EGC output, and generated emotion.

Figure 9.7 is the procedure to extract the emotions of "Confirmation." At first, whether the event finished or not is checked according to the existence of the past aspect. Next, the event is retrieved from the prospective event list that accumulates the expected events. When the event exists in the prospective event list, we compare affirmative/negative expression of the input event with that of the expected event based on Table 9.6. Then, the user's emotion for the prospective event is calculated by EGC. When the event happens and it pleases the user, the user feels satisfaction. Other emotions are extracted in the same way as shown in Table 9.7.

There is another process to extract emotions about confirmation. If the adverb that suggests "predicted result" exists in the event, we consider the fact that the event was expected because we can guess that the event had already been expected even through the user did not inform us about the prospect. On the other hand, we

TABLE 9.6. Relationship Between FVs and Generated Emotion

	Confirmed Event	
Prospective Event	Affirmative	Negative
Affirmative	Happened	Not happened
Negative	Not happened	Happened

TABLE 9.7. Generated Emotions for the Result of Confirmation and the EGC Output

EGC Result	Confirmation	
	Happened	Not Happened
Pleasure	Satisfaction	Disappointment
0	0	0
Displeasure	Fears confirmed	Relief

consider the fact that the event was not expected when there is an adverb that suggests an "unpredicted result" in the event. We chose 17 adverbs that suggest confirmation in "present-day adjective using a dictionary" [14].

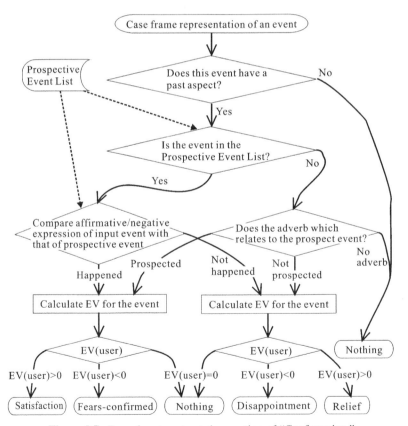

Figure 9.7. Procedure to extract the emotion of "Confirmation."

Well-Being. The emotions in the "Well-being" group are aroused when the user feels pleasure or displeasure for the event. When the user feels pleasure about an event, the user is feeling "joy;" and when the user feels displeasure for an event, the displeasure means "distress." The "Emotion Eliciting Condition Theory" suggests that joy is elicited when he/she is pleased about an event. However, this condition can be confirmed by the other emotions such as *happy for, gloating, hope, satisfaction*, and *relief.*

In these events, eliciting *joy* is judged by adopting the EGC output for the event. Furthermore, when the user elicits *happy for, gloating, hope, satisfaction*, and *relief*, the user elicits *joy*, too, because the eliciting condition of these emotions also meets a demand of the condition of *joy.* The condition about *distress* is dealt with in the same way.

If an event elicits opposite emotions at the same time, the situation is called *conflict.* For example, for an event such as "my son was jilted by a bimbo," the speaker is *sorry for* his son but feels *relief* at the same time. Any special processes are not supplied for the conflict, but just extract two opposite emotions.

Attribution. There are "pride," "admiration," "shame," and "reproach" in a group of "Attribution." The condition for the emotion is "approving/disapproving of one's own/another action." We propose the methods to judge whether the event is approving or not and who caused the event.

First, we propose a method to judge whether the event is approving or not. The event is approved/disapproved by the one's own judgment. There are various criteria for the standard character based on many factors like the users' senses of values, experience, living environment, social environment, and so on. However, it is impossible to compare all the events with all the moral values whenever the agent recognizes the event, because there are countless different values in the world and we have to prepare a system for complex reasoning to confirm that the event is in keeping with the values for each case. Furthermore, there are no knowledge databases, which can deal with such complex reasoning. Therefore, we deal with only one moral value, "An event that gives me pleasure is a good thing," because it is the simplest and the most instinctive moral. "An event that gives me pleasure" is defined as "the event that the EGC result is pleasure."

Next, we propose a method to check who caused the event. The actor of the event is also needed for detecting attribution emotion. We adopt this method only when we use the transitive verb, because the concept of the actor is expressed as the subject of such an event. The event types with the transitive verb are type $V(S,O,{}^*)$. Then we classify the emotions based on "the actor of the event is one's own or not" and "the event is pleasure for me" as shown in Table 9.8.

Figure 9.8 is the procedure to extract the emotion of "attribution." At first, whether the predicate of the event is the transitive verb or not is checked. The event with the transitive verb means that the situation is "the object has been affected by someone." Next, the emotion about the event is calculated by the EGC. When the user feels pleasure or displeasure about the event, we pay attention to the actor, who brings about the event. When the EV of the event is pleasure and is created by the

TABLE 9.8. Relationship Between the Actor, EGC Result, and Generated Emotion

	Actor	
EGC Result	One's Own	Another
Pleasure	Pride	Admiration
0	0	0
Displeasure	Shame	Reproach

user, the user feels *pride*, and when it is created by another, the user feels *admiration*. On the other hand, when the EV of the event is displeasure and it is created by the user, the user feels *shame*, and when it is created by another, the user feels *reproach*.

Well-Being/Attribution. The emotions in the group of "Well-being/Attribution" are elicited as compound emotions. There are four emotions—*gratitude*, *anger*, *gratification*, and *remorse*—in the "Well-being/Attribution" group. As shown in Table 9.9, these emotions are compounded from "Well-being" emotions and "Attribution" emotions based on the "Emotion Eliciting Condition Theory." Some conflicts are elicited in this table, however, any special processes are not supplied for the conflict.

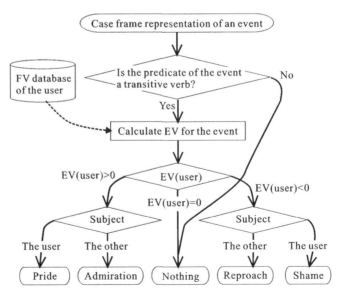

Figure 9.8. Procedure to extract the emotion of "Attribution."

TABLE 9.9. Emotion Compound Rules from "Well-Being" Emotions and "Attribution" Emotions

Well-Being Emotion	Emotion of Attribution			
	Admiration	Reproach	Pride	Shame
Joy	Gratitude	(Conflict)	Gratification	(Conflict)
Distress	(Conflict)	Anger	(Conflict)	Remorse

9.2.6 Dependency Among Emotion Groups

We consider the dependency among emotion groups, as shown in Fig. 9.9, based on the eliciting condition of each emotion. At first, we calculate pleasure/displeasure of the user concerning the event using the EGC method from the user's viewpoint. When the event is prospective, the emotion in the "Prospect-based" group is extracted. When the prospective event is confirmed or unconfirmed, the emotion in the "Confirmation" group is extracted. Furthermore, the EGC is applied to the event from the other's viewpoint, too; and when the other feels pleasure or displeasure, the emotion in the "Fortunes of others" group is extracted. The emotions in the "Prospect-based," "Confirmation," and "Fortunes of others" groups are aroused when the user is pleased/displeased about the event. Therefore, the emotion in the "Well-being" group is extracted when these emotions are extracted or the user feels pleasure/displeasure for the event. On the other hand, the EGC output also

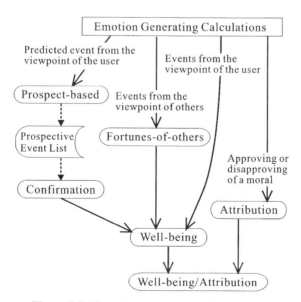

Figure 9.9. Dependency among emotion groups.

shows the moral value. When a moral is approved/disapproved of by the event, we can extract the emotion in the "Attribution" group. At last, the emotion in the "Well-being/Attribution" group is compounded from "Well-being" emotions and "Attribution" emotions.

9.2.7 Example of Complicated Emotion Allocating Method

We show an example to calculate complicated emotions for an example event "Romeo dates with Juliet" from Romeo's viewpoint.

Emotion Generating Calculations Method

Event: "Romeo dates with Juliet."

Predicate (P) = "date with":	+0.6
Subject (S) = "Romeo":	+1.0
Object-Mutual (OM) = "Juliet":	+0.9

Event Type: "date with" $\rightarrow$ V(S, OM)

Degree of EV $= (f_S, f_{OM}, f_P)$

$$= (+1.0, +0.9, +0.6)$$
$$= \sqrt{(+1)^2 + (+0.9)^2 + (+0.6)^2} = 1.47$$

Distinguish pleasure/displeasure $= (f_S, f_{OM}, f_P)$

$$= (+1.0, +0.9, +0.6) \rightarrow \text{Area I (Pleasure)}$$

Complicated Emotion Allocating Method

1. Fortunes of others

   (a) Fortunes of "Juliet"

Predicate (P) = "date with":	+0.7
Subject (S) = "Romeo":	+0.9
Object-Mutual (OM) = "Juliet (myself)":	+1.0

   Event Type: "date with" $\rightarrow$ V(S, OM)

   Distinguish pleasure/displeasure $= (f_S, f_{OM}, f_P)$

   $$= (+0.9, +1.0, +0.7) \rightarrow \text{Area I (Pleasure)}$$

   EV of the event from "Juliet's" viewpoint = Pleasure
   & Romeo *likes* "Juliet"

   (FV of "Juliet" from Romeo's viewpoint: +0.9)

   $\downarrow$

   Happy for "Juliet"

   (b) Fortunes of "Lord Montague (Romeo's father)"

Predicate (P) = "date with":	+0.3
Subject (S) = "Romeo":	+0.8
Object-Mutual (OM) = "Juliet":	−0.5

   Event Type: "date with" $\longrightarrow$ V(S, OM)

   Distinguish pleasure/displeasure $= (f_S, f_{OM}, f_P)$

$$= (+0.8, -0.5, +0.3) \rightarrow \text{Area IV (Displeasure)}$$

EV of the event from "Lord Montague" viewpoint = *Displeasure*

& Romeo *likes* "Lord Montague"

(FV of "Lord Montague" from Romeo's viewpoint: +0.5)

$\downarrow$

Sorry for "Lord Montague"

2. Well-being

(a) "*Happy for* Juliet" is generated by the event

$\downarrow$

Joy about the event

(b) "*Sorry for* Lord Montague" is generated by the event

$\downarrow$

Distress about the event

9.2.8 Experimental Results

The adequacy of the generated emotion by our proposed method was reviewed through the analysis of compared the generated emotions of the system, with the result of the questionnaire. At first, we adopted our method to dialogue corpus and we extracted 30 sentences from the conversation log. Then, we asked 15 university students to tell us which emotion was aroused by the content of each sentence.

First, we evaluated how the system generates emotions, similar to that aroused in the subjects. At first, we showed 30 sentences to 15 subjects, and they selected adequate emotions from the 20 emotions that our system can generate. Table 9.10 shows the comparative result between the system output and the subjects' answers. The system extracted all the emotions that all subjects selected, and it extracted 75% of emotions that most of the subjects (80%) selected. From this result, we consider that our method can estimate common emotions, which the people generally feel for the event.

Next, how the system generates adequate emotions is reviewed. We showed the generated emotions by the system to 15 subjects, and they answered the adequacy of the emotions by the five grade evaluations (very poor to very good). Table 9.11 shows the median of the questionnaire result. We gave 0.5 for each when the result has two modes. Note that 68.6% of the generated emotions by the system were evaluated as good, and 11.4% of the generated emotions were evaluated as

TABLE 9.10. Reappearance Rate

Agreement Rate	100	90	80	70	60
Selected number	2	4	20	29	47
Reappearance number	2	3	15	20	31
Reappearance rate (%)	100.0	75.0	75.0	69.0	66.0

TABLE 9.11. Adequacy Rate

	Very Poor	Poor	Adequate	Good	Very Good
Median	4	4	14	21	27

inadequate. The number of emotions evaluated as good is not so high. However, we can regard highly that 88.6% of the emotions were evaluated as adequate, because although aroused emotions are quite different individually, we can accept such an emotion except when we feel inadequate.

9.3 EMOTION-ORIENTED INTERACTION SYSTEMS

In this section, we propose a method to generate the user's facial expressions based on the extracted emotions by the EGC method. Some common methods to generate facial expression pay attention to the action units of the face. The action units are the symbols, and the concept is based on HC. However, it is difficult to express the subtle difference of the facial expression by using HC techniques, and it is also difficult to choose adequate action units to represent his/her real face corresponding to his/her own emotion. Moreover, it is much more difficult to formulate the relationship between the facial expression and the emotion. Therefore, we use the "parallel sand-glass-type neural network" [8], which is a kind of hierarchical neural network. First, we classify the emotions for the facial expressions as "happiness," "sadness," "disgust," "anger," "fear," and "surprise" as proposed by Ekman [21]. By training the neural network based on such types of facial expressions, each emotion is partitioned on the two-dimensional emotional space constructed by the outputs of the third layer in the neural network.

In order to employ the emotional space, we assign the EGC output (20 kinds of emotions) to the input of the two-dimensional emotional space (6 kinds of emotions). Next, one point on the two-dimensional emotional space is determined from the assigned emotions.

9.3.1 Facial Expression Generating Method by Neural Network

Ichimura constructed "two-dimensional emotional space" by learning the facial expressions of some people (including men and women) using a parallel sand-glass-type neural network, which connects N kinds of the five-layer neural networks at the third layer as shown in Fig. 9.10 [8,9]. This network can deal with N kinds of data simultaneously.

We use emotional facial expressions of some people as teaching signals. For the individual, there are six basic kinds of emotional faces: "happiness," "sadness," "disgust," "anger," "fear," "surprise," and a neutral one [21,22]. Two facial images are readied for each emotion. Therefore, we have 13 pieces of pictures for the individual.

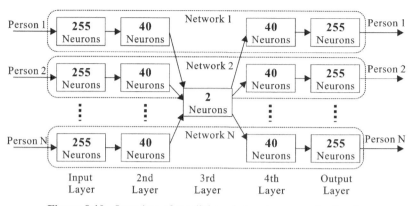

Figure 9.10. Overview of parallel sand-glass-type neural network.

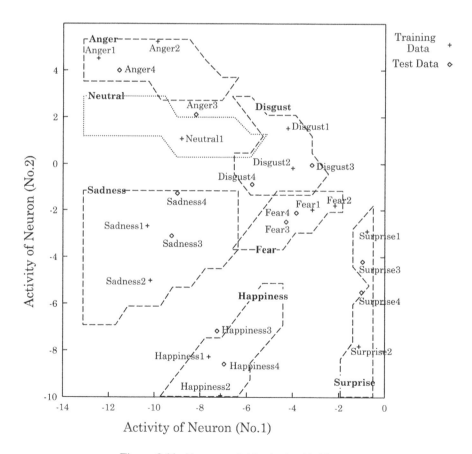

Figure 9.11. Neuron activities in the third layer.

After training the network, we investigated the output activities in the third layer. Figure 9.11 shows the neuron output activities in the third layer. It represents the distributions of the emotions for the facial images on the two-dimensional emotional space—through the horizontal axis, which shows the output activity of the first neuron in the third layer, and the vertical axis, which shows the output activity of the second neuron in the third layer. We define this two-dimensional map based on the activities of the third layer as "two-dimensional emotional space."

The area of each emotion as shown in Fig. 9.11 shows the groups of the points where the error at the output layer is less than $0.25 \times N$ when the emotional space is partitioned into 20×20 grids and the center point of each grid is given as the input for the fourth layer.

Furthermore, the network outputs 400 facial images when we input 400 points allocated to the grids as shown in Fig. 9.11. This indicates that each facial image can be created for the optional point and that the points which do not belong in any emotion areas also have each facial image. We plotted the facial images at the same positions of the points on the emotional space as shown in Fig. 9.12. In this figure, we can see that the emotional facial expressions appear to be

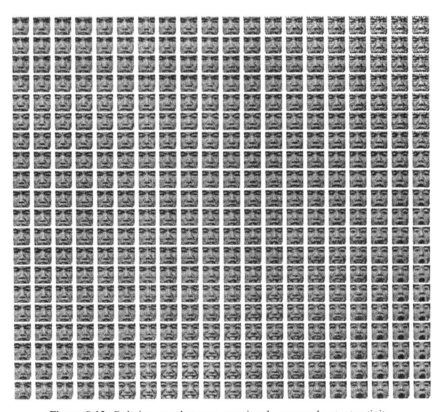

Figure 9.12. Relation map between emotional space and output activity.

almost in the same area as shown in the emotional space of Fig. 9.11. Furthermore, we can confirm that the intermediate facial expressions among the inputted facial images are complemented, similar to a complex emotion that is composed of some basic emotions.

9.3.2 Assign Rules to the Facial Expressions

We give the assign rules from the emotion type by the EGC to facial emotion types as shown in Table 9.12. At first, there is the emotion "*Fear*," which is characterized by the EGC and the facial emotion types. Therefore, the emotion "*Fear*" is equal to the facial emotion type "Fear." In the same way, there is the emotion "*Anger*," which is characterized by the EGC and the facial emotion types. "*Resentment*" and "*Reproach*" are also assigned to the "Anger" group, because these emotions indicate the aggressions to someone. Next, the emotions aroused by "pleasure" (*Joy, Happy for, Gloating, Hope Relief, and Satisfaction*) are equal to the facial emotion type "Happiness." However, we only assign "*Joy*," "*Happy for*," and "*Gloating*" to the "Happiness" group, because the concept of "*Joy*" embraces the one of "*Hope*," "*Relief*," and "*Satisfaction.*" In the same way, the emotions "*Distress*," "*Sorry for*," and "*Resentment*" by the EGC are equal to the facial emotion type "Sadness." The emotion "Surprise" is the action of assailing unexpectedly or attacking without warning. Emotions such as "*Relief*" and "*Disappointment*" are equal to the "Surprise" group, because these emotions are generated when the prospective event is not confirmed. The "Disgust" is caused when the situation is completely unacceptable. There are four types of emotions (*Reproach, Anger, Shame, and Remorse*) relating to "unacceptable" in the EGC output. We assign "*Shame*" and "*Remorse*" to the "Disgust" group, because "*Reproach*" and "*Anger*" are already assigned to the "Anger" group. Each EV is added to the corresponding values attached to each emotional facial type. Each facial expression's value by the EGC is calculated from the EVs preset in the whole conversation.

Next, a point on the emotional space should be determined from these six emotions in the content of the dialogue. These values are inputted to two neurons in the third layer of the trained sand-glass-type neural network. We define the points, which output the facial image teaching data for each emotion, as each center of the emotion types on the emotional space. Successively, the sums of

TABLE 9.12. Assign Rules to the Facial Expression

Facial Expression	Emotion by the EGC Method
Fear	Fear
Anger	Anger, Resentment, Reproach
Happiness	Joy, Happy for, Gloating
Sadness	Distress, Sorry for, Resentment
Surprise	Relief, Disappointment
Disgust	Shame, Remorse

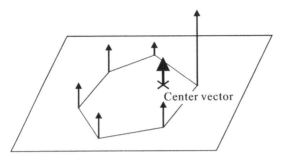

Figure 9.13. Center of each emotion vector.

emotion values for each emotion are set on the emotional space as the vectors, and the center of gravity of the emotional space is calculated as shown in Fig. 9.13. Then, the network obtains the facial expression by the given input emotion types and values. This facial image indicates the facial expression for the whole conversation.

However, this method sometimes generates a neutral facial expression when there are two conflicting emotions (e.g., happiness and sadness). In our study, we do not consider such conflicting situations because there are many variations of the reactions to some situation [23] and the facial expressions appear according to the reactions.

9.4 APPLICATIONS OF EMOTION-ORIENTED INTERACTION SYSTEMS

We applied this method into mail software and a chat system. The mail software (JavaFaceMail [8]) calculates the emotions from the content of the mail, generates one facial expression image of the sender, and sends the mail with the type of facial image. The chat system (JavaFaceChat [10]) also generates a facial expression image like JavaFaceMail. Furthermore, JavaFaceChat analyzes the variances of emotions for each user, and it invites two users to a new closed chat room when their tendencies of variances are alike.

9.4.1 JavaFaceMail

This mail software can analyze and express the emotions that the user will generate from the content of the email. Figure 9.14 shows the overview of the system. Email is inputted using the interface on the client system, and it is sent to the server through the Internet. The server has six processes: mail receiving process, morphological analyzing and parsing process, case frame extracting process, the EGC process, facial expression selecting process, and mail sending process. The client system

From User

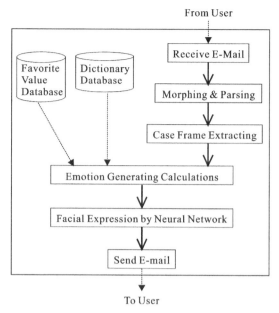

To User

Figure 9.14. Overview of JavaFaceMail.

has the functions not only for general email tools but also for displaying the facial image.

Server Side. The morphological analyzing and parsing process analyzes the sentences in the mail morphologically and parses them. The process is done for each sentence. We used JUMAN as a morphological analyzer and KNP as a parser. Both JUMAN and KNP were developed in Kyoto University [24]. Then, the case frame representations are made from the result of KNP. If the input sentence includes some misspellings and typing errors, our method will not estimate any emotions because JUMAN and KNP will fail to parse the sentence and cannot generate the case frame expression.

Next, the EGC method is applied to the case frame representations. The process sometimes does not generate any emotions when there are not any like/dislike objects in the sentence or the event type of the predicate is not registered. We do not consider that such sentences have any effect on the whole emotion for the mail content.

After the EGC method outputs 20 kinds of emotions, they are translated to six kinds of emotions for facial expression by using "assign rules" as described in Section 9.3.2. The server delivers the received mail with the emotion analyzing result to the receive address. When the sender's facial images have already been registered in the server, the server attaches the type of facial image output by the trained neural network to the mail. When the sender has not registered his/her facial images in the server, the server attaches the default facial picture as shown

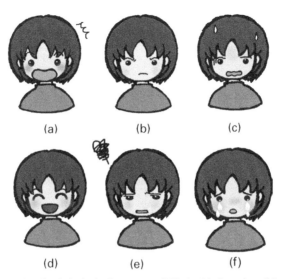

(a)   (b)   (c)

(d)   (e)   (f)

Figure 9.15. Example of original six face types (Mika): (a) Surprise. (b) Anger. (c) Fear. (d) Happiness. (e) Disgust. (f) Sadness.

in Fig. 9.15. The sender can select the type of facial image when he/she sends an email message, but cannot select the emotion.

Now, mail data consist of two parts: "header," which has the information about the sending route, the name of the mail software, and so on; and "body," which includes the inputted sentences. This system attaches the type of the facial image and analyzing result to the header area. Accordingly, in order to display the facial images, the user has to use special mail software as described in the next subsection for JavaFaceMail.

Client Side. To display the facial images, special mail software that has the functions to display the facial images is needed. We named the mail software JavaFaceMail, and it is developed by Java Swing.

When the user starts JavaFaceMail for the first time, he/she has to register his/her information with the JavaFaceMail server, because the server distinguishes the face type from the user's mail address and retrieves the facial images. The information about face images is managed using PostgreSQL, a kind of database software. All the software for the server can be installed in the standard Linux OS.

Next, the user has to configure the client system. Because JavaFaceMail has a usual mail function via Authenticated Post Office Protocol (APOP) and Simple Mail Transfer Protocol (SMTP), the user inputs a Full Qualified Domain Name (FQDN) with each server like standard mail software. Furthermore, the user inputs his/her name, password, a place of mail spool, and the face type previously registered with the server. Although the face type of the sender can be retrieved from the email address and the face type registered by the user, the "From" information in the mail can be changed optionally on the mail software. Then, the system requires the face type.

The mail software also has an address book that is a tool to convert the sender's name into a mail address. The items for face type are in the address book. This address book can receive some information from the server directly. The server cannot analyze the mail sent from the other mail software because of a lack of information for generating the facial image.

Received mails have information about the face type and the value that indicates emotion at the header area. The client system displays an adequate facial image using such information. However, the facial image itself is not attached to the mail, but it is downloaded from the server directly. All the downloaded images are accumulated in the client's machine. Figure 9.16 shows the analyzing result of the sentences.

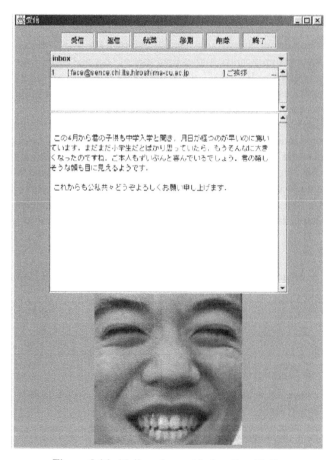

Figure 9.16. Mail reader part in JavaFaceMail.

Mental Effects by Outputting Facial Expressions. We evaluated the mental effects of displaying the facial expressions using our method by the following questionnaire. The subjects read an email message on three types of mail windows that are (A) displaying only the context, (B) inserting face marks for each sentence, and (C) displaying the facial expression image with the context. Then, they evaluated these three methods from the following viewpoints by five grade evaluations (very poor to excellent):

1. It gives you pleasure to read the mail.
2. It helps to communicate the sender's emotion well to you.
3. You feel familiar with the output of the mail software.

The subjects were randomly chosen university students (34 men, 3 women) because we carried out the questionnaire for the students in our university. Table 9.13 shows the average ratios and the standard deviations for each item. There were some significant differences at the 1% level among the items by one-factor analysis of variance.

For the first condition, "It gives you pleasure to read the mail," the average ratios of (B) and (C) were significantly higher than that of (A), and there were no significant differences between (B) and (C) using the t-test. This indicates that "displaying facial expressions" using the JavaFaceMail increases the fun of reading email messages similar to inserting the face marks.

For the second condition, "It helps to communicate the sender's emotion well to you," the average ratio of (B) was significantly higher than that of (A) at ($p < 0.01$), and the average ratio of (C) was significantly higher than that of (A) at ($p < 0.05$), where p indicates "significance level." This indicates that both (B) and (C) are effective, but inserting face marks is more effective than JavaFaceMail. A possible explanation for this is that face marks are inserted for each sentence in an email message. On the other hand, JavaFaceMail displays only one facial expression for the total

TABLE 9.13. Average Ratings and the Standard Deviations for Each Displaying Method

	(A) Only Sentences	(B) With Face Marks	(C) With Facial Expression	One Factor ANOVA
1. It gives you pleasure to read the mail.	2.57 (0.83)	3.57 (1.01)	3.51 (0.93)	$p < 0.01$
2. It helps to communicate the sender's emotion well to you.	2.86 (0.98)	3.81 (0.96)	3.49 (0.96)	$p < 0.01$
3. You feel familiar with the output of the mail software.	1.81 (1.00)	3.22 (1.25)	3.95 (1.18)	$p < 0.01$

content of an email. Therefore, a displayed facial expression can be neutralized if a number of emotions are aroused simultaneously in an email. There is no problem when the content of the email is short. However, we have to improve our method for analyzing emails with a large content—for example, displaying the facial expressions for each paragraph that arouse the same emotion, or displaying the facial expression just after a sentence if the sentence arouses an emotion, and so on.

For the third condition, "You feel familiar with the output of the mail software," there were some significant differences among all the situations. The average ratio of (C) was the highest, and the ratio of (B) was higher than that of (A). For the effect of familiarity, JavaFaceMail was significantly more effective than the face marks. This indicates that the JavaFaceMail system is effective for introducing face-to-face communication onto the human computer interaction.

9.4.2 JavaFaceChat

We created a "chat system" called JavaFaceChat, which represents facial expressions corresponding to the user's emotion. "Chat rooms" are one of the most popular communication tools used on the Internet. "Chat rooms," which extend to Internet TV phones such as xDSL connections, have become popular due to the connection being very fast and inexpensive.

JavaFaceChat supplies the usual functions for "chat rooms." We applied the EGC method to analyze all messages, and all the generated emotion types were concentrated in six kinds of emotions. The system in the server calculated the facial image from the six emotion types and values described in Section 9.3.2. This facial image indicates a facial expression against one utterance by each user, respectively. The system sends a sentence and a facial image to all users upon receiving every new message. JavaFaceChat server has plural agents. An agent receives the message from a user, and it sends the message and the face type using the EGC method to the other users. Each agent has the user's facial images for the six kinds of emotions. Procedures for JavaFaceChat when a user "A" inputs something is described as follows. The JavaFaceChat system analyzes the other's sentences based on one's own FVs, and it guesses the variances of the other's intention and emotion, like a person who uses a standard chat room.

1. Start system:
   a. Download six types of emotional facial images for each chat participant when a chat session starts.
2. Do the following processes at the client terminal of "A":
   a. Send an input sentence to the server.
   b. Calculate Emotion Value E_A by applying the EGC method to the sentence, and send E_A to the server.
   c. Generate one facial expression image based on the EGC result.
   d. Display the sentence and the facial image of "A" on the display of A's terminal.

3. Do the following processes at the client terminals excluding A's own terminal:

   a. Receive A's sentence from the server.

   b. Calculate emotion value by applying the EGC method to the sentence. FV database accumulated in each terminal is employed for the EGC method.

   c. Generate one facial expression image based on the EGC result.

   d. Display the sentence and the facial image of "A" on the display of each terminal.

4. Do the following processes at the server:

   a. Send the sentence from "A" to all the chat participants.

   b. Check the variances of the output emotions that are sent from all the chat participants. When there are some variances, the server calculates their norms and checks whether they are less than threshold or not.

   c. Ask participant 1 and 2 whether they want to go to another chat room or not, when $\|E_1 - E_2\| \leq \alpha$ is satisfied. E_1 and E_2 mean the vectors of generated emotions by participant 1 and participant 2, respectively.

   d. Create a new chat room if both of the participants agree to it. Information about generated emotions is duplicated into the new chat room.

In the initial stage of the chat, all agents attend the same chat room, which is opened for an aim or a common topic. If an agent wants to talk only with a specified agent, and the specified agent agrees to it, the system can open a new closed chat room for the two agents. The system then copies the agents' attributes from Room 1 to Room 2 as shown in Fig. 9.17. Agent A and Agent B are still in Chat Room 1, but they can enjoy their own conversations in Chat Room 2, too. Figure 9.18 shows the terminal of JavaFaceChat. All utterances of the users are outputted with the facial expressions.

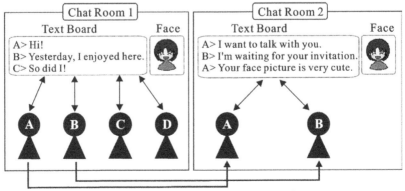

Figure 9.17. Agents attend two chat rooms simultaneously.

Figure 9.18. Terminal of JavaFaceChat.

9.5 FUSION OF SOFT COMPUTING AND HARD COMPUTING

The interfaces between man and machine are important to use the functions effectively. Most conventional interface tools are constructed based on the idea of hard computing where work is performed according to the fixed procedures of our inputted information and the flow of processes for the binary like "Yes" or "No." However, as the interface is equipped with more functions, the machine requires more complicated procedures in their operations. It is very hard for us to understand and to control all operations completely, because human behavior is always ambiguous and sensitive about feeling. In spite of that, we have to use the machines with such behaviors every day. In particular, the development of interface for elderly people or handicapped people is very late.

In order to improve various functions in their interfaces, we should fuse the technologies of soft computing and hard computing. Although humans have ambiguous feelings in a face-to-face communication, the traditional interface did not consider feelings to be a human specification like Kansei or emotion. Moreover, we use computers on the Internet, and many new types of communication tools are developing. We may consider that the interface can recognize such feelings as in direct human-to-human communication.

Therefore, we proposed a method that includes two types of SC techniques: the "limitation of fuzzy linguistic truth value" and the "parallel sand-glass-type neural network." The first one is the "limitation of fuzzy linguistic truth value" method. We use the FVs of the objects to calculate emotions as described in Section 9.2.1 and Section 9.2.3. However, the FVs are widely different according to their contents of the modifiers even if they are corresponding to the same object. It is difficult to calculate the modifier's effect by using HC technique, because it changes too ambiguously. Therefore, we applied the "limitation of fuzzy linguistic truth value" method. It can calculate the "truth value" of the object with modifier. On the process calculating the object's FV, the fusion type of SC and HC is classified into *soft-computing-assisted hard computing* (SC//HC) as shown in Fig. 1.8 (Chapter 1). In this case, HC is the standard FV calculating process; and when the object is modified, the effect from the modifier is calculated by using the "limitation of fuzzy linguistic truth value" method, which is a kind of SC.

Next, we show the "parallel sand-glass-type neural network." Our method can calculate 20 types of emotions and their degrees from the inputted event as described in Section 9.2. The calculated emotions are expressed by a facial expression, because the emotions expressed numerically are difficult to understand for the people. Generally, we use action units of the face to represent his/her facial expression. However, it is difficult to choose adequate action units, and it is even more difficult to formulate the relationship between the facial expression and the emotion. Therefore, we train a neural network based on the types of facial expression images as it stands, and we compress the information based on the output of the middle layer in the neural network. In order to do it, the "sand-glass-type neural network" is available. Furthermore, to train the neural network by plural people's facial expressions, we apply *parallel* sand-glass-type neural network. On the process calculating the emotions from the events and expressing the emotions by a facial expression, the fusion type of SC and HC is classified into a *cascade of hard computing and soft computing* (HC-SC) as shown in Fig. 1.5 (Chapter 1). In this case, HC is the process of analyzing sentences linguistically and calculating emotion values based on the event type, and SC is the "parallel sand-glass-type neural network" method of generating a facial expression.

9.6   CONCLUSION

This chapter presented a method of generating some emotions from the user's viewpoint. First, we proposed the "Emotion Generating Calculations" method. This method generates pleasure/displeasure emotion for an event, an attribute, and for an "is-a" relationship in utterance using the user's taste information (FV). Furthermore, the method calculates the degree of the pleasure/displeasure. Second, the EGC method has been developed to distinguish generated emotions into 20 various emotions based on "Emotion Eliciting Condition Theory." The method distinguishes emotions based on the pleasure/displeasure and some conditions. Third, we proposed a method to represent emotions with facial expressions. Extracted emotions by the EGC method are inputted into trained "sand-glass-type neural networks," and one facial image was calculated from the emotional space. We constructed a mail tool and a chat tool as applications of the EGC method. We are going to apply the method into an interface of the "Web-based analytical system of health service needs among healthy elderly" [25].

In our method, we used two types of SC techniques: the "limitation of fuzzy linguistic truth value" and the "parallel sand-glass-type neural network" to calculate the modifier's effect and to generate a facial expression for calculated emotions. However, emotional process is highly complex, so we should obviously incorporate more SC techniques. At present, we have been researching about the enfeeblement process of the emotion intensity.

Recently, the Japanese government started a project called "e-Japan strategy II." It aims to improve computer usability in order that all Japanese can use computer freely. We hope that our method will serve in the future a natural human–computer interface considering the user's emotion, and our method will aid to construct a good relationship between human and computer.

REFERENCES

1. O. Hasegawa, S. Morishima, and M. Kaneko, "Processing of Facial Information by Computer," *Transaction of the Institute of Electronics, Information, and Communication Engineers* **J80-D-II**, 2047–2065 (1997), in Japanese.

2. P. Ekman and W. V. Friesen, "The Repertoire of Nonverbal Behavior," *Semiotica* **1**, 49–98 (1969).

3. A. Mehrabian, *Nonverbal Communication*, Aldine-Atherton, Chicago, 1972.

4. R. W. Picard, E. Vyzas, and J. Healey, "Toward Machine Emotional Intelligence: Analysis of Affective Physiological State," *IEEE Transactions on Pattern Analysis and Machine Intelligence* **23**, 1175–1191 (2001).

5. K. Mera, "Emotion Oriented Intelligent Interface," Doctoral Dissertation, Tokyo Metropolitan Institute of Technology, Graduate School of Engineering, Tokyo, Japan, 2003.

6. K. Mera, T. Ichimura, T. Aizawa, and T. Yamashita, "Invoking Emotions in a Dialog System Based on Word Impressions," *Journal of Japanese Society of Artificial Intelligence* **17**, 186–195 (2002), in Japanese.

7. K. Mera, T. Ichimura, and T. Yamashita, "Complicated Emotion Allocating Method Based on Emotional Eliciting Condition Theory," *Journal of the Biomedical Fuzzy Systems and Human Sciences* **9**, 1–10 (2003).

8. T. Ichimura, H. Ishida, K. Mera, S. Oeda, A. Sugihara, and T. Yamashita, "Approach to Emotion Oriented Intelligent System by Parallel Sand Glass Type Neural Networks and

Emotion Generating Calculations," *Journal of Human Interface Society* **3**, 225–238 (2001), in Japanese.

9. T. Ichimura, K. Mera, H. Ishida, S. Oeda, A. Sugihara, and T. Yamashita, "An Emotional Interface with Facial Expression by Sand Glass Type Neural Network and Emotion Generating Calculations Method," *Proceedings of the International Symposium on Measurement, Analysis and Modeling of Human Functions*, Hokkaido, Japan, Sept. 2001, pp. 275–280.

10. T. Ichimura, K. Mera, Y. Miki, and T. Yamashita, "Emotional Interface for Human Feelings by Mobile Phone," *Proceedings of the 6th International Conference on Knowledge-Based Intelligent Engineering Systems & Allied Technologies (Part I)*, Crema, Italy, Sept. 2002, pp. 708–712.

11. N. Okada, *Representation and Accumulation of the Concepts of Words*, IEICE Publishers, Tokyo, Japan, 1991, in Japanese.

12. K. Mera, T. Ichimura, T. Yamashita, and Y. Miki, "Approach of Noun Modifier with Verb by Linguistic Truth Value," *Journal of Japan Society for Fuzzy Theory and Intelligent Informatics* **15**, 465–473 (2003).

13. C. Elliott, "The Affective Reasoner: A Process Model of Emotions in a Multi-Agent System," Doctoral Dissertation, Northwestern University, The Institute for the Learning Sciences, Evanston, IL, 1992.

14. Y. Hida and H. Asada, *Present-Day Adjective Using Dictionary*, Tokyo Dou Publishers, Tokyo, Japan, 1991, in Japanese.

15. K. Mera, S. Kawamoto, T. Ichimura, T. Yamashita, and T. Aizawa, "A Learning Method of Individual's Taste Information," *Proceedings of the 5th International Conference on Knowledge-Based Intelligent Engineering Systems & Allied Technologies (Part II)*, Osaka, Japan, Sept. 2001, pp. 1217–1221.

16. K. Mera and T. Ichimura, "Knowledge Structure for Acquiring Personal Taste Information," *Proceedings of the 7th International Conference on Knowledge-Based Intelligent Engineering Systems & Allied Technologies (Part II)*, Oxford, UK, Sept. 2003, pp. 454–460.

17. M. B. Arnold, *Emotion and Personality*, Columbia University Press, New York, 1960.

18. Japan Society of Fuzzy Theory and Systems, *Fuzzy Logic—Course of Fuzzy* **4**, 1993.

19. A. Ortony, G. L. Clore, and A. Collins, *The Cognitive Structure of Emotions*, Cambridge University Press, New York, 1988.

20. P. O'Rorke and A. Ortony, "Explaining Emotions," *Cognitive Science* **11**, 283–323 (1994).

21. P. Ekman and W. V. Friesen, *Unmasking the Face: A Guide to Recognizing Emotions from Facial Clues*, Prentice-Hall, Englewood Cliffs, NJ, 1975.

22. N. Ueki, S. Morishima, H. Yamada, and H. Harashima, "Expression Analysis/Synthesis System Based on Emotional Space Constructed by Multi-Layered Neural Network," *Transaction of the Institute of Electronics, Information, and Communication Engineers* **J77-D-II**, 573–582 (1993), in Japanese.

23. T. Kumamoto, A. Ito, and T. Ebina, "Recognizing User Communicative Intention in a Dialogue-Based Consultant System—A Statistical Approach Based on the Analysis of Spoken Japanese Sentences," *Transaction of the Institute of Electronics, Information, and Communication Engineers* **J77-D-II**, 1144–1123 (1994), in Japanese.

EDITOR'S INTRODUCTION TO CHAPTER 10

Since the late 1990s, data mining (DM) has been an active and fruitful field of multidisciplinary research and development. Data mining combines the three necessary constituents that have earlier evolved and matured as individual disciplines [1]:

1. Statistical analysis
2. Machine learning
3. Database management

These three disciplines have a complementary role in the computerized data mining process. Machine learning and database management matured in the 1980s, but the *collective approach* of data mining can still be considered as an emerging technology. Data mining is usually defined as the automated extraction of novel, interesting, and nonobvious information from large databases [2].

The three individual constituents of data mining process are typically implemented using a heterogeneous set of algorithms and methods. On the other hand, the entire DM process can be divided into five consecutive phases [1]:

1. Integration of data sources
2. Preprocessing of available data
3. Mining the data
4. Examination and complexity control of results
5. Visualizing and reporting of final results

Computationally Intelligent Hybrid Systems. Edited by Seppo J. Ovaska
ISBN 0-471-47668-4 © 2005 the Institute of Electrical and Electronics Engineers, Inc.

Also these five phases require a diverse set of sophisticated techniques and tools.

Bioinformatics is an expanding application area of scientific data mining (a vital subclass of data mining), where the data consist of scientific measurements and possibly of simulation results. The common approach is to *let the data tell what some of the underlying hypotheses could be*, while it remains a human task to understand and interpret the DM results. Chapter 10 of the present book, "Introduction to Scientific Data Mining: Direct Kernel Methods and Applications," authored by Mark J. Embrechts, Boleslaw Szymanski, and Karsten Sternickel, provides a concise introduction to scientific data mining, and it introduces direct kernel methods and their use for DM applications. The authors point out that data mining problems are often challenging tasks because of a *data mining dilemma*: "Even if it is possible to obtain better models from larger datasets because there is more useful and relevant information out there, it is actually harder to extract that information." Finally, a bioinformatics application of predicting the occurrence of ischemic heart disease from recorded magnetocardiogram data is presented.

In the beginning of their chapter, Embrechts et al. introduce *the standard data mining problem*. It is a regression problem of predicting the response from a set of descriptive features. The elementary problem is used throughout the introductory sections for illustrating the different phases of data mining process. However, practical data mining tasks differ from this small-scale problem in many ways, because real-world data sets are often very large.

Direct kernel methods form a general methodology to convert linear modeling tools into nonlinear regression techniques. They apply some kernel transformation as a preprocessing phase of the available data. Direct kernel methods can be seen as a fusion of soft computing (SC) and hard computing (HC), because they are actually layered neural networks, and their weights are obtained using linear algebra. Based on the categorization of fusion structures in Chapter 1, this particular fusion type can be classified as HC-designed SC, and its fusion grade is high.

The operation and performance of direct kernel and other methods in scientific data mining is demonstrated with three case studies:

1. Predicting the binding energy for amino acids
2. Predicting the region of origin for olive oils
3. Predicting ischemia from magnetocardiography (MCG)

The first two examples are standard textbook case studies, while the third one is a demanding real-world application. There is a goal to automate the interpretation of MCG measurements to minimize physician's input for the analysis of data-rich recordings. Altogether, 11 different machine learning methods were benchmarked for pattern recognition and classification to separate abnormal heart patterns from normal ones. In that comparison, the direct kernel partial least-squares (DK-PLS) method gave a superior performance compared to the other methods. DK-PLS detected 83% of heart patterns correctly, while the more traditional self-organizing map (SOM) was able to recognize only 63% of those patterns. Moreover, the computation time of DK-PLS was drastically reduced from that of SOM. In both of these cases, the MCG data were first preprocessed by a wavelet transform.

As a conclusion, it is natural to see data mining as a versatile application domain for the fusion of SC and HC, as well as for implementing robust and computationally efficient algorithms [3].

REFERENCES

1. B. Thuraisingham, "A Primer for Understanding and Applying Data Mining," *IT Professional* **2**, 28–31 (Jan./Feb. 2000).

2. Y. Bengio, J. M. Buhmann, M. J. Embrechts, and J. M. Zurada, "Introduction to the Special Issue on Neural Networks for Data Mining and Knowledge Discovery," *IEEE Transactions on Neural Networks* **11**, 545–549 (2000).

3. S. Mitra, S. K. Pal, and P. Mitra, "Data Mining in Soft Computing Framework: A Survey," *IEEE Transactions on Neural Networks* **13**, 3–14 (2002).

CHAPTER 10

INTRODUCTION TO SCIENTIFIC DATA MINING: DIRECT KERNEL METHODS AND APPLICATIONS

MARK J. EMBRECHTS and BOLESLAW SZYMANSKI
Rensselaer Polytechnic Institute, Troy, New York

KARSTEN STERNICKEL
Cardiomag Imaging Inc., Schenectady, New York

10.1 INTRODUCTION

The purpose of this chapter is to give a brief overview of data mining and to introduce direct kernel methods as a general-purpose and powerful data mining tool for predictive modeling, feature selection, and visualization. Direct kernel methods are a generalized methodology to convert linear modeling tools into nonlinear regression models by applying the kernel transformation as a data preprocessing step. We will illustrate direct kernel methods for ridge regression and the self-organizing map and apply these methods to some challenging scientific data mining problems. Direct kernel methods are introduced in this chapter because they transform the powerful nonlinear modeling power of support vector machines in a straightforward manner to more traditional regression and classification algorithms. An additional advantage of direct kernel methods is that only linear algebra is required.

Direct kernel methods will be introduced as a true fusion of soft and hard computing. We will present such direct kernel methods as simple multilayered neural networks, where the weights can actually be determined based on linear algebra, rather than following the traditional neural network approach. Direct kernel methods are inherently nonlinear methods, and they can be represented as a multilayered neural network that now combines elements of soft and hard computing. The hard-computing takes place in the scientific domain where data are generated, in a way that often involves elaborate hard-computing algorithms. Hard computing is also used here to

Computationally Intelligent Hybrid Systems. Edited by Seppo J. Ovaska
ISBN 0-471-47668-4 © 2005 the Institute of Electrical and Electronics Engineers, Inc.

make up the kernel and to calculate the weights for the underlying neural networks in direct kernel methods. Soft computing occurs because of the underlying neural network framework and in estimating the hyperparameters for direct kernel models. These hyperparameters usually deal with the proper choice for the nonlinear kernel, as well as with the selection of a close-to-optimal regularization penalty term.

Support vector machines (SVMs) have proven to be formidable machine learning tools because of their efficiency, model flexibility, predictive power, and theoretical transparency [1–3]. While the nonlinear properties of SVMs can be exclusively attributed to the kernel transformation, other methods such as self-organizing maps (SOMs) [4] are inherently nonlinear because they incorporate various neighborhood-based manipulations. This way of accounting for nonlinearity effects is similar to the way that K-nearest-neighbor algorithms incorporate nonlinearity. Unlike SVMs, the prime use for SOMs is often as a visualization tool [5] for revealing the underlying similarity/cluster structure of high-dimensional data on a two-dimensional map, rather than for regression or classification predictions. SOMs have the additional advantage that they incorporate class ordinality in a rather natural way—that is, via their self-organization properties that preserve the topology of a high-dimensional space in the two-dimensional SOM. SOMs are therefore quite powerful for multiclass classification, especially when the classes are not ordinal—a problem that is far from trivial. They are also very effective for outlier and novelty detection.

Before explaining direct kernel methods, we will present a brief overview of scientific data mining. The standard data mining problem will be introduced as the underlying framework for different data mining tasks. We will then build a simple linear regression model, explain the data mining and machine learning dilemmas, and provide a straightforward solution to overcome this type of uncertainty principle. These linear methods will then be translated into an equivalent, but still linear, neural network model, for which the weights can be obtained with hard computing. The linear regression model or predictive data mining model can be transformed into powerful nonlinear prediction method by applying the kernel transformation as a data transformation rather than an inherent ingredient in the mathematical derivation of the modeling algorithm. Many traditional linear regression models can be transformed into nonlinear direct kernel methods that share many desirable characteristics with support vector machines: They can incorporate regularization and they do not involve the controversial heuristics, common in the neural network approach. We will finally apply this methodology to a challenging scientific data mining problem and illustrate predictive modeling, feature selection, and data visualization based on direct kernel methods for predicting ischemia from magnetocardiogram data.

10.2 WHAT IS DATA MINING?

10.2.1 Introduction to Data Mining

Data mining is often defined as the automated extraction of novel and interesting information from large data sets. Data mining, as we currently know it, has its roots in statistics, probability theory, neural networks, and the expert systems wing of artificial intelligence (AI). The term *data mining* used to have a negative connotation, meaning the existence of spurious correlations, indicating that if one looks far enough in a variety of data sets, one might find a coincidental rise in the stock market when there is a peak of two-headed sheep born in New Zealand. This out-of-date interpretation of data mining can be summarized as "the torturing the data until they confess approach." The current popularity of the term *data mining* can be attributed largely to the rise of the Knowledge Discovery and Data Mining (KDD) Conference. The KDD conference started in the early 1990s as a small workshop, spearheaded by Usama Fayyad, Gregory Piatetsky-Shapiro, Padhraic Smyth, and Ramasamy Uthurusamy. The KDD conference is now an annual event and has a good attendance. In the book that resulted from the 1995 KDD conference in Montreal [6], data mining was defined as follows: "Data mining is the process of automatically extracting valid, novel, potentially useful, and ultimately comprehensible information from large databases." We will adhere to this definition to introduce data mining in the present chapter. Recommended books on data mining are summarized in references 7–10. One of the underlying principles of knowledge discovery in data is to promote the process of building data-driven expert systems as an extension of the more traditional AI expert systems approach. The idea is now that experts learn from new findings in the data as well.

Data mining is not a narrowly focused discipline, but requires a combination of multiple disciplines and techniques. Data mining distinguishes itself from traditional statistics in the sense that we now deal with potentially very large data sets that can range from gigabytes to petabytes. For a while, a problem was considered a data mining problem only if the data could not be stored in the working memory of a computer all-at-once. Other definitions of data mining insisted for a while that the data have to come from a variety of different databases. Of course, interesting and challenging problems such as gene discovery and protein folding in bioinformatics would not qualify as legitimate data mining problems under these restrictive definitions. Data mining is different from the more traditional methods in the sense that for large amounts of data, many classical algorithms, such as the K-means algorithm for clustering, do not scale well with ever-larger data sets. In general, one can summarize as follows for a typical data mining case: (1) the data set can be quite large; (2) the problem is generally challenging and is often not well-defined; (3) there are missing and faulty data; (4) there are redundancies in the data fields, but the redundant fields do not all have the same quality; that is, two columns in a data description matrix might represent the same feature, but one column might have more data entry errors than the other column; and (5) it is not sufficient to build a predictive model, but it is necessary to feed back notions of a deeper understanding as well—for example, by generating a data-driven (possibly fuzzy rule based) expert system that enhances the knowledge of the domain expert.

Data mining distinguishes itself also from statistics and artificial intelligence (AI) in the sense that the expert now exercises a different role. While the goal of AI expert systems was to query the experts in order to come up with a rule base that captures their expertise, that approach often led to failure because the experts, even though knowledgeable and mostly right, are not necessarily in the best position to formulate an explicit set of rules. In data mining, rather than letting the expert formulate the rules up front, the idea is now to let the rules appear in a more or less automated and data-driven way. The expert comes in at the end stage of this data-driven rule discovery/formulation process and applies his domain knowledge to validate the rules.

The first very successful data mining applications were often motivated by database marketing and business applications. Typical applications of database marketing are the use of a database to decide on a mail-order campaign, or linking a sales campaign in a supermarket with product positioning and discounting. A classical case study for data mining points out that beer sales go up when the beer is positioned close to the diapers in a supermarket, because dad is likely to buy a six-pack of beer when he comes to the store to buy diapers. The tongue-in-cheek corollary is here that the reverse is not true. Other early successful applications of data mining relate to credit card fraud, establishing lending and refinancing policies, and telephone fraud.

Data mining is an interdisciplinary science ranging from the domain area and statistics to information processing, database systems, machine learning, artificial intelligence, and soft computing. The emphasis in data mining is not just building predictive models or good classifiers for out-of-sample real-world data, but obtaining a novel or deeper understanding. In real-world problems, data distributions are usually not Gaussian. There also tend to be outliers and missing data. Often there are faulty and imprecise data to deal with as well. Data mining emphasizes the use of effective data visualization techniques, such as self-organizing maps [4], that can go way beyond the common bar and pie charts. The exact purpose and outcome of a data mining study should probably not be clearly defined up front. The idea of data mining is to look at data in a different way and, in a sense, to let the data speak for themselves.

10.2.2 Scientific Data Mining

Scientific data mining is defined as data mining applied to scientific problems, rather than database marketing, finance, or business-driven applications. Scientific data mining distinguishes itself in the sense that the nature of the data sets is often very different from traditional market-driven data mining applications. The data sets might now involve vast amounts of precise and continuous data, and accounting for underlying system nonlinearities can be extremely challenging from the machine learning point of view.

Applications of data mining to astronomy-based data is a clear example of the case where data sets are vast, and dealing with such vast amounts of data now poses a challenge on its own. On the other hand, for bioinformatics-related applications such as gene finding and protein folding, the data sets are more modest, but the modeling part can be very challenging. Scientific data mining might involve just building an on-the-fly predictive model that mimics a large computer program that is too slow to be used in real time. Other interesting examples of scientific data mining can be found in bioengineering, and they might present themselves as challenging pattern recognition problems based on images (e.g., brain scans) or multivariate time series signals (e.g., electrocardiograms and magnetocardiograms).

An interesting application relates to in-silico drug design [11]. The idea is to identify and select small molecules (ligands) with superior drug qualities from a huge library of potential often not yet synthesized molecules. The challenge is that the library of molecules with known pharmaceutical properties is often relatively small (e.g., 50–2000), but that there is a large number of descriptive features or attributes (e.g., 500–20,000). We define such problems where the number of descriptive features exceeds the number of data considerably, as data strip mining problems [12]. We call them data strip mining problems, because if the data are placed in an Excel sheet, all the data seem to be now on the surface rather than going on and on for thousands and thousands of rows of cells. There is one additional interesting aspect here: Many computer programs such as editors and the Excel spreadsheet were not design to handle this type of data. A key challenge for in-silico drug design problems is now to identify a reasonably small subset of relevant features that explain the pharmaceutical properties of the molecule. One ultimate aim of in-silico drug design is real-time invention and synthesis of novel drugs to mitigate natural or man-made society-threatening diseases. A second type of strip mining problem occurs in the use of gene expression micro-arrays for the identification of relevant genes that are indicative for the presence of a disease. A typical case is a dataset of 72 microarray data with 6000 descriptive features related to the identification of leukemia.

In a data mining context, common techniques such as clustering might now be used in a very different way. The clustering procedure does not necessarily have to provide a good overall clustering, but just finding one relatively small and fairly homogeneous cluster might offer a significant pay-off in database marketing. Kohonen's self-organizing map has been extensively applied as an efficient visualization tool for high-dimensional data on a two-dimensional map while preserving important aspects of the underlying topology.

10.2.3 The Data Mining Process

Many data mining applications can be represented in a cartoon model that we will call the standard data mining process. This process involves the gathering of data, data cleansing, data preprocessing and transforming a subset of data to a flat file, building one or more models that can be predictive models, clusters, or data visualizations that lead to the formulation of rules, and finally piecing together the larger picture. This process is outlined in Fig. 10.1.

Often a large amount of effort is required before the data can be presented in a flat file. Data cleansing and data preprocessing might take up a large part of the resources committed to a typical data mining project and might involve 80% of the effort. It is often necessary to experiment with different data transformations (e.g., Fourier and wavelet transforms) in the data preprocessing stage.

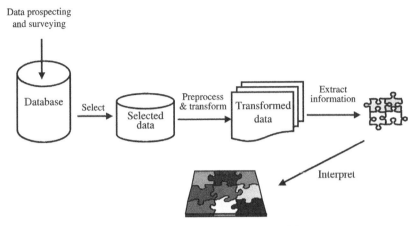

Figure 10.1. Cartoon illustration of the data mining process.

Another representation of the data mining process is the data mining wisdom pyramid in Fig. 10.2, where we progress from raw data to information, knowledge, understanding, and ultimately wisdom. The art of data mining is to charm the data into a confession. An informal way to define data mining is to say that we are looking for a needle in a haystack without knowing what a needle looks like and where the haystack is located.

10.2.4   Data Mining Methods and Techniques

A wide variety of techniques and methods are commonly used in data mining applications. Data mining often involves clustering, the building of predictive regression

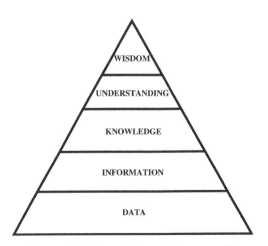

Figure 10.2. Data mining wisdom pyramid.

or classification models, attribute and/or feature selection, the formation of rules, and outlier or novelty detection. These techniques can be based on statistics, probability theory, Bayesian networks, decision trees, association rules, neural networks, evolutionary computation, and fuzzy logic.

While the reader may already be familiar with some of these techniques, they often have an additional flavor to them, when it comes to data mining. It is not the purpose of this introduction to discuss data mining in wide breadth, but rather to emphasize the proper use of soft-computing techniques for scientific data mining in the context of the fusion of soft-computing and hard-computing methodologies.

We will introduce direct kernel methods for predictive data mining, feature detection, and visualization. Direct-kernel based techniques will then be applied to a challenging problem related to the prediction of ischemia from magnetocardiogram data.

10.3 BASIC DEFINITIONS FOR DATA MINING

10.3.1 The MetaNeural Data Format

In this section, the standard data mining problem will be introduced and it will be shown how the standard data mining problem actually relates to many interesting types of real-world applications. It is assumed here that the data are already prepared and available in the form of a single (i.e., flat) data file, rather than a relational database. Note that extracting such flat files from different databases is often a challenging task on its own. Consider the flat file data from Table 10.1, provided by Wold et al. [13]. They represent a cartoon example for a QSAR or QSPR (quantitative structural activity and quantitative structural property relationship) problem [11], where it is often the purpose to predict chemical properties in the case of QSPR and bioactivities in the case of QSAR from other basic properties (or molecular descriptors) of a molecular data set. In this case, the activity of interest (or in data mining lingo, the response) for which we would like to make a model is in the second column, represented by DDGTS.

Table 10.1 is a spreadsheet-like table, with 20 horizontal row entries and 9 vertical fields. The first row contains acronyms MOL, DDGTS, PIE, PIF, DGR, SAC, MR, LAM, and Vol, which describe entries in each vertical field. The first column contains the abbreviations for 19 amino acid (AA) names (i.e., all the coded amino acids, except arginine). The second column contains the free energy for unfolding a protein. This free energy, nicknamed DDGTS, is called the response. In this case, we want to build a predictive model for the response based on the remaining seven fields, which contain the chemical properties for the 19 amino acids listed here. Data entries that are used in predictive models are called descriptors, attributes, or descriptive attributes. Sometimes they are also called features. In a machine learning context, a feature, strictly speaking, is not the same as an attribute, but rather a combination of descriptors, such as principal components in principal component

TABLE 10.1. Example of a Flat Data File

MOL	DDGTS	PIE	PIF	DGR	SAC	MR	LAM	Vol
Ala	8.5	0.23	0.31	−0.55	254.2	2.126	−0.02	82.2
Asn	8.2	−0.48	−0.60	−0.51	303.6	2.994	−1.24	112.3
Asp	8.5	−0.61	−0.77	1.20	287.9	2.994	−1.08	103.7
Cys	11.0	0.45	1.54	−1.40	282.9	2.933	−0.11	99.1
Gln	6.3	−0.11	−0.22	0.29	335.0	3.458	−1.19	127.5
Glu	8.8	−0.51	−0.64	0.76	311.6	3.243	−1.43	120.5
Gly	7.1	0.00	0.00	0.00	224.9	1.662	0.03	65.0
His	10.1	0.15	0.13	−0.25	337.2	3.856	−1.06	140.6
Ile	16.8	1.20	1.80	2.10	322.6	3.350	0.04	131.7
Leu	15.0	1.28	1.70	−2.00	324.0	3.518	0.12	131.5
Lys	7.9	−0.77	−0.99	0.78	336.6	2.933	−2.26	144.3
Met	13.3	0.90	1.23	−1.60	336.3	3.860	−0.33	132.3
Phe	11.2	1.56	1.79	−2.60	366.1	4.638	−0.05	155.8
Pro	8.2	0.38	0.49	−1.50	288.5	2.876	−0.32	106.7
Ser	7.4	0.00	−0.04	0.09	266.7	2.279	−0.40	88.5
Thr	8.8	0.17	0.26	−0.58	283.9	2.743	0.53	105.3
Trp	9.9	1.85	2.25	−2.70	401.8	5.755	−0.31	185.9
Tyr	8.8	0.89	0.96	−1.70	377.8	4.791	−0.84	162.7
Val	12.0	0.71	1.22	−1.60	295.1	3.054	−0.13	115.6

analysis (PCA) [14] and latent variables in the case of partial least-squares or PLS methods [13]. In this case, PIE and PIF are the lipophilicity constants of the AA side, DGR is the free energy of transfer of an AA side chain from protein interior to water, SAC is the water-accessible surface area, MR is the molecular refractivity, LAM is a polarity parameter, and Vol represents the molecular volume.

While this table is definitely informative, we will introduce some conventions and standard formats here to make it easier for a computer program to automate the data analysis procedure. It is our experience that when looking at the data related to many different industrial applications, there is no standard way of presenting data. Each application has its own different way of presenting data, and often a lot of time is spent just for trying to read and organize these data before actually doing an analysis or starting the data mining cycle. We will therefore first rearrange and format data into a standard shape, so that we can feed them into a computer program or data mining software. We will be strict when it comes to adhering to this standard format, in order to reduce the amount of potential computer problems. There is no uniform flat file standard in the data mining community, and each data mining program assumes that the data are organized and presented differently. We will introduce here just one way to organize data: the MetaNeural format. The MetaNeural format will be assumed as the standard format for data representation in this chapter.

An intermediate step toward the MetaNeural format is presented in Table 10.2, which contains almost the same information as Table 10.1, but with a few

TABLE 10.2. Different Representation for the Data of Table 10.1

Attribute_1	Attribute_2	Attribute_3	Attribute_4	Attribute_5	Attribute_6	Attribute_7	Response	ID
0.23	0.31	−0.55	254.2	2.126	−0.02	82.2	8.5	1
−0.48	−0.60	−0.51	303.6	2.994	−1.24	112.3	8.2	2
−0.61	−0.77	1.20	287.9	2.994	−1.08	103.7	8.5	3
0.45	1.54	−1.40	282.9	2.933	−0.11	99.1	11.0	4
−0.11	−0.22	0.29	335.0	3.458	−1.19	127.5	6.3	5
−0.51	−0.64	0.76	311.6	3.243	−1.43	120.5	8.8	6
0.00	0.00	0.00	224.9	1.662	0.03	65.0	7.1	7
0.15	0.13	−0.25	337.2	3.856	−1.06	140.6	10.1	8
1.20	1.80	−2.10	322.6	3.350	0.04	131.7	16.8	9
1.28	1.70	−2.00	324.0	3.518	0.12	131.5	15.0	10
−0.77	−0.99	0.78	336.6	2.933	−2.26	144.3	7.9	11
0.90	1.23	−1.60	336.3	3.860	−0.33	132.3	13.3	12
1.56	1.79	−2.60	366.1	4.638	−0.05	155.8	11.2	13
0.38	0.49	−1.50	288.5	2.876	−0.32	106.7	8.2	14
0.00	−0.04	0.09	266.7	2.279	−0.40	88.5	7.4	15
0.17	0.26	−0.58	283.9	2.743	−0.53	105.3	8.8	16
1.85	2.25	−2.70	401.8	5.755	−0.31	185.9	9.9	17
0.89	0.96	−1.70	377.8	4.791	−0.84	162.7	8.8	18
0.71	1.22	−1.60	295.1	3.054	−0.13	115.6	12.0	19

changes. (1) The column containing the names for each data entry is now placed last, and the names are translated into numerical identifiers (IDs) 1–19. (2) The response of interest, DDGTS, is now made the next to last column field, and the descriptive alphanumerical entry is now called Response. (3) The first row, or header row, now contains different names, indicating the columns with descriptive features or attributes (Attribute_1 ... Attribute_7), followed by one or more names for the response, followed by the identifier.

In order to convert this flat data file to the MetaNeural format, all the alphanumerical information in the file will be discarded. This is done by just eliminating the first header row in the file, as shown in Table 10.3. Basically, the MetaNeural format contains only numerical information, where the data are ordered as follows: First are the descriptors or attributes, next is the response (or responses, in the rarer case of multiple responses), and finally some record identifier. If the original data contained symbolic or descriptive attribute entries, they have to be converted to numbers.

Data sets often have missing data elements. It is a standard practice to code missing data as "−999". Before processing the data, it is often common practice to drop columns and/or rows containing many data entries with −999, or replace the −999 data entries with the average value for the corresponding data descriptor.

10.3.2 The "Standard Data Mining Problem"

We will define the standard (predictive) data mining problem as a regression problem of predicting the response from the descriptive features. In order to do

TABLE 10.3. The MetaNeural Format as a Standard Format for Presenting a Flat Data File

0.23	0.31	−0.55	254.2	2.126	−0.02	82.2	8.5	1
−0.48	−0.60	−0.51	303.6	2.994	−1.24	112.3	8.2	2
−0.61	−0.77	1.20	287.9	2.994	−1.08	103.7	8.5	3
0.45	1.54	−1.40	282.9	2.933	−0.11	99.1	11.0	4
−0.11	−0.22	0.29	335.0	3.458	−1.19	127.5	6.3	5
−0.51	−0.64	0.76	311.6	3.243	−1.43	120.5	8.8	6
0.00	0.00	0.00	224.9	1.662	0.03	65.0	7.1	7
0.15	0.13	−0.25	337.2	3.856	−1.06	140.6	10.1	8
1.20	1.80	−2.10	322.6	3.350	0.04	131.7	16.8	9
1.28	1.70	−2.00	324.0	3.518	0.12	131.5	15.0	10
−0.77	−0.99	0.78	336.6	2.933	−2.26	144.3	7.9	11
0.90	1.23	−1.60	336.3	3.860	−0.33	132.3	13.3	12
1.56	1.79	−2.60	366.1	4.638	−0.05	155.8	11.2	13
0.38	0.49	−1.50	288.5	2.876	−0.32	106.7	8.2	14
0.00	−0.04	0.09	266.7	2.279	−0.40	88.5	7.4	15
0.17	0.26	−0.58	283.9	2.743	−0.53	105.3	8.8	16
1.85	2.25	−2.70	401.8	5.755	−0.31	185.9	9.9	17
0.89	0.96	−1.70	377.8	4.791	−0.84	162.7	8.8	18
0.71	1.22	−1.60	295.1	3.054	−0.13	115.6	12.0	19

so, we will first build a predictive model based on training data, evaluate the performance of this predictive model based on validation data, and finally use this predictive model to make actual predictions on a test data set for which we generally do not know, or pretend not to know, the response value. There are many different ways to build such predictive regression models. Just to mention a few alternatives here, such a regression model could be a linear statistical model, a Neural-Network-based model (NN), or a Support Vector Machine (SVM)-based model. Examples for linear statistical models are Principal Component Regression models (PCR) and Partial Least-Squares models (PLS). Typical examples of neural network-based models include feedforward neural networks (trained with a particular learning method), Self-Organizing Maps (SOM), and Radial Basis Function Networks (RBFN). Examples of Support Vector Machine algorithms include (a) the perceptron-like SVM for classification and (b) Least-Squares Support Vector Machines (LS-SVM), also known as kernel ridge regression.

It is customary to denote the data matrix as X_{nm} and denote the response vector as $\vec{y}_n$. In this case, there are n data points and m descriptive features in the data set. We would like to infer $\vec{y}_n$ from X_{nm} by induction, denoted as $X_{nm} \Rightarrow \vec{y}_n$, in such a way that our inference model works not only for the training data, but also for the out-of-sample data (i.e., validation data and test data). In other words, we aim at building a linear predictive model of the type

$$\hat{\vec{y}}_n = X_{nm}\vec{w}_m \tag{10.1}$$

The hat symbol indicates that we are making predictions that are not perfect (especially for the validation and test data). Equation (10.1) answers the question of which "wisdom vector" should be applied to provide the answer. The vector $\vec{w}_n$ is that wisdom vector and is formally called the weight vector in machine learning. By introducing the standard data mining problem we are doing a lot of oversimplifying. In a typical data mining study, the questions related to what we are trying to find out are not a priori defined. In this context, precisely formulating the right questions might actually be a more difficult task than answering them. A typical data mining case is therefore more complex than the standard data mining problem. There might be many regression models involved, and there might be a whole set of additional constraints as well. For example, a more realistic problem for data mining that is still close to the standard data mining problem might be picking an a priori unspecified small subset of the chemically most transparent descriptive features or descriptors from Table 10.3, in order to make a good model for the protein folding energy. Note that now we are using qualitative terms that are not precisely defined such as "small subset," "chemically most transparent," and "pretty good model." Also, keep in mind that the predictive model that was proposed so far is strictly linear. It therefore cannot be expected that the model is going to be very accurate, but that will change soon.

It should be pointed out that many problems that are typical for data mining can be posed as a variation of the standard data mining problem. In the above case, we considered a regression problem. Note that a classification problem can be treated as a special case of a regression problem; for example, the data entries for the response could be just -1 and $+1$ in the case of a two-class classification problem. For a multiclass classification problem, the different classes could be presented as 1, 2, 3, and so on. However, there is one difficulty for multiclass classification. If the multiclass classification problem is posed as a regression problem, the classes should be ordinal; that is, class 2 should be indicative for a response that is in between class 1 and class 3. In practice, that is often the case; for example, consider the case where we have five alert levels from 1 to 5, where a higher alert number means a more severe type of alert. On the other hand, when we have a classification problem where the classes represent five cities, they are usually not fully ordinal. In that case, it is common not to represent the response as a single response, but to encode the response as an orthogonal set of five response vectors of the type {0, 0, 0, 0, 1}, {0, 0, 0, 1, 0}, {0, 0, 1, 0, 0}, and so on. Nonorthogonal classification problems are often not trivial to solve, and we refer the reader to the literature [3] for a further discussion.

A different and difficult classification problem is the case with just two classes that have very unbalanced representation—that is, cases in which there are much more samples from one class than from the other. Consider the cartoon problem of a trinket manufacturing case where a product line produces 1,000,000 good trinkets that pass the inspection line and 1000 defect trinkets that should not pass the inspection line before the product is shipped out. It is often difficult to build good models for such problems without being aware that we are dealing here with an outlier problem. Naively applying machine learning models could result in the case where the model now predicts that all trinkets belong to the majority class. Concluding that now only 1000 out of 1,001,000 cases are missed, and that the classification is therefore 99.9% correct, does not make sense, because in reality 100% of the cases that we are interested in catching are now missed altogether. It therefore should be a common practice for classification problems to represent the results in the form of a confusion matrix. In case of a binary classification problem where the classification results can be presented as four numbers: the number of true negatives, the number of false negatives, the number of true positives, and the number of false positives. The false negatives and false positives are called Type I and Type II errors. For medical applications, it is customary to convert these numbers further into sensitivity and specificity measures.

Note that outlier problems occur not only in classification problems, but also in regression problems. Predicting the swing for the stock market is a regression problem, and predicting a stock market crash is an outlier problem in that context. Predicting rare events such as stock market crashes, earthquakes, or tornados can also be considered as extreme outlier problems or rare event problems. Such cases are usually very difficult if not impossible to deal with using data mining techniques.

A special case of an outlier problem is novelty detection, where we often have a data set consisting of normal cases and maybe a few instances of abnormal cases. The different categories for abnormal cases are often not known a priori. The problem is now to devise a detection model that tags data samples that are very different from what has been seen before.

A difficult type of data mining problem is a data strip mining problem. Data strip mining is a special case of predictive data mining, where the data have much more descriptors than there are data. Such problems are common, for example, for in-silico drug design and the analysis of gene-expression arrays. The task is now to identify a combination of subsets of the most relevant features and make a predictive model that works well on external test data.

A whole different class of data mining relates to signal and time-series analysis. Time-series analysis problems are of common interest to the financial world, process control, and medical diagnostics. Challenging time-series analysis problems deal with multivariate time series, problems where the time series exhibits complex dynamics (such as nonlinear chaotic time sequences), or cases with the nonstationary time series.

Note that for a legitimate data mining case, we are not just interested in building predictive models. What is of real interest is the understanding and explaining of these models (e.g., in the form of a fuzzy rules system). It is often revealing for such a rule set to identify the most important descriptors and/or features and then explain what these descriptors or features do for the model. Feature detection is a subdiscipline on its own and an important part of the data mining process. There are many different ways for feature detection, and the most appropriate method depends on the modeling method, the data characteristics, and the application domain. It is important to point out here that the most interesting features are often not the most correlated features.

10.3.3 Predictive Data Mining

In this section, a simple statistical regression solution to the standard data mining problem will be introduced. In this context, the standard data mining problem can be interpreted as a predictive data mining problem.

Looking back at Eq. (10.1), let us try now whether we can produce simple estimates for the weights of the model for the cartoon QSAR data of Wold et al. from Table 10.3. In this case, the aim is to predict the free energy for protein folding, or the entry next to last column, based on the descriptive features in the prior columns. A model will be constructed here by finding an approximate solution for the weights in Eq. (10.1). Note that the data matrix is generally not symmetric. If that were the case, it would be straightforward to come up with an answer by using the inverse of the data matrix. We will therefore apply the pseudo-inverse transformation, which will generally not lead to precise predictions for y, but will predict y in a way that is optimal in a least-squares sense. The pseudo-inverse solution for the weight vector is illustrated in Eq. (10.2):

$$X_{mn}^T X_{nm} \vec{w}_m = X_{mn}^T \vec{y}_n$$

$$(X_{mn}^T X_{nm})^{-1} (X_{mn}^T X_{nm}) \vec{w}_m = (X_{mn}^T X_{nm})^{-1} X_{mn}^T \vec{y}_n \qquad (10.2)$$

$$\vec{w}_m = (X_{mn}^T X_{nm})^{-1} X_{mn}^T \vec{y}_n$$

Predictions for the training set can now be made for y by substituting Eq. (10.2) in Eq. (10.1):

$$\hat{\vec{y}}_n = X_{nm} (X_{mn}^T X_{nm})^{-1} X_{mn}^T \vec{y}_n \qquad (10.3)$$

Before applying this formula for the prediction of the free binding energy of amino acids, we have to introduce one more important stage of the data mining cycle: data preprocessing. The seven descriptors for the amino acids have very different underlying metrics and scales; that is, some columns have all very small entries and other columns have relatively large entries. It is therefore a common procedure in data mining to center all the descriptors and to bring them to a unity variance. The same process is then applied to the response. This procedure of centering and variance normalization is known as Mahalanobis scaling or normalizing the data. While Mahalanobis scaling is not the only way to preprocess the data, it is a general and robust way to preprocess data. If we represent a feature vector as $\vec{z}$, Mahalanobis scaling will result in a rescaled feature vector $\vec{z}'$ that can be expressed as

$$\vec{z}' = \frac{\vec{z} - \bar{z}}{\text{std}(\vec{z})} \tag{10.4}$$

where $\bar{z}$ represents the average value and $\text{std}(\vec{z})$ represents the standard deviation for attribute $\vec{z}$. After Mahalanobis scaling, the data matrix from Table 10.3 now changes to Table 10.4.

The modeling results obtained from Eq. (10.3) after de-scaling the "predictions" back to the original distribution are shown in Fig. 10.3. After a first inspection, these "predictions" do not look bad. However, there is one caveat: These are "predictions" for training data. It is imperative for predictive data mining to verify how good the model really is on a validation set—that is, a set of data that was not used for

TABLE 10.4. Amino Acid Protein Folding Data After Mahalanobis Scaling During Preprocessing

−0.205	−0.240	0.195	−1.340	−1.233	0.881	−1.344	−0.502	1
−1.149	−1.155	1.067	−0.204	−0.336	−1.022	−0.318	−0.611	2
−1.322	−1.326	1.635	−0.565	−0.336	−0.772	−0.611	−0.502	3
0.088	0.997	−0.504	−0.680	−0.399	0.740	−0.768	0.405	4
−0.657	−0.773	0.886	0.518	0.144	−0.944	0.200	−1.300	5
−1.189	−1.195	1.273	−0.020	−0.079	−1.318	−0.039	−0.393	6
−0.511	−0.552	0.647	−2.013	−1.713	0.959	−1.930	−1.010	7
−0.311	−0.421	0.442	0.569	0.555	−0.741	0.646	0.078	8
1.086	1.259	−1.080	0.233	0.032	0.974	0.343	2.508	9
1.193	1.158	−0.998	0.265	0.206	1.099	0.336	1.855	10
−1.535	−1.547	1.289	0.555	−0.399	−2.612	0.772	−0.719	11
0.687	0.686	−0.669	0.548	0.559	0.397	0.363	1.239	12
1.566	1.249	−1.492	1.234	1.363	0.834	1.164	0.477	13
−0.005	−0.059	−0.587	−0.551	−0.458	0.413	−0.509	−0.611	14
−0.511	−0.592	0.721	−1.052	−1.075	0.288	−1.129	−0.901	15
−0.284	−0.290	0.170	−0.657	−0.596	0.085	−0.557	−0.393	16
1.951	1.712	−1.574	2.055	2.518	0.428	2.189	0.006	17
0.674	0.414	−0.751	1.503	1.522	−0.398	1.399	−0.393	18
0.434	0.676	−0.669	−0.399	−0.274	0.709	−0.206	0.767	19

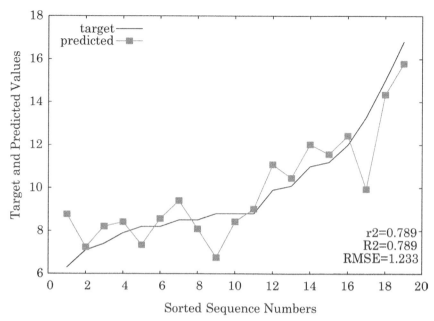

Figure 10.3. Predictions for training model for the 19-amino-acid data from Table 10.4.

training. Of course, there is now a problem here: There are only 19 data points. If we would build a model using 13 data points and test on the remaining 6 data points, the model is probably not going to be as accurate as it potentially could be, because all the available data were not used for model building. There are several ways out of that dilemma. (1) Because data mining usually deals with large data sets, there are normally enough data available to split the data set up into a training set and a test set. A good practice would be to use a random sample of two-thirds of the data for the training and one-third for testing. (2) If one is truly concerned about compromising the quality of the model, one can follow the leave-one-out (LOO) method. In this case, one would build 19 different models, each time using 18 data points for training and then using the one remaining data point for testing. The 19 individual tests would then be combined and displayed in a simple plot similar to the plot of Fig. 10.4. (3) An obvious extension to the LOO practice is to leave several

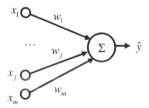

Figure 10.4. Neural network representation for the simple regression model.

samples out. This procedure is called bootstrapping and in analogy with the LOO method will be indicated by the acronym BOO. By using the bootstrapping, it is possible to generate multiple models from the 19 data samples, leaving three samples out each time for testing and then combining the predictions by averaging the models.

A model for testing is created in a very similar way as for training: The "wisdom vector" or the weight vector will be applied to the test data to make predictions according to

$$\hat{\vec{y}}_k^{\text{test}} = X_{km}^{\text{test}}\vec{w}_m \tag{10.5}$$

In the above expression it was assumed that there are k test data, and the superscript "test" is used to explicitly indicate that the wisdom vector will be applied to a set of k test data with m attributes or descriptors. If one considers testing for one sample data point at a time, Eq. (10.5) can be represented as a simple neural network with an input layer and just a single neuron, as shown in Fig. 10.4. The neuron produces the weighted sum of the input attributes. Note that the activation function, commonly found in neural networks, is not present here. Note also that the number of weights for this one-layer neural network equals the number of input descriptors or attributes.

Let us proceed with training the simple learning model on the first 13 data points, and make predictions on the last six data points. The results are shown in Fig. 10.5.

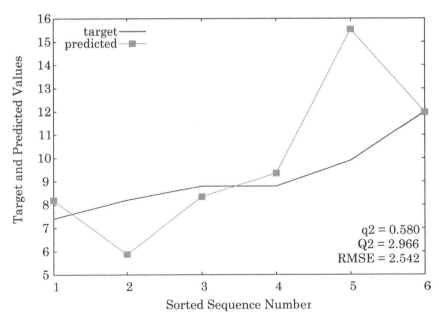

Figure 10.5. Test data predictions for the simple regression model trained on the first 13 data samples in Table 10.4 and tested on the six last data samples.

It is clear that this model looks less convincing for being able to make good predictions on the test data.

10.3.4 Metrics for Assessing Model Quality

An obvious question that now comes to mind is how to assess or describe the quality of a model for training data and test data, such as is the case for the data shown in Figs. 10.4 and 10.6. In the case of a classification problem that would be easy, and one would present the number of hits and misses in the form of a confusion matrix as described earlier. For a regression problem, a common way to capture the error is by the root mean square error index (RMSE), which is defined as the square root of the average value of the squared error (either for the training set or the test set) according to

$$\text{RMSE} = \sqrt{\frac{1}{n} \sum_i (\hat{y}_i - y_i)^2} \tag{10.6}$$

While the root mean square error is a straightforward way to compare the performance of different prediction methods on the same data, it is not an absolute metric in the sense that the RMSE will depend on how the response for the data was scaled. In order to overcome this handicap, additional error measures will be introduced that are less dependent on the scaling and magnitude of the response value. A first metric that will be used for assessing the quality of a trained model is r^2, where r^2 is defined as the correlation coefficient squared between target values and predictions for the response according to

$$r^2 = \frac{\sum_{i=1}^{n_{\text{train}}} (\hat{y}_i - \bar{y})(y_i - \bar{y})}{\sqrt{\sum_{i=1}^{n_{\text{train}}} (\hat{y}_i - \bar{y})^2} \sqrt{\sum_{i=1}^{n_{\text{train}}} (y_i - \bar{y})^2}} \tag{10.7}$$

where n_{train} represents the number of data points in the training set. r^2 takes values between zero and unity, and the higher the r^2 value, the better the model. An obvious drawback of r^2 for assessing the model quality is that r^2 only expresses a linear correlation, indicating how well the predictions follow a line if $\hat{y}$ is plotted as function of y. While one would expect a nearly perfect model when r^2 is unity, this is not always the case, because an r^2 of unity only indicates that when $\hat{y}$ is plotted as function of y, the points fall on a straight line. A second and more powerful measure to assess the quality of a trained model is the so-called "Press r squared," or R^2, often used in chemometric modeling [15], where R^2 is defined as [16]:

$$R^2 = 1 - \frac{\sum_{i=1}^{n_{\text{train}}} (y_i - \hat{y}_i)^2}{\sum_{i=1}^{n_{\text{train}}} (y_i - \bar{y})^2} \tag{10.8}$$

We consider R^2 as a better measure than r^2, because it accounts for the residual error as well. The higher the value for R^2, the better the model. Note that in certain cases the R^2

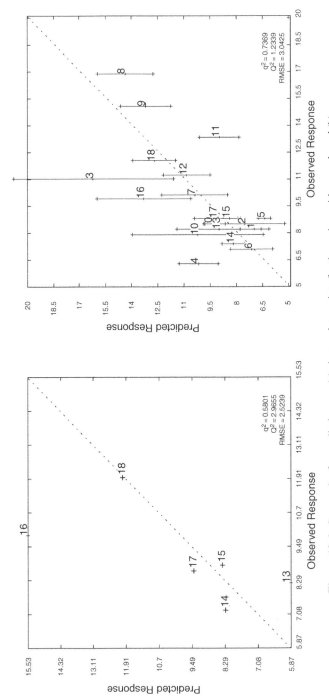

Figure 10.6. Scatterplot for predictions on (a) six test data points for the amino acid example and (b) 200 bootstraps with six sample test data each.

metric can actually be negative. The R^2 metric is frequently used in chemometrics and is generally smaller than r^2. For large data sets, R^2 tends to converge to r^2, and the comparison between r^2 and R^2 for such data often reveals hidden biases.

For assessing the quality of the validation set or a test set, we will introduce similar metrics, q^2 and Q^2, where q^2 and Q^2 are defined as $1 - r^2$ and $1 - R^2$ for the data in the test set. For a model that perfectly predicts on the test data, we now would expect q^2 and Q^2 to be zero. The reason for introducing metrics that are symmetric between the training set and the test set is to avoid confusion. Q^2 and q^2 values will always apply to a validation set or a test set, and we would expect these values to be quite low in order to have a good predictive model. R^2 and r^2 values will always apply to training data, and they should be close to unity for a good training model. For the example above, trained on 13 training data points, we obtained RMSE = 0.1306, $r^2 = 0.826$, and $R^2 = 0.815$ for the training data. Similarly, with a model in which the six data points are put aside for the validation set, we obtained 2.524, 0.580, 2.966, for the RMSE, q^2, and Q^2, respectively.

Note that for the above example, Q^2 is significantly larger than unity (2.966). While $0 < q^2 < 1$, inspecting Eq. (10.8) reveals that this upper limit does not hold anymore for Q^2. The Q^2 measure for the six test data points indicates that the predictions on the test data are poor. The large difference between q^2 and Q^2 indicates that the model also has a lot of uncertainty. Looking at Fig. 10.6a, this conclusion is not entirely obvious: the predictions in this figure seem to follow the right trend, and there are two data points that are clearly missed in the predictions. A better type of plot, that clearly supports the conclusions from the q^2 and Q^2 analysis, is the scatterplot. A scatterplot is a plot where the true values are indicated on the horizontal axis and the predicted values correspond to the y-axis. For a perfect predictive model, all the data should fall on the main diagonal. Figure 10.6b shows the scatterplot for the six test data points for the amino acid example. From looking at the scatterplot, it now becomes immediately clear that the predictive model is not good at all in predicting on test data. The scatterplot on the left-hand side is for the six test data points (the last six samples from Table 10.3), while the scatterplot on the right-hand side is obtained from running 200 different bootstraps and then testing on a random selection of six test samples. The variance on the bootstrap predictions for this case is indicated with error bars on the figure.

10.4 INTRODUCTION TO DIRECT KERNEL METHODS

10.4.1 Data Mining and Machine Learning Dilemmas for Real-World Data

The example above is a simple toy problem. Real-world data mining problems differ in many ways. Real-world data sets can be vast. They are often so large that they cannot be elegantly presented and looked at in a spreadsheet anymore. Furthermore, real-world data sets have missing data, errors, outliers, and minority classes.

There is also the problem of diminishing "information density" in large data sets. As data sets become larger and larger, we would expect, on the one hand, that there is more information out there to build good and robust models. On the other hand, there might also be so much spurious and superfluous data in the data set that the information density is generally lower. Even if it is possible to obtain better models from larger data sets because there is more useful and relevant information out there, it is actually harder to extract that information. We call this the phenomenon "the data mining dilemma."

Another observation will be even more fundamental for predictive data mining. Looking back at Eqs. (10.2) and (10.3) it can be noticed that they contain the inverse of the feature kernel, K_F, defined as

$$K_F = X_{mn}^T X_{nm} \tag{10.9}$$

The feature kernel is an $m \times m$ symmetric matrix where each entry represents the similarity between features. Obviously, if there were two features that would be completely redundant, the feature matrix would contain two columns and two rows that are identical, and the inverse does not exist. For the case of data strip mining problems, where there are more descriptors than data, this matrix would be rank deficient and the inverse would not exist. Consequently, the simple regression model we proposed above would not work anymore. One can argue that all is still well and that in order to make the simple regression method work, one would just make sure that the same descriptor or attribute is not included twice. By the same argument, highly correlated descriptors (i.e., "cousin features" in data mining lingo) should be eliminated as well. While this argument sounds plausible, the truth of the matter is subtler. Let us repeat Eq. (10.2) again and go just one step further as shown below:

$$X_{mn}^T X_{nm} \vec{w}_m = X_{mn}^T \vec{y}_n$$
$$(X_{mn}^T X_{nm})^{-1} (X_{mn}^T X_{nm}) \vec{w}_m = (X_{mn}^T X_{nm})^{-1} X_{mn}^T \vec{y}_n$$
$$\vec{w}_m = (X_{mn}^T X_{nm})^{-1} X_{mn}^T \vec{y}_n \tag{10.10}$$
$$\vec{w}_m = X_{mn}^T (X_{nm} X_{mn}^T)^{-1} \vec{y}_n$$

Equation (10.10) is the derivation of an equivalent linear formulation to Eq. (10.2), based on the so-called right-hand pseudo-inverse or Penrose inverse, rather than using the more common left-hand pseudo-inverse. It was not shown here how that last line followed from the previous equation, but the proof is straightforward and left as an exercise to the reader. Note that now the inverse is needed for a different entity matrix, which now has an $n \times n$ dimensionality and is called the data kernel, K_D, as defined by

$$K_D = X_{nm} X_{mn}^T \tag{10.11}$$

The right-hand pseudo-inverse formulation is less frequently cited in the literature, because it can only be non-rank-deficient when there are more descriptive attributes than data points, which is not the usual case for data mining problems, except for data strip mining cases. The data kernel matrix is a symmetrical matrix that contains entries representing similarities between data points. The solution to this problem seems to be straightforward. We will first explain here what seems to be an obvious solution, and then we will show why this would not work. Looking at Eqs. (10.10) and (10.11), it can be concluded that, except for rare cases where there are as many data records as there are features, either the feature kernel is rank-deficient (in case that $m > n$, i.e., there are more attributes than data) or the data kernel is rank-deficient (in case that $n > m$, i.e., there are more data than attributes). It can be now argued that for the $m < n$ case one can proceed with the usual left-hand pseudo-inverse method of Eq. (10.2), and that for the $m > n$ case one should proceed with the right-hand pseudo-inverse (or Penrose inverse) following Eq. (10.10).

While the approach just proposed above seems to be reasonable, it will not work. Learning occurs by discovering patterns in data through redundancies present in the data. Data redundancies imply that there are data present that seem to be very similar to each other (and that have similar values for the response as well). An extreme example for data redundancy would be a data set that contains the same data point twice. Obviously, in that case, the data matrix is ill-conditioned and the inverse does not exist. This type of redundancy, where data repeat themselves, will be called here a "hard redundancy." However, for any data set that one can possibly learn from, there have to be many "soft redundancies" as well. While these soft redundancies will not necessarily make the data matrix ill-conditioned, in the sense that the inverse does not exist because the determinant of the data kernel is zero, in practice this determinant will be very small. In other words, regardless of whether one proceeds with a left-hand or a right-hand pseudo-inverse, if data contain information that can be learned from, there have to be soft or hard redundancies in the data. Unfortunately, Eqs. (10.2) and (10.10) cannot be solved for the weight vector in that case, because the kernel will be either rank-deficient (i.e., ill-conditioned) or poor-conditioned; that is, calculating the inverse will be numerically unstable. This phenomenon is "the data mining dilemma": (1) Machine learning from data can only occur when data contain redundancies; (2) but, in that case the kernel inverse in Eq. (10.2) or Eq. (10.10) is either not defined or numerically unstable because of poor conditioning. Taking the inverse of a poor-conditioned matrix is possible, but most numerical methods, with the exception of methods based on single value decomposition (SVD), will run into numerical instabilities. The data mining dilemma has some similarity with the uncertainty principle in physics, but we will not try to draw that parallel too far.

Statisticians have been aware of the data mining dilemma for a long time, and they have devised various methods around this paradox. In the next sections, we will propose several methods to deal with the data mining dilemma, and we will obtain efficient and robust prediction models in the process.

10.4.2 Regression Models Based on the Data Kernel

In this section, we will consider the data kernel formulation of Eq. (10.10) for predictive modeling. Not because we have to, but because this formulation is just in the right form to apply the kernel transformation on test data. There are several well-known methods for dealing with the data mining dilemma by using techniques that ensure that the kernel matrix will not be rank-deficient anymore. Two well-known methods are principal component regression [17] and ridge regression [18,19]. In order to keep the mathematical diversions to its bare minimum, only ridge regression will be discussed.

Ridge regression is a very straightforward way to ensure that the kernel matrix is positive definite (or well-conditioned), before inverting the data kernel. In ridge regression, a small positive value, λ, is added to each element on the main diagonal of the data matrix. Usually the same value for λ is used for each entry. Obviously, we are not exactly solving the same problem anymore. In order to not deviate too much from the original problem, the value for λ will be kept as small as we reasonably can tolerate. A good choice for λ is a small value that will make the newly defined data kernel matrix barely positive definite, so that the inverse exists and is mathematically stable. In data kernel space, the solution for the weight vector that will be used in the ridge regression prediction model now becomes

$$\vec{w}_n = X_{mn}^T (X_{nm} X_{mn}^T + \lambda I)^{-1} \vec{y}_n \tag{10.12}$$

and predictions for y can now be made according to

$$\begin{aligned} \hat{\vec{y}} &= X_{nm} X_{mn}^T (X_{nm} X_{mn}^T + \lambda I)^{-1} \vec{y}_n \\ &= K_D (K_D + \lambda I)^{-1} \vec{y}_n \\ &= K_D \vec{w}_n \end{aligned} \tag{10.13}$$

where a very different weight vector was introduced: $\vec{w}_n$. This new weight vector is applied directly to the data kernel matrix (rather than the training data matrix) and has the same dimensionality as the number of training data. To make a prediction on the test set, one proceeds in a similar way, but applies the weight vector on the data kernel for the test data, which is generally a rectangular matrix, and projects the test data on the training data according to

$$K_D^{\text{test}} = X_{km}^{\text{test}} \left(X_{mn}^{\text{train}} \right)^T \tag{10.14}$$

where it is assumed that there are k data points in the test set.

10.4.3 Kernel Transformations

The kernel transformation is an efficient way to make a regression model nonlinear. The kernel transformation goes back at least to the early 1900s, when Hilbert addressed kernels in the mathematical literature. A kernel is a matrix containing similarity measures for a data set: either between the data of the data set itself or with other data (e.g., support vectors [1]). A classical use of a kernel is the correlation matrix used for determining the principal components in principal component analysis, where the feature kernel contains linear similarity measures between (centered) attributes. In support vector machines, the kernel entries are similarity measures between data rather than features; these similarity measures are usually nonlinear, unlike the dot product similarity measure that we used before to define a kernel. There are many possible nonlinear similarity measures, but in order to be mathematically tractable the kernel has to satisfy certain conditions, the so-called Mercer conditions [1–3].

$$
\overset{\leftrightarrow}{K}_{nn} =
\begin{bmatrix}
k_{11} & k_{12} & \cdots & k_{1n} \\
k_{21} & k_{22} & \cdots & k_{2n} \\
& & \cdots & \\
k_{n1} & k_{n2} & \cdots & k_{nn}
\end{bmatrix}
\tag{10.15}
$$

The expression above introduces the general structure for the data kernel matrix, $\overset{\leftrightarrow}{K}_{nm}$, for n data. The kernel matrix is a symmetrical matrix where each entry contains a (linear or nonlinear) similarity between two data vectors. There are many different possibilities for defining similarity metrics such as the dot product, which is a linear similarity measure, and the radial basis function kernel or RBF kernel, which is a nonlinear similarity measure. The RBF kernel is the most widely used nonlinear kernel, and the kernel entries are defined by

$$
k_{ij} \equiv e^{-(\|\vec{x}_j - \vec{x}_i\|_2^2)/2\sigma^2}
\tag{10.16}
$$

Note that in the kernel definition above, the kernel entry contains the square of the Euclidean distance (or two-norm) between data points, which is a dissimilarity measure (rather than a similarity), in a negative exponential. The negative exponential also contains a free parameter, σ, which is the Parzen window width for the RBF kernel. The proper choice for selecting the Parzen window is usually determined by additional tuning, also called hyper-tuning, on an external validation set. The precise choice for σ is not crucial; there usually is a relatively broad range for the choice of σ for which the model quality should be stable.

Different learning methods distinguish themselves in the way by which the weights are determined. Obviously, the model in Eqs. (10.12)–(10.14) is meant to produce linear estimates or predictions for y. Such a linear model has a handicap in the sense that it cannot capture inherent nonlinearities in the data. This handicap can easily be overcome by applying the kernel transformation directly as a data transformation. We will therefore not operate directly on the data, but on a nonlinear transform of the data—in this case the nonlinear data kernel. This is very similar to what is done in principal component analysis, where the data are substituted by their principal components before building a model. A similar procedure will be applied here, but rather than substituting data by their principal components, the data will be substituted by their kernel transform (either linear or nonlinear) before building a predictive model.

The kernel transformation is applied here as a data transformation in a separate preprocessing stage. We replace in this case the data by a nonlinear data kernel and apply a traditional linear predictive model. Methods where a traditional linear algorithm is used on a nonlinear kernel transform of the data are introduced in this chapter as "direct kernel methods." The advantage of direct kernel methods is that the nonlinear aspects of the problem are captured entirely in the kernel and are transparent to the applied algorithm. If a linear algorithm was used before introducing the kernel transformation, the required mathematical operations remain linear. It is now clear how linear methods such as principal component regression, ridge regression, and partial least squares can be turned into nonlinear direct kernel methods, by using exactly the same algorithm and code: Only the data are different, and we operate on the kernel transformation of the data rather than the data themselves. This same approach for converting algorithms to direct kernel methods can also be applied to nonlinear algorithms such as the self-organizing map [4]. In order to make out-of-sample predictions on test data, a similar kernel transformation needs to be applied to the test data, as shown in Eq. (10.14). The idea of direct kernel methods is illustrated in Fig. 10.7, by showing how any regression model can be applied to kernel-transformed data. One could also represent the kernel transformation in a neural network type of flow diagram; the first hidden layer would now yield the kernel-transformed data, and the weights in the first layer would be just the descriptors of the training data. The second layer contains the weights that can be calculated with a hard-computing method, such as kernel ridge regression. When a radial basis function kernel is used, this type of neural network would be similar to a radial basis function neural network [14,20], except that the weights in the second layer are calculated differently.

10.4.4 Dealing with Bias: Centering the Kernel

There is still one important detail that was overlooked so far and that is necessary to make direct kernel methods work. Looking at the prediction equations in which the weight vector is applied to data as in Eq. (10.1), there is no constant offset term or bias. It turns out that for data that are centered, this offset term is always zero and does not have to be included explicitly. In machine learning lingo the proper name for this offset term is the bias; and rather than applying Eq. (10.1), a more general predictive model that includes this bias can be written as

$$\hat{\vec{y}}_n = X_{nm}\vec{w}_m + b \tag{10.17}$$

Training Mode

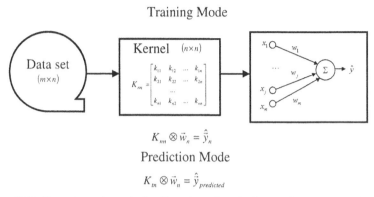

$$K_{nn} \otimes \vec{w}_n = \hat{\vec{y}}_n$$

Prediction Mode

$$K_{tn} \otimes \vec{w}_n = \hat{\vec{y}}_{predicted}$$

Figure 10.7. Operation schematic for direct kernel methods as a data preprocessing step.

where b is the bias term. Since we made it a practice in data mining to center the data first by Mahalanobis scaling, this bias term is zero and can be ignored.

When dealing with kernels, the situation is more complex, because they need some type of bias as well. Here, we will give only a recipe that works well in practice, and we will refer the reader to the literature for a detailed explanation [3,21–23]. Even when the data were Mahalanobis-scaled, before applying a kernel transform, the kernel still needs some type of centering to be able to omit the bias term in the prediction model. A straightforward way for kernel centering is to subtract the average of the data entries for each column of the training data kernel, and store this average for later recall, when centering the test kernel. A second step for centering the kernel is going through the newly obtained vertically centered kernel again, this time row by row, and subtracting the row average from each row entry.

The kernel of the test data needs to be centered in a consistent way, following a similar procedure. In this case, the stored column centers from the kernel of the training data will be used for the vertical centering of the kernel of the test data. This vertically centered test kernel is then centered horizontally; that is, for each row, the average of the vertically centered test kernel is calculated, and each horizontal entry of the vertically centered test kernel is substituted by that entry minus the row average.

Mathematical formulations for centering square kernels are explained in the literature [21–23]. The advantage of the kernel-centering algorithm introduced (and described above in words) in this section is that it also applies to rectangular data kernels. The flow chart for preprocessing the data, applying a kernel transform on this data, and centering the kernel for the training data, validation data, and test data is shown in Fig. 10.8.

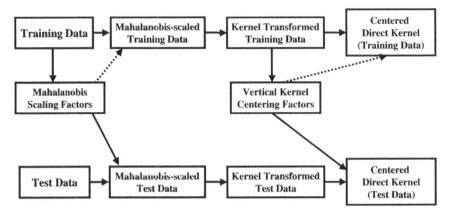

Figure 10.8. Data preprocessing with kernel centering for direct kernel methods.

10.5 DIRECT KERNEL RIDGE REGRESSION

10.5.1 Overview

So far, the argument was made that by applying the kernel transformation in Eqs. (10.13) and (10.14), many traditional linear regression models can be transformed into a nonlinear direct kernel method. The kernel transformation and kernel centering proceed as data preprocessing steps (Fig. 10.8). In order to make the predictive model inherently nonlinear, the radial basis function kernel will be applied, rather than the (linear) dot product kernel, used in Eqs. (10.2) and (10.10). There are several different choices for the kernel [1–3,14], but the RBF kernel is the most widely applied kernel. In order to overcome the machine learning dilemma, a ridge can be applied to the main diagonal of the data kernel matrix. Since the kernel transformation is applied directly on the data, before applying ridge regression, this method is called direct kernel ridge regression.

Kernel ridge regression and direct kernel ridge regression are not new. The roots for ridge regression can be traced back to the statistics literature [19]. Methods equivalent to kernel ridge regression were recently introduced under different names in the machine learning literature (e.g., proximal SVMs were introduced by Fung and Mangasarian [24], kernel ridge regression was introduced by Poggio et al. [25–27], and least-squares support vector machines were introduced by Suykens et al. [28,29]). In those works, kernel ridge regression is usually introduced as a regularization method that solves a convex optimization problem in a Langrangian formulation for the dual problem that is very similar to traditional SVMs. The equivalency with ridge regression techniques then appears after a series of mathematical manipulations. By contrast, in the present chapter direct kernel ridge regression was introduced with few mathematical diversions in the context of the machine learning dilemma. For all practical purposes, kernel ridge regression is similar to support vector machines, works in the same feature space as support vector machines, and was therefore named least-squares support vector machines by Suykens et al. [28,29].

Note that kernel ridge regression still requires the computation of an inverse for an $n \times n$ matrix, which can be quite large. This task is computationally demanding for large data sets, as is the case in a typical data mining problem. Since the kernel matrix now scales with the number of data squared, this method can also become prohibitive from a practical computer implementation point of view, because both memory and processing requirements can be very demanding. Krylov-space-based methods and conjugate gradient methods are efficient ways to speed up the matrix inverse transformation of large matrices, where the computation time now scales as n^2, rather than n^3. Krylov-space methods are discussed in reference 30. Conjugate gradient-based methods for inverting large matrices are discussed in references 1 and 29. The Analyze/StripMiner [31] code used for the analysis presented here applies Møller's scaled conjugate gradient method to calculate the matrix inverse [32].

The issue of dealing with large data sets is even more profound. There are several potential solutions that will not be discussed in detail. One approach would be to use a rectangular kernel, where not all the data are used as bases to calculate the kernel, but a good subset of "support vectors" is estimated by chunking [1] or other techniques such as sensitivity analysis (explained further on in this chapter). More efficient ways for inverting large matrices are based on piecewise inversion. Alternatively, the matrix inversion may be avoided altogether by adhering to the support vector machine formulation of kernel ridge regression and solving the dual Lagrangian optimization problem and applying the sequential minimum optimization or SMO algorithm as explained in reference 33.

10.5.2 Choosing the Ridge Parameter

It has been shown in the literature [29] that kernel ridge regression can be expressed as an optimization method, where rather than minimizing the residual error on the training set, according to

$$\sum_{i=1}^{n_{\text{train}}} \|\hat{\vec{y}}_i - \vec{y}_i\|_2 \tag{10.18}$$

we now minimize

$$\sum_{i=1}^{n_{\text{train}}} \|\hat{\vec{y}}_i - \vec{y}_i\|_2 + \frac{\lambda}{2} \|\vec{w}\|_2 \tag{10.19}$$

The above equation is a form of Tikhonov regularization [34,35] that has been explained in detail by Cherkassky and Mulier [18] in the context of empirical versus structural risk minimization. Minimizing the norm of the weight vector is in a sense similar to an error penalization for prediction models with a large number of free parameters. An obvious question in this context relates to the proper choice for the regularization parameter or ridge parameter λ.

In machine learning, it is common to tune the hyperparameter λ by making use of a tuning/validation set. This tuning procedure can be quite time-consuming for large data sets, especially in consideration that a simultaneous tuning for the RBF kernel width must proceed in a similar manner. We therefore propose a simple heuristic formula for the proper choice of the ridge parameter, which has proven to be close to optimal in numerous practical cases [36]. If the data were originally Mahalanobis scaled, it was found by scaling experiments that a good choice for λ is

$$\lambda = \min\left\{1; \quad 0.05\left(\frac{n}{200}\right)^{3/2}\right\} \tag{10.20}$$

where n is the number of data for the training set.

Note that in order to apply the above heuristic formula, the data have to be Mahalanobis scaled first. Equation (10.20) was validated on a variety of standard benchmark data sets from the UCI data repository [36], and it provided results that are close to an optimally tuned λ on a tuning/validation set. In any case, the heuristic formula for λ should be an excellent starting choice for the tuning process of λ. The above formula proved to be also useful for the initial choice for the regularization parameter C of SVMs, where C is now taken as $1/\lambda$.

10.6 CASE STUDY #1: PREDICTING THE BINDING ENERGY FOR AMINO ACIDS

In this section, predicting the free energy for unfolding amino acids will be revisited by applying direct kernel ridge regression with a Gaussian or RBF kernel. The ridge parameter λ was chosen as 0.00083, following Eq. (10.20), and the Parzen window parameter, σ, was chosen to be unity (obtained by tuning with the leave-one-out method on the training set of 13 data). The predictions for the six amino acids are shown in Fig. 10.9. The lower values for q^2, Q^2, and RMSE show a clear improvement over the predictions in Fig. 10.5. Figure 10.10 illustrates the scatterplot for 200 bootstrap predictions on six randomly selected samples. The values of q^2 and Q^2 are now 0.366 and 0.374, compared to 0.737 and 1.233 for the corresponding values in the linear bootstrap model shown in Fig. 10.6b. The execution time for the 200 bootstraps was 13 s for kernel ridge regression, compared to 0.5 s with the simple regression model using the Analyze/StripMiner code on a 128-MHz Pentium III computer. Note also that the bootstrapped values for q^2 and Q^2 (i.e., 0.366 and 0.374) are now almost equal. The similar values for q^2 and Q^2 indicate that there is no bias in the models and that the choices for the hyperparameters σ and λ are at least close to optimal.

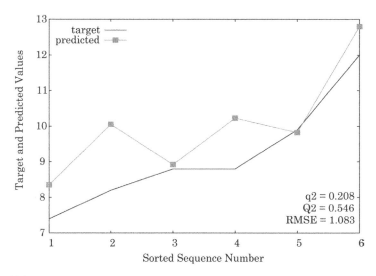

Figure 10.9. Predictions for DDGTS for the last six amino acids from Table 10.4 with direct kernel ridge regression.

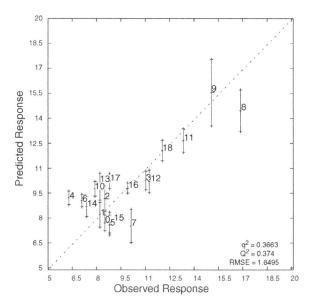

Figure 10.10. Scatterplot for predictions on six test data points for DDGTS with 200 bootstraps with six sample test data points each.

10.7 CASE STUDY #2: PREDICTING THE REGION OF ORIGIN FOR ITALIAN OLIVE OILS

The second case study deals with classifying 572 Italian olive oils by their region of origin, based on eight fatty acid contents (Fig. 10.11). We chose this problem because it is a multiclass problem with nine classes that are not ordinal. By the term *nonordinal* we mean that the class numbers are not hierarchical and do not reflect a natural ordering.

The olive oil data were introduced by Forina and Armanino [37] and extensively analyzed by Zupan and Gasteiger [38]. They can be downloaded from the web site referenced in reference 37. Following reference 38, the data were split into 250 training data and 322 test data, but the split is different from the one used in reference 38.

The data were preprocessed as shown in Fig. 10.8. The response for the nine classes is now coded as {1 ... 9}, and it is Mahalanobis scaled before applying kernel ridge regression. σ is tuned on the training set and assumed a value of 2. The ridge parameter, λ, is 0.07, based on Eq. (10.20). The errors on the test set, after de-scaling, are shown in Fig. 10.12. Figure 10.13 shows the scatterplot for the same data.

In this case, 84% of the classes were correctly predicted. This is significantly better than the 40% prediction rate with a neural network with one output neuron for the classes, as reported in reference 38, but also clearly below the 90% prediction rate with a neural network with nine output neurons and an orthogonal encoding reported in the same reference. In order to improve the prediction results, one could either (a) train nine different kernel ridge models and predict for one-class versus the other eight classes at a time or (b) train for all possible 36 combinations on two class problems and let a voting scheme decide on the final class predictions. While this latter scheme is definitely not as straightforward as training a single neural network with nine orthogonally encoded output neurons, the results are more comparable to the best neural network results.

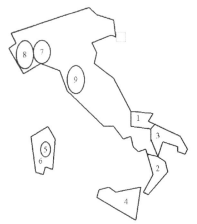

Class	Region	#Samples
1	North Apulia Calabria	25
2	Calabria	56
3	South Apulia	206
4	Sicily	36
5	Inner Sardinia	65
6	Coastal Sardinia	33
7	East Liguria	50
8	West Liguria	50
9	Umbria	51
		572

Figure 10.11. Five hundred and seventy-two Italian olive oil samples by nine regions of origin [37,38].

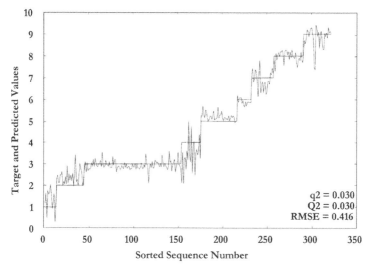

Figure 10.12. Test results for nine olive oil classes on 322 test data points (kernel ridge regression). Steady line: target. Oscillating line: predicted.

Note that there is a near-perfect separation for distinguishing the olive oils from regions in southern Italy from the olive oils from the northern regions. Most of the misses in the prediction in Figs. 10.12 and 10.13 are off by just one class, locating the olive oils that were misclassified close to the actual region of origin. The single-field

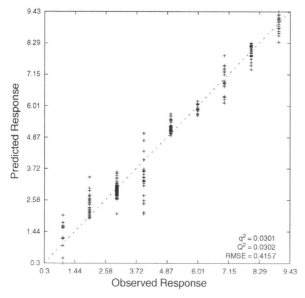

Figure 10.13. Scatterplot for nine olive oil classes on 322 test data points (kernel ridge regression).

encoding for the output class still works reasonably well on this nonordinal classification problem, because the classes were labeled in an almost ordinal fashion. By this we mean that class numbers that are close to each other (e.g., 1, 2, and 3), are also geographically located nearby on the map in Fig. 10.11.

Direct kernel partial least squares (DK-PLS) is a direct kernel implementation form of the PLS algorithm, popular in chemometrics and similar to kernel-PLS first introduced in reference 39. DK-PLS yields an 83% correct classification rate, using the same preprocessing procedure and 12 latent variables [13]. In this case, latent variables are the equivalent of principal components in PCA. The traditional (linear) PLS algorithm yields a 28% correct classification rate. Direct kernel principal component analysis with 12 principal components yields a 54% correct classification rate, while principal component analysis with six principal components results in a 30% correct classification rate. The classification results reported in this section indicate a clear improvement of direct kernel methods over their linear counterpart. The excellent comparison between kernel ridge regression and direct kernel PLS is also a good confidence indicator for the heuristic formula, Eq. (10.20), for selecting the ridge parameter.

Rather than reporting improved results from combining binary classification models, we will illustrate Kohonen's self-organizing map or SOM [4]. Since self-organizing maps already inherently account for nonlinear effects, it is not necessary to apply a direct kernel self-organizing map (DK-SOM). Figure 10.14 shows a 13 × 20 Kohonen map based on 250 training data. Ninety-three percent of the 322 test samples are now correctly classified as shown by the confusion matrix in Table 10.5. The classification performance of the DK-SOM is similar to that of the SOM, but the DK-SOM in this case requires 3 min of training, rather than 6 s of training for the SOM. This is not entirely surprising because the DK-SOM operates on data with 250 features or kernel entries, while the SOM operates on the eight original features. While in this case there seems to be little advantage in applying a DK-SOM, it should be noted that for cases where there are significantly more features than data, the DK-SOM can be significantly faster than the traditional SOM.

An efficient SOM module was incorporated in the Analyze/StripMiner software [31] with a goal of keeping user decisions minimal by incorporating robust default parameter settings. To do so, the SOM is trained in its usual two-stage procedure: an ordering phase and a fine-tuning phase. The weights are trained by competitive learning where the winning neuron and its neighboring neurons in the map are iteratively updated, according to

$$\vec{w}_m^{\text{new}} = (1 - \alpha)\vec{w}_m^{\text{old}} + \alpha\vec{x} \qquad (10.21)$$

where $\vec{x}$ is a pattern vector with m features, α is the learning parameter, and $\vec{w}$ represents the weight vector.

Data patterns are presented at random, and the learning parameter α is linearly reduced from 0.9 to 0.1 during the ordering phase. During this phase, the neighborhood size of the SOM is reduced from six to one on a hexagonal grid in a linear

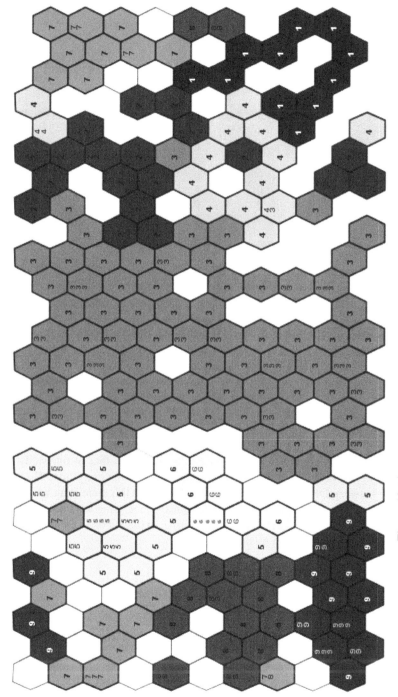

Figure 10.14. SOM for 250 training data points for olive oil region of origin.

TABLE 10.5. Confusion Matrix for 332 Olive Oil Test Data Points for Nine Nonordinal Classes

Region										Total Number of Test Data Points
North Apulia	10	1	1	1	0	0	0	0	0	13
Calabria	0	25	6	0	0	0	0	0	0	31
South Apulia	0	1	108	0	0	0	0	0	0	109
Sicily	1	5	3	13	0	0	0	0	0	22
Inner Sardinia	0	0	0	0	40	1	0	0	0	41
Coastal Sardinia	0	0	0	0	0	16	0	0	0	16
East Liguria	0	0	0	0	1	0	23	1	0	25
West Liguria	0	0	0	0	0	0	0	33	0	33
Umbria	0	0	0	0	0	0	0	0	32	32
										322

fashion. The number of iterations with Eq. (10.24) can be user-specified: 100 times the number of samples is a robust default for the ordering phase. During the fine iteration stage, α is reduced from 0.1 to 0.01 in a linear fashion. The code defaults to 20,000 iterations for the ordering phase and 50,000 iterations in the fine-tuning phase. The map size defaults to a 9×18 hexagonal grid. Following Kohonen [4], the initial weights are random data samples and a supervised Learning Vector Quantization (LVQ) algorithm was implemented in the fine-tuning stage following [4]. The cells in the Kohonen map are colored by applying semi-supervised learning. By this, we mean that the weight vector is augmented by an additional entry for the class, which is called the color. The color code entry is not used in the distance metrics used in the SOM, but is otherwise updated in the same manner as the other weights in the SOM. A second optional cell-coloring scheme implemented in the code is based on a cellular automaton rule [40]. Note also that in our study the data were preprocessed by Mahalanobis scaling each column entry first. The only difference between DK-SOM and SOM is that for DK-SOM, there is an additional preprocessing stage where the data are kernel-transformed using a Gaussian kernel. The Parzen width, σ, for the default Gaussian kernel in the SOM is kept the same as for the kernel ridge regression model.

10.8   CASE STUDY #3: PREDICTING ISCHEMIA FROM MAGNETOCARDIOGRAPHY

10.8.1   Introduction to Magnetocardiography

We describe in this section the use of direct kernel methods and support vector machines for pattern recognition in magnetocardiography (MCG) that measures magnetic fields emitted by the electrophysiological activity of the heart. A

SQUID (or superconducting interference device) measures MCGs in a regular, magnetically unshielded hospital room. The operation of the system is computer-controlled and largely automated. Procedures are applied for electric/magnetic activity localization, heart current reconstruction, and derivation of diagnostic scores. However, the interpretation of MCG records remains a challenge since there are no databases available from which precise rules could be formulated. Hence, there is a need to automate interpretation of MCG measurements to minimize human input for the analysis. In this particular case we are interested in detecting ischemia, which is a loss of conductivity because of damaged cell tissue in the heart and the main cause of heart attacks, the leading cause of death in the United States.

10.8.2 Data Acquisition and Preprocessing

MCG data are acquired at 36 locations above the torso for 90 s using a sampling rate of 1000 Hz leading to 36 individual time series. To eliminate noise components, the complete time series is lowpass-filtered at 20 Hz and averaged using the maximum of the R peak of the cardiac cycle as trigger point (Fig. 10.15). For automatic classification, we used data from a time window within the ST segment [41] of the cardiac cycle in which values for 32 evenly spaced points were interpolated from the measured data. The training data consist of 73 cases that were easy to classify visually by trained experts. The testing was done on a set of 36 cases that included patients whose magnetocardiograms misled or confused trained experts doing visual classification.

We experimented with different preprocessing strategies. Data are preprocessed in this case by first subtracting the bias from each signal; each signal is then wavelet transformed by applying the Daubechies-4 wavelet transform [42]. Finally, there is a horizontal Mahalanobis scaling for each patient record over all the 36 signals combined. The data are then vertically Mahalanobis scaled on each attribute (except for the SOM based methods, where no further vertical scaling was applied).

10.8.3 Predictive Modeling for Binary Classification of Magnetocardiograms

The aim of this application is the automatic pattern recognition and classification for MCG data in order to separate abnormal from normal heart patterns. For unsupervised learning, we used DK-SOMs, because SOMs are often applied for novelty detection and automated clustering. The DK-SOM has a 9×18 hexagonal grid with unwrapped edges. Three kernel-based regression algorithms were used for supervised learning: support vector machines, DK-PLS, and kernel ridge regression (also known as least-squares support vector machines). The Analyze/StripMiner software package was used for this analysis. LibSVM was applied for the SVM model [43]. The parameter values for DK-SOM, SVM, DK-PLS, and LS-SVM were tuned on the training set before testing. The results are similar to the quality of classification achieved by the trained experts and similar for all these methods.

A typical data set for 36 signals that are interpolated to 32 equally spaced points in the analysis window [41] and after Mahalanobis scaling on each of the individual signals is shown in Fig. 10.15. The results for different methods are shown in Table 10.6. Table 10.6 also indicates the number of correctly classified patterns and the number of misses on the negative and the positive cases.

Better results were generally obtained with wavelet-transformed data than with pure time-series data. For wavelet-transformed data, the Daubechies-4 or D4 wavelet transform [42] was chosen, because of the relatively small set of data (32) in each of the interpolated time signals. The agreement between K-PLS as proposed by Rosipal [43], direct kernel PLS or DK-PLS, LibSVM, and LS-SVM is generally excellent, and there are no noticeable differences between these methods on these data. In this case, DK-PLS gave a superior performance, but the differences between kernel-based methods are typically insignificant. After tuning, σ was chosen as 10, a λ of 0.011 was used following Eq. (10.20), and the regularization parameter, C, in LibSVM was set as $1/\lambda$ as suggested in reference 39.

The excellent agreement between the direct kernel methods (DK-PLS and LS-SVM) and the traditional kernel methods (K-PLS and LibSVM) shows the robustness of the direct kernel methods and also indicates that Eq. (10.20) results in a near-optimal choice for the ridge parameter.

Equation (10.20) applies not only to the selection of the ridge parameter, but also to the selection of the regularization parameter, C, in support vector machines, when C is taken as $1/\lambda$. Linear methods such as partial least squares result in an inferior predictive model as compared to the kernel methods. For K-PLS and DK-PLS we chose five latent variables, but the results were not critically dependent on the exact choice of the number of latent variables. We also tried Direct Kernel Principal Component Analysis (DK-PCA), the direct kernel version of K-PCA [3,21–23], but the results were more sensitive to the choice for the number of principal components and were not as good as for the other direct kernel methods.

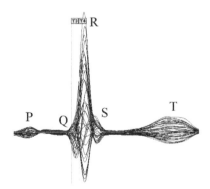

Figure 10.15. Superposition of all traces of the 36-lead MCG. The typical waveforms as seen in ECG are the P wave (P, atrial activation), the Q wave (Q, septal activation), the R peak (R, left ventricular depolarization), the S wave (S, late right ventricular depolarization), and the T wave (T, ventricular repolarization).

TABLE 10.6. RMSE, q^2, Q^2, Number of Correct Patterns and Number of Misses, and Execution Time on 35 Test Data Points for Magnetocardiogram Data

Method	Domain	q^2	Q^2	RMSE	% Correct	Number of Misses	Time (s)	Comments
SVMLib	Time	0.767	0.842	0.852	74	4 + 5	10	$\lambda = 0.011$, $\sigma = 10$
K-PLS	Time	0.779	0.849	0.856	74	4 + 5	6	5 latent vars, $\sigma = 10$
DK-PCA	D4-wavelet	0.783	0.812	0.870	71	7 + 3	5	5 prinicipal components
PLS	D4-wavelet	0.841	0.142	1.146	63	2 + 11	3	5 latent variables
K-PLS	D4-wavelet	0.591	0.694	0.773	80	2 + 5	6	5 latent vars, $\sigma = 10$
DK-PLS	D4-wavelet	0.554	0.662	0.750	83	1 + 5	5	5 latent vars, $\sigma = 10$
SVMLib	D4-wavelet	0.591	0.697	0.775	80	2 + 5	10	$\lambda = 0.011$, $\sigma = 10$
LS-SVM	D4-wavelet	0.590	0.692	0.772	80	2 + 5	0.5	$\lambda = 0.011$, $\sigma = 10$
SOM	D4-wavelet	0.866	1.304	1.060	63	3 + 10	960	9×18 hexagonal grid
DK-SOM	D4-wavelet	0.855	1.011	0.934	71	5 + 5	28	9×18 hex grid, $\sigma = 10$
DK-SOM	D4-wavelet	0.755	0.859	0.861	77	3 + 5	28	18×18 hex grid, $\sigma = 8$

Typical prediction results for the magnetocardiogram data based on wavelet-transformed data and DK-PLS are shown in Fig. 10.16. We can see from this figure that the predictions miss 6 of 36 test cases (1 healthy or negative case and 5 ischemia cases). The missed cases were also difficult for the trained expert to identify, based on a 2-D visual display of the time-varying magnetic field, obtained by proprietary methods.

For medical data, it is often important to be able to make a trade-off between false-negative and false-positive cases, or between sensitivity and specificity (which are different metrics related to false positives and false negatives). In machine-learning methods, such a trade-off can easily be accomplished by changing the threshold for interpreting the classification (e.g., in Fig. 10.16), rather than using the zero as the discrimination level; one could shift the discrimination threshold toward a more desirable level, thereby influencing the false positive/false negative ratio. A summary of all possible outcomes can be displayed in a receiver operator characteristics (ROC) curve as shown in Fig. 10.17 for the above case. The concept of ROC curves originated from the early development of the radar in the 1940s for identifying airplanes and is summarized in reference 44. All points of the ROC curve are possible operating points, and they depend on the chosen threshold value to distinguish ischemia cases from nonischemia cases. A particular point on the ROC curve indicates the fraction of ischemia cases that were correctly identified as such (true positives), and the fraction of healthy cases that were incorrectly identified as ischemia cases (false positives).

Figure 10.18 shows a projection of 73 training data, based on (1) Direct Kernel Principal Component Analysis (DK-PCA) and (2) Direct Kernel PLS (DK-PLS). Diseased cases are shown as filled circles, and the test data are not shown on

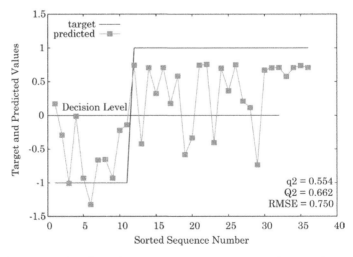

Figure 10.16. Error plot for 35 test cases, based on K-PLS for wavelet-transformed magnetocardiograms.

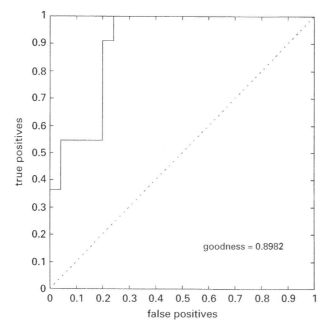

Figure 10.17. ROC curve showing possible trade-offs between false positive and false negatives.

these plots. The training data show a clear separation between cases with and without ischemia.

A typical 9 × 18 self-organizing map on a hexagonal grid in wrap-around mode, based on the direct kernel SOM, is shown in Figure 10.19. The wrap-around mode means that the left and right boundaries (and also the top and bottom boundaries) flow into each other and that the map is an unfolding of a toroidal projection. The dark hexagons indicate diseased cases, while the light hexagons indicate healthy cases. Fully colored hexagons indicate the positions for the training data, while the white and dark-shaded numbers are the pattern identifiers for healthy and diseased test cases. Most misclassifications usually occur on boundary regions in the map. The cells in the map are colored by semisupervised learning; that is, each data vector, containing 36 × 32 or 1152 features, is augmented by an additional field that indicates the color. The color entry in the data vectors are updated in a similar way as for the weight vectors, as indicated by Eq. (10.21), but are not used to calculate the distance metrics for determining the winning cell. The resulting map for a regular SOM implementation is very similar to the corresponding map based on direct kernel DK-SOM. The execution time for generating DK-SOM on a 128-MHz Pentium III computer was 28 s, rather than 960 s required for generating the regular SOM. The kernel transformation caused this significant speedup, because the data dimensionality dropped from the original 1152 descriptive features to 73 after the kernel transformation. The fine-tuning stage for the SOM and DK-SOM

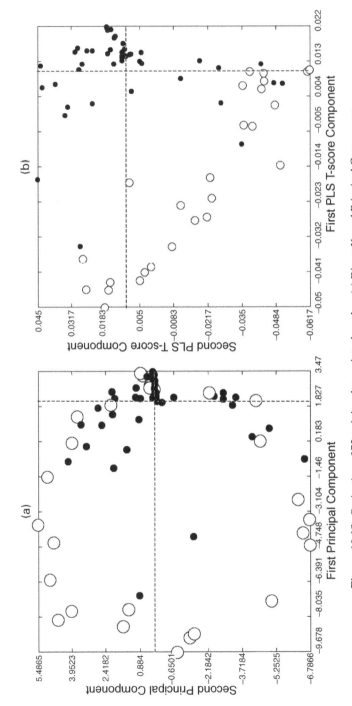

Figure 10.18. Projection of 73 training data points, based on (a) Direct Kernel Principal Analysis (DK-PCA) and (b) Direct Kernel PLS (DK-PLS). Diseased cases are shown as filled circles. Figure 10.18b shows a clearer separation and wider margin between different classes, based on the first two components for DK-PLS as compared to DK-PCA in Fig. 10.18a.

Figure 10.19. Test data displayed on the self-organizing map based on a 9 × 18 DK-SOM in wrap-around mode. Light-colored cells indicate healthy cases, and dark-colored cells diseased cases. Patient identifiers for the test cases are displayed as well.

was done in a supervised mode with learning vector quantization [4], following Kohonen's suggestion for obtaining better classification results. While the results based on SOM and DK-SOM are still excellent, they are not as good as those obtained with the other kernel-based methods (LibSVM, LS-SVM, and K-PLS).

10.8.4 Feature Selection

The results in the previous section were obtained using all 1152 (36×32) descriptors. It would be most informative to the domain expert if we were able to identify where exactly in the time or wavelet signals, and for which of the 36 magnetocardiogram signals that were measured at different positions for each patient, the most important information necessary for good binary classification is located. Such information can be derived from feature selection.

Feature selection—that is, the identification of the most important input parameters for the data vector—can proceed in two different ways: the filtering mode and the wrap-around mode. In the filtering mode, features are eliminated based on a prescribed and generally unsupervised procedure. An example of such a procedure could be the elimination of descriptor columns that contain four-sigma outliers, as is often the case in PLS applications for chemometrics. Depending on the modeling method, it is often common practice to drop the cousin descriptors (descriptors that show more than 95% correlation between each other) and only retain the descriptors that either (1) show the highest correlation with the response variable or (2) have the clearest domain transparency to the domain expert for explaining the model.

The second mode of feature selection is based on the wrap-around mode. It is the aim to retain the most relevant features necessary to have a good predictive model. Often the modeling quality improves with a good feature subset selection. Determining the right subset of features can proceed based on different concepts. The particular choice for the features subset often depends on the modeling method. Feature selection in a wrap-around mode generally proceeds by using a training set and a validation set. In this case, the validation set is used to confirm that the model is not overtrained by selecting a spurious set of descriptors.

Two generally applicable methods for feature selections are based on the use of genetic algorithms and sensitivity analysis. The idea with the genetic algorithm approach is to be able to obtain a good representative subset of features from the training set, showing a good performance on the validation set as well. The concept of sensitivity analysis [12] exploits the saliency of features; that is, once a predictive model has been built, the model is used for the average value of each descriptor, and the descriptors are tweaked, one at a time between a minimum and maximum value. The sensitivity for a descriptor is the change in predicted response. The premise is that when the sensitivity for a descriptor is low, it is probably not an essential descriptor for making a good model. A few of the least sensitive features can be dropped during one iteration step, and the procedure of sensitivity analysis is repeated many times until a near-optimal set of features is retained. Both the genetic algorithm approach and the sensitivity analysis approach are soft-computing methods and require quite a few heuristics and experience. The advantage of both approaches here is that the genetic algorithm and sensitivity approach are general methods that do not depend on the specific modeling method.

10.9 FUSION OF SOFT COMPUTING AND HARD COMPUTING

In this chapter the fusion of soft and hard computing occurred on several levels. On the one hand, scientific data mining applications operate on data that are generated based on computationally intense algorithms. Examples of the hard-computing algorithms are the extensive filtering and preprocessing algorithms in the case of the heart disease example. Other examples of hard computing in scientific data mining occur when the purpose of the soft-computing model is to mimic a more traditional computationally demanding hard-computing problem. This type of fusion of soft and hard computing is labeled in Chapter 1 as the SC=HC type.

In this chapter the fusion of soft and hard computing occurs on a different level as well. The direct kernel modeling methods highlighted in this chapter are in essence neural networks (soft computing). On the other hand, the kernel transform itself, as well as how the weights of support vector machines, kernel ridge regression, and kernel-PLS are determined, are all hard-computing methods. From this point of view, this type of fusion of hard and soft computing is labeled as the HC=SC type in Chapter 1. The optimal choice for the hyperparameters in these models (e.g., the kernel σ, as well as λ for the regularization parameter in ridge regression), is often based on a soft-computing approach as well. By this we mean that the model performance is rather insensitive to the exact (hard) optimal choice and that approximate procedures for determining the hyperparameters suffice for most applications.

10.10 CONCLUSIONS

In this chapter, we provided an introduction to predictive data mining, introduced the standard data mining problem and some basic terminology, and developed direct kernel methods as a way out of the machine learning dilemma and as a true fusion between hard and soft computing. Direct kernel methods were then applied to three different case studies for predictive data mining. In this introduction, a narrow view on data mining was presented. We did not address explicitly how to feed back novel and potentially useful information to the expert. While feature selection is definitely an important step to provide such meaningful feedback, the final discovery and rule formulation phase is often highly application-dependent. The use of innovative visualization methods, such as the so-called pharmaplots in Fig. 10.18, and self-organizing maps is often informative and helpful for the knowledge discovery process.

Three case studies showed the applicability of direct kernel methods to a typical variety of data mining problems. The prediction of binding energies for amino acids is a toy problem, based on real data, that has all the aspects of a typical QSAR problem. This case clearly illustrated the prediction improvement that could be obtained by using nonlinear models and regularization. The olive oil region of origin problem is a nine-class nonordinal classification problem that could be resolved with SOMs and DK-SOMs. The case study for predicting ischemia is a realistic data mining problem where we introduced, applied, and compared several direct kernel methods with other linear methods and other nonlinear kernel methods.

ACKNOWLEDGMENTS

The authors thank Thanakorn Naenna, Robert Bress, and Ramathilagam Bragaspathi for the computational support for this work. The authors also thank Professors Kristin Bennett and Curt Breneman for interesting and stimulating discussions during developing the framework of direct kernel methods for data mining applications.

The authors acknowledge the National Science Foundation support of this work (IIS-9979860) and SBIR Phase I #0232215.

REFERENCES

4. N. Cristianini and J. Shawe-Taylor, *Support Vector Machines and Other Kernel-Based Learning Methods*, Cambridge University Press, Cambridge, MA, 2000.

5. V. Vapnik, *Statistical Learning Theory*, Wiley, New York, 1998.

6. B. Schölkopf and A. J. Smola, *Learning with Kernels*, MIT Press, Cambridge, MA, 2002.

7. T. Kohonen, *Self-Organizing Maps*, 2nd ed., Springer, Berlin, 1997.

8. G. Deboeck and T. Kohonen, eds., *Visual Explorations in Finance with Self-Organizing Maps*, Springer, Berlin, 1998.

9. U. M. Fayyad, G. Piatetsky-Shapiro, P. Smyth, and R. Uthurusamy, eds., *Advances in Knowledge Discovery and Data Mining*, MIT Press, Cambridge, MA, 1996.

10. M. A. Berry and G. Linoff, *Data Mining Techniques for Marketing, Sales, and Customer Support*, Wiley, New York, 1997.

11. J. P. Bigus, *Data Mining with Neural Networks*, McGraw-Hill, New York, 1996.

12. S. M. Weiss and N. Indurkhya, *Predictive Data Mining: A Practical Guide*, Morgan Kaufmann Publishers, San Francisco, 1998.

13. Z. Chen, *Data Mining and Uncertain Reasoning*, Wiley, New York, 2001.

14. C. M. Breneman, K. P. Bennett, M. Embrechts, S. Cramer, M. Song, and J. Bi, "Descriptor Generation, Selection and Model Building in Quantitative Structure-Property Analysis," in *QSAR Developments*, J. N. Crawse, ed., Wiley, New York, 2003, Ch. 11, pp. 203–238.

15. R. H. Kewley and M. J. Embrechts, "Data Strip Mining for the Virtual Design of Pharmaceuticals with Neural Networks," *IEEE Transactions on Neural Networks* **11**, 668–679 (2000).

16. S. Wold, M. Sjöström, and L. Eriksson, "PLS-Regression: A Basic Tool of Chemometrics," *Chemometrics and Intelligent Laboratory Systems* **58**, 109–130 (2001).

17. S. Haykin, *Neural Networks: A Comprehensive Foundation*, 2nd ed., Prentice Hall, Upper Saddle River, NJ, 1999.

18. A. Golbraikh and A. Tropsha, "Beware of q^2!" *Journal of Molecular Graphics and Modelling* **20**, 269–276 (2002).

19. R. A. Johnson and D. W. Wichern, *Applied Multivariate Statistical Analysis*, 2nd ed., Prentice Hall, Upper Saddle River, NJ, 2000.

20. F. M. Ham and I. Kostanic, *Principles of Neurocomputing for Science & Engineering*, McGraw-Hill, New York, 2001.

21. V. Cherkassky and F. Mulier, *Learning from Data: Concepts, Theory, and Methods*, Wiley, New York, 1998.

22. A. E. Hoerl and R. W. Kennard, "Ridge Regression: Biased Estimation for Non-orthogonal Problems," *Technometrics* **12**, 69–82 (1970).

23. J. Principe, N. R. Euliano, and W. C. Lefebre, *Neural and Adaptive Systems: Fundamentals through Simulations*, Wiley, New York, 2000.

24. B. Schölkopf, A. Smola, and K.-R. Müller, "Nonlinear Component Analysis as a Kernel Eigenvalue Problem," *Neural Computation* **10**, 1299–1319 (1998).

25. W. Wu, D. L. Massarat, and S. de Jong, "The Kernel PCA Algorithm for Wide Data. Part I: Theory and Algorithms," *Chemometrics and Intelligent Laboratory Systems* **36**, 165–172 (1997).

26. W. Wu, D. L. Massarat, and S. de Jong, "The Kernel PCA Algorithm for Wide Data. Part II: Fast Cross-Validation and Application in Classification of NIR Data," *Chemometrics and Intelligent Laboratory Systems* **37**, 271–280 (1997).

27. G. Fung and O. L. Mangasarian, "Proximal Support Vector Machine Classifiers," *Proceedings of the 7th ACM SIGKDD International Conference on Knowledge Discovery and Data Mining*, San Francisco, CA, Aug. 2001, pp. 786–886.

28. T. Evgeniou, M. Pontil, and T. Poggio, "Statistical Learning Theory: A Primer," *International Journal of Computer Vision* **38**, 9–13 (2000).

29. T. Evgeniou, M. Pontil, and T. Poggio, "Regularization Networks and Support Vector Machines," *Advances in Computational Mathematics* **13**, 1–50 (2000).

30. T. Poggio and S. Smale, "The Mathematics of Learning: Dealing with Data," *Notices of the AMS* **50**, 537–544 (2003).

31. J. A. K. Suykens and J. Vandewalle, "Least-Squares Support Vector Machine Classifiers," *Neural Processing Letters* **9**, 293–300 (1999).

32. J. A. K. Suykens, T. Van Gestel, J. De Brabanter, B. De Moor, and J. Vandewalle, *Least Squares Support Vector Machines*, World Scientific Publishing Company, Singapore, 2003.

33. I. C. F. Ipsen and C. D. Meyer, "The Idea Behind Krylov Methods," *American Mathematical Monthly* **105**, 889–899 (1998).

34. The *Analyze/StripMiner* code is available on request for academic use, or can be downloaded from <http://www.drugmining.com>.

35. M. F. Møller, "A Scaled Conjugate Gradient Algorithm for Fast Supervised Learning," *Neural Networks* **6**, 525–534 (1993).

36. S. S. Keerthi and S. K. Shevade, "SMO Algorithm for Least Squares SVM Formulations," *Neural Computation* **15**, 487–507 (2003).

37. A. N. Tikhonov "On Solving Incorrectly Posed Problems and Method of Regularization," *Doklady Akademii Nauk USSR* **151**, 501–504 (1963).

38. A. N. Tikhonov and V. Y. Arsenin, *Solutions of Ill-Posed Problems*, W. H. Winston, Washington, DC, 1977.

39. K. P. Bennett and M. J. Embrechts, "An Optimization Perspective on Kernel Partial Least Squares Regression," in J. A. K. Suykens et al., eds., *Advances in Learning Theory: Methods, Models and Applications*, NATO-ASI Series in Computer and System Sciences, IOS Press, Amsterdam, The Netherlands, 2003, pp. 227–246.

40. M. Forina and C. Armanino, "Eigenvector Projection and Simplified Non-linear Mapping of Fatty Acid Content of Italian Olive Oils," *Annali di Chimica (Rome)* **72**, 127–155 (1981).

41. J. Zupan and J. Gasteiger, *Neural Networks in Chemistry and Drug Design*, Wiley-VCH, Weinheim, Germany, 1999.

42. R. Rosipal and L. J. Trejo, "Kernel Partial Least Squares Regression in Reproducing Kernel Hilbert Spaces," *Journal of Machine Learning Research* **2**, 97–128 (2001).

43. S. Wolfram, *A New Kind of Science*, Wolfram Media, Inc., Champaign, IL, 2002.

44. M. S. Thaler, *The Only EKG Book You'll Ever Need*, 3rd ed., Lippincott Williams & Wilkins, New York, 1999.

45. I. Daubechies, *Ten Lectures on Wavelets*, Siam, Philadelphia, 1992.

46. C.-C. Chang and C.-J. Lin, *LIBSVM: A library for Support Vector Machines*, 2001, Software available at <http://www.csie.ntu.edu.tw/~cjlin/libsvm>.

47. J. A. Swets, R. M. Dawes, and J. Monahan, "Better Decisions Through Science," *Scientific American* **286**(10), 82–87 (2000).

EDITOR'S INTRODUCTION TO CHAPTER 11

The use of Internet or World Wide Web (WWW) has been growing drastically since its introduction in the early 1990s. In the beginning of 1994, the total number of servers was about 2 million, while at the beginning of 2004, there were 200 million servers around the world [1]. These rough numbers correspond to the number of IP (Internet Protocol) addresses that have been assigned a name. On the other hand, the projected number of global Internet users for 2004 is 945 million by the Computer Industry Almanac Inc.

Montgomery and Faloutsos point out in their noteworthy study on browsing trends and patterns [2] that "Although Internet usage has increased exponentially since the World Wide Web's inception, many browsing behaviors have remained surprisingly stable." They found out, for example, that the growth in the usage of Internet is mostly due to more frequent, not necessarily any longer, browsing sessions.

In parallel with the huge growth of Internet usage, also Web usage mining has become a lively and important field of research and development. When an Internet server receives a request from some user, it creates a new transaction entry in its log files. Those log records include three types of files [3]:

1. Access log file
2. Referrer log file
3. Agent log file

Computationally Intelligent Hybrid Systems. Edited by Seppo J. Ovaska
ISBN 0-471-47668-4   © 2005 the Institute of Electrical and Electronics Engineers, Inc.

Web usage mining extracts users' browsing trends and patterns by applying data mining techniques to those lengthy log records. The key motivations behind Web usage mining are usually related to

- Optimizing the capacity of server hardware and the used network connection
- Refining the logical structure of Web site and providing more individualized services
- Determining effective presentation schemes for offered products or services
- Construction of user profiles by combining users' navigation paths with other data features—for example, page viewing time and page content
- Business intelligence that could be applied to manage activities related to e-business, e-services, and e-education

Chapter 11 of the present book, "World Wide Web Usage Mining," is authored by Ajith Abraham. He presents multistage Web usage mining frameworks integrating a few clustering and function approximation algorithms. Preclustering of the filtered access log data is suggested when developing robust methods to predict the dynamical trends of Web usage. The clustering phase involves the task of dividing data elements into homogenous clusters; items in the same cluster are as similar as possible, while items in different clusters are greatly dissimilar. To demonstrate the performance of proposed frameworks, Web access log data of one Australian university was used for evaluative experiments. Those log records contain formatted information from a period of six months in 2002. The empirical results are graphically illustrated, and their practical meaning is discussed in detail.

This particular chapter is not only on the fusion of soft-computing (SC) and hard-computing (HC) methodologies between different functional layers, but also on the fusion of individual soft computing paradigms. The applied categories of the fusion of SC and HC are straightforward cascades of soft-computing and hard-computing elements.

Cleaning and preprocessing of access log data is done by pure hard-computing methods. For clustering, Abraham uses three alternative algorithms: the self-organizing map (SOM), evolutionary-fuzzy clustering, and ant colony optimization. Of those techniques, the ant colony optimization is obviously on the borderline between soft computing and hard computing. Furthermore, neural networks, linear genetic programming, and fuzzy inference system are used for function approximation—that is, prediction of hourly and daily Web usage trends. All three soft-computing methods perform well in trend prediction. It is observable from Abraham's empirical results that the root-mean-square errors of hourly and daily predictions are highly similar. Thus, the prediction time frame is not any problematic issue.

The presently available access log information does not make it possible to distinguish between different users sharing the same host or one proxy server. Simple methods, such as cookies or user registration, would naturally make the identification of each user possible. However, those methods raise privacy concerns among many people; therefore, their usage is not generally preferred [3]. Hence, in addition to the development of more advanced data mining techniques, also the development of "friendly" user identification schemes is needed to be able to enhance the results of Web usage mining. Such explicit identification methods together with computationally intelligent hybrid systems would provide a sound basis for the development of future Web usage mining tools.

REFERENCES

1. Internet Software Consortium, "Internet Domain Survey, Jan. 2003," WWW page, 2003. Available from < http://www.isc.org/ds/WWW-200301/index.html > .

2. A. L. Montgomery and C. Faloutsos, "Identifying Web Browsing Trends and Patterns," *Computer* **34**, 94–95 (July 2001).

3. F. Zhang and H.-Y. Chang, "Research and Development in Web Usage Mining System— Key Issues and Proposed Solutions: A Survey," *Proceedings of the IEEE International Conference on Machine Learning and Cybernetics*, Beijing, China, Nov. 2002, pp. 986–990.

CHAPTER 11

WORLD WIDE WEB USAGE MINING

AJITH ABRAHAM

Oklahoma State University, Tulsa, Oklahoma

11.1 INTRODUCTION

The World Wide Web (WWW) continues to grow at an amazing rate as an information gateway and as a medium for conducting business. Web mining is the extraction of interesting and useful knowledge and implicit information from artifacts or activity related to the WWW. Based on several research studies, we can broadly classify Web mining into three domains: content, structure, and usage mining [1–3]. Web content mining is the process of extracting knowledge from the content of the actual Web documents (text content, multimedia, etc.). Web structure mining is targeting useful knowledge from the Web structure, hyperlink references, and so on. Web usage mining attempts to discover useful knowledge from the secondary data obtained from the interactions of the users with the Web. Web usage mining has become very critical for effective Web site management, creating adaptive Web sites, business and support services, personalization, and network traffic flow analysis.

Web servers record and accumulate data about user interactions whenever requests for resources are received. Analyzing the Web access logs can help understand the user behavior and the Web structure. From the business and applications point of view, knowledge obtained from the Web usage patterns could be directly applied to efficiently manage activities related to e-business, e-services, and e-education. Accurate Web usage information could help to attract new customers, retain current customers, improve cross-marketing/sales, improve effectiveness of promotional campaigns, improve tracking leaving customers, and find the most effective logical structure for their Web space. User profiles could be built by combining users' navigation paths with other data features, such as page viewing time, hyperlink structure, and page content [4]. What makes the discovered knowledge interesting had been addressed by several works. Results previously known are very often considered as not interesting. Therefore, the key concept to make the

Computationally Intelligent Hybrid Systems. Edited by Seppo J. Ovaska
ISBN 0-471-47668-4 © 2005 the Institute of Electrical and Electronics Engineers, Inc.

discovered knowledge interesting will be its novelty or unexpected appearance. A typical Web log format is depicted in Fig. 11.1. Whenever a visitor accesses the server, it leaves, for example, the IP address, authenticated user ID, time/date, request mode, status, bytes, referrer, and agent. The available data fields are specified by the HTTP protocol. There are several commercial software packages that could provide Web usage statistics [5]. These statistics could be useful for Web administrators to get a sense of the actual load on the server. For small Web servers, the usage statistics provided by conventional Web site trackers may be adequate to analyze the usage patterns and trends. However, as the size and complexity of the data increases, the statistics provided by existing Web log file analysis tools alone may prove inadequate, and more knowledge mining and intelligent information processing will be necessary [6–8].

A generic Web usage-mining framework is depicted in Fig. 11.2. In the case of Web mining, data could be collected at the server level, client level, or proxy level or could use some consolidated data. These data could differ in terms of content and the way it is collected. The usage data collected at different sources represent the navigation patterns of different segments of the overall Web traffic, ranging from single-user, single-site browsing behavior to multiuser, multisite access patterns. Web server log does not accurately contain sufficient information for inferring the behavior at the client side as they relate to the pages served by the Web server. The raw Web log data after preprocessing and cleaning could be used for pattern discovery, pattern analysis, Web usage statistics, and generating association/sequential rules. Much work has been performed on extracting various pattern information from Web logs, and the applications of the discovered knowledge range from improving the design and structure of a web site to enabling business organizations to function more efficiently [9–13].

Jespersen et al. [8] proposed a hybrid approach for analyzing the visitor click sequences. A combination of Hypertext Probabilistic Grammar (HPG) and click fact table approach is used to mine Web logs, which could be also used for general sequence mining tasks. In HPG, a nonterminal symbol corresponds to a Web page and a production rule corresponds to a hypertext link. Mobasher et al. [14] proposed the Web personalization system that consists of (a) off-line tasks related to the mining of usage data and (b) on-line process of automatic Web page customization based on the knowledge discovered. LOGSOM, proposed by Smith and Ng [15], utilizes self-organizing map to organize Web pages into a two-dimensional map based solely on the users' navigation behavior, rather than the content of the Web pages. LumberJack proposed by Chi et al. [16] builds up user profiles by combining both user session clustering and traditional statistical traffic analysis using K-means algorithm. Joshi et al. [17] used a relational on-line analytical processing approach for creating a Web log warehouse using access logs and mined logs (association rules and clusters). A comprehensive overview of Web usage mining research is found in references 2 and 8.

We present a hybrid Web usage-mining framework using soft-computing and hard-computing techniques. A summary of the different methodologies used is illustrated in Fig. 11.3. Data preprocessing involves mundane tasks such as merging multiple server logs into a central location and parsing the log into data

```
136.142.22.177 - - [12/Nov/2002:02:30:09 -0600] "GET /~cs4323/lect11.html HTTP/1.1" 304 -
136.142.22.177 - - [12/Nov/2002:02:30:15 -0600] "GET /~cs4323/lect12.html HTTP/1.1" 304 -
138.238.190.5 - - [12/Nov/2002:02:30:36 -0600] "GET /~dpravee/msrit.html HTTP/1.0" 404 288
138.238.190.5 - - [12/Nov/2002:02:30:36 -0600] "GET /~dpravee/msrit.html HTTP/1.0" 404 288
139.78.98.195 - - [12/Nov/2002:02:30:43 -0600] "GET / HTTP/1.1" 200 6894
139.78.98.195 - - [12/Nov/2002:02:30:43 -0600] "GET /graphics/currentbanner.jpg HTTP/1.1" 200 17581
139.78.98.195 - - [12/Nov/2002:02:30:43 -0600] "GET /graphics/topleftcorner.gif HTTP/1.1" 200 671
139.78.98.195 - - [12/Nov/2002:02:30:43 -0600] "GET /graphics/toprightcorner.gif HTTP/1.1" 200 674
139.78.98.195 - - [12/Nov/2002:02:30:43 -0600] "GET /graphics/ms222.gif HTTP/1.1" 200 14432
139.78.98.195 - - [12/Nov/2002:02:30:43 -0600] "GET /graphics/arrow.gif HTTP/1.1" 200 70
139.78.98.195 - - [12/Nov/2002:02:30:55 -0600] "GET /facstaff/index.html HTTP/1.1" 200 7768
```

Figure 11.1. Sample entries from a Web server access log.

369

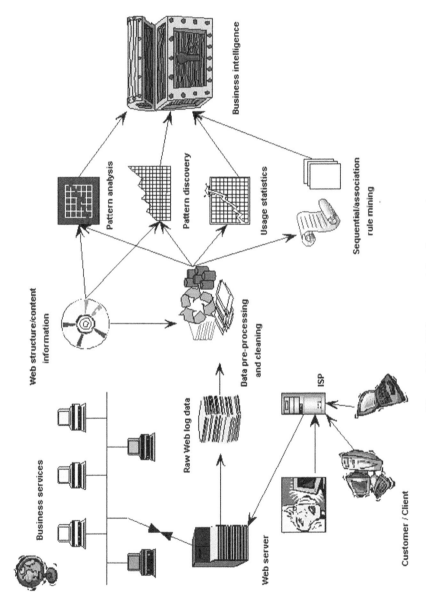

Figure 11.2. Web usage mining framework.

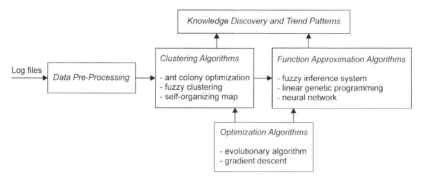

Figure 11.3. Intelligent Web mining framework.

fields followed by data cleaning. Graphic file requests, agent/spider crawling, and so on, could be easily removed by only looking for HTML file requests. Normalization of URLs is often required to make the requests consistent. For example, requests for `http://www.okstate.edu` and `http://www.okstate.edu/index.html` are both for the same file. All these tasks could be achieved by conventional hard-computing techniques that involve text processing, string matching, association rules, simple statistical measures, and so on.

Our preliminary research indicated that clustering of the Web data improves the trend analysis [5]. Clustering of the log data helps to segregate similar visitors, and the function approximation algorithm takes care of analyzing the visitor patterns and developing some trends. We started this research using a simple architecture consisting of a preprocessing block followed by a self-organizing map (clustering) and a neural network (function approximation). To improve the performance, we further investigated various hybrid combinations of soft-computing and hard-computing paradigms to cluster similar visitors based on the domain of origin, number of pages requested, time of access, and so on. For data clustering, we used self-organizing maps, the evolutionary fuzzy clustering algorithm, and the ant colony optimization (ACO) algorithm. The clustered data are then used to analyze the trends using (a) several function approximation algorithms like neural networks, (b) the Takagi–Sugeno fuzzy inference system (TSFIS) trained using neural network learning [19], and (c) linear genetic programming. Table 11.1 illustrates the different hybrid combinations of clustering and function approximation algorithms, which will be presented in this chapter.

To demonstrate the efficiency of the proposed frameworks, Web access log data at the Monash University's Web site [20] were used for experimentations. The university's central Web server receives over 7 million hits in a week; therefore, it is a challenge to find and extract hidden usage pattern information. Due to the enormous traffic volume and chaotic visitor access behavior, the prediction of the user access patterns becomes difficult and complex.

We used the Web log data from January 1, 2002 to July 7, 2002. Selecting useful data (contributing variables) is an important task in the data preprocessing block.

TABLE 11.1. Hybrid Combinations of Clustering and Function Approximation Algorithms

Preprocessing	Clustering Algorithm	Function Approximation Algorithm
Hard-computing techniques: text processing, string matching, association rules, simple statistical measures, etc.	Self-organizing map (SOM)	Neural network (NN) Linear genetic programming (LGP) Takagi–Sugeno fuzzy inference system (TSFIS)
	Fuzzy clustering method (FCM) optimized using evolutionary algorithm	Fuzzy inference system optimized using evolutionary algorithm (*i-Miner*)
	Ant colony optimization (ACO)	Linear genetic programming (LGP)

After some preliminary analysis, we selected the statistical data comprising of domain byte requests, hourly page requests, and daily page requests as focus of the cluster models for finding Web users' usage patterns. The most recently accessed data were indexed higher, while the least recently accessed data were placed at the bottom. In Section 11.2, we present some fundamental concepts of clustering algorithms and the different soft-computing paradigms used for experiments. Various clustering results are depicted in Section 11.2 followed by the usage trend analysis in Section 11.3. The results are graphically illustrated, and the practical significance is discussed in detail. Empirical results clearly show that the proposed Web usage-mining framework is efficient.

11.2 DAILY AND HOURLY WEB USAGE CLUSTERING

11.2.1 Ant Colony Optimization

It is well known that social insects like ants, bees, termites, and wasps exhibit a collective problem-solving ability [21,22]. Several ant species are capable of selecting the shortest path, among a set of alternative pathways, from their nest to a food source. Taking advantage of this ant-based optimization, recently such algorithms have been used for to clustering data [7,23]. In several species of ants, workers have been reported to sort their larvae or form piles of corpses (cemeteries) to clean up their nests. If sufficiently large parts of corpses are randomly distributed in space at the beginning of the experiment, the workers form cemetery clusters within a few hours, following a behavior similar to segregation. If the experimental arena is not sufficiently large, or if it contains spatial heterogeneities, the clusters will be formed along the edges of the arena or, more generally, following the heterogeneities. The basic mechanism underlying this type of aggregation phenomenon is an attraction between dead items mediated by the ant workers: Small clusters of items grow by attracting workers to deposit more items. It is this positive and autocatalytic feedback that leads to the formation of larger and larger clusters. In this case, it is therefore the distribution of the clusters in the environment that plays the role of a stigmergic variable. Deneubourg et al. [22] have proposed a clustering approach with the general idea of picking up isolated items and dropping at some other location where more items of that type are present.

Exploration of regions without any type of object clusters is generally counter-productive and time-consuming. Ramos et al. [23] proposed the ACLUSTER algorithm in which bioinspired spatial transition probabilities are incorporated into the system, avoiding randomly moving agents, which encourage the distributed algorithm to explore regions manifestly without interest. Since these types of transition probabilities depend on the spatial distribution of pheromone across the environment, the behavior reproduced is also a stigmergic one. Moreover, the strategy allows guiding ants to find clusters of objects in an adaptive way as the use of embodied short-term memories is avoided. Ants are not allowed to have any memory, and the individual's spatial knowledge is restricted to local information about the whole colony pheromone density.

In order to model the behavior of ants associated with different tasks, such as dropping and picking up objects, a combination of different response thresholds has been suggested. There are two major factors that should influence any local action taken by the ant-like agent: the number of objects in the neighborhood and their similarity (including the hypothetical object carried by one ant). Lumer and Faieta [24] use an average similarity, mixing distances between objects with their number and then incorporating this number simultaneously into a response threshold function like the one of Deneubourg's [22]. ACLUSTER uses combinations of two independent response threshold functions, each associated with a different environmental factor (or stimuli intensity)—that is, the number of objects in the area, along with their similarity. The computation of average similarities is avoided in the ACLUSTER algorithm, since this strategy could be blind to the number of objects present in one specific neighborhood. Technical details of the ACLUSTER algorithm could be obtained from reference 23.

Experimental Setup and Clustering Results. The raw data from the log files are cleaned and preprocessed. Preprocessing consists of converting the text, image, scripts, and other multimedia files that are useful for the mining process. Data cleaning involves parsing the log into data fields and removing all multimedia file requests. Using the IP address, agent, and server side click streams, users and server sessions are further identified. By analyzing the server session files, several statistical measures could be further obtained—for example, frequency of visitors, page views, viewing time, and so on. Most of the commercially available Web site trackers are able to provide such information. Using the preprocessed and cleaned statistical and text data, we used the ACLUSTER algorithm to identify Web access patterns (data clusters). The algorithm was run twice (for $t = 1$ to

1×10^6) in order to check if the results were similar. The classification space is always two-dimensional, nonparametric, and toroidal. Experiment results for the daily and hourly clustering of Web traffic data are presented in Figs. 11.4 and 11.5. The snapshots represent the spatial distribution of daily Web traffic data (25×25 nonparametric toroidal grid) and hourly Web traffic data (45×45 nonparametric toroidal grid) at several time steps (i.e., 1, 500, 1,000,000). At $t = 1$, data items are randomly allocated into the grid. From the figures, it could be observed that as time evolves, several homogeneous clusters emerge due to the ant colony action. Type 1 probability function was used with $k_1 = 0.1$ and $k_2 = 0.3$. The probability function determines the chance to pick up or drop a data point by a randomly moving ant. Depending on the value of k_1 and k_2 (threshold constants), the similar data points are picked up or dropped. We used 14 ants for daily Web traffic data and 48 ants for hourly Web traffic data, respectively.

11.2.2 Fuzzy Clustering Algorithm

One of the widely used clustering methods is the fuzzy c-means (FCM) algorithm developed by Bezdek [25]. FCM partitions a collection of n vectors, x_i, $i = 1$, $2, \ldots, n$, into c fuzzy groups and finds a cluster center in each group such that a

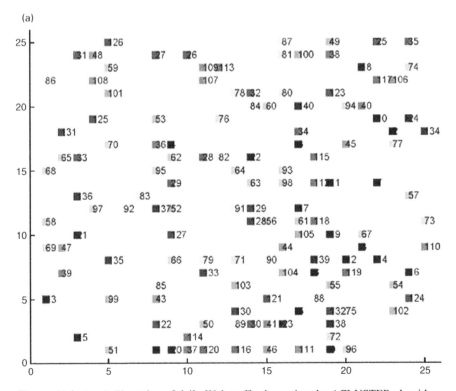

Figure 11.4. (a–c) Clustering of daily Web traffic data using the ACLUSTER algorithm.

(b)

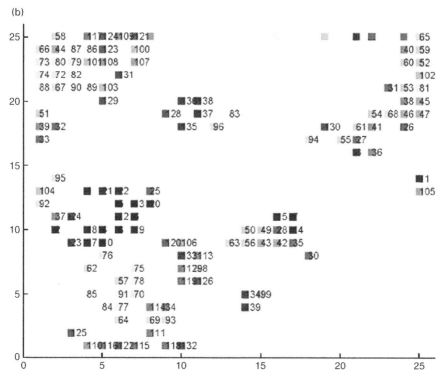

Figure 11.4. *Continued.*

cost function of dissimilarity measure is minimized. This criterion is usually to optimize an objective function that acts as a performance index of clustering. The end
result of fuzzy clustering can be expressed by a partition matrix U such that

$$U = [u_{ij}] \quad \text{with } i = 1, \ldots, c \quad \text{and} \quad j = 1, \ldots, n \quad (11.1)$$

where u_{ij} is a numerical value between $[0, 1]$ and expresses the degree to which the
element x_j belongs to the ith cluster. To accommodate the introduction of fuzzy partitioning, the membership matrix U is allowed to have elements with values between
0 and 1. The FCM objective function takes the form

$$J(U, c_1, \ldots, c_c) \sum_{i=1}^{c} J_i = \sum_{i=1}^{c} \sum_{j=1}^{n} u_{ij}^m d_{ij}^2 \quad (11.2)$$

where c_i is the cluster center of fuzzy group i; $d_{ij} = \|c_i - x_j\|$ is the Euclidian distance
between ith cluster center and jth data point; and m is called the exponential weight,
which influences the degree of fuzziness of the membership (partition) matrix.
Usually a number of cluster centers are randomly initialized, and the FCM algorithm

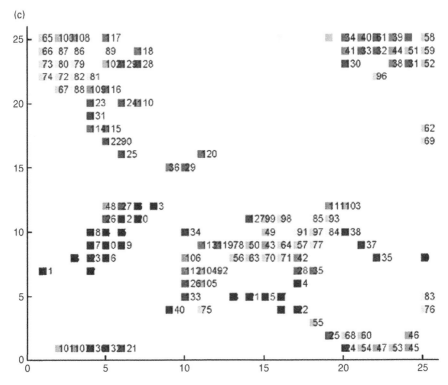

Figure 11.4. *Continued.*

provides an iterative approach to approximate the minimum of the objective function starting from a given position and leads to any of its local minima [25]. No guarantee ensures that FCM converges to an optimum solution (can be trapped by local minima in the process of optimizing the clustering criterion). The performance is very sensitive to initialization of the cluster centers. An evolutionary algorithm is used to decide the optimal number of clusters and their cluster centers to give the best performance in the next stage—that is, trend prediction. The algorithm is initialized by constraining the initial values to be within the space defined by the vectors to be clustered. A very similar approach is proposed in reference 26. The various parameter settings of the evolutionary fuzzy clustering algorithm are given in Table 11.2. The evolutionary–FCM approach created seven data clusters (Fig. 11.6) for the hourly traffic according to the input features compared to nine data clusters (Fig. 11.7) for the daily traffic. Cluster centers are marked in the respective figures.

11.2.3   Self-Organizing Map

The self-organizing map (SOM) is an algorithm used to visualize and interpret large high-dimensional data sets. The map consists of a regular grid of processing units,

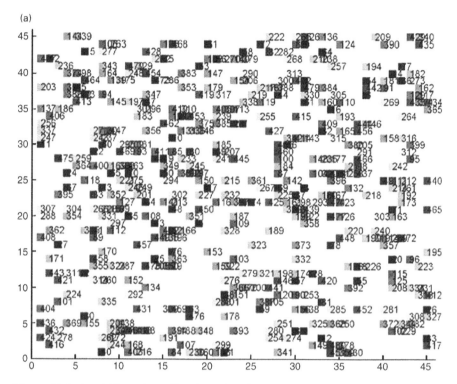

Figure 11.5. (a–c) Clustering of hourly Web traffic data using the ACLUSTER algorithm.

namely, neurons. A model of some multidimensional observation, eventually a vector consisting of features, is associated with each unit. The map attempts to represent all the available observations with optimal accuracy using a restricted set of models. At the same time, the models become ordered on the grid so that similar models are close to each other and dissimilar models are far from each other. We compared the normalized distortion and quantization error to decide the various parameter settings of the SOM algorithm and finally decided the parameter setting, which could minimize both the error measures. The obtained two-dimensional cluster map showing the day/hour of traffic, volume of requests/pages, and index of records according to the country of origin (domain) is shown in Figs. 11.8 and 11.9.

11.2.4 Analysis of Web Data Clusters

Useful knowledge could be discovered from the clusters developed by ACO, FCM, and SOM algorithms. As illustrated in Figs. 11.10, 11.11, and 11.12, many interesting access behaviors could be obtained from the different clusters. Self-organizing map created seven data clusters (daily traffic volume) and four data clusters (hourly traffic volume), respectively. As evident, FCM approach resulted in the

(b)

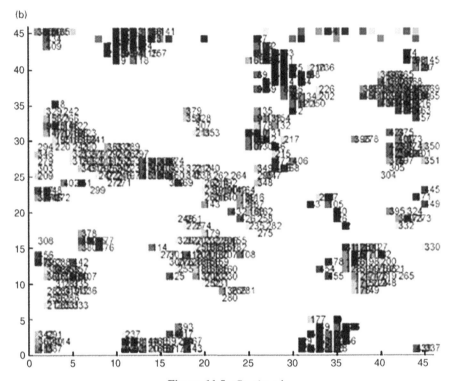

Figure 11.5. *Continued.*

formation of additional data clusters. Figure 11.10 depicts the hourly visitor information according to domain names from an FCM cluster. The sample cluster represented mainly the domestic domains and a few others from the South-/ Far-East Asia according to the hour of access. Figure 11.11 illustrates the volume of visitors in each FCM cluster according to the day of access. It is interesting to note that cluster 6 accounted for 82% of the traffic volume.

Since majority of the visitors originated from Australia, there was an SOM cluster to account for the various Australian-based domains. Depending on the hour of access, certain SOM clusters accounted for the peak hour traffic (09:00–18:00 hrs) and some clusters represented the off-peak traffic (Fig. 11.12). The same trend was evident in the daily traffic. While five clusters took care of the weekday traffic, two clusters accounted for the weekend traffic. The visitors were clustered based on the country of origin (domain) and the volume of requests.

11.3 DAILY AND HOURLY WEB USAGE ANALYSIS

Different soft-computing (SC) paradigms were used to analyze the hourly and daily visitor access patterns. SC provides an attractive framework by unifying the individual paradigms and even by incorporating other complementary methods.

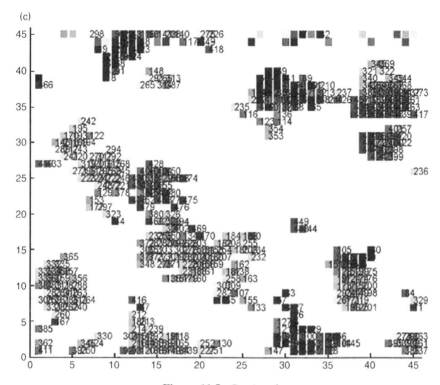

Figure 11.5. *Continued.*

11.3.1 Linear Genetic Programming

Linear genetic programming is a variant of the genetic programming (GP) technique that acts on linear genomes [27]. Its main characteristic in comparison to tree-based GP is in that the evolvable units are not expressions of a functional programming language (like LISP), but programs of an imperative language (like C/C++) instead. An alternate approach is to evolve a computer program at the machine

TABLE 11.2. Parameter Settings of *i-Miner*

Population size	30
Maximum number of generations	35
Number of cluster centers	4–12
Rule antecedent membership functions	Three Gaussian membership functions
Rule consequent parameters	Linear parameters
Gradient descent learning	Ten epochs
	Learning parameter (0.05–0.20)
Rank-based selection	0.50
Elitism	5%
Starting mutation rate	0.50

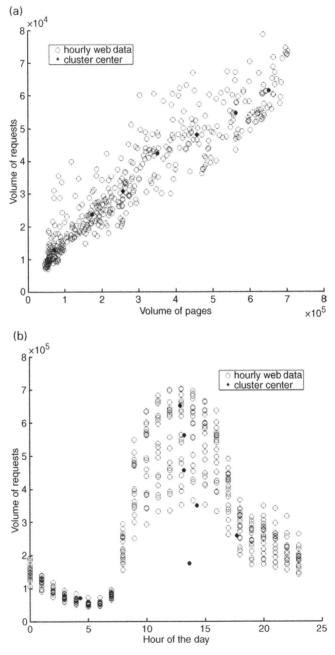

Figure 11.6. FCM clustering: (**a**) Hourly volume of requests versus volume of pages accessed and (**b**) volume of requests according to the hour of the day.

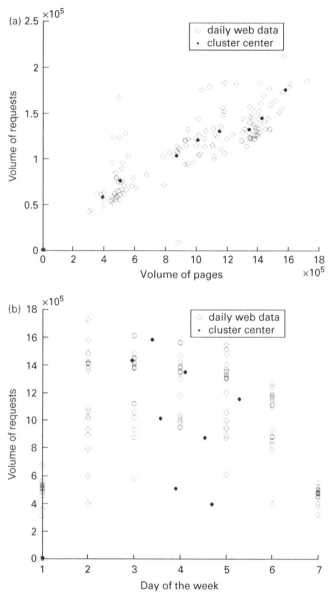

Figure 11.7. FCM clustering: (**a**) Daily volume of requests versus volume of pages accessed and (**b**) volume of requests according to the day of the week.

code level, using lower-level representations for the individuals. When compared to conventional genetic algorithms, this can tremendously hasten up the evolution processes, no matter how an individual is initially represented. The basic unit of evolution here is a native machine code instruction that runs on the floating-point

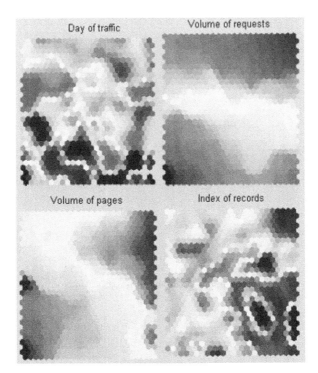

Figure 11.8. Developed SOM clusters showing the different input variables (title of each map) for daily Web traffic.

processor unit (FPU). Since different instructions may have different sizes, here instructions are clubbed up together to form instruction blocks of 32 bits each. The instruction blocks hold one or more native machine code instructions, depending on the sizes of the instructions. A crossover point can occur only between instructions and is prohibited from occurring within an instruction. However, the mutation operation does not have any such restriction.

11.3.2 Fuzzy Inference Systems

Several adaptation techniques have been investigated to optimize fuzzy inference systems (FIS). Neural network learning algorithms have been used to determine the parameters of fuzzy inference system. Such models are often called integrated neuro-fuzzy models. In an integrated neuro-fuzzy model, there is no guarantee that the neural network learning algorithm converges and the tuning of fuzzy inference system will be successful. Success of evolutionary search procedures for optimization of fuzzy inference systems is well-proven and established in many application areas [28]. We used the intelligent-miner (*i-Miner*) to optimize the concurrent architecture of a fuzzy clustering algorithm (to discover data clusters)

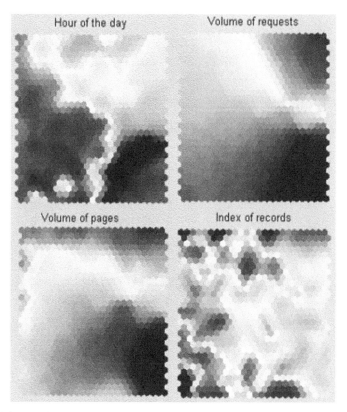

Figure 11.9. Developed SOM clusters showing the different input variables (title of each map) for hourly Web traffic.

and a fuzzy inference system to analyze the trends. The hybrid framework optimizes a fuzzy clustering algorithm using an evolutionary algorithm, and it optimizes a Takagi–Sugeno fuzzy inference system using a combination of evolutionary algorithm and neural network learning. In the *i-Miner* framework, the developed clusters of data are fed to a Takagi–Sugeno fuzzy inference system to analyze the trend patterns. The *if-then* rule structures are learned using an iterative learning procedure [29] by an evolutionary algorithm, and the rule parameters (consequent and antecedent) are fine-tuned using a backpropagation algorithm. The hierarchical architecture of the *i-Miner* is depicted in Fig. 11.13. The arrow direction depicts the speed of the evolutionary search [28]. The optimization of clustering algorithm progresses at a faster time scale in an environment determined by the inference method and the problem environment. For every fuzzy inference system, there exist a global search of neural network learning algorithm parameters, parameters of fuzzy operators, *if-then* rules, and membership functions in an environment decided by the problem. The evolution of the fuzzy inference system will evolve at the slowest time scale while the evolution of the quantity and type of membership functions

384

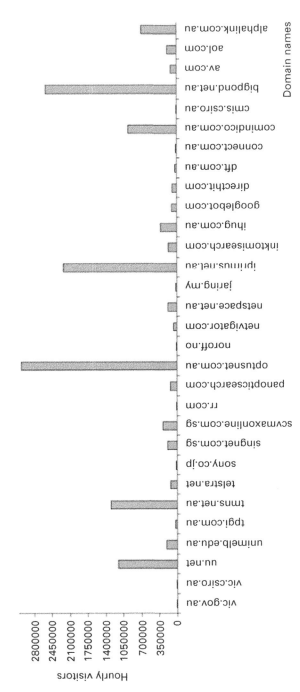

Figure 11.10. Hourly visitor information according to the domain names from an FCM cluster.

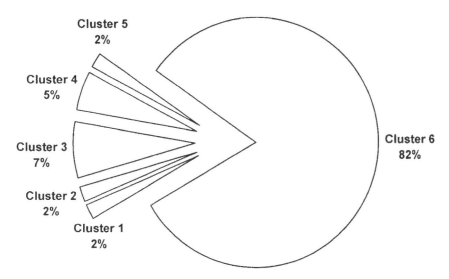

Figure 11.11. Clustering of visitors based on the day of access from an FCM cluster.

(MF) will evolve at the fastest rate [28]. The function of the other layers could be derived similarly.

Chromosome Modeling and Representation. Hierarchical evolutionary search process has to be represented in a chromosome for successful modeling of the *i-Miner* framework. A typical chromosome of the *i-Miner* would appear as shown in Fig. 11.14, and the detailed modeling process is as follows. **Layer 1:** The optimal number of clusters and initial cluster centers is represented in this layer. **Layer 2:** This layer is responsible for the optimization of the rule base. This includes deciding the total number of rules, as well as representation of the

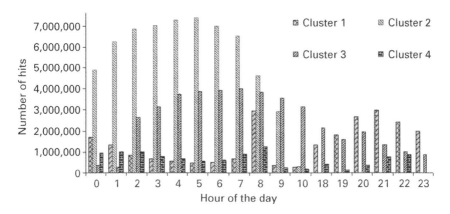

Figure 11.12. Hourly clustering of visitors using self-organizing maps.

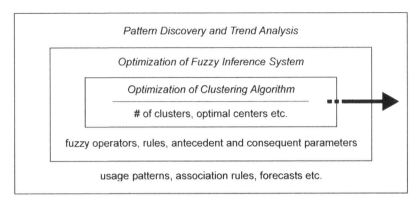

Figure 11.13. Hierarchical architecture of *i-Miner*.

antecedent and consequent parts. The number of rules grows rapidly with an increasing number of variables and fuzzy sets. We used the grid-partitioning algorithm to generate the initial set of rules. An iterative learning method is then adopted to optimize the rules [29]. The existing rules are mutated and new rules are introduced. The fitness of a rule is given by its contribution (strength) to the actual output. To represent a single rule, a position-dependent code with as many elements as the number of variables of the system is used. Each element is a binary string with a bit per fuzzy set in the fuzzy partition of the variable, meaning the absence or presence of the corresponding linguistic label in the rule. **Layer 3:** This layer is responsible for the selection of optimal learning parameters. Performance of the gradient descent algorithm directly depends on the learning rate according to the error surface. The optimal learning parameters decided by this layer will be used to tune the parameterized rule antecedents and consequents as well as the fuzzy operators. The rule antecedent/consequent parameters and the fuzzy operators are fine-tuned using a gradient descent algorithm

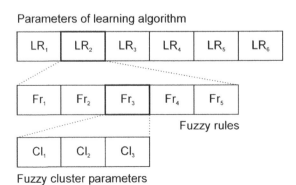

Figure 11.14. Chromosome structure of the *i-Miner*.

to minimize the output error

$$E_r = \sum_{k=1}^{N} (d_k - x_k)^2 \qquad (11.3)$$

where d_k is the kth component of the rth desired output vector and x_k is the kth component of the actual output vector by presenting the rth input vector to the network. All the gradients of the parameters to be optimized are computed, namely the consequent parameters $\partial E/\partial P_n$ for all rules R_n and the premise parameters $\partial E/\partial \sigma_i$ and $\partial E/\partial c_i$ for all fuzzy sets F_i (σ and c represents the membership function width and center of a Gaussian function).

Once the three layers are represented in a chromosome C, the learning procedure could be initiated as follows:

1. Generate an initial population of N number of C chromosomes. Evaluate the fitness of each chromosome depending on the output error.
2. Depending on the fitness and using suitable selection methods, reproduce a number of offspring for each individual in the current generation.
3. Apply genetic operators to each offspring individual generated above and obtain the next generation.
4. Check whether the current model has achieved the required error rate or whether the specified number of generations has been reached. If not, go to Step 2.
5. End.

11.3.3 Experimentation Setup, Training, and Performance Evaluation

Besides the inputs *volume of requests* and *volume of pages (bytes)* and *index number*, we also used the *cluster information* provided by the clustering algorithm as an additional input variable. The data were re-indexed based on the cluster information. Our task is to predict (few time steps ahead) the Web traffic volume on an hourly and daily basis. We used the data from February 17, 2002 to June 30, 2002 for training, and we used the data from July 1, 2002 to July 6, 2002 for testing and validation purposes.

The initial populations were randomly created based on the parameters shown in Table 11.2. We used a special mutation operator, which decreases the mutation rate as the algorithm proceeds in the search space [29]. If the allelic value x_i of the ith gene ranges over the domain a_i and b_i, the mutated gene x_i' is drawn randomly (uniformly) from the interval $[a_i, b_i]$.

$$x_i' = \begin{cases} x_i + \Delta(t, b_i - x_i), & \text{if } \omega = 0 \\ x_i + \Delta(t, x_i - a_i), & \text{if } \omega = 1 \end{cases} \qquad (11.4)$$

where ω represents an unbiased coin flip prob($\omega = 0$) = prob($\omega = 1$) = 0.5, and

$$\Delta(t, x) = x(1 - \gamma^{\tau}) \quad \text{with } \tau = \left(1 - \frac{t}{t_{\max}}\right)^{b} \qquad (11.5)$$

defines the mutation step, where γ is the random number from the interval [0, 1], t is the current generation, and $t_{\max}$ is the maximum number of generations. The function Δ computes a value in the range [0, x] such that the probability of returning a number close to zero increases as the algorithm proceeds with the search. The parameter b determines the impact of time on the probability distribution Δ over [0, x]. Large values of b decrease the likelihood of large mutations in a small number of generations. The parameters mentioned in Table 11.2 were determined after a few trial-and-error approaches. Experiments were repeated three times, and the average performance measures are reported. Figures 11.15 and 11.16 illustrate the meta-learning approach combining evolutionary learning and gradient descent techniques (fusion of soft computing and hard computing) during the 35 generations.

Table 11.3 summarizes the performance of the different SC paradigms for training and test data [1–3,25]. The correlation coefficient (CC) for the training/test data set is also given in Table 11.3. For *i-Miner*, 35 generations of the meta-learning approach created 62 *if-then* Takagi–Sugeno-type fuzzy rules for daily traffic trends and 64 rules for hourly traffic trends.

Adaptive Neuro Fuzzy Inference System Learning. We also trained the adaptive neuro-fuzzy inference system (ANFIS), which is a Takagi–Sugeno fuzzy inference system adapted using a direct neural learning technique. Three Gaussian membership functions were assigned to each input variable. Eighty-one fuzzy *if-then* rules were generated using the grid-based partitioning method, and the rule antecedent/consequent parameters were learned after 50 epochs.

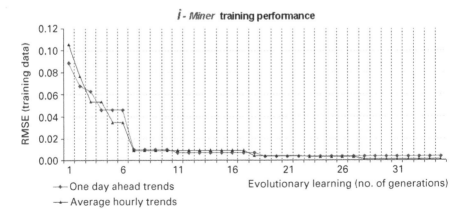

Figure 11.15. Meta-learning performance (training) of *i-Miner*.

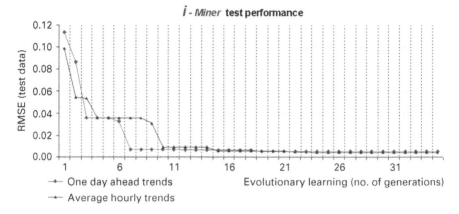

Figure 11.16. Meta-learning performance (testing) of *i-Miner*.

Neural Network Learning. We used a feedforward neural network with 14 and 17 neurons (single hidden layer), respectively, for forecasting the daily and hourly requests. The learning rate and momentum parameter were set at 0.05 and 0.2, respectively, and the network was trained for 3×10^4 epochs. The network parameters, including the number of neurons, were determined by a trial-and-error approach.

Linear Genetic Programming Learning. We used a population size of 500, a tournament size of 2×10^5, a crossover and mutation rate of 0.9, and limited to the maximum program size of 256. Figures 11.17 and 11.18 illustrate the actual and predicted trends for the test data set using the proposed techniques.

11.4 FUSION OF SOFT COMPUTING AND HARD COMPUTING

The Web usage-mining framework presented in this chapter introduces the fusion of soft computing and hard computing (HC) at several levels. Referring to the

TABLE 11.3. Performance of the Different Hybrid Paradigms

	Period					
	Daily (1 day ahead)			Hourly (1 hour ahead)		
	RMSE			RMSE		
Method	Training	Test	CC	Training	Test	CC
i-Miner	0.004	0.005	0.997	0.001	0.004	0.998
ACO-LGP	0.019	0.029	0.996	0.256	0.035	0.992
SOM-NN	0.035	0.048	0.929	0.055	0.064	0.949
SOM-LGP	0.054	0.075	0.932	0.065	0.052	0.945
SOM-TSFIS	0.018	0.040	0.995	0.043	0.043	0.984

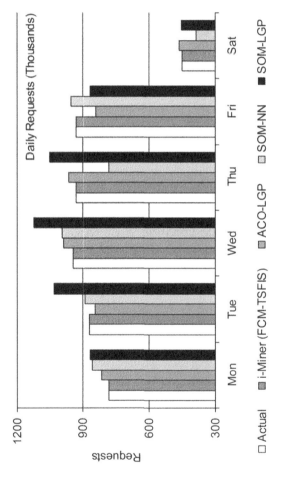

Figure 11.17. Comparison of different SC paradigms for daily Web traffic trends.

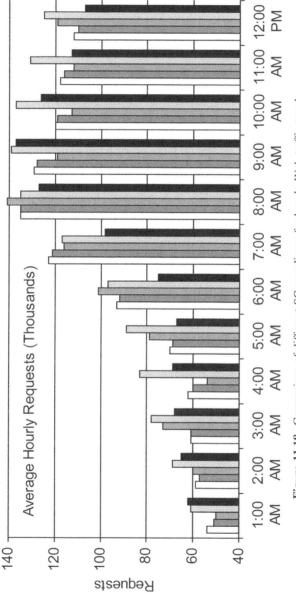

Figure 11.18. Comparison of different SC paradigms for hourly Web traffic trends.

framework presented in Fig. 11.3 the computational tasks comprise of three layers: data preprocessing, clustering, and function approximation. Data preprocessing is a pure HC task. For clustering, evolutionary fuzzy clustering algorithm was used, which could be considered as an SC+SC+HC fusion (Chapter 1). For trend prediction the fuzzy inference system was optimized using evolutionary learning and gradient descent technique, which could be considered as HC+SC+SC. At a very high level, we could see the proposed framework as a hybrid of HC-(SC+SC+HC)-(HC+SC+SC).

Data preprocessing involves merging log files from multiple locations and parsing the chunks of text (Fig. 11.1) into data fields. In some cases, graphic file requests are removed and the URLs are normalized after parsing any common gateway interface (CGI) data. Simple statistical analysis, association rules, and classification of the preprocessed data would help us to generate the simple server access statistics. This method is widely adopted by several types of Web log analyzer software.

Table 11.4 illustrates the importance of the clustering layer for improving the function approximation performance [5]. SOM was used for clustering. The empirical results depicted are obtained by using a Takagi–Sugeno fuzzy inference system trained using neural learning. As evident, the performance is improved by about 50% or more by providing the clustering information generated by SOM.

Clustering involves the task of dividing data points into homogeneous classes or clusters so that items in the same class are as similar as possible and items in different classes are as dissimilar as possible. Evolutionary fuzzy clustering could be considered as an SC-assisted SC+HC fusion (Chapter 1). In nonfuzzy or hard clustering, data are divided into crisp clusters, where each data point belongs to exactly one cluster. In fuzzy clustering, the data points can belong to more than one cluster, and associated with each of the points are membership grades that indicate the degree to which the data points belong to the different clusters. No guarantee ensures that FCM converges to an optimum solution (can be trapped by local minima in the process of optimizing the clustering criterion). The performance is very sensitive to initialization of the cluster centers and the number of clusters. Hence, an evolutionary algorithm is used to decide the optimal number of fuzzy clusters and their cluster centers. Such a methodological fusion could improve the overall performance of conventional clustering. For comparison purposes, SOM and ACO clustering were used independently.

Neural networks (NN), linear genetic programming (LGP), and fuzzy inference system were used in the function approximation layer. While NN and LGP were

TABLE 11.4. Function Approximation Performance

	TSFIS (with cluster info)			TSFIS (without cluster info)		
	RMSE			RMSE		
Period	Train	Test	CC	Train	Test	CC
Daily	0.018	0.040	0.995	0.065	0.096	0.988
Hourly	0.043	0.044	0.984	0.065	0.096	0.977

used without any fusion, fuzzy inference system was optimized using evolutionary computation and gradient descent. This could be again considered as an HC-assisted SC+SC fusion (Chapter 1). The presented *i-Miner* framework (Fig. 11.13) combines the clustering and function approximation blocks into a single layer by sharing the data structure and knowledge representation. Empirical results clearly illustrate the importance of fusion in the function approximation layer regardless of the prediction time frame.

11.5 CONCLUSIONS

Recently, Web usage mining has been gaining a lot of attention because of its potential commercial benefits. We have analyzed six months of Web server logs of Monash University, which receives over 7 million hits in a week. Empirical results show that the proposed hybrid framework seems to work very well. The empirical results also reveal the importance of the fusion of SC and HC paradigms for mining useful information. As evident from the research outcome, by incorporating more fusion techniques, there was a significant improvement in the performance. Useful information could be discovered from the clustered data. FCM clustering resulted in more clusters than did the SOM approach. Perhaps more clusters were required to improve the accuracy of the trend analysis. The main advantage of SOM comes from the easy visualization and interpretation of clusters formed by the map. As illustrated in Table 11.3, incorporation of the ACO clustering algorithm helped to improve the performance of the LGP model (when compared to clustering using self-organizing maps). *i-Miner* framework gave the best results with the lowest root-mean-squared error (RMSE) on test data and the highest correlation coefficient. The comparison of knowledge discovered from the developed ACO, FCM, and SOM clusters could be a good comparison study and is left as a future research topic.

i-Miner framework gave the overall best results with the lowest RMSE on test error and the highest correlation coefficient. It is interesting to note that the three SC paradigms could easily pickup the daily and hourly Web-access trend patterns. When compared to LGP, the developed neural network performed better (in terms of RMSE) for daily trends but for hourly trends LGP gave better results. An important disadvantage of *i-Miner* is the computational complexity of the algorithm. When optimal performance is required (in terms of accuracy and smaller structure), such algorithms might prove to be useful as evident from the empirical results.

So far, most analysis of Web data have involved basic traffic reports that do not provide much pattern and trend analysis. By linking the Web logs with cookies and forms, it is further possible to analyze the visitor behavior and profiles that could help an e-commerce site to address several business questions. Our future research will be oriented in this direction by incorporating more data mining paradigms to improve knowledge discovery and association rules from the clustered data.

ACKNOWLEDGMENTS

The initial part of the research was done during the author's stay at Monash University, Australia. The author wishes to thank Dr. Vitorino Ramos and Ms. Xiaozhe Wang for all the valuable discussions and contributions during the different stages of this research. This work was partially supported by the 2003 summer support received through the Oklahoma State University, Presidential Challenge Grant.

REFERENCES

1. A. Abraham, "Business Intelligence from Web Usage Mining," *Journal of Information & Knowledge Management* **2**, 375–390 (2003).

2. R. Cooley, "Web Usage Mining: Discovery and Application of Interesting Patterns from Web Data," Ph.D. Thesis, University of Minnesota, Department of Computer Science, Minneapolis, 2000.

3. R. Kosala and H. Blockeel, "Web Mining Research: A Survey," *ACM-SIGKDD Explorations* **2**, 1–15 (2000).

4. J. Heer and E. H. Chi, "Identification of Web User Traffic Composition Using Multi-modal Clustering and Information Scent," *Proceedings of the Workshop on Web Mining, SIAM Conference on Data Mining*, Chicago, 2001, pp. 51–58.

5. X. Wang, A. Abraham, and K. A. Smith, "Soft Computing Paradigms for Web Access Pattern Analysis," *Proceedings of the 1st International Conference on Fuzzy Systems and Knowledge Discovery*, Singapore, 2002, pp. 631–635.

6. A. Abraham, "*i-Miner*: A Web Usage Mining Framework Using Hierarchical Intelligent Systems," *Proceedings of the IEEE International Conference on Fuzzy Systems*, St. Louis, 2003, pp. 1129–1134.

7. A. Abraham and V. Ramos, "Web Usage Mining Using Artificial Ant Colony Clustering and Genetic Programming," *Proceedings of the IEEE Congress on Evolutionary Computation*, Canberra, Australia, Dec. 2003, pp. 1384–1391.

8. S. E. Jespersen, J. Thorhauge, and T. Bach, "A Hybrid Approach to Web Usage Mining, Data Warehousing and Knowledge Discovery," in Y. Kambayashi, W. Winiwarter, and M. Arikawa, eds., Lecture Notes in Computer Science **2454**, Springer-Verlag, Heidelberg, Germany, 2002, pp. 73–82.

9. F. Masseglia, P. Poncelet, and R. Cicchetti, "An Efficient Algorithm for Web Usage Mining," *Networking and Information Systems Journal* **2**, 571–603 (1999).

10. S. K. Pal, V. Talwar, and P. Mitra, "Web Mining in Soft Computing Framework: Relevance, State of the Art and Future Directions," *IEEE Transactions on Neural Networks* **13**, 1163–1177 (2002).

11. M. Perkowitz and O. Etzioni, "Adaptive Web Sites: Automatically Synthesizing Web Pages," *Proceedings of the 15th National Conference on Artificial Intelligence*, Madison, WI, 1998, pp. 727–732.

12. P. Pirolli, J. Pitkow, and R. Rao, "Silk from a Sow's Ear: Extracting Usable Structures from the Web," *Proceedings on Human Factors in Computing Systems*, ACM Press, 1996.

13. M. Spiliopoulou and L. C. Faulstich, "WUM: A Web Utilization Miner," *Proceedings of the EDBT Workshop on the Web and Data Bases*, Valencia, Spain, 1999, pp. 109–115.

14. Mobasher, R. Cooley, and J. Srivastava, "Creating Adaptive Web Sites through Usage-Based Clustering of URLs," *Proceedings of the Workshop on Knowledge and Data Engineering Exchange*, Chicago, 1999, pp. 19–25.

15. K. A. Smith and A. Ng, "Web Page Clustering Using a Self-Organizing Map of User Navigation Patterns," *Decision Support Systems* **35**, 245–256 (2003).

16. E. H. Chi, A. Rosien, and J. Heer, "LumberJack: Intelligent Discovery and Analysis of Web User Traffic Composition," *Proceedings of the ACM-SIGKDD Workshop on Web Mining for Usage Patterns and User Profiles*, Edmonton, Canada, 2002.

17. K. P. Joshi, A. Joshi, Y. Yesha, and R. Krishnapuram, "Warehousing and Mining Web Logs," *Proceedings of the 2nd ACM-CIKM Workshop on Web Information and Data Management*, Kansas City, MO, 1999, pp. 63–68.

18. J. Srivastava, R. Cooley, M. Deshpande, and P. N. Tan, "Web Usage Mining: Discovery and Applications of Usage Patterns from Web Data," *ACM SIGKDD Explorations* **1**, 12–23 (2000).

19. A. Abraham, "Neuro-Fuzzy Systems: State-of-the-Art Modeling Techniques," in J. Mira and A. Prieto, eds., *Connectionist Models of Neurons, Learning Processes, and Artificial Intelligence*, Springer-Verlag, Heidelberg, Germany, 2001, pp. 269–276.

20. Monash University, Clayton, Victoria, Australia. Web site < http://www.monash.edu.au > .

21. E. Bonabeau, G. Théraulaz, and J. L. Deneubourg, "Quantitative Study of the Fixed Response Threshold Model for the Regulation of Division of Labour in Insect Societies," *Proceedings of the Royal Society of London Series B* **263**, 1565–1569 (1996).

22. J. L. Deneubourg, S. Goss, N. Franks, A. Sendova-Franks, C. Detrain, and L. Chretien, "The Dynamic of Collective Sorting Robot-like Ants and Ant-like Robots," in J. A. Meyer and S. W. Wilson, eds., *SAB'90 — 1st Conference On Simulation of Adaptive Behavior: From Animals to Animats*, MIT Press, Cambridge, MA, 1991, pp. 356–365.

23. V. Ramos, F. Muge, and P. Pina, "Self-Organized Data and Image Retrieval as a Consequence of Inter-Dynamic Synergistic Relationships in Artificial Ant Colonies," *Proceedings of the Soft Computing Systems—Design, Management and Applications, 2nd International Conference on Hybrid Intelligent Systems*, IOS Press, Amsterdam, The Netherlands, 2002, pp. 500–509.

24. E. D. Lumer and B. Faieta, "Diversity and Adaptation in Populations of Clustering Ants," in D. Cliff, P. Husbands, J. Meyer, and S. Wilson, eds., *From Animals to Animats 3, Proceedings of the 3rd International Conference on the Simulation of Adaptive Behavior*, MIT Press/Bradford Books, Cambridge, MA, 1994.

25. J. C. Bezdek, *Pattern Recognition with Fuzzy Objective Function Algorithms*, Plenum Press, New York, 1981.

26. L. O. Hall, I. B. Ozyurt, and J. C. Bezdek, "Clustering with a Genetically Optimized Approach," *IEEE Transactions on Evolutionary Computation* **3**, 103–112 (1999).

27. W. Banzhaf, P. Nordin, E. R. Keller, and F. D. Francone, *Genetic Programming: An Introduction on the Automatic Evolution of Computer Programs and Its Applications*, Morgan Kaufmann Publishers, San Francisco, CA, 1998.

28. A. Abraham, "EvoNF: A Framework for Optimization of Fuzzy Inference Systems Using Neural Network Learning and Evolutionary Computation," *Proceedings of the 17th IEEE International Symposium on Intelligent Control*, Vancouver, Canada, 2002, pp. 327–332.

29. O. Cordón, F. Herrera, F. Hoffmann, and L. Magdalena, *Genetic Fuzzy Systems: Evolutionary Tuning and Learning of Fuzzy Knowledge Bases*, World Scientific Publishing Company, Singapore, 2001.

INDEX

Computationally Intelligent Hybrid Systems. Edited by Seppo J. Ovaska
ISBN 0-471-47668-4 © 2005 the Institute of Electrical and Electronics Engineers, Inc.

ABOUT THE EDITOR

Dr. Seppo J. Ovaska is a Professor of Industrial Electronics at the Department of Electrical and Communications Engineering, Helsinki University of Technology, Espoo, Finland. His international experience in industrial electronics spans 24 years and includes research and development (R&D) contributions in elevator group dispatching, overlay modernization of high-rise elevator banks, and motion control. Dr. Ovaska is a prolific author in soft computing and digital signal processing, having published more than 70 journal articles, more than 110 conference publications, and four book chapters. In addition, he has co-edited the book *Soft Computing in Industrial Electronics* (Physica-Verlag, Germany, 2002) and holds nine patents in the area of elevator systems and control.

Dr. Ovaska received a D.Sc. degree in electrical engineering from the Tampere University of Technology, Finland, in 1989. He earned an Lic.Sc. degree in computer science and engineering from the Helsinki University of Technology in 1987, and an M.Sc. in electrical engineering from the Tampere University of Technology in 1980. Prior to joining the Helsinki University of Technology in 1996, Dr. Ovaska was a Professor of Electronics at the Lappeenranta University of Technology, Finland (1992–1996). From 1980 to 1992, he held engineering, research, and R&D management positions with Kone Corporation and Nokia Research Center, both in Finland and Kentucky. He has taught university courses at the graduate and undergraduate level in soft computing, signal processing, real-time systems, microcomputer hardware design, and computer architectures. He serves as associate editor for the *IEEE Transactions on Industrial Electronics* and the *IEEE Transactions on Systems, Man, and Cybernetics—Part C: Applications and Reviews*. In addition, he was the coordinating chair of technical committees in the area of systems (2000–2003), and an elected member of the board of governors (2001–2003), IEEE Systems, Man, and Cybernetics Society.

Dr. Ovaska served as a Visiting Scientist at the Muroran Institute of Technology, Japan, in the summer of 1999; at the Virginia Polytechnic Institute and State University in the summers of 2000 and 2001; and at the Utah State University in the summers of 2002–2004. He is a senior member of the IEEE, a member of the International Society for Computers and Their Applications, and a member of the

Computationally Intelligent Hybrid Systems. Edited by Seppo J. Ovaska
ISBN 0-471-47668-4 © 2005 the Institute of Electrical and Electronics Engineers, Inc.

American Society for Engineering Education. He was the founding general chair of the IEEE Midnight-Sun Workshop on Soft Computing Methods in Industrial Applications in 1999 and was the general chair of the 5th Online World Conference on Soft Computing in Industrial Applications in 2000. Dr. Ovaska is a recipient of two Outstanding Contribution Awards of the IEEE Systems, Man, and Cybernetics Society.

Printed and bound by CPI Group (UK) Ltd, Croydon, CR0 4YY

27/10/2024

14580254-0004